PART 2: ANALYZING ENVIRONMENTS   40

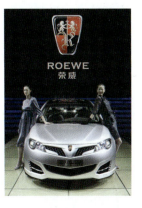

In the Preface to the first edition of our book, we noted that "firms are important to all of us." This is as true as we introduce the second edition of our text to you as it was a few years ago. Think about the importance of firms to a variety of people in the following ways. As customers, we buy products (goods and services) from firms producing them; as employees, we work for them; as suppliers, we sell raw materials to them; and, as perhaps many of us would agree, firms often are a vital part of the communities in which we live. Thus, for many reasons, all of us benefit when firms perform well. Indeed, when firms are successful, they are (1) producing, selling, and servicing products that you and I as customers want to buy, (2) providing employees with good-paying jobs, and (3) contributing in various ways to the communities in which they are located. But what influences a firm's performance? Why do some perform exceptionally well while others fail to perform adequately and end up in bankruptcy?

Corporate experiences as well as insights resulting from completing academic studies suggest that the strategic management process, which is the focus of this book, strongly influences firm performance. Stated simply, firms with leaders and personnel who understand how to effectively use the strategic management process tend to succeed. In contrast, firms without leaders and personnel who understand the strategic management process depend more on luck and often experience deteriorating performance that leads to failure.

Our purpose in writing the second edition of this successful text is to present to you a succinct and action-oriented explanation of how to manage a firm strategically. To do this, we explain a number of important concepts in ten concise chapters. As you can see from examining the following list of features, this book is exceptionally reader-friendly.

Let's examine some examples of how this book is accessible to readers.

- The writing style is lively, engaging, and application-oriented. You'll find examples in each chapter of how firms that you likely know actually use strategic management concepts and tools. These examples bring the strategic management process to life and highlight its relevance to real firms around the globe. Most of these examples are new to this edition of our text and the others have been substantially updated.
- Each chapter is organized around **"Knowledge Objectives."** Appearing at the beginning of each chapter, these objectives clarify what you can expect to learn as a result of studying the materials in the individual chapters.
- Key terms are placed in the margins for easy mastery of terminology that is important to understanding the strategic management process.
- We open each chapter with a feature called **"Focusing on Strategy."** Each **Focusing on Strategy** illustrates how a particular company uses the part of the strategic management process that is explained in the chapter. These features bring strategic management issues to life by showing their application in actual firms. All of the **Focusing on Strategy** features are new to this edition.

- In each chapter, we also include a feature ("**Understanding Strategy: Learning from Success**") to explain how one or more actual firms have benefited by successfully using a particular part of the strategic management process. We include a related feature in each chapter ("**Understanding Strategy: Learning from Failure**") to explain how one or more firms suffered poor performance because of their failure to effectively use one or more parts of the strategic management process. All of the **Understanding Strategy** features are new to this edition.

- Current references (from business publications such as *The Wall Street Journal*, *Business Week*, and *Fortune* and from academic publications) appear at the end of each chapter. The references we use demonstrate the currency of the firm-specific examples appearing in each chapter as well as our commitment to use results from recent academic research to provide you with the latest thinking about strategic management. Additionally, our presentation of the strategic management process is grounded in proven business practices as well as "classic" research from the academic literature.

- The "**Strategy Toolbox**" end-of-chapter feature, expertly prepared by Paul N. Friga of Indiana University, presents you with a tool or technique firms actually use with the strategic management process. In addition to learning how firms use strategic management, you will be able to use these helpful tools to help analyze cases. Most of these tools are new to this edition while the others have been completely updated.

- An especially exciting feature located at the end of each chapter is "**Biz Flix**," prepared by Joseph E. Champoux of the University of New Mexico. This feature consists of a carefully selected video segment taken from popular motion pictures that have appeared over the last 25 years. These short video segments reinforce main text concepts in a fresh and compelling way and are highly interesting and appealing. The discussion questions integrate video and chapter content. The Biz Flix video clips are available on the Instructor Resource DVD for ease on use in the classroom and also in WebTutor for Blackboard and WebCT.

- At the end of each chapter, we present a "**Mini-Case**" that deals with an actual firm and explains, in some detail, how that firm uses one or more parts of the strategic management process. Each **Mini-Case** is more comprehensive than the **Focusing on Strategy** and **Understanding Strategy** features. To help you learn more about the firm discussed in the case and to enhance your strategic management skills, each case closes with a set of discussion questions. These questions are designed to help you think about the issues in the case and enhance your learning of the chapter's concepts. Three of the **Mini-Cases** (Chapters 1, 4, and 6) are new to this edition while the others have been substantially updated.

- Two "**Experiential Exercises**" are included in the end-of-chapter content. We are grateful to Charles M. Byles (Virginia Commonwealth University) for preparing these exercises. Each cognitive or experiential exercise involves you, as an active learner, in a way that will help you develop a better understanding of the chapter's topics. Typically, you are provided with some discussion questions that facilitate efforts to apply the learning gained from each exercise. More than half of the experiential exercises are new to this edition while others have been updated.

- To increase the book's visual appeal, full color is used to enhance the presentation of the concepts presented in the book's ten chapters. The full-color format enables us to include interesting color photographs to further illustrate each chapter's content.

Acknowledgments

We are especially grateful to those preparing end-of-chapter content: Paul N. Friga, Indiana University, who wrote the "Strategy Toolbox" materials; Joseph E. Champoux, University of New Mexico, who developed the "Biz Flix" items; and Charles M. Byles, Virginia Commonwealth University, who developed the "Experiential Exercises."

The feedback and guidance provided by our reviewers for this text were especially helpful. We are grateful for their insights about how to present you with an interesting, accessible, and complete explanation of strategic management.

Todd M. Alessandri
Syracuse University

Sonny Ariss
University of Toledo

Kunal Banerji
Florida Atlantic University

Janice A. Black
New Mexico State University

Keith Brigham
Texas Tech University

Carol A. Decker
Tennessee Wesleyan College

Rocki-Lee DeWitt
University of Vermont

Scott Droege
Western Kentucky University

Bahman Paul Ebrahimi
University of Denver

Tamela D. Ferguson
University of Louisiana at Lafayette

Cameron M. Ford
University of Central Florida

Debora J. Gilliard
Metropolitan State College—Denver

Steven Hamilton
University of Alaska, S.E.

Peter Horn
Arizona State University

Delores James
University of Maryland—University College

Reza Karim
California State University, Fullerton

Franz W. Kellermanns
Mississippi State University

Raihan Khan
SUNY Oswego

Leslie A. Korb
Georgian Court University

Joseph W. Leonard
Miami University

Joseph T. Mahoney
University of Illinois at Urbana-Champaign

Paul Mallete
Colorado State University

Brian L. Maruffi
Fordham University

George D. Mason
Providence College

Dennis Mathern
University of Findlay

Brett P. Matherne
Loyola University New Orleans

Donald Neubaum
Oregon State University

Frank Novakowski
Davenport University

Daewoo Park
Xavier University

Clifton D. Petty
Drury University

Laura H. Poppo
Virginia Tech University

Jude Rathburn
University of Wisconsin, River Falls

Janice J. Reily
Mt. Mercy College

Mitrabarun Sarkar
University of Central Florida

Khaled Sartawi
Fort Valley State University

Deepak Sethi
Old Dominion University

Amit J. Shah
Frostburg State University

Katsuhiko Shimizu
University of Texas, San Antonio

Thomas D. Sigerstad
Frostburg State University

f. i. Smith
Missouri Western State University

William L. Smith
Emporia State University

Jeffrey E. Stambaugh
Texas Tech University

Linda Thacker
El Centro College

Laszlo Tihanyi
Texas A&M University

Klaus Uhlenbruck
University of Montana

Floyd G. Willoughby
Oakland University

Joette Wisnieski
Indiana University of Pennsylvania

Our focus group participants helped us a great deal in understanding instructors' and students' needs in teaching and learning about strategic management in an action-oriented manner. We are grateful for the excellent observations the following scholar-teachers provided.

Donald Baack
Ball State University

Ed Murphy
Embry Riddle University

Rick Crandall
Appalachian State University

Tyge Payne
Texas Tech University

Fred Doran
University of Mississippi

Bill Ritchie
Florida Gulf Coast University

Chuck Englehart
Salem International University

Michelle Slagle
University of South Alabama

Steven Hamilton
University of Alaska, S.E.

Eva Smith
Spartanburg Technical College

We also want to express our sincere appreciation for the excellent support we've received from our editorial and production team at South-Western, Cengage Learning. In particular, we want to very sincerely thank Michele Rhoades, senior acquisitions editor, our editor and product champion; John Abner, our managing developmental editor; Darrell Frye, our content project manager; and Clint Kernan, our marketing manager. We are truly grateful for their dedication, professionalism, and commitment to work closely with us to prepare a high-quality book and an excellent and comprehensive package of support materials. It has been a great team effort.

Supplements

Instructor's Resource DVD

Place resources at your fingertips with this efficient Instructor's Resource DVD, including Instructor's Resource Manual, Test Bank, ExamView Testing software, PowerPoint, and Case Notes. Easily access the text's two sets of videos. Brief BizFlix clips from popular Hollywood movies correspond with end-of-chapter exercises for use in class, while longer new videos from 50Lessons feature world business leaders.

Test Bank

This thorough test bank contains more than 1,000 questions, including multiple-choice, true/false, and essay questions for every chapter. Answers are cross-referenced to pages within the text making it easy to pinpoint related material. The AACSB assurance of learning standards reflected in each Test Bank question have been identified to allow for the assessment of student achievement as it relates to these key measures. The Test Bank is available on the Instructor's Resource DVD or international.cengage.com.

ExamView®

The ExamView test creation software, which is an easy-to-use Windows-based program, contains all of the questions in the printed test bank. Instructors can add or edit questions, instructions, and answers, and select questions by previewing them on the screen, selecting them randomly, or selecting them by number. Instructors can also create and administer quizzes online, whether over the Internet, a local area network (LAN), or a wide area network (WAN). ExamView is included on the Instructor's Resource DVD or international.cengage.com.

Instructor's Resource Manual

One of the most exciting, useful instructor's aids available, this Manual offers comprehensive chapter overviews and outlines, instructor's notes, and answers to end-of-chapter questions. The Manual is available on the Instructor's Resource DVD or international.cengage.com.

PowerPoint Slide Presentations

Bring your lectures to life with this comprehensive set of PowerPoint slides that highlight figures from the text, reinforces all main concepts and terms, and assists with classroom discussion questions. Encourage active learning in each chapter with these slides, available on the Instructor's Resource DVD or international.cengage.com.

All-New 50Lessons Video Collection

Bring the latest challenges of today's business leaders throughout the world into your course with new videos by Fifty Lessons. Available on the Instructor's Resource DVD, these short, powerful videos offers a comprehensive, compelling resource of management and leadership lessons as leaders share their business acumen and outline principles guiding their business decisions and careers.

Biz Flix Video Clips

Put business strategy in action for your students as unique Biz Flix videos feature short scenes from popular Hollywood movies. Corresponding text chapter exercises further describe the business strategy at work in the movie scene with questions that help students connect the video to abstract strategy concepts. Teaching notes in the Instructor's Manual help guide classroom discussion. BizFlix Videos are available on the Instructor's Resource DVD for ease of use in the classroom and are also included as part of WebTutor for Blackboard and WebCT for use in online courses.

WebTutor for Blackboard
WebTutor for WebCT

Jumpstart your course with customizable, rich, text-specific content within this Course Management System! Access a wealth of interactive resources in addition to those on the companion website to supplement the classroom experience and further prepare students for professional success. This resource is ideal as an integrated solution for your distance learning or web-enhanced course.

Product Support Web Site
international.cengage.com

Our product support web site contains all ancillary products for the instructor as well as a variety of content reinforcement materials for students including a tutorial on the effective analysis of cases and also the Your Career series which focuses on applying the strategic management process in one's professional life.

Robert E. Hoskisson

Robert E. Hoskisson is a Professor of Strategic Management and he holds the W. P. Carey Chair in the Department of Management at the W. P. Carey School of Business at Arizona State University. He received his Ph.D. from the University of California–Irvine. His interest in strategic management topics has allowed him to teach overview as well topical courses in strategic management at the undergraduate, master's, and doctoral levels. His teaching and research expertise in these areas have been recognized. For example, in 1998, he received an award for Outstanding Academic Contributions to Competitiveness, American Society for Competitiveness. He also received the William G. Dyer Distinguished Alumni Award given at the Marriott School of Management, Brigham Young University. He is a Fellow of the Academy of Management and a member of the Fellows Group of the Strategic Management Society. These recognitions come from his academic oriented publications in top peer-reviewed journals including the Academy of Management Journal, Academy of Management Review, Strategic Management Journal, Organization Science, Journal of Management, Journal of Business Venturing, Entrepreneurship: Theory and Practice and Journal of Management Studies. Because of his interest in managerial practice and application, he has also published in journals with this focus such as the California Management Review, Academy of Management Executive, Long Range Planning, and Journal of World Business. He has also coauthored a number of textbooks to foster instruction in Strategic Management including the eighth edition of Strategic Management: Competitiveness and Globalization and Competing for Advantage (second edition). He has also coauthored Downscoping: How to Tame the Diversified Firm (Oxford University Press), a masters' level text on restructuring large businesses. In serving the academic community, Hoskisson has served on several editorial boards for publications such as the Academy of Management Journal (including Consulting Editor and Guest Editor of a special issue), Strategic Management Journal, Journal of Management (including Associate Editor), Journal of International Business Studies (Consulting Editor), Organization Science, and Journal of Management Studies (Guest Editor of two special issues). He completed three years of service as a representative-at-large on the Board of Governors of the Academy of Management and currently is on the Board of Directors of the Strategic Management Society.

Michael A. Hitt

Michael A. Hitt is a Distinguished Professor and holds the Joe B. Foster Chair in Business Leadership at Texas A&M University. He received his Ph.D. from the University of Colorado. He has authored or coauthored over 160 journal articles and coauthored or coedited 26 separate books. Those books include: Downscoping: How to Tame the Diversified Firm (1994); Mergers and Acquisitions: A Guide to Creating Value for Stakeholders (2001); Handbook of Strategic Management (2001); Strategic Entrepreneurship: Creating a New Integrated Mindset (2002); Managing Knowledge for Sustained Competitive Advantage (2003); The Blackwell Entrepreneurship Encyclopedia (2005); Great Minds in Management: The Process of Theory Development (2005). The Global Mindset (2007); Competing for Advantage (2008); and Strategic Management: Competitiveness and Globalization (2009). He has served on the editorial review boards of multiple journals and served as Consulting Editor (1988–1990) and Editor (1991–1993) of the Academy of Management Journal. He is the current Co-editor of the Strategic Entrepreneurship Journal. He serves as President of the Strategic Management Society and is a past president of the Academy of Management. He received the 1996 Award for Outstanding Academic Contributions to Competitiveness and the 1999 Award for Outstanding Intellectual Contributions to Competitiveness Research from the American Society for Competitiveness. He is a Fellow in the Academy of Management and the Strategic Management Society and a Research Fellow in the National Entrepreneurship Consortium. He received an honorary doctorate from the Universidad Carlos III de Madrid for his contributions to the field. He received the Irwin Outstanding Educator Award and the Distinguished Service Award from the Academy of Management.

R. Duane Ireland

R. Duane Ireland is a Distinguished Professor and holds the Foreman R. and Ruby S. Bennett Chair in Business in the Mays Business School, Texas A&M University. He teaches courses at all levels (undergraduate, master's, doctoral, and executive). He has won multiple awards for his teaching and research. His research, which focuses on diversification, innovation, corporate entrepreneurship, and strategic entrepreneurship, has been published in a number of journals including Academy of Management Journal, Academy of Management Review, Academy of Management Executive, Administrative Science Quarterly, Strategic Management Journal, Journal of Management, Entrepreneurship Theory and Practice, Journal of Business Venturing, Human Relations, and Journal of Management Studies. His published books include Competing for Advantage, second edition (2008), Strategic Management: Competitiveness and Globalization, eighth edition (2009), Entrepreneurship: Successfully Creating New Ventures, second edition (2008), and What's Stopping You? Shatter the 9 Most Common Myths Keeping You from Starting Your Own Business (2008). He is serving or has served as a member of the editorial review boards for a number of journals such as Academy of Management Journal, Academy of Management Review, Academy of Management Executive, Journal of Management, Journal of Business Venturing, Entrepreneurship Theory and Practice, Journal of Business Strategy, and European Management Journal. He has co-edited special issues of Academy of Management Review, Academy of Management Executive, Journal of Business Venturing, Strategic Management Journal, Organizational Research Methods, and Journal of High Technology and Engineering Management. He is the current editor of the Academy of Management Journal. He received awards for the best article published in Academy of Management Executive (1999) and Academy of Management Journal (2000). In 2001, his article published in Academy of Management Executive won the Best Journal Article in Corporate Entrepreneurship Award from the U.S. Association for Small Business & Entrepreneurship (USASBE). He is a Fellow of the Academy of Management and a Research Fellow in the National Entrepreneurship Consortium. He received the 1999 Award for Outstanding Intellectual Contributions to Competitiveness Research from the American Society for Competitiveness and the USASBE Scholar in Corporate Entrepreneurship Award (2004) from USASBE. Previously, he served as a representative-at-large on the Board of Governors of the Academy of Management.

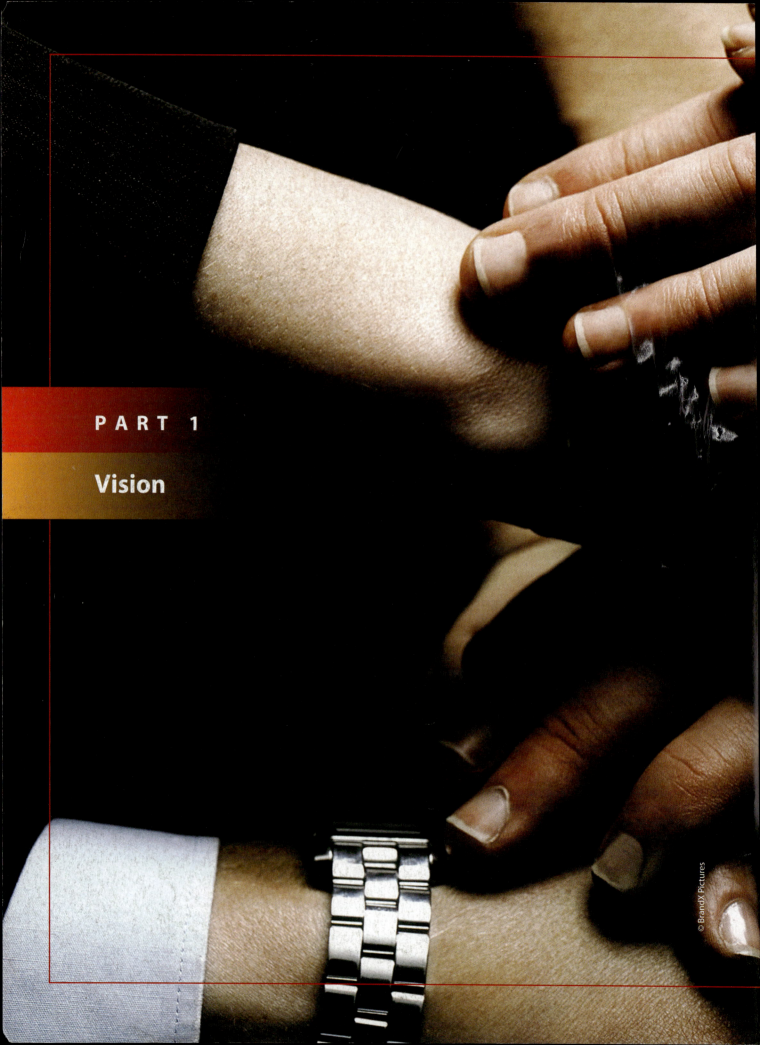

PART 1

Vision

CHAPTER 1
Managing Strategy

Knowledge Objectives

Reading and studying this chapter should enable you to:

1. Define strategic management.

2. Discuss why firms use the industrial organization model to analyze their external environment.

3. Discuss why firms use the resource-based view of the firm model to analyze their internal environment.

4. Define stakeholders and understand their importance.

5. Explain the work of strategic leaders.

© BrandX Pictures

Integrating Solutions to Handle Cash:
The Foundation for Loomis's Continuing Success

"People talk about a cash-free world. I see cash never going away." (Calvin Murri, Chief Operating Officer, Loomis)

Launched more than 100 years ago in Portland, Oregon, Loomis got its start by using dog sleds to haul gold from Alaska to other parts of the United States. In addition to transporting gold in its early life, Loomis has focused on making certain that its customers "have the right amount of cash, in the right place at the right time." To meet this goal today, Loomis uses 5,800 secure vehicles from its 440 branch offices in 11 different countries to serve three core customer groups: banks, multilocation retailers, and other commercial enterprises. (In actuality, Loomis, as we know the firm today, is the name commonly used in the United States for Loomis, Fargo & Co. This company was created in 1997 when Loomis and competitor Wells Fargo Armored merged their operations. Subsequently, Loomis, Fargo & Co. merged with Sweden-based Securitas in 2001.)

Courtesy, Loomis

Loomis's vision is to "manage the public flow of cash." Banks, cash-handling centers, and ATMs (automated teller machines) are examples of the variety of participants involved with managing the public flow of cash. On occasions, the viability of Loomis's vision has been challenged by changes in conditions that emerge in the external environment. (We explain the parts of a firm's external environment and their effects in Chapter 3.) The changes affecting Loomis occur mainly in the *economic* part of the external environment. For example, some thought that the appearance of written checks would put armor car companies (such as Loomis) out of business in that checks do not require the movement of cash. This expectation has not come true. The growth of ATMs brought additional "the sky is falling warnings" from investors and other observers of the armor car business; this warning too proved untrue.

However, those leading Loomis and responsible for forming its strategies do recognize that even though the odds of cash ever becoming obsolete are indeed slim, paper money and coins are being used less frequently in today's economies across the globe. In light of this understanding, Loomis is busy recasting itself and altering its strategy, using technology as the means of doing so. The major objective of these efforts is for Loomis to differentiate itself from competitors by providing customers with broader cash logistics services. The fact that banks (a key customer group for Loomis) are trying to outsource more of their activities (in order to increase their efficiency and reduce their costs) creates opportunities for Loomis to provide cash logistics services. For example, Loomis now stocks ATMs for many of its bank customers. Additionally, the company processes and sorts cash, rolls and wraps coins, scans and processes checks, weeding out counterfeit and deteriorated bills in the process, and sells safes "that can scan for counterfeits and verify deposit amounts to save time and money for retailers."

As these examples illustrate, Loomis seeks to use technology as the foundation for integrating the activities of virtually all players involved with managing the public flow of cash. To increase the scale of its operations, Loomis selectively acquires firms such as Guardian Armored Security, Inc., a Michigan-based cash handling services provider. With this transaction, Loomis became the largest cash-handling services provider in the state of Michigan.

Sources: B. Hem, 2008, Loomis cashes in on technology, *The Houston Chronicle Online*, www.chron.com, March 1; 2008, Loomis, www.lomis.com; 2008, Loomisfargo, http://loomisfargo.com, March 1; 2001, Loomis, a cash-handling business, will be bought out, *The New York Times Online*, www.nytimes, May 16.

Do you sometimes wonder why some firms are more adaptive and successful than others? Why, for example, is Loomis able to alter its strategy in ways that allow it to remain successful? Why is Best Buy continuing to outperform Circuit City, its closest competitor? (The performance gap between these two firms is wide. Circuit City lost $300 million in 2007. In contrast, Best Buy posted net income of $228 million in the third quarter alone.)[1] Why is Helicopter Services of Houston, Texas (a pilot training school), successful at a time when Silver State Helicopters of Las Vegas, Nevada, filed for bankruptcy? (*Hint*: Some believe that the success of Helicopter Services is a function of the firm's ability to control its costs while providing highly personal attention to each of its customers.)[2]

Although the reasons for Loomis's, Best Buy's, and Helicopter Services' success as well as the successes of many other firms sometime seem mysterious, they really aren't a secret. As with these three companies, firms use the strategic management process to achieve success. The purpose of this book is to explain each part of the strategic management process—*vision, analysis*, and *strategy*. We think you will enjoy learning about the strategic management process and know that you will benefit from doing so.

What Is Strategic Management?

Strategic management is the ongoing process companies use to form a *vision, analyze* their external environment and their internal environment, and select one or more *strategies* to use to create value for customers and other stakeholders, especially shareholders. Let's define the parts of the strategic management process so we can see the differences among them. In this chapter, we will merely introduce you to the parts of this important process. You'll learn more about each part in the book's remaining chapters. We'll also define a number of terms that are used throughout the book.

The **vision** contains at least two components—a mission that describes the firm's DNA and the "picture" of the firm as it hopes to exist in a future time period.[3] DNA includes the core information and characteristics necessary for the firm to function. The vision is intended to inspire the firm's employees to realize or "picture" the future aspirations of what the firm can become and to help establish a framework for ethical behavior. The vision for Intoweb Design is "to become the best Web Developers in South Africa."[4] The vision for this Internet service provider should inspire the firm's employees in their daily work. A **strategy** is an action plan designed to move an organization toward achievement of its vision. The mission of the firm is focused on the markets it serves and the products (either goods or services) it provides. The **mission** defines the firm's core intent and the business or businesses in which it intends to operate. Loomis's mission, for the firm to "Be a world class provider in delivering quality, secure services for managing cash in society," demonstrates these characteristics.[5] The **external environment** is a set of conditions outside the firm that affect the firm's performance. Changes in population trends and income levels, competition between firms, and economic changes are examples of the many conditions in a firm's external environment that can affect its performance. For example, think of the effect of the home mortgage crisis in the United States in 2008 and beyond on homeowners, home builders, and local communities among others. (Mortgage rates and institutional lending practices are a part of the *economic* segment of the external environment.) The **internal environment** is the set of conditions (such as strengths, resources, capabilities, and so forth) inside the firm affecting the choice and use of strategies.

Strengths are resources and capabilities that allow the firm to complete important tasks. Being able to effectively manage the flow of its inventory is one of Best Buy's strengths that help it complete the important task of having the right merchandise on its shelves for customers to buy. (This strength also helps Best Buy

strategic management

the ongoing process companies use to form a *vision, analyze* their external environment and their internal environment, and select one or more *strategies* to use to create value for customers and other stakeholders, especially shareholders

vision

contains at least two components—a mission that describes the firm's DNA and the "picture" of the firm as it hopes to exist in a future time period

strategy

an action plan designed to move an organization toward achievement of its vision

mission

defines the firm's core intent and the business or businesses in which it intends to operate

external environment

a set of conditions outside the firm that affect the firm's performance

internal environment

the set of conditions (such as strengths, resources and capabilities, and so forth) inside the firm affecting the choice and use of strategies

strengths

resources and capabilities that allow the firm to complete important tasks

outperform Circuit City.) **Resources** are the tangible and intangible assets held by the firm. A strong balance sheet is one of Coca-Cola's tangible assets, while the knowledge held by its employees is one of Microsoft's intangible assets. **Capabilities** result when the firm integrates several different resources to complete a task or a series of related tasks.[6] 3M integrates the knowledge of its scientists (an intangible asset) with other resources, including its sophisticated scientific equipment (a tangible asset), to create its innovation capability.

Core competencies are capabilities the firm emphasizes and performs especially well while pursuing its vision. Sony Corporation's ability to miniaturize components as the foundation for developing small, value-creating products is an important core competence for this global giant. The Walkman is an example of a successful product introduction resulting from Sony's miniaturization core competence.

Core competencies that differ from those held by competitors are called **distinctive competencies.** Miniaturization is a distinctive competence for Sony as is innovation for Gillette. An example of a product Gillette developed by using its innovative competence is the Sensor razor. Introduced in 1990, the Sensor gave way to Gillette's newer innovation (the Mach3) in 1998.[7] When core competencies allow the firm to create value for customers by performing a key activity (such as innovation at Gillette) *better* than competitors, it has a **competitive advantage.** Today, Lenovo Group Ltd. is trying to develop a competitive advantage in design and style. Lenovo believes that developing design and style competencies that are superior to those of firms such as Dell, Acer, and Hewlett-Packard can be a source of differentiation (and competitive advantage) for its personal computers compared to the products its competitors are producing.[8] A firm can also have a competitive advantage when a distinctive competence allows it to perform an activity that creates value for customers that competitors can't perform.

Figure 1.1 presents a diagram of the strategic management process, while the key characteristics of strategic management are listed in Table 1.1. We continue our introduction of the parts of the strategic management process in the next few sections.

resources
the tangible and intangible assets held by the firm

capabilities
result when the firm integrates several different resources to complete a task or a series of related tasks

core competencies
capabilities the firm emphasizes and performs especially well while pursuing its vision

distinctive competencies
core competencies that differ from those held by competitors

competitive advantage
when the firm's core competencies allow it to create value for customers by performing a key activity *better* than competitors or when a distinctive competence allows it to perform an activity that creates value for customers that competitors can't perform

Figure 1.1 The Strategic Management Process

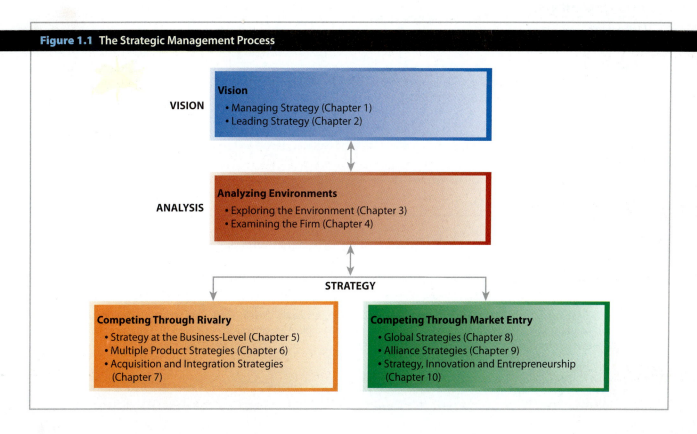

Table 1.1 Key Characteristics of Strategic Management

Strategic management is:
- Performance oriented
- Ongoing in nature
- Dynamic rather than static
- Oriented to the present and the future
- Concerned with conditions both outside and inside the firm
- Concerned with performing well and satisfying stakeholders

The Three Parts of the Strategic Management Process

As suggested in Figure 1.1, strategic leaders are responsible for forming a firm's vision and mission (which we talk about in greater detail in Chapter 2). As noted earlier, an effective mission provides direction to the firm, while an effective vision inspires people to ethical actions. We present additional vision statements and mission statements from different organizations in Table 1.2. Which of the vision statements shown in Table 1.2 inspire you? Which mission statement does the best job of telling you about the direction a firm is taking? Would you make changes to any of the vision or mission statements shown in Table 1.2? If so, why and what would those changes be?

Figure 1.1 also suggests that firms must *analyze* their external environment and their internal environment before strategies can be chosen and *implemented*. Here's an example of how this process is taking place today at Circuit City.

Table 1.2 Vision and Mission Statements

VISION STATEMENTS

McDonald's

To give each customer, every time, an experience that sets new standards in value, service, friendliness, and quality.

NASDAQ

To build the world's first truly global securities market . . . A worldwide market of markets built on a worldwide network of networks . . . linking pools of liquidity and connecting investors from all over the world . . . assuring the best possible price for securities at the lowest possible cost.

Petsmart

To be the premier organization in nurturing and enriching the bond between people and animals.

Wachovia

Wachovia's vision is to be the best, most trusted and admired financial services company.

MISSION STATEMENTS

Bristol-Myers Squibb

Our mission is to extend and enhance human life by providing the highest-quality pharmaceuticals and health care products.

GlaxoSmithKline

GSK's mission is to improve the quality of human life by enabling people to do more, feel better and live longer.

Merck

The mission of Merck is to provide society with superior products and services by developing innovations and solutions that improve the quality of life and satisfy customer needs, and to provide employees with meaningful work and advancement opportunities, and investors with a superior rate of return.

Wipro

The mission is to be a full-service, global outsourcing company.

Recall that Circuit City's performance today is falling short of expectations. In fact, the firm's shares lost 76 percent of their value in 2007.[9] Spotting an opportunity in the external environment to offer customers deep insights about individual products, the firm is opening new concept stores called City. Smaller (20,000 square feet compared to 34,000 square feet in a typical Circuit City store) and more focused in terms of product lines (a City store is restricted to five main product areas—photo, computer, games, home entertainment, and portable gear), each City unit has highly trained staff members. Carrying tablet PCs with them at all

times, employees are capable of providing in-depth knowledge to customers about a focused array of products. Circuit City is using the skills of its workforce and its product purchasing competence to serve customers seeking in-depth knowledge about products before deciding to make a purchase. Will the City stores help to reverse Circuit City's fortunes? Only time will time. However, one customer's reaction to shopping at a City store, as follows, is encouraging: "It's pretty neat. I was very impressed with the overall process and the intelligence of the people I was involved with."[10]

As mentioned earlier, a strategy is an action plan designed to move an organization toward achievement of its vision. Strategy is about finding ways for the firm to be different from its competitors. The most effective companies avoid using "me-too" strategies—strategies that are the same as those of their competitors. A firm's strategy should allow it to deliver a unique mix of value to customers.[11]

As shown in Figure 1.1, firms use business-level strategies, multiproduct strategies, and merger and acquisition strategies to directly compete with rivals. With product names such as Mastiff and Pitbull, Big Dog Motorcycles uses its focused differentiation business-level strategy to build premium, heavyweight motorcycles that are targeted for customers with needs for this unique product. (We discuss five types of business-level strategies in Chapter 5.) Big Dog competes directly against Harley-Davidson with its business-level strategy. Procter & Gamble uses a related diversification multiproduct strategy (discussed in Chapter 6) in battles with global competitors such as Unilever, Kimberly Clark, and Johnson & Johnson. We won't provide examples here of companies using the other strategy (mergers and acquisitions) that is a means of competing directly with competitors or of the three strategies (see Figure 1.1) firms use to compete against competitors by entering additional markets. We will, however, provide examples of how firms use these strategies in the relevant chapters (Chapters 7 through 10).

Once chosen, strategies must be put into use. **Strategy implementation** is the set of actions firms take to use a strategy after it has been selected. Advertising itself as "America's Largest Pet Pharmacy," 1-800-PetsMed.com offers the largest selection of prescription and nonprescription pet medications to consumers at competitive prices. Using the Internet and telemarketing to sell products to customers is a critical part of how the firm implements its cost leadership (see Chapter 5) strategy.[12]

In Understanding Strategy: Learning from Success, we describe Wal-Mart's success as a grocer. (You will learn more about Wal-Mart and other parts of its operations in Focusing on Strategy that opens Chapter 5.) The world's largest public corporation by revenue, Wal-Mart uses its famous and widely recognized inventory management and distribution core competencies to drive its continuing success. Because Wal-Mart's inventory management and distribution core competencies are superior to those of its competitors, they are competitive advantages for the firm.

After reading the Understanding Strategy about Wal-Mart as a grocer, are you able to conclude that the company is effectively using the strategic management process? What future do you envision for Wal-Mart as a grocer? Can you anticipate Wal-Mart taking its grocery store concepts to other countries? Might Wal-Mart choose to enter Tesco's core market in order to compete directly against its

strategy implementation

the set of actions firms take to use a strategy after it has been selected

Wal-Mart's Grocery Business: Can the Momentum and Success Be Maintained?

Operating more than 4,100 stores in the United States and approximately 2,800 global outlets that span 13 countries, Wal-Mart's size and the breadth of its product offerings strike many as amazing. In an analyst's words, "The $374.5 billion behemoth sells everything from electronics and groceries to medication at everyday low prices."

© Jonathan Alcorn/Bloomberg News/Landov

is the world's third-largest retailer (behind Wal-Mart and France's Carrefour). In the fall of 2007, Tesco opened its first U.S. stores in Los Angeles. Called Fresh & Easy Neighborhood Markets, these units are about half the size of Wal-Mart's Neighborhood Markets. Impressed by Tesco's competitive abilities and concerned about its foray into the United States, Wal-Mart is now test marketing small-format grocery stores in Arizona. Using the name Marketside, these units measure about 20,000 square feet (half the size of Wal-Mart's initial grocery store format and equivalent to the size of Tesco's stores). As with Tesco's concept, Marketside stores are emphasizing fresh foods and greater customer convenience.

With the first unit established in Bentonville, Arkansas, in 1998, Wal-Mart "the grocer" is relatively new. Called Neighborhood Markets, these grocery stores average 42,000 square feet and offer a variety of products, including pharmaceuticals, health and beauty aids, and photo-developing services in addition to groceries. Using its inventory management and distribution competitive advantages, Wal-Mart implements the cost leadership strategy in its grocery stores as it does in its other units such as Wal-Mart Supercenters and Sam's Clubs. Given that it took Wal-Mart less than a decade to become the largest grocer in the United States, isn't it possible that the firm is successfully using the strategic management process as the foundation for operating its grocery store business?

However, success begets competition. None of the competitive challenges Wal-Mart faces as a grocer is potentially more serious than Tesco PLC's decision to enter the U.S. market. A British-based international grocery and general merchandise retail chain, Tesco

Constantly seeking to use its competitive advantages to create additional types of value for its customers, Wal-Mart recently registered new trade names such as City Thyme and Field & Vine. Some industry analysts believe that Wal-Mart might develop these concepts as a means of selling its soon-to-be-available private-label fresh-food offerings. Additionally, by 2010, Wal-Mart intends to establish walk-in medical care facilities in 400 of its stores. The firm will partner with local hospitals and medical practices to operate these "stores within a store."

Sources: J. Birchall, 2008, Wal-Mart goes small to take on UK's Tesco, *Financial Times Online*, www.ft.com, January 14; M. Freudenheim, 2008, Wal-Mart will expand in-store medical clinics, *The New York Times Online*, www.nytimes, February 7; 2008, Wal-Mart opens smaller grocery stores as test, *MSNBC.com*, www.msnbc.com, January 14; 2008, Wal-Mart Stores, *Market Edge Research*, www.marketedgeresearch.com, March 2.

British rival on its home turf? What about CompUSA? Read Understanding Strategy: Learning from Failure to learn about this company's situation. What is your assessment of CompUSA's use of the strategic management process? What might you have done differently if you were leading CompUSA? In your opinion, did CompUSA ever find a unique way to pursue a unique opportunity in its external environment?

As the CompUSA example shows, organizational success (certainly success over time) is not guaranteed for any firm. Indeed, success is strongly influenced by how well a firm uses the strategic management process. In your opinion, was this process used successfully and consistently at CompUSA?

Moreover, even for successful companies, success can be transitory. Firms must always be aware of their surroundings and about what is happening in the global business world. Patricia Sueltz, executive vice president of Salesforce.com, believes

"CompUSA Is Closing All of Its Stores," the Headlines Read. What Happened?

With the name Soft Warehouse, the firm that came to be known as CompUSA was founded in 1984 as a seller of software. The firm then expanded its operations in order to sell consumer electronics products and personal computers. In 1991, when it went public, the company's name was changed to CompUSA.

During the 1990s, CompUSA struggled to find its identity. Was it primarily a seller of software or of products using software applications and consumer electronics products? Continuing declines in the prices of personal computers as well as competition from direct seller Dell, Inc., damaged the company as did intense competition from big box retailers Best Buy and Circuit City and from Wal-Mart as well. Because of their size, these three competitors were able to offer greater selection and lower prices on consumer electronics products (e.g., televisions) that CompUSA was carrying.

Throughout its turbulent history though, some saw value in CompUSA. In 1999, for example, Mexican telephone and retailing magnate Carlos Slim took a stake in the firm and then acquired other companies to increase its size. Slim later spent roughly $800 million to take the firm private. Over time, Slim's total investment in CompUSA was close to $2 billion.

Although "the chain went through several CEOs and tried different turnaround strategies such as a move (in 2007) to focus on core customers such as gadget lovers and small business owners," nothing really worked. As a result, Slim decided in late 2007 to close the firm's remaining stores (severely underperforming units were previously closed). CompUSA was then sold to retail-store liquidator Gordon Brothers Group.

But all may not be lost! Saying that "We believe the value of the CompUSA brand remains very high," Systemax CEO Richard Leeds announced about a month after Gordon Brothers took control of CompUSA's assets that his firm was purchasing CompUSA's brand, trademarks, and e-commerce business. The intention was to integrate CompUSA with Systemax's TigerDirect, which is a popular computer parts reseller. Primarily an online seller for computer enthusiasts, TigerDirect will replace the CompUSA name with its own name in retail stores as a means of expanding its presence in retail storefronts.

Sources: J. Cheng, 2008, Back from the dead: CompUSA assets snapped up by TigerDirect, *Answers from Laptop Experts*, www.arstechnica.com, January 7; 2008, Systemax agrees to purchase CompUSA assets, *IT Business Edge*, www.itbusinessedge.com, January 28; G. McWilliams, 2007, Slim to close last CompUSA stores, *The Wall Street Journal Online*, www.wsj.com, December 7; 2007, CompUSA to close corporate operations in March, *The Houston Chronicle Online*, www.chron.com, December 27; 2007, CompUSA to close stores after holidays, *The Motley Fool*, www.fool.com, December 7.

that she has to keep looking over her shoulder to see what competitors are doing to determine whether those actions are a threat to her firm's performance.[13]

We've now introduced you to the strategic management process, provided examples of vision statements and mission statements, and described in some detail how Wal-Mart is using the strategic management process. We also examined CompUSA as an example of a situation in which more effective use of the strategic management process might have had a positive effect on the firm's performance.

We'll use the remainder of this chapter to tell you a bit more about how firms analyze their external environment and their internal environment. Decision makers use the information gathered from the analyses of their firm's external and internal environments to select one or more strategies (see Figure 1.1). Before closing the chapter with a brief discussion of the contents of the book's remaining chapters, we'll introduce you to stakeholders and strategic leaders. In essence, stakeholders are the individuals and groups that firms try to satisfy when using the strategic management process, while strategic leaders are responsible for making certain their firms use the process effectively.

The Industrial Organization Model

Firms use what is called the industrial organization (I/O) model to analyze their external environment. We introduce you to this model here and provide you with a fuller discussion of it and its use in Chapter 3.

Firms use the I/O model to identify opportunities and threats. **Opportunities** are conditions in the firm's external environment that may help the firm reach its vision. **Threats** are conditions in the firm's external environment that may prevent the firm from reaching its vision. Performance often declines in firms that do not carefully study the threats and opportunities in their external environment. Firms use their resources to pursue environmental opportunities and to overcome environmental threats.

The experiences of Levi Strauss demonstrate how important it is for firms to recognize threats (and opportunities as well) in their external environment. During the late 1980s and into the 1990s, Levi failed to detect changes in its external environment such as those in customers' preferences. Changing preferences mandated that the firm begin to produce more fashionable jeans and related clothing items. Additionally, in contrast to competitors such as Jordache, Ralph Lauren, and Gloria Vanderbilt, Levi chose to remain focused on traditional distribution channels, avoiding discounters Target and Wal-Mart in the process. Thus, changes in Levi's external environment (in the form of customer demand and retail distribution patterns)—changes that had negative effects on the firm's financial performance—threatened the success of the world-famous branded products company.

In response to the challenges facing it, Levi decided to change virtually every aspect of how it conducts business. The firm now interacts with customers more frequently and with greater intensity to understand their product preferences. Levi also enhanced its product innovation capabilities and "implemented a new business planning and performance model that clarifies roles, responsibilities, and accountabilities and improves [the firm's] operational effectiveness."[14] These efforts are proving worthwhile in that the firm's financial performance continues to improve compared to the 1980s and 1990s.

Similar to Levi Strauss, the global airline industry illustrates the influence of the external environment on a firm's choice of strategy. Let's describe this influence.

Economic conditions, which as we said before are part of the firm's external environment, influence travel decisions. During poor economic times, for example, people might choose not to travel at all or to reduce the number of times they travel by air. Unrest in the global environment created by war and international tensions also affect the demand for airline services. The cost of fuel can have a dramatic effect on each airline company's profitability; in mid-2008, for example, increasing fuel costs were exerting an extremely negative effect on airline firms' ability to earn profits.

To deal with influences in their external environment, several carriers continue to contemplate the possibility of using a different strategy to compete. Essentially, many carriers are evaluating the use of a merger strategy (described in Chapter 7) in which firms agree to combine their operations on a relatively equal basis as the foundation for forming a single company. In early 2008, Delta and Northwest announced their intention to merge. Recognizing this possibility, US Airways officials commented that the industry needed to consolidate to reduce the number of major carriers from six to four. The compelling rationale for merging "in the airline executives' and analysts' views is how much money they believe they could save by combining their jet fleets, workforces, airport facilities, frequent-flyer programs, and headquarters."[15]

In Figure 1.2, we diagram how firms use the I/O model to analyze their external environment. The information gained from this analysis is used to help strategic leaders choose one or more strategies.

The Resource-Based View of the Firm Model

While the I/O model focuses on the firm's external environment, the resource-based view (RBV) model describes what firms do to analyze their internal environment. The purpose of analyzing the internal environment is to identify the

opportunities

conditions in the firm's external environment that may help the firm reach its vision

threats

conditions in the firm's external environment that may prevent the firm from reaching its vision

Figure 1.2 Using the Industrial Organization (I/O) Model to Analyze the External Environment

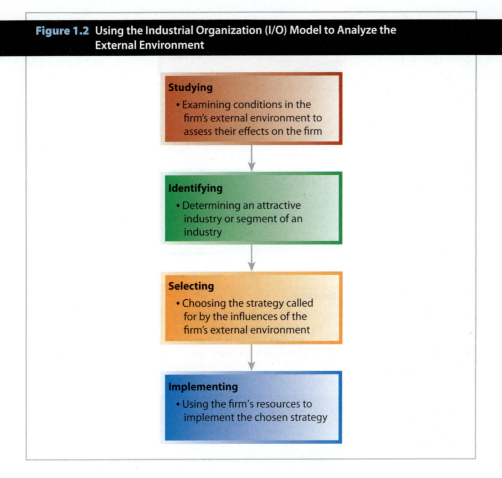

Studying
- Examining conditions in the firm's external environment to assess their effects on the firm

Identifying
- Determining an attractive industry or segment of an industry

Selecting
- Choosing the strategy called for by the influences of the firm's external environment

Implementing
- Using the firm's resources to implement the chosen strategy

firm's strengths, resources, capabilities, core competencies, and distinctive competencies, all of which are the source or foundation of the firm's competitive advantages. Thus, the I/O and RBV models complement each other; one (the I/O model) deals with conditions outside the firm, and the other (the RBV model) deals with conditions inside the firm. We introduce you to the RBV model here and offer a fuller description of it in Chapter 4.

The RBV model suggests that effective management of the firm's operations creates resources and capabilities that are unique to that firm. Therefore, the bundle of productive resources across firms can vary quite substantially.[16] Louis Vuitton's resources and capabilities, for example, differ from those of competitors Prada, Gucci, Hermes, and Coach. With resources and capabilities that differ from its competitors, each of these firms has a chance to develop distinctive competencies that it can use to produce a product that creates value for a group of customers. Let's describe how Louis Vuitton uses its unique resources and capabilities to develop core competencies and perhaps distinctive competencies that in turn allow the firm to create value for a group of customers.

The world's most profitable luxury brand, Vuitton has design skills and manufacturing efficiencies that are considered superior to those of its competitors. These distinctive competencies contribute to Louis Vuitton's ability to generate higher operating margins. Because of this superiority relative to its competitors, its distinctive competencies are the foundation for Vuitton's competitive advantages in product design and manufacturing that are critical to the firm's effective use of its focused differentiation strategy (see Chapter 5).

Figure 1.3 Using the RBV Model to Analyze the Internal Environment

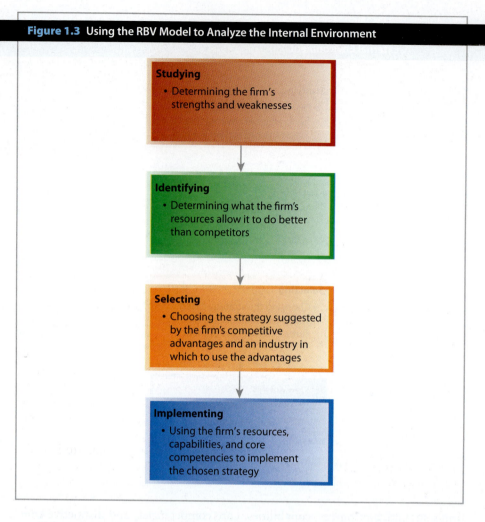

Although expensive, the firm's products do create value for a group of customers. One customer sees this value as "buying into a dream." In this particular customer's words, "You buy into the dream of Louis Vuitton. We're part of a sect, and the more they put their prices up, the more we come back. They pull the wool over our eyes, but we love it."[17]

Unlike the external environment, firms have direct control over conditions in their internal environment. Each firm's strategic leaders make choices about the resources and capabilities the firm wants to control and about how they'll be nurtured and used. The ability to control the firm's resources, capabilities, and core competencies and to develop them in ways that differ from those of the competitors increases the number of strategic options. Thus, from the RBV perspective, the uniqueness of the firm's resources, capabilities, and core competencies influences the choice of one or more strategies.

Figure 1.3 diagrams how firms use the RBV model to analyze their internal environment. Notice how the firm's resources, capabilities, and core competencies influence the choice of a strategy.

Next, we discuss stakeholders—the individuals and groups the firm seeks to satisfy by using the strategy or strategies it has selected.

Stakeholders

stakeholders

individuals and groups who have an interest in a firm's performance and an ability to influence its actions

Stakeholders are individuals and groups who have an interest in a firm's performance and an ability to influence its actions.[18] In essence, stakeholders influence firms by deciding the degree to which they will support the firm's strategy.

Figure 1.4 Stakeholder Groups

Owners
Shareholders
- Individual
- Institutional

External Stakeholders
- Customers
- Suppliers
- Local communities
- Government agencies
- General society

Internal Stakeholders
- Employees
- Managers

Shareholders, customers, and suppliers are stakeholders, as are a firm's employees and the communities in which the firm conducts business. Shareholders, for example, exercise their influence by deciding whether they will keep their shares in the firm or sell them. Employees decide whether they will remain with their employer or work for another firm, perhaps even a competitor. Not surprisingly, firms use the strategic management process to select and implement strategies that create value for stakeholders.[19]

As shown in Figure 1.4, firms have three major stakeholder groups: owners (shareholders), external stakeholders, and internal stakeholders. Each stakeholder wants the firm in which it has an interest to satisfy its needs. Generally speaking, stakeholders continue to support firms that satisfy their needs. However, in general, stakeholders withdraw their support from firms failing to meet their needs.

Stakeholders' interest in performance, coupled with their ability to influence the firm through their decisions to support the firm or not, suggests that companies have important *relationships* with their stakeholders. These relationships must be managed in a way that keeps the stakeholders committed to the firm. Firms that are able to use their resources and capabilities to manage relationships with their stakeholders better than their competitors may gain a competitive advantage.[20] These firms see stakeholders as their partners and keep them well informed about the company's actions.[21]

Firms and stakeholders have relationships because they need each other. To launch a company and operate it on a continuing basis, firms need capital (that is, money) provided by investors (such as stockholders) and financial institutions (such as banks), materials from suppliers that are used to produce a good or provide a service, and employees to complete necessary tasks. In addition and importantly, firms need customers to buy their good or service. Similarly, investors (individual stockholders and institutional stockholders such as pension funds) need to find viable businesses in which they can invest and earn a return on their capital. Employees need to work for organizations for income and at least some personal satisfaction. Customers want to buy goods and services from companies that will satisfy their various needs. Thus, firms need stakeholders, but stakeholders also need firms.

Managing relationships between the firm and its stakeholders is difficult because satisfying one stakeholder's needs may come at the expense of another stakeholder. Consider, for example, employees' desire to be paid more for their work. If wages are increased without an identical increase in productivity to offset the higher costs, the firm's cost of goods sold will increase, reducing the return on investment for shareholders. Alternatively, think of customers wanting to buy higher-quality products from a firm at ever-decreasing prices. The net result of the firm's lowering the price of its good or service without reducing the cost to produce it is fewer resources for wages and salaries and for returns to shareholders.

Although other examples could be offered, the main point here is that firms must manage their relationships with stakeholders in ways that will keep all stakeholders at least minimally satisfied. In other words, the firm wants to retain quality suppliers, loyal customers, and satisfied employees while providing returns to shareholders that cause them to retain their investment in the firm. As these comments show, managing relationships among various stakeholders is a challenging, yet important task for the firm's strategic leaders.

Strategic Leaders

Strategic leaders are the individuals who practice strategic leadership. (We define and fully discuss strategic leadership in the next chapter.) Strategic leaders make certain that actions are being taken that will lead to their firm's success.[22] As CEO of Apple Computer, for example, Steve Jobs must make certain that his firm uses the strategic management process to continue benefiting from its highly successful iPod digital music player and the more recently introduced iPhone. Because the iPhone has the power of a computer, the potential software applications are generating enthusiasm among both programmers and consumers. Part of Apple's product strategy for the iPhone is to develop the array of software applications that creates the most value for customers.[23]

© Christoph Dernbach/DPA/Landov

A firm's board of directors holds the CEO and top management team responsible for ensuring that an effective strategic management process is developed and properly used throughout the organization. When doing their work, top-level managers concentrate on the big picture to envision their firm's future and the strategies necessary to achieve that vision.[24] Increasingly, CEOs are being drawn from a global talent pool. Currently, the "head of the Altria Group was born in Egypt, PepsiCo's is from India, the Liberty Mutual Group's is a native of Ireland, and Alcoa's was born in Morocco."[25] Diversity at the helm of companies makes it more likely that an all-important global perspective will be adopted throughout the firm.

In small firms, the CEO may be the sole owner and may not report to a board of directors. In this instance, of course, that person is responsible for both designing and using the strategic management process. Decisions that strategic leaders make when using the strategic management process include determining what resources are acquired, what prices are paid for those resources, and how to manage those resources.[26] Through the firm's vision statement, strategic leaders try to stimulate their employees' creativity to develop new products, new processes to produce the firm's products, and the administrative routines necessary to successfully implement the firm's strategies.[27]

The CEO and top management team are also responsible for shaping and nurturing the firm's culture. **Organizational culture** is the set of values and beliefs that are shared throughout the firm. *Values* reflect what is important, while *beliefs* speak to how things should be done. In 3M's organizational culture, respect for the contribution of each employee and continuous innovation are important values.[28] The most effective organizational cultures let people know that they are appreciated, which provides strong motivation toward excellent performance by employees.[29]

Intangible in nature, culture can't be touched or seen, but its presence is felt throughout every organization. Think of companies where you've worked, university classes you've attended, or other groups to which you've belonged. Consider the values and beliefs held by each of those groups. How did it feel to be a member of those groups? The groups you are thinking about are different in

strategic leaders

the individuals who practice strategic leadership

organizational culture

the set of values and beliefs that are shared throughout the firm

terms of their values and beliefs, aren't they? The same can be said of business organizations.

Increasingly, strategic management is becoming more decentralized in companies. The logic behind this is to have the people who are "closest to the action" making decisions and taking actions.[30] Thus, the strategic management process is often shared among many people in an organization.[31] As a result, we need to be prepared to take on leadership roles regardless of our position in an organization. Additionally, frequent communication among all involved with the strategic management process helps ensure that changes are made when and where they are needed. Because of changing conditions, adjustments are often necessary when implementing strategies.

However, we should understand that even though many different people may be involved, the final responsibility for effective use of the strategic management process rests with the firm's top-level strategic leaders (i.e., the chief executive officer and the top management team). In addition, it is important to note that the best strategic leaders as well as all others throughout the firm also act ethically.

Ethics are concerned with the standards for deciding what is good or bad, right or wrong[32] as defined by most members of a particular society.[33] In an organizational context, ethics reveal a value system that has been widely adopted by the firm's employees[34] and that other stakeholders recognize as an important driver of decisions and actions. Firms can record their ethics in documents such as a code of conduct. On a daily basis, however, ethics can be inferred by observing the actions of the firm's stakeholders, especially its employees.[35] Even a brief review of events in the business world shows that an organization's ethics are of interest to the general society as well as to other stakeholders whose interests can be negatively affected when a firm acts unethically. Thus, as explored further in Chapter 2, ethical practices are a vital part of effective strategic leadership and strategic management.

How the Book Is Organized

The book has three major parts corresponding to the three parts of the strategic management process. Part One of this book comprises two chapters. This first chapter introduces you to the strategic management process. In Chapter 2, we describe leadership from a strategic perspective. Strategic leadership is being effectively practiced when everyone in a firm is aware of the vision being pursued and the important role each person plays in pursuing that vision. We also describe the most important actions strategic leaders take to guide their organizations. Being an effective strategic leader (especially an effective CEO) is challenging. And the fact that CEO turnover continues to increase suggests that stakeholders have high performance expectations of the person serving as the firm's CEO.[36]

In Part Two, which also has two chapters, we focus on two analyses firms use to gather and evaluate the information needed to choose strategies for pursuing the firm's vision. Chapter 3 focuses on the external environment. A firm analyzes the external environment to identify factors outside the company that can affect the strategic actions the firm is taking to achieve its vision. Firms can influence but not control conditions in their external environment. The focus of Chapter 4 is inside the firm. Here, the purpose is to understand how the firm's unique resources, capabilities, and core competencies can be used to create value for customers. Using resources, capabilities, and core competencies in ways that create value means that the firm has one or more competitive advantages.

Part Three examines different types of strategies. The strategies the firm chooses are a product of the vision and the conditions in the firm's external environment and its internal environment. The insights gained from the topics presented in the book's first four chapters strongly guide the selection of strategies. In Chapters 5, 6, and 7, our concern is with different strategies (business-level, multiproduct, and mergers and acquisitions) that firms use to successfully compete in different markets. Each chapter also provides guidelines for implementing different strategies. We follow these discussions with explanations in Chapters 8, 9, and 10 of strategies (international, cooperative alliances, and new ventures) that firms use to enter new markets.

SUMMARY

Our primary purpose with this chapter is to introduce you to the strategic management process and to discuss how firms use this important organizational tool to continuously improve their performance for stakeholders. To reach this purpose, we examined the following topics:

- **Strategic management** is the ongoing process firms use to form a vision, analyze their external and internal environments, and select one or more strategies to create value for customers and satisfy other stakeholders. The external and internal environments are analyzed to determine what strategies the firm should use (and how to use those strategies) to achieve the vision. Strategic management is concerned with both formulation (selection of one or more strategies) and implementation (actions taken to ensure that the chosen strategies are used as intended).
- Firms use the industrial organization model (the I/O model) to examine their **external environment** in order to identify opportunities and threats in that environment. Firms use the resource-based view of the firm model (the RBV model) to analyze their **internal environment** in order to identify their resources, capabilities, and core competencies. A firm must use both models to

have the knowledge it needs to choose strategies that will enable it to achieve its vision.

- **Stakeholders** are individuals and groups who have an interest in how the firm performs and who can influence the firm's actions. Firms and their stakeholders are dependent on each other. Firms must operate in ways that satisfy the needs of each stakeholder (such as shareholders, customers, suppliers, and employees). Firms failing to satisfy those needs likely will lose a stakeholder's support. Owners, external stakeholders, and internal stakeholders are the three primary stakeholder groups with which firms are involved. But stakeholders need firms as well. Consider, for example, that investors (as owners of the firm) want to invest in profitable firms, employees want to work for acceptable wages, and customers want to buy products that create value for them.
- **Strategic leaders** practice strategic leadership when they make certain that their firm is effectively using the strategic management process. Increasingly, effective strategic management results when many people are involved with the strategic management process and when strategic leaders demand that everyone in the firm act responsibly and ethically in all that they do.

KEY TERMS

DISCUSSION QUESTIONS

1. What is strategic management? Describe strategic management's importance to today's organizations.
2. What is the industrial organization (I/O) model? Why do firms use it to analyze their external environment?
3. What is the resource-based view of the firm model? Why do firms use this model to examine their internal environment?

4. Who are stakeholders? Why are stakeholders important to firms? What does it mean to say that the firm has relationships with its stakeholders?
5. What is the nature of the strategic leader's work?

STRATEGY TOOLBOX

Introduction

A major problem facing strategic leaders is maintaining focus within a firm given the dynamic and complex nature of today's competitive environment. Effective strategic leaders use the strategic management process (which we define in this chapter) to increase the probability that their firm will properly conduct an external analysis and an internal analysis—two core activities that are the foundation for selecting the company's strategy.

Strategic Management Steps

External Analysis

- Examine the trends in the Macro Environment (including customers)
- Profile the Industry (including competitors)
- **Outcomes:**
  - Document and prioritize "Threats"
  - Document and prioritize "Opportunities"

Internal Analysis

- Inventory the company's resources
- Assess the company's capabilities
- **Outcomes:**
  - Document and link "Strengths" and "Weaknesses" to opportunities
  - Identify "Core Competencies"
  - Identify current and potential "Distinctive Competencies"

Strategy

- Establish the "Mission" (who we are)
- Communicate the "Vision" (where we are going)
- Roll out the "Strategies" (how we are going to get there)
- **Outcomes:**
  - Successful implementation
  - Decision-making alignment
  - Motivated employees

MINI-CASE

Are Still Better Days Ahead for Hewlett-Packard?

Technology giant Hewlett-Packard (HP) makes computers and printers and provides technology consulting services. Printers are perhaps the firm's most famous and durable products. In early 2008, HP celebrated the twentieth anniversary of its Deskjet printer, which the firm notes is "the world's top-selling printer brand," serving more than 240 million customers worldwide. HP generates more than $100 billion annually in sales revenue, making it one of the world's largest information technology companies.

Mark Hurd became HP's CEO in March 2005, following Carly Fiorina in this role. From a financial perspective, HP's early results during Hurd's tenure were quite positive as indicated by the fact that from his first day as CEO through the end of 2007, "HP's stock surged 132%, about five times the return of the Standard & Poor's 500-stock

index." Results such as this one clearly have the potential to satisfy stakeholders, especially those owning stock in HP.

Known for his operational management skills, Hurd's cost-cutting and improvements in the firm's operations techniques were the source of HP's impressive financial gains during the initial phase of Hurd's service. But times may be changing for Hurd and HP. As 2008 unfolded and in light of industry-wide predictions of reductions in the amounts companies around the globe would invest in technology in the next several years, some thought that as HP's key strategic leader, Hurd needed to take different actions. One analyst saw it this way: "The first three years of [Hurd's] tenure have been about profit growth through cost-cutting and restructuring and raising efficiencies." Looking to the years ahead, this analyst suggested that "HP is [now] entering a phase where it needs to get future profit growth from sales growth and not cost cutting." Another way of capturing the essence of this analyst's perspective is to say that Hurd needs to display visionary leadership in addition to execution-oriented leadership in order for HP to remain successful.

Hurd gives every indication that he intends to serve as a visionary leader for HP. Innovation may be the foundation for the HP of the future that Hurd envisions. With an interest in driving technological innovations for its customers, HP allocated $3.6 billion to research and development (R&D) in 2006. Recently, Hurd stated that he is "determined to keep [HP's] pipeline stocked with promising new products and services." More fundamentally, Hurd believes that investing heavily in R&D today is the path to best position HP for long-term success.

One part of the innovation-focused vision Hurd and other strategic leaders at HP have for the company revolves around a strategy to leverage the Internet. Specifically, relying on Hurd's support and the vision of Vyomesh I. Joshi, the senior vice president in charge of the firm's printing division, HP is trying to figure out a way to encourage people to print more Web pages, especially when using their home computers. In 2008, HP acquired Tabblo, a privately held developer of Web-based software. HP completed this transaction to gain access to Tabblo's software application that "creates templates that reorganize the photos and text blocks on a Web page to fit standard sizes of paper." HP's interest is to make this software a standard like Adobe's Flash and Reader or Sun Microsystems' Java. This intention demonstrates Joshi's belief that HP is in the "content consumption business" rather than the printing business.

Sources: L. Lee, 2008, HP's Hurd is about to be tested, *BusinessWeek*, February 25, 59–60; J. Scheck, 2008, HP posts 38% quarterly profit gain, *The Wall Street Journal Online*, www.wsj.com, February 20; 2008, HP makes big investment in consumer tech support, *The Wall Street Journal Online*, www.wsj.com, February 28; 2008, Hewlett-Packard, www.hp.com, March 3; D. Darlin, 2007, HP tries to create printers that love the Web, *The New York Times Online*, www.nytimes.com, April 9.

Questions

1. Using materials available to you, including the Internet, learn as much as you can about Mark Hurd as a strategic leader. See if you can determine the type of organizational culture Hurd is developing at HP. Given what you learn and in light of comments included in the case, would you want to work for Hurd? Why or why not?

2. Go to Hewlett-Packard's Web site (www.hp.com) to discover the firm's current actions regarding "printing from the Web." Has HP acquired more companies to support the effort to leverage the Internet? If so, what are those actions and how successful are they?

3. The industrial organization (I/O) model and the resource-based view of the firm model are introduced in this chapter. Find evidence in the case showing that HP was being influenced by its external environment and that the firm has unique capabilities it intends to use to be successful.

EXPERIENTIAL EXERCISES

Exercise One: The Culture, Vision, and Strategy Linkage

Vision and mission statements of firms need to be aligned with organizational culture. Together they give employees direction in any situation by providing them with values and purpose that set key priorities and orient action.

In Small Groups

In a small group, determine what your group thinks is the culture for each of the following companies. Then link that culture to your view of the firm's vision or mission as you understand it. How does your concept of the firm's culture and vision fit with what you understand about its strategy, which is the basis for its success?

- Target
- Mary Kay Cosmetics
- UPS
- Starbucks

Whole Class

Groups should then compare their answers to the question that was answered in small groups. The purpose of this activity is to highlight differences as well as similarities in the small groups' answers. Finally, go to each firm's Web site and find its mission or vision statement. How well does the statement align with the culture and strategy you identified?

BIZ FLIX

U-571: Setting Strategy

Watch the scene from *U-571*. It shows several aspects of strategic management and strategic planning described earlier in this chapter.

This action-packed World War II thriller shows a U.S. submarine crew's efforts to retrieve an Enigma encryption device from a disabled German submarine. After the crew gets the device, a German vessel torpedoes and sinks their submarine. The survivors must now use the disabled German submarine to escape from the enemy with their prize. The film's almost nonstop action and extraordinary special effects look and sound best with a home theater system.

The scene comes from the "160 meters" segment toward the film's end. Lt. Andrew Tyler (Matthew McConaughey) is now the submarine's commander following the drowning death of Lt. Commander Mike Dahlgren (Bill Paxton), the original commander. Lt. Tyler says, "Chief." Chief Petty Officer (CPO) Henry Klough (Harvey Keitel) approaches the map table. The film continues to its dramatic end with the execution of the strategy Tyler described.

What to Watch for and Ask Yourself
1.   Does Lt. Tyler analyze the submarine's external environment?
2.   What is Lt. Tyler's assessment of the submarine's resources and competitive advantage?
3.   Does Lt. Tyler consider threats and opportunities in forming his strategic plan?

ENDNOTES

1.   D. Kaplan, 2008, Aiming big by going small, *The Houston Chronicle Online*, www.chron.com, February 25; P. B. Kavilanz, 2007, Best Buy's profit, sales top view, *CNNMoney.com*, www.cnnmoney.com, December 18.
2.   S. Bretting, 2008, Helicopter school fills a niche need, *The Houston Chronicle Online*, www.chron.com, February 15.
3.   D. Rigby, 2007, Management tools, Bain & Company, www.bain.com, August 25.
4.   2008, Intoweb, www.intoweb.co.za, March 1.
5.   2008, Loomis, www.loomis.com, February 26.
6.   D. J. Teece, 2007, Explicating dynamic capabilities: The nature and microfoundations of (sustainable) enterprise performance, *Strategic Management Journal*, 28: 1319–1350.
7.   R. B. Tucker, 2008, Innovation: Core competency for the 21st century, *The Innovation Resource*, www.innovationresource.com, February 15.
8.   J. Spencer, 2008, Lenovo puts style in new laptop, *The Wall Street Journal Online*, www.wsj.com, January 3.
9.   G. McWilliams, 2008, Wattles nominates slate of 5 to Circuit City board, *The Wall Street Journal Online*, www.wsj.com, February 26.
10. Kaplan, 2008, Aiming big by going small.
11. C. A. Montgomery, 2008, Putting leadership back into strategy, *Harvard Business Review*, 86(1): 54–60; M. E. Porter, 1996, What is strategy? *Harvard Business Review*, 74(6): 61–78.
12. 2008, 1-800-PetsMed.com, www.petsmed.com, February 22.
13. J. Kerstetter, 2004, A long climb to Salesforce.com, *BusinessWeek Online*, www.businessweek.com, May 12.
14. 2008, Levi Strauss, *Company Transformation*, www.levistrauss.com, March 2.
15. T. Belden, 2008, Likely Delta and Northwest merger could signal a trend, *The Philadelphia Inquirer*, www.philly.com, February 8.
16. E. T. Penrose, 1959, *The Theory of the Growth of the Firm*, New York: Wiley.
17. C. Matlack, R. Tiplady, D. Brady, R. Berner, & H. Tashiro, 2004, The Vuitton machine, *BusinessWeek*, March 22: 98–102.
18. K. Basu & G. Palazzo, 2008, Corporate social responsibility: A process model of sensemaking, *Academy of Management Review*, 33: 122–136; S. L. Hart & S. Sharma, 2004, Engaging fringe stakeholders for competitive imagination, *Academy of Management Executive*, 18(1): 7–18.
19. T. P. Moliterno & M. F. Wiersema, 2007, Firm performance, rent appropriation, and the strategic resource divestment capability, *Strategic Management Journal*, 28: 1065–1087; M. Beer & R. A. Eisenstat, 2004, How to have an honest conversation about your business strategy, *Harvard Business Review*, 82(2): 82–89.
20. A. King, 2007, Cooperation between corporations and environmental groups: A transaction cost perspective, *Academy of Management Review*, 32: 889–900;

A. J. Hillman & G. D. Keim, 2001, Shareholder value, stakeholder management, and social issues: What's the bottom line? *Strategic Management Journal*, 22: 125–139.
21. J. L. Campbell, 2007, Why would corporations behave in socially responsible ways? An institutional theory of corporate social responsibility, *Academy of Management Review*, 32: 946–967.
22. P. F. Drucker, 2004, What makes an effective executive, *Harvard Business Review*, 82(6): 58–63.
23. N. Wingfield, 2008, Apple is transparent in bid to broaden iPhone's reach, *The Wall Street Journal Online*, www.wsj.com, March 1.
24. T. A. Stewart & A. P. Raman, 2007, Lessons from Toyota's long drive, *Harvard Business Review*, 85(7/8): 74–83.
25. L. Story, 2007, Seeking leaders, U.S. companies think globally, *The New York Times Online*, www.nytimes.com, December 12.
26. D. G. Sirmon, M. A. Hitt, & R. D. Ireland, 2007, Managing resources in dynamic environments to create value: Looking inside the black box, *Academy of Management Review*, 32: 273–292.
27. M. Gottfredson, S. Schaubert, & H. Saenz, 2008, The new leader's guide to diagnosing the business, *Harvard Business Review*, 86(2): 62–73.
28. 2008, About 3M, 3M, www.3m.com, February 28.
29. D. C. Kayes, D. Stirling, & T. M. Nielsen, 2007, Building organizational integrity, *Business Horizons*, 50: 61–70.
30. A. T. Hall, M. G. Bowen, G. R. Ferris, M. T. Royle, & D. E. Fitzgibbons, 2007, The accountability lens: A new way to view management issues, *Business Horizons*, 50: 405–413.
31. R. D. Ireland & J. W. Webb, 2007, Strategic entrepreneurship: Creating competitive advantage through streams of innovation, *Business Horizons*, 50: 49–59; H. M. Guttman & R. S. Hawkes, 2004, New rules for strategic management, *Journal of Business Strategy*, 25(1): 34–38.
32. B. W. Heineman, Jr., 2007, Avoiding integrity land mines, *Harvard Business Review* 85(4): 100–108.
33. J. S. Harrison, 2004, Ethics in entrepreneurship, in M. A. Hitt & R. D. Ireland (eds.), *Entrepreneurship Encyclopedia*, Oxford, UK: Blackwell, 122–125.
34. D. Pastoriza, M. A. Arino, & J. E. Ricart, 2008, Ethical managerial behavior as an antecedent of organizational social capital, *Journal of Business Ethics*, 78: 329–341.
35. M. A. Hitt & J. D. Collins, 2007, Business ethics, strategic decision making, and firm performance, *Business Horizons*, 50: 353–357; M. A. Hitt, R. D. Ireland, & G. W. Rowe, 2005, Strategic leadership: Strategy, resources, ethics and succession, in J. Doh & S. Stumpf (eds.), *Handbook on Responsible Leadership and Governance in Global Business*, New York: Edward Elgar Publishers.
36. 2008, A second life for CEOs, *The Bryan-College Station Eagle*, March 2, E1.

CHAPTER 2
Leading Strategy

Knowledge Objectives

Reading and studying this chapter should enable you to:

1. Define and explain strategic leadership.

2. Explain how vision and mission create value.

3. Define the meaning of a top management team and the value of having a heterogeneous top management team.

4. Explain the importance of managerial succession.

5. Define human capital and social capital and describe their value to the firm.

6. Describe an entrepreneurial culture and its contribution to a firm.

7. Explain the importance of managerial integrity and ethical behavior.

8. Discuss why firms should have a control system that balances the use of strategic controls and financial controls.

© BrandX Pictures

Changes in Corporate Governance Have Reformed the Role of the CEO in Strategic Leadership

The role of the chief executive officer (CEO), especially in the United States, has been changing due to increased scrutiny by boards of directors and corporate governance trends in general. One of the most visible changes has been the division of the CEO role from that of the chairperson of the board of directors. Historically, many CEOs resisted sharing power by insisting on holding both roles simultaneously. For example, in 2002, 73 percent of public companies had combined roles whereas by 2007, 55 percent had a nonemployee chairperson of the board. Furthermore, the chairperson being independent of the board has created a situation such that "the age of the imperial CEO" is declining. Where the roles are separate, boards often have separate planning meetings in which board members might examine important strategy or executive succession issues. Additionally, in such boards, members are more likely to engage investors in concerns around executive pay and takeover defenses. Much of the unease regarding corporate governance has been due to the enactment of the Sarbanes-Oxley Act of 2002, which was a response to the accounting scandals such as those by Enron and WorldCom in 2001.

© Kevin Winer/Getty Images

However, because of the separation of the board chairperson and CEO roles, questions arise as to how these roles should be carried out in regard to important strategic issues. The basic question is "Who has the power to formulate strategy?" Interestingly, U.S. executives have been looking to Great Britain, which forced major public companies to divorce the two roles in 1992 during a period of corporate governance reform. As such, the board chairperson in large British companies usually comes from outside company ranks. Increasingly, boards of U.S. firms have likewise been naming former CEOs with no affiliation to the focal company to fill the chairperson role, which is now the case in 7.2 percent of S&P companies.

Critics, however, have warned that this new breed of chairpersons may be tempted to get involved in management issues that are reserved for the actual CEO, creating confusion for shareholders as to who is actually in charge. Often, under the new board reforms, the board will have an outside director who is not part of the firm's employment structure historically. Although this person will not necessarily be the board chair, he/she can hold independent meetings without executives from the board and can consult with other outsider directors regarding issues that pertain to strategy and management succession without political influence from the current CEO. Accordingly, these new changes and other changes associated with the Sarbanes-Oxley Act of 2002 mean more power sharing in important issues related to strategy of the overall firm.

Examples of recent companies that have divided the roles and have hired a strong external chairperson of the board are Walt Disney Company, Marsh & McLennan Cos., and Bristol Meyers Squibb Co. Some of these companies were seeking to reassure stockholders after a scandal or bad corporate report that they would pursue better corporate governance procedures. These changes in corporate governance have led to a decrease in the CEO's power and an increase in power sharing among board members and the CEO in regard to overall strategic responsibilities and direction of the company. Thus, the CEO is not only accountable to shareholders, but also more accountable to a chairperson or a lead outside director who can consult with an increasing number of independent outside directors on boards regarding important strategic issues.

Power sharing has also occurred because firms have more diffuse supply chains as well as numerous and often complex strategic alliances or joint ventures with numerous partner firms. As such, strategic leaders find that they must manage with more involvement of employees and of managers of these complex partnering arrangements. In essence, this situation requires less top-down strategic leadership and more power sharing and joint decision making with middle managers, strategic partners, and supplier and customer firms in regard to important strategic decisions.

In summary, strategic leadership is more diffuse because of corporate governance as well as other strategic partnering arrangements that are necessary to manage a large firm both domestically and globally. Consequently, strategy becomes more of a dynamic process that involves continual evaluation rather than a set solution to establish long-term sustainable competitive advantage. Thus, strategy has become a process of continual creation and recreation rather than a stable set of characteristics that differentiate the company from its competitors.

Sources: R. M. Kanter, 2008, Transforming giants, *Harvard Business Review*, 86(1): 43–52; J. S. Lublin, 2008, When chairman and CEO roles get a divorce, *Wall Street Journal*, January 14, B1; S. Mishra, 2008, Counting progress; The state of boards five years after Sarbanes-Oxley, *The Corporate Governance Advisor*, January/February, 12; C. A. Montgomery, 2008, Putting leadership back into strategy, *Harvard Business Review*, 86(1): 54–60; S. E. Needleman, 2008, Corporate governance (a special report); Too many cooks? Companies are tapping outside CEOs to run their boards; It makes sense—but it could be a recipe for conflict, *Wall Street Journal*, January 14, R4; K. Elsayed, 2007, Does CEO duality really affect corporate performance? *Corporate Governance: An International Review*, 15: 1203–1204.

Strategic leadership involves developing a vision for the firm, designing strategic actions to achieve this vision, and empowering others to carry out those strategic actions. As defined in Chapter 1, *strategic leaders* are the individuals practicing strategic leadership. Strategic leaders hold upper-level organizational positions. As Focusing on Strategy indicated, today's strategic leaders are involving people throughout the firm as well as other governance participants (board of director members and other stakeholders (suppliers and customers) in strategic management. Thus, any person in the firm (and outside) responsible for designing strategic actions and ensuring that they are carried out in ways that move the firm toward achievement of the vision is essentially playing the role of a strategic leader.

Is strategic leadership important? A substantial amount of research suggests that it is.[1] Richard Clark became CEO of Merck, a large pharmaceutical firm, in mid-2005 shortly after the drug Vioxx was recalled, which led to a number of lawsuits and a dramatic drop in Merck's share price. Clark immediately began to reshape the company's strategy and rebuild Merck's reputation. Working with other leaders (for example, chief scientist Peter Kim and former legal counsel Ken Frazier), Clark sought to unite Merck operationally by seeking "a more integrated approach." Clark is quoted as saying, "From the moment we begin talking about a particular drug franchise, I want researchers, marketers, and manufacturing people sitting in the same room."[2] Besides having a stronger purpose and developing a more integrated approach internally and through its partners, it also had to rebuild its reputation given the Vioxx disaster. It helped that by late 2007, of the 20 Vioxx cases that had gone to trial, Merck won 12 (although two of those verdicts have been set aside) and lost five. This winning record helped to restore investor confidence. Although Merck's problems may not be over, without the strategic leadership of CEO Richard Clark and other top executives, Merck's situation would likely be much worse.

In this chapter, we examine important strategic leadership actions: establishing the firm's vision and mission, developing a management team and planning for succession, managing the resource portfolio, building and supporting an entrepreneurial culture, promoting integrity and ethical behavior, and using effective organizational controls. These strategic leadership actions are displayed in Figure 2.1. We begin with a discussion of how vision and mission are used to direct the firm's future.

strategic leadership

developing a vision for the firm, designing strategic actions to achieve this vision, and empowering others to carry out those strategic actions

Figure 2.1 Strategic Leadership Actions

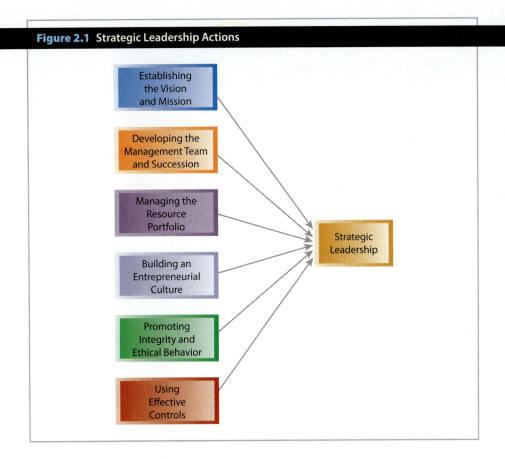

Establishing the Vision and Mission

Most strategic plans are designed for a 3- to 5-year time period, but a vision is usually targeted for a longer time, generally 10 to 20 years. As explained in Chapter 1, the *vision* contains at least two components—a statement describing the firm's DNA and the "picture" of the firm as it is hoped to exist in a future time period. The second part of the vision is *mission*, which defines the firm's core intent and the business or businesses in which it intends to operate. The mission flows from the vision and compared to the vision is more concrete in nature.

Visions can differ greatly across firms depending on the strategic leaders' intentions. For example, Steven Jobs, CEO of Apple, continues to develop visions of new products and markets. He developed not only Apple, but also Pixar—an extremely successful animation company that teamed with Disney to make the movie *Finding Nemo*. He created the Mac revolution with the Apple Macintosh computer; reshaped the music industry with Apple's iPod and iTunes online music venture; and more recently introduced the iPhone and Apple TV Take Two, a revamped version of the company's living-room media server. These new products are part of Jobs's vision to dramatically change the computer, music, cell phone, and media industries.[3]

Other firms have simpler visions even though they still may be difficult to achieve. For example, some firms may envision being among the most admired firms for their performance and effective management. A number of organizations now rank firms on a regular basis. For example, *Fortune* publishes a list of the world's most admired companies based on an annual survey; the top 20 firms for 2005, 2006, and 2007 are shown in Table 2.1. Although *Fortune*'s ranking includes only U.S. firms, the ranks change over time as some firm's strategies fall out of favor or strategic leaders make errors of strategic judgment. For example, Dell has been having a hard time relative to competitors such as Hewlett-Packard. Similarly, Wal-Mart's reputation has declined as it finds itself on the negative side

Table 2.1 *Fortune's* Most Admired Companies Ranking

2008	2007	2006
1. Apple	1. General Electric	1. General Electric
2. Berkshire Hathaway	2. Starbucks	2. FedEx
3. General Electric	3. Toyota Motor	3. Southwest Airlines
4. Google	4. Berkshire Hathaway	4. Procter & Gamble
5. Toyota	5. Southwest Airlines	5. Starbucks
6. Starbucks	6. FedEx	6. Johnson & Johnson
7. FedEx	7. Apple	7. Berkshire Hathaway
8. Procter & Gamble	8. Google	8. Dell
9. Johnson & Johnson	9. Johnson & Johnson	9. Toyota Motor
10. Goldman Sachs Group	10. Procter & Gamble	10. Microsoft
11. Target	11. Goldman Sachs Group	11. Apple Computer
12. Southwest Airlines	12. Microsoft	12. Wal-Mart Stores
13. American Express	13. Target	13. United Parcel Service
14. BMW	14. 3M	13. Home Depot
15. Costco Wholesale	15. Nordstrom	15. PepsiCo
16. Microsoft	16. United Parcel Service	15. Costco Wholesale
17. United Parcel Service	17. American Express	17. American Express
18. Cisco Systems	18. Costco Wholesale	18. Goldman Sachs Group
19. 3M	19. PepsiCo	19. International Business Machines
20. Nordstrom	20. Wal-Mart Stores	20. 3M

Source: A. Fisher, 2008, America's most admired companies, *Fortune*, March 17, 65; A. Fisher, 2007, America's most admired companies, *Fortune*, March 19, 88; A. Fisher & T. Demos, 2006, America's most admired companies, *Fortune*, March 6, 65.

of much media attention. On the other hand, General Electric has been able to maintain a strong reputation, most likely due to strong strategic leadership.

An effective strategic leader not only can develop a vision of the future, but also can inspire stakeholders to commit to achieving it. It is especially important for the leader to gain the support of the company's shareholders and employees. If the shareholders do not support the vision, they may pressure the board of directors to change it or find new strategic leaders. Similarly, employee commitment to the vision is needed because they must help implement the strategy designed to achieve the vision. Consider the case of Porsche. Company officials believe that they have a clear strategy in place to develop a group of new models through 2012. The firm's vision entails growth and maintenance of its strong brand image by introducing these new products. More specifically, CEO Wendelin Wiedeking has an "emphasis on turning out high performance cars that are as durable as Japanese sedans."[4] This vision has helped establish Porsche's brand as the number one rank in J.D. Power & Associates' survey of initial quality in the automobile industry. Wiedeking has also maintained a Japanese-like focus on reducing costs such that Porsche cars have the "performance of an exotic car but the reliability of a Honda." In 2009, Porsche plans to introduce a new four-door coupe, the Panamera. To make sure that the new model meets the standards of its vision and image, marketers and engineers communicate almost daily about quality, seeking to make sure that even minor problems are ironed out before the company starts delivery.

As we mentioned earlier, and as exemplified by Porsche, strategic leaders often use their team of managers as well as others in the firm to help make major decisions, especially to define and implement a vision for the firm. This team also helps formulate the firm's strategy. Next, we examine the teams of managers that strategic leaders use in the decision process.

Developing the Top Management Team and Succession

Top Management Team

Because of the complexity of their roles, most strategic leaders form teams to help them complete their work. A **top management team** is the group of managers charged with the responsibility to develop and implement the firm's strategies. Generally, the top management team is composed of officers of the company with the title of vice president and higher.[5]

Typically, when people select individuals for a team to work with, they prefer to choose people who think like them and are more likely to agree with them. Although such a team can facilitate making fast decisions (because members of the team more easily agree), these teams are more prone to making mistakes. A team of people with similar backgrounds (a *homogeneous team*) may achieve a quick consensus about issues but may lack sufficient knowledge and information needed to make an effective decision. Additionally, because they "think alike," they may overlook important issues and make errors in judgment. Therefore, to be most effective, strategic leaders need a management team composed of members who see and think differently. The team members may have different types of education (such as engineering, chemistry, and business) or varying amounts and types of experience (working in different functional areas, companies, or industries). We refer to this type of group as a *heterogeneous team*. A heterogeneous team is likely to take more time to make decisions but also likely to make better decisions. However, such teams may hinder strategic expansion if they have problems relating socially to one another.[6]

Historically, Nissan included only Japanese employees in its management teams. However, in 2000, it was nearly bankrupt when Carlos Ghosn took over as CEO of the Japanese-centered company. Ghosn was born in Brazil; reared in Lebanon; and attended school in Paris, France. As such, he had a broad understanding of global issues and was able to help Nissan recover dramatically. He also was promoted to be the CEO of Renault, which has a joint venture with Nissan. Part of Ghosn's success at Nissan was due to the diversity of the management team that he brought in to help revive Nissan. Although Nissan subsequently stumbled, it has had recent successes with the subcompact Versa. In the future, with his diverse management team, he seeks to put an electric car on the road by 2011 and eventually partner with a Detroit car maker through an auto alliance with Renault and/or Nissan. But even though he is as popular as a rock star at industry events, he won't succeed as a one-person team. So he needs to continue to develop his top management team.[7]

Management Succession

In addition to forming the management team, strategic leaders must develop people who can succeed them. In fact, having people with skills to take over a job when needed is important to a firm's success. Some companies use sophisticated leadership screening systems to select people with the skills needed to perform well as a strategic leader.[8] The people selected then normally participate in an intensive management development program to further hone their leadership skills. The "ten-step talent" management development program at General Electric (GE) is considered one of the most effective programs for developing strategic leaders. Because of the quality of its programs, General Electric "is famous for developing leaders who are dedicated to turning imaginative ideas into leading products and services."[9]

Obviously, a change in CEO is a critical succession event in firms. The effects of CEO succession can be different based on whether the new CEO is from inside or outside the firm. The majority of CEO successions are from the inside, with a person groomed for the position by the former CEO or the board of directors. "Hiring from the inside" motivates employees because they believe that they have opportunities to receive promotions and more challenging jobs if they perform well. A recent inside CEO succession was announced at PepsiCo. Having worked for PepsiCo since 1994, Indra Nooyi proved herself worthy to the board and was

top management team
the group of managers charged with the responsibility to develop and implement the firm's strategies

nominated and promoted to CEO in late 2006. She had served as a CFO and helped integrate the acquisition of Quaker Oats and the Gatorade brands.[10]

Most new CEOs selected for the job in an inside succession are unlikely to change in any drastic way the strategies designed under the leadership of the former CEO.[11] However, when the firm is performing poorly, it is more common to select an outside successor.

When new CEOs are chosen from outside the organization, the board often does so with the desire to change the firm's strategies. A change in strategies may be desired because the firm is performing poorly or because opportunities and threats in the competitive landscape require adjustments to avoid performing poorly in the future.[12] For example, Lou Gerstner helped to provide significant change at IBM when he was recruited from a consumer goods firm to become CEO of IBM. Gerstner transformed IBM into a successful performer again with a major change in its strategy.[13] Under Gerstner, IBM moved from a strategy based on selling separate pieces of hardware to a strategy calling for the firm to emphasize its service solutions and consulting services.

At times, it is more difficult to determine whether a succession is from the inside or outside. For example, in 2008, John Donahoe was selected to be the new CEO of eBay Inc. to replace Meg Whitman who planned to retire. Donahoe was recruited in 2005 to become the president of eBay's main auction business unit. He was a managing partner of Bain Consulting Company and thus came to eBay as an outsider. However, he is considered an insider given that he has been managing the core auction business for several years. Thus, it is hard to tell at times whether a successor is an insider or an outsider.[14] Interestingly, research shows that companies perform significantly better when they appoint insiders to the job of CEO. However, this research also suggests that many companies do not have succession plans; as such, when it comes time to find a new CEO, many firms turn to outsiders.

Of course as already noted, both insiders and outsiders have strengths and weaknesses depending on the conditions of the firm. Nonetheless, utilizing a strong succession plan and developing a strong set of training programs for managers firms can develop internal candidates who have a strong outside perspective. These executives in training can spend much of their time away from the main operations of the organization, that is, away from headquarters and working with new businesses that are different from the dominant business. They can be appointed CEOs of these business units and thus have the opportunity to manage the whole business. They can also be mentored to preserve their outside perspective and learn how to turn their new ideas into successful businesses that are protected from the dominant culture in the organization. Ultimately they can be CEOs who have an understanding of the inside approach to management, but also have the ability to transform the dominant organization in new ways should this be required.[15]

As discussed next, managing the firm's resource portfolio is another critical component of strategic leadership.

Managing the Resource Portfolio

Resources are the basis for a firm's competitive advantages and strategies (see Chapter 4). Even though we often think of tangible resources such as buildings, manufacturing plants, offices, machinery, and computers as being important, intangible resources may be more important. Indeed, recent estimates suggest that as much as 75 percent of a firm's value may be contained in its intangible resources.[16] Intangible resources include human capital, social capital, and organizational capital (such as the organizational culture). Additionally, financial capital is a critically important resource.

Intellectual property can be an especially valuable intangible resource in high-technology companies. For example, TiVo, a company that popularized digital video recorders (DVRs), lost much of its value when more generic DVRs were produced and undercut its success. However, because TiVo was a first mover in this market of 20 million users, the Patent and Trademark Office recognizes TiVo's patent on "time-warp" technology, which allows users to record one program while watching another. Because TiVo sees itself as a technology company, it has been creating partnerships and licenses with firms such as NBC Universal and cable companies such as Comcast and Cox that pay a premium to download TiVo's software on their generic DVRs. Previously, where others had been copying its technology, TiVo filed lawsuits in order to protect its intellectual property. For instance it filed a suit against EchoStar Communications, a satellite television producer. TiVo continues to move from a focus on hardware to an increased emphasis on software and processing advertising data as part of its strategy to facilitate advertising media expenditures through DVR systems. Additionally, it is seeking to help the television industry move to a media-on-demand strategy that will allow content delivery directly to people's television sets and to their PCs.[17]

A firm's intellectual property such as TiVo's is developed by its human capital. **Human capital** includes the knowledge and skills of those working for the firm. Employees' knowledge and skills are critical for all organizations. According to Ed Breen, CEO of Tyco International Ltd., "Companies compete with their brains as well as their brawn. Organizations today must not only outgun and outhustle competitors, they must also outthink them. Companies win with ideas."[18] To outthink competitors, a firm must depend on the knowledge of its workforce (managers and nonmanagerial employees) and continuously invest in developing their knowledge and skills. Such organizations are focused on learning. Knowledge can be acquired in training programs or through experience on the job. Learning from failure is a quality that leaders will experience repeatedly. The difference between some people and others is that some "fail better than others." In other words, it is not whether you fail but how you fail and what you learn from it that really matters.[19] It is the strategic leader's responsibility to help the firm learn faster and persevere better than others when mistakes are made.

Effective strategic leaders base their strategies on the organization's human capital.[20] They do so because the human capital in the organization must have the skills and motivation needed to implement chosen strategies. As such, leaders must help develop skills throughout the firm's workforce, motivate employees to use their skills when working to implement strategies, and reward them for doing so.[21] Steven K. Green, chairperson of the board of directors of the large global bank HSBC, suggests, "If we don't create the proper climate internally and live up to our brand name, we won't be able to achieve our strategic objective—managing for corporate growth."[22]

Another important resource is social capital. **Social capital** includes all internal and external relationships that help the firm provide value to customers and ultimately to its other stakeholders. *Internal social capital* refers to the relationships among people working inside the firm. These relationships help each organizational unit effectively complete its work while contributing to the overall value of the firm's human capital. "Most companies continue to assume that innovation comes from that individual genius, or best sequestered teams that vanish from sight and then return with big ideas, but the truth is most innovations are created through networks—groups of people working in concert."[23]

External social capital refers to relationships between those working within a firm and others (individuals and organizations) outside the firm. Such relationships

human capital

includes the knowledge and skills of those working for the firm

social capital

includes all internal and external relationships that help the firm provide value to customers and ultimately to its other stakeholders are essential because they provide access to needed resources. Few firms have all of the resources they need. Furthermore, most firms cannot do everything well. It may be better to outsource some activities to partner companies who can perform those activities exceptionally well, thereby increasing the quality of the focal firm's ability to produce products. External social capital can also help firms enter new markets. New companies may seek the financial support and expertise of venture capitalists, whereas more established companies often develop alliances with reliable suppliers or joint ventures with highly competent partners. In a sense, strategic leaders serve as key points of effective linkages for their firm in a network of relationships with other organizations. Some relationships involve strong ties where trust exists between the parties and reciprocity is expected, whereas other relationships represent weaker ties that serve more informational roles and allow strategic leaders to stay on top of the latest developments—even outside their industry—that may affect their firm (such as technology developments). So both strong and weak ties are important in strategic leaders' networks.[24]

The most effective social capital occurs when partners trust each other (strong ties). Effective strategic leaders have well-developed relational skills that help them establish trusting relationships with others inside and outside the organization. Andrea Jung, CEO of Avon Products, suggests that compassion is one of the key characteristics of effective leaders. As such, she believes that leaders should treat people fairly, with dignity and respect. In so doing, leaders are leading with their heart as well as their head.[25] One analysts suggested that leaders of today such as Jung need "the essential qualities of what we now call a Cross-Enterprise Leader—a leader adept at building, fostering and influencing a complex web of relationships across all levels—from employees, partners and suppliers to customers, citizens, and even competitors."[26]

Other resources such as financial capital are also important. In fact, firms with strong human capital and social capital are more likely to build a good base of financial capital.[27] Some also believe that an organization's culture can be a valuable resource. We discuss that topic next.

Building an Entrepreneurial Culture

Strategic leaders are concerned about the organization's culture because it can have major effects on employees' actions. An organizational culture is based on the core values of an organization, largely espoused by its leaders. When these values support opportunities to innovate, an entrepreneurial culture may develop. An **entrepreneurial culture** encourages employees to identify and exploit new opportunities. It encourages creativity and risk taking but also tolerates failure. Championing innovation is rewarded in this type of culture.[28] Building an entrepreneurial culture is of particular importance to strategic leaders.

Because of the pressure to be innovative yet profitable, many leaders try to focus their firm's innovation to increase the chances of success. For example, as explained in Understanding Strategy: Learning from Success, General Mills recently focused on innovative activities designed to provide foods that are healthier and products that meet government agency health standards.[29] As this example illustrates, such an approach has improved its new product growth rates and profitability.

Innovation is important in high-technology industries such as computers and in creative industries such as music and film animation. Steve Jobs is an appropriate strategic leader for Apple with his emphasis on creativity and innovation. However, 3M operates in several different industries with lower technology, such as adhesives (i.e., Scotch tape), traffic signs, and sandpaper. Yet the firm has been a pioneer, being the first to introduce products in its markets, such as the Post-it note. Therefore, an entrepreneurial culture is important in both firms.

entrepreneurial culture

encourages employees to identify and exploit new opportunities

General Mills Creates Wealth with a Focus on Healthier Products

In 2007, Kendall Powell replaced Steve Sanger as the CEO at General Mills. Powell has had a 28-year career at General Mills. As such, his promotion is seen as an inside succession. He managed the Yoplait Yogurt and Big G cereal divisions. He was also the chief executive for Cereal Partners Worldwide, a Switzerland-based joint venture with Nestle SA. His most recent position was president and chief operating officer (COO), to which he was appointed in June 2006. Powell's appointment is part of the company's long-time succession plan.

In his most recent role as COO, he worked at developing the company's long-term growth strategies, which included "broadening the channels through which the company sells its products, expanding overseas, and bringing more innovation to the business." For instance, half of its sales in Cascadian Farm and Muir Glen, which are organic brands, were sold through natural and organic specialty stores such as Whole Foods Market. Additionally, a new line of Pillsbury miniature desserts will be sold in convenience stores. General Mills has also been expanding internationally by reaching out to new consumers, such as with the Chinese brand Wanchai Ferry. The company has also been pushing to develop new innovative products such as Fizzix, a carbonated yogurt.

Probably one of the biggest changes has been its success in pursuing healthier product lines. Susan Crockett, who runs the company's Bell Institute of Health and Nutrition, an internal group of scientists who study and conduct health research, has been pushing the company to pursue healthier products. In this effort, the division heads, as well as Sanger and Powell, have found that they had to compensate managers for meeting more healthy product goals. The consumer trend in the food industry is toward healthier packaged food products. Also, Kellogg's, Kraft Foods, Campbell Soup Company, and Sara Lee have all been pushed by regulators and consumer advocates to increase nutrition in their products.

© Susan Van Etten

At General Mills, the company found that its fastest-growing sales were in products that carried some type of U.S. Food and Drug Administration approval health claim. In the mid-1990s, General Mills "established a goal of having its products preferred by 60 percent of consumers in market tests." In 2004, it established an additional goal that 20 percent of its sales should include products that "meet certain nutritional standards." A measurable goal was set such that divisions could meet these objectives by "a 10 percent reduction in fat, sugar, or sodium content; a 10 percent increase in healthful ingredients, including vitamins and fiber; or by meeting FDA guidelines that allow the product to carry labels such as 'reduced sodium' or 'lower fat.'" Interestingly, the company met its goals ahead of schedule and in 2006, the top executives set another standard that 20 percent more of its sales should meet the more stringent healthful product standards by 2010. Executives attribute the progress toward these healthy goals to linking 25 percent of the annual bonuses to these health and wellness objectives.

For example, to get children to eat more vegetables, the Green Giant brand spent two years on focused research with parents and developed a product that included "10 ounces of vegetables" in small packages. Although it costs more money to put the vegetables into individual microwavable trays, the company was convinced by the consumer research it carried out to create a "just for one" advertising campaign. Although it experienced some failures with this innovative approach, 34 percent of its products now meet its new standards for healthier products. Overall, the company reformulated more than 200 products and introduced at least 100 new ones. Even more important, significant firm sales growth and profits have come from these new lines.

Sources: J. Jargon, 2008, General Mills sees wealth via health: New recipe for profit, sales growth: More whole grains, less salt, fat, *Wall Street Journal*, February 25, A9; J. Jargon, 2007, General Mills taps Powell as next CEO: Successor to Steve Sanger is seeing continual plans for long-term growth, *Wall Street Journal*, September 25, B8; J. Birchall, 2007, General Mills's chief executive to bow out, *Financial Times*, September 25, 22.

The preceding discussions suggest the importance of innovation and strategic leadership. Even though the type and focus of innovation may vary, it is important in nearly all industries. As a result, building an entrepreneurial culture is a vital task for strategic leaders. Strategic leaders also must demonstrate ethical behavior. Next, we discuss the importance of integrity and ethical behavior for strategic leaders.

Promoting Integrity and Ethical Behavior

Strategic leaders not only develop standards for behavior among employees, but also serve as role models in meeting and exceeding those standards. Even though quality of performance is an important criterion, showing integrity and behaving ethically are also essential. So strategic leaders should determine the boundaries of acceptable behavior; establish the tone for organizational actions; and ensure that ethical behaviors are expected, praised, and rewarded. Lack of integrity and unethical behavior can be serious and extremely costly for a firm and for the person lacking integrity and behaving unethically. In fact, extraordinary unethical behavior can even lead to a firm's demise; Enron is a well-known example.

Recently, cases in which strategic leaders acted opportunistically in managing their firms have been a major concern. Acting opportunistically means that managers are making decisions that are in their own best interests rather than in the firms' best interests. Enron and Tyco are examples of what happens when leaders allow opportunistic behavior.

Because of opportunistic behavior in a number of companies, significant emphasis has been placed on how firms govern themselves (*corporate governance*). Corporate governance begins with the board of directors, whose members are responsible for overseeing managerial activities and approving (or disapproving) managerial decisions and actions. As illustrated in the opening Focusing on Strategy, the outcry from shareholders and the public in general has placed pressure on board members to be more diligent in examining managerial behavior. Legislation (such as Sarbanes-Oxley) passed in the United States requires greater managerial responsibility for the firm's activities and outcomes. Institutional owners in particular have pressured boards to enact better governance practices. For example, they generally want more independent outsiders than inside officers on the board. They believe that independent outside board members will be more objective and are less likely to agree with the CEO if he/she takes actions that appear not to be in the firm's best interests. In this way, managers' opportunistic actions can be curtailed.[30]

related-party transactions

paying a person who has a relationship with the firm extra money for reasons other than his or her normal activities on the firm's behalf

One form of potential opportunism, **related-party transactions,** involves paying a person who has a relationship with the firm extra money for reasons other than his or her normal activities on the firm's behalf. For example, Apple CEO Steve Jobs was reimbursed $1.2 million for costs he incurred while using his personal jet on company business. Two directors for Ford Motor Company, William Clay Ford and Edsel Ford, receive hundreds of thousands of dollars in consulting fees in addition to their compensation for serving as directors. Many of these transactions are legitimate, but some can be for questionable purposes as well. The Securities and Exchange Commission has started to carefully scrutinize related-party deals because of the opportunity for unethical behavior. Related-party deals were curtailed in the United States by Sarbanes-Oxley.[31]

Often worse than opportunistic actions by managers are fraudulent and other unlawful activities in which managers and companies' representatives engage. As an example, Jerome Kerviel was a night trader who pursued secret deals at the French Bank, Societe Generale, which cost the company

© Benoit Tessier/Reuters/Landov

$7 billion. Kerviel was adept at covering his tracks and was able to slip through several of the banks security firewalls. Even more critical is that many of his coworkers thought that there was something wrong, but none of them spoke to a manager about their concerns. A system to detect these problems is essential, but it functions best when individuals are encouraged to report such activities in order to prevent fraudulent behavior.[32]

Only leaders who demonstrate integrity and values respected by all constituents of the company will be able to sustain effective outcomes over time. Those who engage in unethical or unlawful activities may go unrecognized or undetected for a time, but eventually they will fail. People working under the leader often demonstrate the same values in their actions that are evident in the leader's behavior. Thus, if the leader engages in unethical activities, the followers are likely to do the same. As a consequence, the leader will suffer from the poor performance that results from his/her own and others' unethical behaviors. However, when the leader displays integrity and strong positive ethical values, the firm's performance will be enhanced over time because the followers will do the same.[33] Opportunism and unethical activities evident in several companies in recent times clearly show the importance of having effective control systems, which are discussed next.

Using Effective Controls

Controls are necessary to ensure that standards are met and that employees do not misuse the firm's resources. Control failures are evident in such dismal outcomes as exemplified by Enron and Tyco. Unfortunately, in both of these cases, the strategic leaders with responsibility for implementing the controls violated them, and the weak governance in both firms was unable to identify and correct the problems until they became excessive and external entities expressed concern about them. However, the potential value of controls goes beyond preventing fraud and managerial opportunism. Properly formed and used controls guide managerial decisions, including strategic decisions. Effective strategic leaders ensure that their firms create and use both financial controls and strategic controls as guides in the strategic management process.

Financial controls focus on shorter-term financial outcomes. These controls help the firm stay on the right path in terms of generating sales revenue, maintaining expenses within reason, and remaining financially solvent. Of course, a prime reason for financial controls is to generate an adequate profit. However, if financial controls are overly emphasized to increase current profits, managers are likely to limit their expenditures more than is necessary. Too many expense reductions in certain categories (such as R&D) can damage the firm's ability to perform successfully in the future. Money spent on R&D helps the firm develop products that customers will want to buy.

Alternatively, **strategic controls** focus on the content of strategic actions rather than on their outcomes. Strategic controls are best employed under conditions of uncertainty. For example, a firm may employ the correct strategy but the financial results may be poor because of a recession or unexpected natural disasters or political actions (such as the 9/11 terrorist attacks). To use strategic controls, the strategic leader or board must have a good understanding of the industry and markets in which the firm or its units operate in order to evaluate the accuracy of the strategy. Using strategic controls encourages managers to adopt longer-term strategies and to take acceptable risks while maintaining the firm's profitability in the current time period. As Understanding Strategy: Learning from Failure indicates, firms without good strategic controls often have significant growth stalls. For example, Dell and Starbucks recently brought back their former CEO's Michael Dell and Howard Schultz, respectively, to reverse problems of slow growth and execution. Four major reasons that pertain to strategic controls are given as reasons for such growth stalls.

financial controls
focus on shorter-term financial outcomes

strategic controls
focus on the content of strategic actions rather than on their outcomes

Understanding Why Growth Stalls and What to Do About It

Recently, two firms that were experiencing stalled growth brought back the former CEO to help save the company. Howard Schultz and Michael Dell were instituted as CEOs at Starbucks and Dell, respectively. In the past, Charles Schwab at Charles Schwab, Inc., Steve Jobs at Apple, and Eli Calloway at Calloway Golf were recruited back to help reestablish a growth trajectory in these firms. Although they may not be the only person in a firm who can solve the problem, former CEOs do help, as the history of these firms seems to indicate.

However, a more important question is "What occurred in these firms that led to the stall in growth and success?" Usually growth stalls because a firm has difficulties in perceiving problems through its strategic and financial control systems. Recent research analyzed points of problems for more than 500 firms that had stalls in their track record of growth. By far, the most important category of factors was labeled "Premium-position captivity: The inability of the firm to respond effectively to new, low-cost competitive challenges or to a significant shift in consumer valuation of product features." In other words, because a firm is captivated by its long history of success, it may find it difficult to evolve relative to external market changes. For instance, Eastman Kodak found it difficult to change to a digital imaging strategy given its strong base of competence and resources invested in film imaging through a chemical base. Levi Strauss faltered in the jean segment, being unable to recognize the threat of the rise of house brand and designer brand jeans.

The second most frequent cause for stalled growth is the breakdown of innovation management systems. At 3M, the company was so focused on creating new products for new strategies that it was unable to execute a strong manufacturing set of competencies and process innovations when it was forced to compete on price. Thus, at times, it is not only the amount of R&D

© Susan Van Etten

spending, but also the focus of the R&D spending. 3M needed to put more focus on process innovations.

A third major cause is premature abandonment of a core product or strategy. An interesting example is the failure of Kmart, which at one point did have a strong position in large-box, low-price retailing. Kmart pursued a strategy of acquisition in a number of disparate businesses including PayLess Drug Stores, The Sports Authority, and Office Max. Alternatively, Wal-Mart was investing significantly in its logistical capabilities. As such, Wal-Mart was able to gain a significant advantage in its inbound logistics costing and inventory management, which enabled it to have a better pricing capacity in the discount retailing segment compared to Kmart.

Another category that affects growth is human resource talent. When the human resource talent falls short, companies suffer. Hitachi had a narrow set of functional managers within its strong engineering culture. However, over time, more top executives with MBAs and other functional backgrounds such as marketing were needed as market changes in telecommunication and information system sectors became important. Thus, the top management team did not have the capabilities required to manage in a different market.

In order to meet these challenges, strong strategic controls as well as financial controls are necessary. But flexibility and a balanced approach in all areas are necessary to meet a more dynamic environment that will continuously challenge strategic leaders.

Sources: J. Adamy, 2008, Starbucks shares rise as CEO returns, *Wall Street Journal*, January 9, A12; J. Birchall, 2008, Starbucks chief plans revamp to restore "coffee authority," *Financial Times*, January 31, 21; H. Greenberg, 2008, Why investors should applaud a CEO's encore performance, *Wall Street Journal*, January 12–13, B3; M. S. Olson, D. van Bever, & S. Verry, 2008, When growth stalls, *Harvard Business Review*, 86(3): 50–61; D. Sewer, 2008, Starbucks fix, *Fortune*, February 4, 14; 2008, Come back kids and the risks of a repeat performance, *Financial Times*, January 16, 14.

The most effective system of controls is balanced using strategic *and* financial controls as illustrated. Controlling financial outcomes is important while simultaneously looking to the longer term and evaluating the content of the strategies used. To obtain the desired balance in control systems, many firms use a **balanced scorecard,**[34] which provides a framework for evaluating the simultaneous use of financial controls and strategic controls.

A balanced scorecard focuses on four areas—*financial* (profit, growth, and shareholder risk), *customers* (value received from the firm's products), *internal business processes* (asset utilization, inventory turnover), and *learning and growth* (a culture that supports innovation and change). In addition to helping implement a balanced control system, the balanced scorecard allows leaders to view the firm from the eyes of stakeholders such as shareholders, customers, and employees. The company's management system is the important link between strategy and operational execution. The company must necessarily begin with a strategic statement and then translate this statement into specific objectives and initiatives that serve as a guide for all employees, especially top management. The plan should map out operations and execution as well as the resources necessary to achieve the objectives. Through the control systems implemented, managers and employees monitor and learn from the strategy performance results and execution of the plan. Periodic assessment and updating of the strategic plan are necessary as emerging strategies show potential and necessitate adaptation and change. Thus, continuous strategic assessment and analysis are required to refine the vision and mission of the corporation that will guide the changes in strategy and execution.[35]

balanced scorecard

provides a framework for evaluating the simultaneous use of financial controls and strategic controls

SUMMARY

The primary purpose of this chapter is to explain strategic leadership and emphasize its value to an organization. In doing so, we examined the following topics:

- **Strategic leadership** involves developing a vision for the firm, designing strategic actions to achieve this vision, and empowering others to carry out those strategic actions. Establishing the firm's vision (and mission), developing a management team and planning for succession, managing the resource portfolio, building and supporting an entrepreneurial culture, promoting integrity and ethical behavior, and using effective organizational controls are the actions of strategic leadership.
- Strategic leaders, those practicing strategic leadership, develop a firm's vision and mission. The vision contains at least two components—a statement describing the firm's DNA and the "picture" of the firm as it is hoped to exist in the future. The mission of the firm focuses on the markets it serves and the goods and services it provides and defines the firm's core intent and the business or businesses in which it intends to operate.
- A **top management team** is the group of managers responsible for developing and implementing the firm's strategies. A heterogeneous team usually develops more-effective strategies than a homogeneous team because it holds a greater diversity of knowledge, considers more issues, and evaluates more alternatives.
- Managerial succession is important for the maintenance of the firm's health. Individuals should be developed and prepared to undertake managerial roles throughout the firm's hierarchy.
- **Human capital** includes the knowledge and skills of those working for the firm. Employees' knowledge and skills are an important resource to all organizations. Another important resource is social capital. **Social capital** includes all internal and external relationships that help the organization provide value to customers and ultimately to its other stakeholders. Strategic leaders must help develop the skills within the firm's workforce, motivate employees to use those skills to implement strategies, and reward them when they successfully use their skills.
- Strategic leaders shape an organization's culture. In the current competitive environment, all firms need to be innovative to remain competitive. Therefore, building an entrepreneurial culture is of particular importance to strategic leaders. An **entrepreneurial culture** encourages employees to identify and exploit new opportunities. It encourages creativity and risk taking and tolerates failures as a result.
- Strategic leaders develop standards for behavior among employees and serve as role models for meeting those standards. Integrity and ethical behavior are essential in today's business environment. Lack of integrity and unethical behavior can be serious and highly costly—to the firm and to individuals lacking integrity and behaving unethically. Ethical strategic leaders guard against managerial opportunism and fraudulent actions.
- Effective controls guide managerial decisions, including strategic decisions. **Financial controls** focus on shorter-term financial outcomes, whereas **strategic controls** focus on the content of the strategic actions rather than their outcomes. An effective control system balances the use of financial controls and strategic controls. The **balanced scorecard** approach is a useful technique that can help balance these two types of control.

KEY TERMS

balanced scorecard, 35
entrepreneurial culture, 30
financial controls, 33

human capital, 29
related-party transactions, 32
social capital, 29

strategic controls, 33
strategic leadership, 24
top management team, 27

DISCUSSION QUESTIONS

1. What is strategic leadership? Describe the major actions involved in strategic leadership.
2. How do a vision and a mission create value for a company?
3. What is a top management team? Why does a heterogeneous top management team usually formulate more effective strategies?
4. Why is it important to develop managers for succession to other managerial jobs?

5. What do the terms *human capital* and *social capital* mean? What is the importance of human capital and social capital to a firm?
6. How can a strategic leader foster an entrepreneurial culture, and why is such a culture valuable to a firm?
7. Why are managerial integrity and ethical behavior important to a firm?
8. Why should strategic leaders develop a control system that balances strategic controls and financial controls?

STRATEGY TOOLBOX

Introduction

Strategic management is the study of how business leaders take their organizations to new heights. A key player in this process is the Chief Executive Officer (CEO). Chapter 2 provides the foundation for the strategic analysis the CEO must perform. With that in mind, we offer for the Strategy Toolbox a "CEO Strategy Checklist" for completion of this awesome responsibility.

"CEO Strategy Checklist"

Key Question	Assessment
Develop—Do we have a strategy that leads to differentiation in the market?	Low – Medium – High
Understand—Could our employees articulate our mission and vision?	Low – Medium – High
Accept—Do our employees believe in our organizational strategy?	Low – Medium – High
Implement—Are our employees making decisions consistent with our strategies?	Low – Medium – High
Modify—Do we have adequate feedback mechanisms to track progress?	Low – Medium – High

Was There Strategic Leadership Failure at Boeing?

Boeing has historically been a global leader in manufacturing commercial airplanes. However, in 2001, Airbus had more orders than Boeing for the first time in their competitive history. In 2006, however, Boeing regained its supremacy with 1,044 versus 790 orders for commercial aircraft. The main turnaround in this battle for competitor orders has been most visible in the super jumbo category with Airbus's A380 versus Boeing's 787 Dreamliner. Boeing's 787 Dreamliner design focused on long-range efficient flight, capable of transporting 250 passengers, whereas Airbus's strategy focused on long-haul flights with the A380 offering 550-plus seats. In their diverging strategies, Airbus focused on flying to larger airports that use the hub-and-spoke system, whereas Boeing concentrated more on a point-to-point system in which smaller airports are more abundant. In reality, the Airbus A380 aircraft, because of its size and weight, is currently able to land at only about 35 airports. The Boeing aircraft, on the other hand, can land at many more airports around the world and the number is growing in emerging economies such as Eastern Europe where smaller airports desire international connections.

Airbus won the competitor battle that occurred between 2001 and 2005 because it focused on the midsized market as well, using the A320 strategy, which competes with Boeing's 737 and 757 aircraft. The A320 was more efficient than the aircraft used by Boeing, and Boeing did not respond to customer demands to create new, efficient aircraft. In fact, it had slowed its innovation process in regard to new models. Besides the lack of new models, the commercial aircraft business was sluggish; new orders ebbed significantly due to the complications associated with the terrorist attacks and the subsequent recession. It was a bleak time for Boeing relative to Airbus.

One analyst described Boeing's problems as a flawed strategy, lax controls, a weak board, and shortcomings in leadership. Philip Condit ascended to CEO in 1996 and became board chairperson in 1997. His time as CEO and board chair was characterized by a number of mergers and acquisitions as well as a struggle with increasing competition with Airbus. Condit was forced to resign in 2003 amidst corruption charges involving his freezing of a contract with the U.S. Air Force. Condit was described as a brilliant engineer with excellent problem-solving skills and a capability to envision elegant designs. Such good decision-making skills and creativity are valuable in a formal leadership role. However, as CEO, Condit did not seem to display those skills.

Some described Condit as indecisive and isolated from Boeing's operations. Condit and his management team failed to understand the determination of the firm's major competitor, Airbus, which by 2003, for the first time ever, had more orders for aircraft than Boeing. Condit and his team also had lapses in judgment, and their actions raised questions of unethical actions. For example, controversial allegations were made about inappropriate contact with Pentagon officials to obtain knowledge about a lower Airbus bid on a contract. In turn, the official providing the information was allegedly offered a job at Boeing. Additionally, the Pentagon placed an indefinite ban on bids by Boeing for military satellite launches because the company possessed documents about rival Lockheed's activities, helping Boeing win contracts.

Harry Stonecipher was the president and COO until 2003, when he filled the shoes of recently resigned Philip Condit as CEO. In 2005, however, Stonecipher resigned at the request of the board after news of a "consensual relationship" with a female board member (violating Boeing's Code of Conduct). The ethical lapses in governance and the defense contract business were especially harmful. In mid-2005, James McNerney was hired from 3M to be Boeing's CEO and to inject the firm with a fresh culture. The new top management team moved quickly to overcome the ethical problems and restore stakeholder confidence. Boeing now has an Ethics and Business Conduct section on its Web site. Included in this section is an Ethics Challenge that employees are encouraged to take.

The new top management team also decided to speed the development of the 787 Dreamliner. In making its decision to move ahead with the 787 Dreamliner versus a more jumbo aircraft comparable to the A380, Boeing made a more concerted effort in connecting and getting input from its airline customers, as well as the ultimate customers, the passengers. Overwhelmingly, the passengers in particular, and thereby the airlines, preferred smaller aircraft that would enable them to get to smaller airports quickly, without as many transfers on a point-to-point system. Additionally, Boeing followed up with the ultimate creditors, the leasing agents who fund airplanes for many airlines, and asked what they would prefer as far as risks were concerned. Again, the leasing agents preferred a smaller aircraft to reduce their risks in financing versus the large super jumbo A380. Boeing's orders for the 787 have been exceeding those for the Airbus A380.

Interestingly, much of the 787 will be produced through a large outsourcing program. Engineers in Everett, Washington, where Boeing is based, will in effect "snap together the parts" that are produced by "risk-sharing partners from Japan, Italy and elsewhere in the United States." This approach is made possible by a switch "to carbon-fibre reinforced plastic for large parts such as the fuselage and wings." The material creates an aircraft that is light and strong and will thereby improve fuel efficiency and cut maintenance costs associated with metal corrosion. "The plastic pieces are built in huge sections, baked in an oven, and shipped from partner plants for final assembly in Everett."

In pursuing this approach, Boeing sought to balance financial controls (to improve its performance today) with strategic controls (to develop innovative products and processes, associated with the 787 Dreamliner) in order to create improved success.

Sources: K. Done, 2008, Boeing bullish in spite of setbacks over Dreamliner, *Financial Times*, January 31, 17; D. Cameron, 2007, "Green" plastic airliner takes off: In the spotlight Boeing 787 Dreamliner, *Financial Times*, July 2, 32; G. Colvin, 2007, Boeing prepares for takeoff, *Fortune*, June 11, 133; C. Matlac & S. Holmes, 2007, Airbus revs up the engines, *BusinessWeek*, March 5, 41; J. Newhouse, 2007, Boeing versus Airbus: The Inside Story of the Greatest International Competition in Business, Toronto, Canada: Alfred A. Knoph; L. Wayne, 2007, A U.S. star turn for the jumbo of jets, *New York Times*, March 20, C1; D. Q. Wilber, 2007, Boeing's 2006 jet orders surpass Airbus, *Washington Post*, January 18, D03; M. Duffy, 2003, How Boeing got lost, *Time*, December 15: 49; S. Holmes, 2003, Boeing: What really happened, *BusinessWeek*, December 15: 33–38.

Questions

1. What are the strategic leadership failures in Boeing that you can identify?
2. Will the actions of Boeing's new top management team resolve the firm's problems? Why or why not?
3. If you were Boeing's CEO, what additional actions would you take to continue to improve the firm's position?

EXPERIENTIAL EXERCISES

Exercise One: Building an Entrepreneurial Culture

In the chapter, building an entrepreneurial culture, one of the important strategic leadership actions, was discussed. An entrepreneurial culture encourages employees to identify and exploit new opportunities, encourages creativity and risk taking, and tolerates failures.

In Small Groups

Each group should choose one of the following five firms. These firms were identified in a recent issue of *Fast Company* as the top five of the 50 most innovative companies in the world. Your group should investigate what the firm does to build an entrepreneurial culture.

- Google
- Apple
- Facebook
- General Electric
- Ideo

Answer the following questions:

1. Does the firm do what was suggested in the chapter? For example, does it encourage risk taking? Does it tolerate failures?
2. What are some examples of how the firm encourages employees to identify or exploit new opportunities? How does the firm encourage risk taking?
3. Does the firm have some other ways of building an entrepreneurial culture that are not discussed in the chapter?

Whole Class

The groups should then compare answers to the questions. What are the similarities and differences in how these innovative companies build an entrepreneurial culture?

BIZ FLIX

Backdraft: Strategic Leadership

Watch the scene from the film *Backdraft* to see dramatic examples of the strategic leadership discussions in this chapter. Use the discussion questions that follow as guides to your viewing of the scene.

Two brothers follow their late father, a legendary Chicago firefighter, and join the department. Stephen "Bull" McCaffrey (Kurt Russell) joins first and rises to the rank of lieutenant. Younger brother Brian (William Baldwin) joins later and becomes a member of Bull's Company 17. Sibling rivalry tarnishes their work relationship, but they continue to fight Chicago fires successfully. Add a plot element about a mysterious arsonist, and you have the basis for an extraordinary film. The intense, unprecedented special effects give the viewer an unparalleled experience of what it is like to fight a fire. Chicago firefighters applauded the realism of the fire scenes.

The scene comes from the "Time to Move On" sequence that appears about 50 minutes into the film. A woman has told the firefighters that her baby is in the burning building. The film continues after this scene with many more dramatic moments in a Chicago firefighter's life.

What to Watch for and Ask Yourself

1. Does Stephen have a vision for how to fight the fire in the burning building? Does he design strategic actions to reach that vision?
2. Does Stephen empower Brian to help reach his vision for fighting the fire? Why or why not?
3. Risk is often part of strategic leadership. What risks does Stephen take? Does he appear to take excessive risks in trying to rescue the child from the fire?

1. L. Bassi & D. McMurrer, 2007, Maximizing your return on people, *Harvard Business Review*, 85(3): 115–23; E. F. Goldman, 2007, Strategic thinking at the top, *MIT Sloan Management Review*, 48(4): 75–81.

2. J. Simons, 2008, From scandal to stardom: How Merck healed itself, *Fortune*, February 18, 94–98.

3. S. Levy, 2008, Hot air from Apple, *Newsweek*, January 28, 61.

4. G. Edmondson, 2007, Pedal to the metal at Porsche: It boasts the speediest growth in the industry, *BusinessWeek*, September 3, 68.

5. A. M. L. Raes, U. Glunk, M. G. Heijltjes, & R. A. Roe, 2007, Top management team and middle managers, *Small Group Research*, 38: 360–386; I. Goll, R. Sambharya, & C. L. Tucci, 2001, Top management team composition, corporate ideology, and firm performance, *Management International Review*, 41(2): 109–129.

6. H. G. Barkema & O. Shvyrkov, 2007, Does top management team diversity promote or hamper foreign expansion? *Strategic Management Journal*, 28: 663–680; M. Jensen & E. Zajac, 2004, Corporate elites and corporate strategy: How demographic preferences and structural position shape the scope of the firm, *Strategic Management Journal*, 25: 507–524; L. Markoczy, 2001, Consensus formation during strategic change, *Strategic Management Journal*, 22: 1013–1031.

7. K. Naughton, 2007, A rock star's rebirth: Carlos Ghosn made history saving Nissan. Then the company stumbled. Now he is trying for a comeback, *Newsweek*, December 24, 50.

8. A. Karaevli, 2007, Performance consequences of new CEO "outsiderness": Moderating effects of pre- and post-succession contexts, *Strategic Management Journal*, 28: 681–706; W. Shen & A. A. Cannella, 2002, Revisiting the performance consequences of CEO succession: The impacts of successor type, post succession, senior executive turnover, and departing CEO tenure, *Academy of Management Journal*, 45: 717–734.

9. D. Ulrich & N. Smallwood, 2007, Building a leadership brand, *Harvard Business Review*, 85(7/8): 93–100.

10. B. Morris, 2008, The Pepsi challenge: Can this snack and soda giant go healthy? CEO Indra Nooyi says yes, but Cola wars and corn prices will test her leadership, *Fortune*, March 3, 55–64.

11. W. Shen & A. A. Cannella, 2003, Will succession planning increase shareholder wealth? Evidence from investor reactions to relay CEO successions, *Strategic Management Journal*, 24: 191–198.

12. L. Greiner, T. Cummings, & A. Bhambri, 2002, When new CEOs succeed and fail: 4-D theory of strategic transformation, *Organizational Dynamics*, 32: 1–16.

13. T. Foremski, 2004, Motorola's new boss aims for Zander-du, *Financial Times*, www.ft.com, May 9.

14. C. Holahan, 2008, eBay's new tough love CEO; John Donahoe will concentrate on winning back users, even at investor's expense, *BusinessWeek*, February 4, 58.

15. J. L. Bower, 2007, Solve the succession crisis by growing inside-outside leaders, *Harvard Business Review*, 85(11): 90–96.

16. G. Kristandl & N. Bontis, 2007, Constructing a definition for intangibles using the resource-based view of the firm, *Management Decision*, 45(9): 1510–1524; M. Reitzig, 2004, Strategic management of intellectual property, *MIT Sloan Management Review*, 45(3): 35–40.

17. N. Aspan, 2007, TiVo shifts to help companies it once threatened, *New York Times*, www.nytimes.com, December 10.

18. B. Breen, 2004, Hidden asset, *Fast Company*, March, 93.

19. S. Brown, 2008, Learning from failure, *Director*, February, 31; S. Finklestein, 2003, *Why Smart Executives Fail: And What You Can Learn from Their Mistakes*, New York: Penguin Group.

20. B. A. Ready & J. A. Conger, 2007, Make your company a talent factory, *Harvard Business Review*, 85(6): 68–77.

21. J. Champ, 2003, The hidden qualities of great leaders, *Fast Company*, November, 139.

22. B. A. Ready & J. A. Conger, 2007, Make your company a talent factory, 71.

23. R. Cross, A. Hargadon, S. Parise, & R. J. Thomas, 2008, Innovation: Together we innovate, *Wall Street Journal*, September 15–16, R6.

24. D. W. Yiu & C.-M. Lau, 2008, Corporate entrepreneurship as resource capital configuration in emerging markets, *Entrepreneurship Theory and Practice*, 32: 37–57; J. Nahapiet & S. Ghoshal, 1998, Social capital, intellectual capital and the organizational advantage, *Academy of Management Review*, 23: 242–266; R. D. Ireland, M. A. Hitt, & D. Vaidyanath, 2002, Alliance management as a source of competitive advantage, *Journal of Management*, 28: 413–446.

25. A. Jung, 2004, You will stand on our shoulders (keynote address at the WWIB Conference), Knowledge @ Wharton, http://knowledge.wharton.upenn.edu, November 5.

26. C. Stephenson, 2008, Dorothy Gale: A compassionate leader, *Financial Times*, January 28, 5.

27. Yiu & Lau, Corporate entrepreneurship as resource capital configuration in emerging markets; R. A. Baron & G. D. Markman, 2003, Beyond social capital: The role of entrepreneurs' social competence in their financial success, *Journal of Business Venturing*, 18: 41–60.

28. S. D. Anthony, N. W. Johnson, & J. B. Sinfield, 2008, Institutionalizing innovation, *MIT Sloan Management Review*, 49(2): 45-50; R. D. Ireland, M. A. Hitt, & D. Sirmon, 2003, A model of strategic entrepreneurship: The construct and its dimensions, *Journal of Management*, 29: 963–989.

29. J. Jargon, 2008, General Mills sees wealth via health: New recipe for profit, sales growth: More whole grains, less salt, fat, *Wall Street Journal*, February 25, A9.

30. S. Mishra, 2008, Counting progress: The state of boards five years after Sarbanes-Oxley, *The Corporate Governance Advisor*, January/February, 12; R. E. Hoskisson, M. A. Hitt, R. A. Johnson, & W. Grossman, 2002, Conflicting voices: The effects of ownership heterogeneity and internal governance on corporate strategy, *Academy of Management Journal*, 45: 697–716.

31. E. A. Gordon, E. Henry, T. J. Louwers, & B. J. Reed, 2007, Are you auditing related-party transactions: A literature overview and research synthesis, *Accounting Horizons*, 21(1): 81–102.

32. J. Welch & S. Welch, 2008, Miscreants among us: Most rogues like SocGen's Jerome Kerviel don't go unnoticed—just unreported, *Business Week*, February 18, 84.

33. D. Pastoriza, M. A. Arino, & J. E. Ricart, 2008, Ethical managerial behavior as an antecedent of organizational social capital, *Journal of Business Ethics*, 78: 329–341.

34. R. S. Kaplan & D. P. Norton, 2008, Mastering the management system, *Harvard Business Review*, 86(1): 62–77.

35. Ibid.

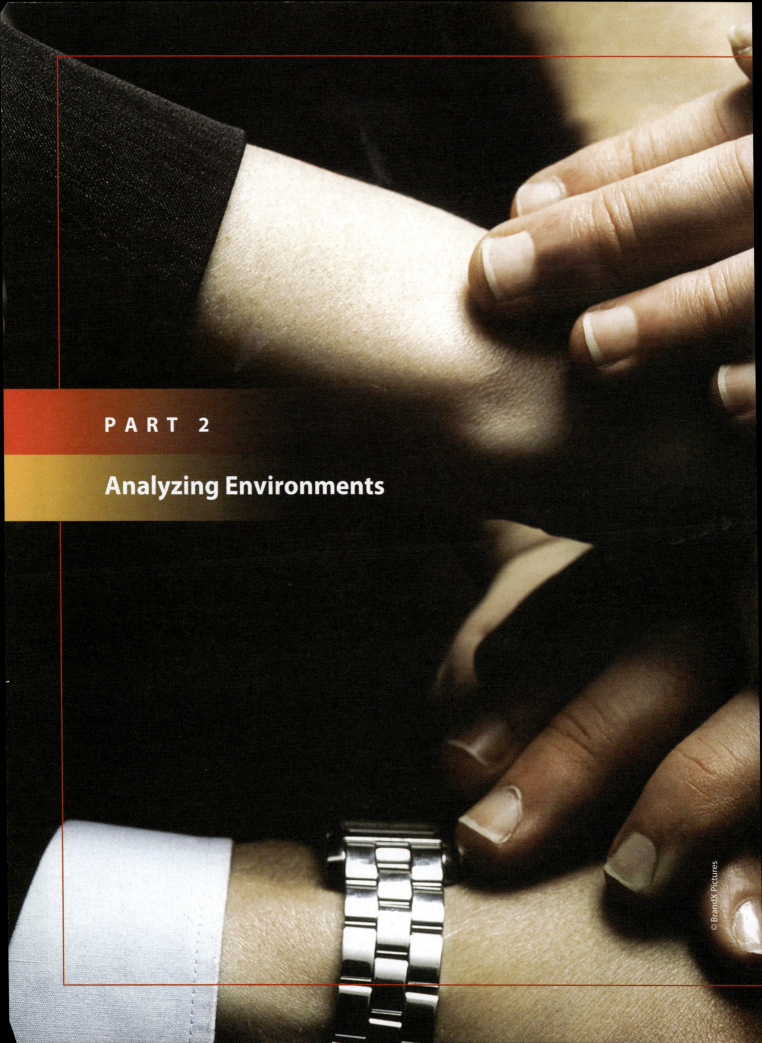

P A R T 2

Analyzing Environments

© BrandX Pictures

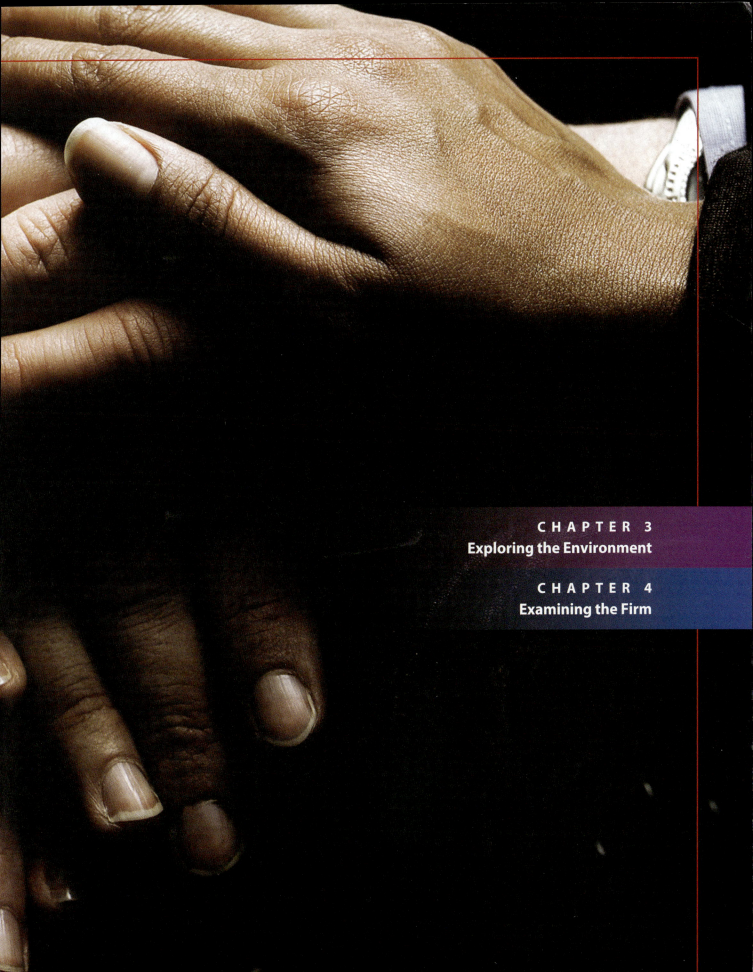

CHAPTER 3

Exploring the Environment

Knowledge Objectives

Reading and studying this chapter should enable you to:

1. Explain the importance of analyzing the firm's external environment.

2. Identify and describe the categories of trends in the general environment that create opportunities or threats for the firm.

3. Describe the five forces of an industry analysis.

4. Understand how to complete a competitor analysis.

5. Identify potential reactions to significant strategic moves by competitors.

6. Understand how complementors support value creation for the firm in a competitive situation.

© BrandX Pictures

Targeting the Bull's-Eye

Target has aimed at and hit the bull's-eye for many of the last 20 years. Started in 1962, the same year that Wal-Mart and Kmart were founded, Target differentiated its approach to the market relative to these two competitors. In the 1980s and 1990s, it solidified its approach and gained market share, especially at the expense of Kmart and Sears.

Target's success has been due largely to its ability to forecast trends in the market, particularly in fashions (clothes and furniture), and to attract those who wanted fashionable goods at a reasonable price. It was known as a discounter, but a step up from Wal-Mart in the market. Kmart learned that it could not beat Wal-Mart in the high discount price market, so it tried to step up and compete with Target and Sears. For example, Kmart obtained Martha Stewart to offer her brand goods. Yet, Target still stole market share from Kmart.

Essentially, Target stores carry high-quality, stylishly designed goods. They are well displayed in clean, well-organized stores with wide aisles. Target has been innovative, willing to bring to the market new and fashionable products. And, yet, the goods are priced reasonably, at a discount from most other retailers except for the super discounters such as Wal-Mart. And in recent years, Target has added Target Superstores, which include their standard goods but add groceries, pharmacies, and even restaurants.

© Justin Sullivan/Getty Images

Target has performed well financially over the years. In 2007, Target was listed at 33 on the *Fortune* 500 list. Target takes in almost $63 billion in annual sales with about 1,500 stores. In 2007, Target was ranked 13 in *Fortune*'s annual survey to identify the best companies. This ranking is ahead of Wal-Mart, which fell to 19 in the rating. Target has been well known for its philanthropy. For example, it gives 5 percent of its annual pretax profits to public education. Its gifts have averaged approximately $2 million per week. Target also has several policies aimed at acting responsibly with regard to the physical environment. The intent is to reduce waste and promote efficient use of energy. For example, Target announced in late 2007 that it would unilaterally reduce the use of PVC in packaging and children's products.

Even though Target has performed well against its competition and managed to serve as a leader in its market niche, it still has to contend with external forces. The slowdown in the U.S. economy in 2007 hurt Target along with most other retailers. The spring of 2007 produced good sales for Target, but the summer and fall months produced lower-than-expected sales. Consumers were affected by the economic slowdown and began cutting back on purchases. When they did make purchases, consumers searched for lower prices. In this environment, Wal-Mart began to prosper at the expense of retailers such as Target. For example, Target and Wal-Mart locked horns in a competitive battle for customers through a price war on drugs. Unfortunately, Wal-Mart is in a better position to offer very low prices on its goods. Target was hurt by its price war with Wal-Mart. Thus, in late 2007 and early 2008, Target missed its expectations because "chic" was out and "cheap" was in.

Sources: 2008, About Target: Fast Facts, www.target.com, January 19; J. Reingold, 2008, New Target CEO aims at bull's-eye, www.cnnmoney.com, January 10; P. Gogoi, 2008, Target: Cheap chic out of style, www.businessweek.com, November 20; S. S. Munoz, 2007, Target will reduce PVC use, www.wsj.com, November 6; A. Farrell, 2007, Target misses the mark, www.forbes.com, September 25; 2007, Target ranks no. 33 on the 2007 *Fortune* 500, www.cnnmoney.com, June 12; P. Gogoi, 2007, Drug wars at the big-box stores, www.businessweek.com, May 24; 2007, Target and Talbots show gains in earnings, www.nytimes.com, May 24; J. Schlosser, 2007, On Target: Fashion, finance, and philanthropy, www.cnnmoney.com, March 9.

Recall from Chapter 1 that the external environment is the set of conditions outside the firm that affects the firm's performance. As Focusing on Strategy suggests, the external environment can indeed affect the firm's choice and use of strategy. Clearly, Target selected its strategy to differentiate its goods and services from competitors Wal-Mart and Kmart, among other retailers. However, economic conditions had a major negative effect on its performance in 2007 and 2008. External events such as the war in Iraq and changes in demographics (e.g., the growing number of Hispanics) illustrate how changes can create opportunities as well as threats for firms. To pursue an opportunity or to protect itself against a threat, the firm might choose to change how it is implementing a current strategy or may even change to a different strategy.

In this chapter, we examine the three parts of a firm's external environment: the general environment, the industry environment, and the competitor environment (see Figure 3.1). Firms analyze their external environment to collect information that will help them select a strategy. For example, conditions in the external environment influence whether a firm might choose to pursue a certain opportunity or to take action to avoid an impending threat. The firm's decisions are also affected by the firm's resources and capabilities, as we discuss in the next chapter. The actual choice of a strategy is a function of conditions in the firm's external environment and the internal conditions of the firm.

As mentioned in Chapter 1, being able to identify opportunities and threats is an important reason why firms study their external environment.[1] *Opportunities* are conditions in the firm's general, industry, and competitor environments that enable the firm to use its core competencies to achieve its vision. *Threats*, on the other hand, are conditions in the firm's general, industry, and competitor environments with the potential to prevent the firm from successfully using its core competencies. Firms evaluate trends in their general environment, assess the effects of competitive forces in the industry in which they compete, and study competitors to identify the opportunities and threats they face.

Firms should not rely on personal opinions and casual observations to assess their external environment. In-depth study is required, and it is important to ask the right questions. Studying all parts of the firm's external environment—the

Figure 3.1 External Environment Analysis

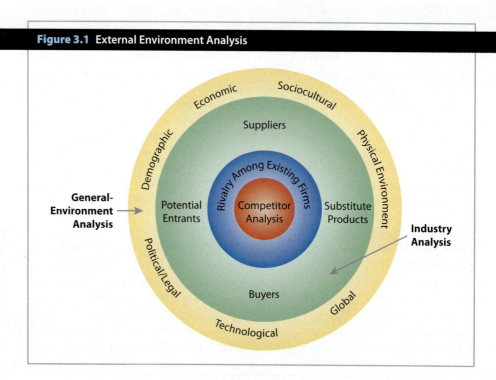

general, industry, and competitor environments—is essential. Beginning with the general environment, we discuss each analysis the firm performs to understand the conditions in its external environment.

Analyzing the General Environment

The **general environment** is composed of trends in the broader society that influence an industry and the firms in it. Firms must pay attention to seven factors in the general environment: demographic, economic, political/legal, sociocultural, technological, global, and physical trends. Each category has conditions that affect the firm's choice of strategy. Conditions in the general environment are outside the firm's direct control; no firm can control demographic trends, for example. Yet, they are important for the company to consider in deciding on its strategy. Think about how conditions in each trend could influence different types of firms and their strategies.

Demographic Trends

Demographic trends are changes in population size, age structure, geographic distribution, ethnic mix, and income distribution. Analysis of these trends is important to determine whether the firm might be able to serve additional customer groups with its products. For example, increasing population rates in international markets might represent opportunities for a firm to sell its products to a new set of consumers. As the largest economies in the world, China and India offer enticing opportunities for a number of firms to use their products to satisfy new customer groups' needs. By 2015, it is predicted that the world population will grow to 7.2 billion, up from 6.1 billion in 2000.

Change in the average age of a population is another important demographic trend. Consider the prediction that the number of Americans over age 65 will increase to 55 million by 2020, up 56 percent from 2000. This prediction could signal an opportunity for pharmaceutical companies to increase their revenues through product innovations.[2]

"As baby boomers get older, they're increasingly going to be less 'do-it-myself' and more 'do-it-for-me,'" and so The Home Depot's and Lowe's customer installation service business is growing more rapidly than their other business segments.[3] Other demographic trends such as changes in a population's ethnic mix can affect the opportunity to enhance diversity in the workforce and also affect patterns of consumer demand.[4] For example, the increasing Hispanic population in the United States and the simultaneous increase in their purchasing power will influence firms' decisions about the customers they seek to serve and the types of products they sell to serve those needs.

Shifts in the geographic distribution of a population can also affect firms. For example, the U.S. population continues to migrate from north and east to west and south. This trend may reduce the number of customers for some firms in the north and east while increasing the number of customers for firms offering similar products in the west and south.

Economic Trends

Economic trends concern the direction of the economy in which a firm competes or may choose to compete. Gross national product, interest and inflation rates, income growth or decline, savings rates, and currency exchange rates in countries across the globe are examples of economic factors that firms examine to understand current future economic trends. Of course, economic trends also affect customers' purchasing decisions. Your current and expected income influences what you decide to buy and from whom.

general environment

the trends in the broader society that influence an industry and the firms in it

demographic trends

changes in population size, age structure, geographic distribution, ethnic mix, and income distribution

economic trends

the direction of the economy in which a firm competes or may choose to compete

In addition, economic trends affect the broader society, such as when a recession occurs. The economic slowdown in 2007 and worries about it becoming a recession (negative economic growth) in 2008 affect the strategic plans of many firms. The Federal Reserve significantly reduced interest rates during this time period to promote economic growth and help avoid a recession.[5] Recessionary conditions have significant effects on firms in most industries. For example, Target and many retailers experienced sales declines during the economic slowdown in 2007. When facing less-than-favorable economic trends, firms must decide how to allocate their resources so they will be positioned to grow when domestic and/or global economies improve.

Political/Legal Trends

Political/legal trends pertain to changes in organizations and interest groups that compete for a voice in developing and implementing the body of laws and regulations that guide interactions among firms and nations. Because political conditions affect how business is conducted, firms try to influence legislation in ways that benefit them through political strategy.[6] The means used to influence political and legal trends must be ethical, moral, and consistent with the laws of the land.

Increasingly, privatization of government-owned and government-regulated businesses has transformed many state-owned enterprises to private firms (as in eastern Europe) and has deregulated formerly regulated businesses (such as U.S. utility firms)[7]; consequently, the global competitive landscape is increasingly dynamic (open to competition) and deregulated. This trend is being fostered by countries' (such as China) admittance to the World Trade Organization (WTO). The Geneva-based WTO helps establish trade rules in the global environment. China's entry into the WTO in late 2001 signaled a significant trend in emerging market countries. Since its entry into the WTO, China has reduced a number of trade barriers and allowed firms from other countries to enter Chinese markets in multiple industries such as telecommunications, banking, automobiles, and professional services.

political/legal trends

the changes in organizations and interest groups that compete for a voice in developing and overseeing the body of laws and regulations that guide interactions among firms and nations

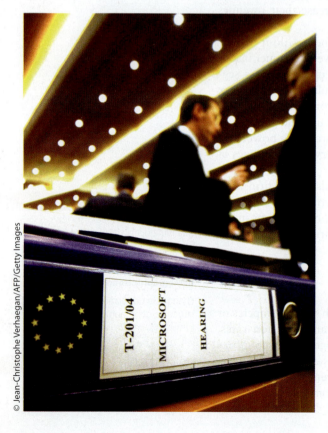

© Jean-Christophe Verhaegan/AFP/Getty Images

Managers must carefully examine political trends in antitrust, taxation, and industry regulations as well as labor laws because of their potential importance to the implementation of strategies. Legal and regulatory constraints reduce the discretion of managers in the strategies that they can select.[8] Often, firms develop political strategies before establishing competitive positions within an industry.

Specific regulatory bodies frequently oversee industry activities. The airline industry in the United States is greatly affected by the Federal Aviation Administration (FAA), and the food and drug industries are strongly influenced by the Food and Drug Administration (FDA). The influence of regulations and antitrust laws on a firm's strategy is shown in the example of Microsoft.

Microsoft is a highly successful company with a market capitalization of $283 billion and annual sales of more than $51 billion. Accordingly, it is a highly profitable company in the technology sector. In 2004, the European Commission announced its judgment that Microsoft was abusing its power in technology markets. In particular, Microsoft's linking of computers and players of music and video clips concerned European regulators. Accordingly, the company was ordered to reveal codes from its "dominant Windows desktop operating system to help rivals competing in similar software." The commission levied a fine on Microsoft of $612.7 million, a single-company record in Europe. Yet,

Microsoft fought the judgment. In 2007, Microsoft lost its appeal of this judgment by the European commission. Late in that year, Microsoft announced that it would accept the judgment and appeal no further.[9] This description of Microsoft's experience shows how political trends in the general environment can affect a firm and its strategy implementation.[10]

Sociocultural Trends

Sociocultural trends deal with changes in a society's attitudes and cultural values. Clearly, national cultures tend to affect managerial work values and thus differ across countries such as the United States, Japan, China and Russia.[11] Likewise, the emphasis on saving the environment is relatively strong in Europe and throughout the developed world; however, until recently, these issues have been less important in emerging economies such as Russia, India, China, and Latin America. Health consciousness is also a trend that has become increasingly important in many countries around the world. Another factor, especially in the United States, is that more women are entering the workforce rather than remaining in traditional family roles, providing new human capital that a firm can hire to pursue an opportunity. What sociocultural trends do you see that you believe are important for U.S. businesses? What should firms do to be prepared to successfully deal with these trends?

Technological Trends

Technological trends concern changes related to creating new knowledge and translating that knowledge into new products, processes, and materials. Some firms require a thorough examination of technological trends because of swift technological changes and shortened product life cycles in their industries. In particular, Internet technology has played an increasingly important role in domestic and global technological change. Furthermore, the Internet is an excellent source of data on the three parts of the external environment. Significant changes in communications technology, especially wireless communications technology, have provided opportunities for many firms. For example, new industries have been created by combining handheld devices and wireless communications equipment in a variety of network-based services. This technology enables individuals to use their handheld computers (such as mobile phones) for scheduling and to send e-mail or conduct Web-based transactions (such as online purchases of stock and other investments).

As suggested earlier, firms study technological trends to identify opportunities and threats. Recent research suggests that new technologies often are applicable across a range of markets. However, new technologies are generally underutilized early in their existence because firms do not realize their full value and applicability to their industry.[12] So those firms that effectively analyze technological trends and identify opportunities with new technologies can achieve an advantage over their competitors.

Global Trends

Global trends concern changes in relevant emerging and developed country global markets, important international political events, and critical changes in cultural and institutional characteristics of global markets. Table 3.1 lists five important global trends that some expect to significantly influence global markets in future years. Examining trends such as the ones shown in Table 3.1 helps the firm identify opportunities and threats outside its domestic market. Undoubtedly, increasing globalization is having a profound effect on national economies and on major political decisions around the world.[13] A major factor increasing the globalization has been the rapid development of some emerging markets such as China and India. They represent markets for multinationals based in developed markets, and

sociocultural trends
changes in a society's attitudes and cultural values

technological trends
changes in the activities involved with creating new knowledge and translating that knowledge into new products, processes, and materials

global trends
changes in relevant emerging and developed country global markets, important international political events, and critical changes in cultural and institutional characteristics of global markets

Table 3.1 Five Important Global Trends

1. **The advent of nanotechnology.** Advances in manipulating organic and inorganic material at the atomic and molecular levels will lead to the ability to create smaller, stronger products. Even though nanotechnology is predicted to usher in a new industrial revolution with effects on global trade and intellectual property, simultaneous developments in information technology and biotechnology will also have substantial effects on standards of living and economic trends.

2. **Globalization.** One of the consequences of globalization is an increasing gulf between rich and poor countries. It has been predicted that many corporations will play an increasingly paternalistic role in Third World countries, developing infrastructure and stepping in where governments have failed. But perhaps the largest development over the next 20 years will be the growth and impact of emerging markets in China, India, and the like.

3. **Global warming.** Earth's average surface temperature has risen by about 1°F in the past century, with accelerated warming during the past two decades, largely due to the buildup of greenhouse gases. Climate change will affect everything from human health and agriculture to forests and water supplies.

4. **Water shortages.** Population growth will increase pressure on water supplies. "Blue gold" is in short supply throughout much of the world. Water shortages are likely to lead to greater political tensions, particularly in drier regions of the world (e.g., the Middle East). Thus, the management and conservation of potable water will become increasingly important.

5. **The employment power shift.** Depending on economic conditions, projections suggest a worker deficit of 10 million people in the years 2008–2010 and a greater shortage beyond those years. These changes will shift the balance of power between employees and companies, and firms will have to compete even more to acquire talent.

Source: L. Pratt, 2003, The 5 most important global trends, *Profit*, December, 24; 2000, Global trends 2015, National Intelligence Council, www.dni.gov/nic/NIC_globaltrend2015.

firms from emerging market countries are increasingly entering international markets.[14] Therefore, managers developing a global mind-set to identify opportunities and threats from global trends can help their firms to grow by pursuing opportunities in other countries.[15]

Global trends can also present significant threats both from foreign competitors and the complexity involved in competing in different countries. Companies must understand the sociocultural and institutional differences in global markets in order to be successful. Significant changes in currency and political risks because of war and nationalization of assets also need to be considered.

Physical Environment Trends

An increasingly important dimension of the general environment focuses on the **physical environment trends.** These trends refer to the changes in the physical environment and business practices that are intended to sustain it.[16] Table 3.1 notes that one of the major global trends is "global warming." Global warming, for example, is the reason that many glaciers such as those in the Los Glaciares National Park in Argentina are melting at an alarming rate.[17] Exemplifying the concern for the environment, Ireland implemented a tax on plastic bags, and in a short period of time, the use of plastic bags decreased by 94 percent. In fact, many people in Ireland now carry cloth bags in which to carry home the grocery purchases. Irish citizens support this law and look askance at the few people who still use plastic bags.[18] Because of the growing concern for sustaining the physical environment around the world, many companies are developing environmentally friendly policies. Some refer to these as "green" policies. Target is a good example (see the chapter opening Focus on Strategy). Target management states that its environmental philosophy is to minimize the firm's environmental footprint. To do so, it has taken several actions; among them are specific waste reduction programs (e.g., recycle millions of garment hangers) and programs to promote efficient use of energy (e.g., lighting in stores).[19] Companies are finding a number of opportunities and threats as they analyze trends in the physical environment.

physical environment trends

changes in the physical environment and the business practices that are intended to sustain it

The Subprime Crisis and the Financial Services Industry: Taking a Bath in Dirty Water

© Paul J. Richards/AFP/Getty Images

Subprime loans became popular with what was hailed as financial innovations. Subprime mortgages are essentially high-interest loans designed for people with prior credit problems. This innovation allowed millions of people to own homes who could not do so otherwise, and mortgage debt in the United States grew from about $6 trillion in 1999 to almost $13 trillion in 2008. However, many of the subprime loans issued during 2004–2006 involved adjustable interest rates that increased after a short term (e.g., two to three years). With the housing boom, prices of homes were escalating. With the increase in prices, homeowners were able to refinance their mortgages when the short-term balloon payments were due.

The loans were then repackaged and sold. Some financial services packaged many of these loans into groups of supposedly varied risk levels and sought investors. Early in the process, many lenders and in turn investors made large profits from these mortgages and packages of loans, respectively. Unfortunately, the whole process was similar to a huge pyramid scheme. The only way it could continue to succeed was for housing prices to regularly increase. When the housing bubble burst, a full-scale financial crisis took hold because of the subprime loans. Even though subprime adjustable rate loans represent only 6.8 percent of the total number of loans, they accounted for approximately 43 percent of the foreclosures in 2007. About 2 million people with subprime loans are predicted to face foreclosure in 2008.

A number of smaller and newer lenders that entered the market to service the subprime market have gone out of business. Many of the larger financial service firms that were major players have had significant negative write-offs. Bear Stearns announced a $1.9 billion write-off in mortgage assets and simultaneously announced its first quarterly loss in its history in the fourth quarter of 2007. Morgan Stanley announced a $9.4 billion write-off of its mortgage assets. Both Citigroup and Morgan Stanley received cash infusions through equity purchases from China and the Middle East. A sad joke on Wall Street was "Shanghai, Dubai, Mumbai, or goodbye." The CEOs at Citigroup and Merrill Lynch lost their jobs over losses their firms suffered because of their investments in the subprime market. The crisis also reached outside the United States and caused problems for foreign financial services firms such as Credit Suisse and Deutsche Bank, both of which took major write-offs.

The U.S. Federal reserve announced in December 2007 its proposals for new restrictions on subprime mortgages. These restrictions will require lenders to certify that loan applicants have the appropriate income and ability to repay the loans granted. Further, they proposed restrictions on hidden fees by lenders and on their ability to refinance these loans. Hopefully, these actions and more reasonable strategies by lenders will disallow future crises such as this one in the financial services industry.

Sources: 2008, 2007 subprime mortgage financial crisis, *Wikipedia*, www.wikipedia.org, January 19; K. Keck, 2007, Looking for ways out of the subprime mortgage crisis, www.cnnmoney.com, March 29; J. Horowitz & J. Flowers, 2007, Mortgage write-downs wound Bear, www.theaustralian.news.com.au, December 22; 2007, Subpar earnings: Companies blame housing, credit problems for weakness, www.wsj.com, December 20; L. Thomas, Jr., 2007, $9.4 billion write-down at Morgan Stanley, www.nytimes.com, December 20; M. Goldstein, 2007, Bear Stearns' subprime bath, www.businessweek.com, June 12; L. Thomas, Jr., 2007, Not a jolly season for 2 top bankers, www.nytimes.com, December 21; E. L. Andrews, 2007, Fed shrugged as subprime crisis spread, www.nytimes.com, December 18; D. Olinger & A. Svaldi, 2007, Examining the subprime lending crisis, www.denverpost.com, December 3.

Firms commonly focus on the future when studying the general environment. However, that future must take place within a particular context. An **industry**, which is a group of firms producing similar products, is the context within which a firm's future is experienced. Firms analyze the industry environment to understand the profitability potential of a particular industry or of a segment within an industry. For example, the financial services industry is not an attractive one in the near term because of poor potential for profitability (see discussion of the industry in Understanding Strategy: Learning from Failure). We discuss how firms study an industry in the next section.

industry

a group of firms producing similar products

49

Analyzing the Industry Environment

Michael Porter developed a framework for classifying and analyzing the characteristics of an industry's environment.[20] His five forces model of competition examines competitive forces that influence the profitability potential in an industry or of a segment within an industry. Each force can reduce the probability that a firm can earn profits while competing in an industry. As shown in Figure 3.2, potential entrants, substitute products, suppliers, buyers, and rivalry among existing firms are the five forces that affect the profitability potential of an industry. Firms competing in an industry want to understand these forces so they can position themselves in the industry to maximize their ability to earn profits. Firms thinking of entering an industry need to understand these forces to decide whether the industry's profitability potential is sufficient to support entry into that industry.

Potential Entrants

Potential entrants can be a threat to firms already competing in an industry; by entering that industry, new firms can take market share away from current competitors. Potential entrants also pose a threat to existing competitors because they bring additional production capacity. If this additional production leads to overcapacity in the industry, prices for consumers will be reduced, but will also cause lower returns for industry firms. On the positive side, new entrants may force incumbent firms to learn new ways to compete. For example, initiating a new Internet-based distribution channel has been important for established pharmacy competitors such as Walgreen's, given new Internet drug distributors in the United States and Canada.

In the highly competitive airline industry, Delta Airlines and American Airlines have been weakened by new entrants such as JetBlue. As smaller, more nimble, and more focused competitors (e.g., Southwest Airlines and JetBlue) increased market share, old-guard airlines with traditionally high cost structures have had to dramatically change their strategies and their implementation to survive. American, unlike United, barely managed to avoid bankruptcy by bargaining for concessions from labor unions and by cutting costs significantly. Though bankruptcy

Figure 3.2 The Five Forces Model

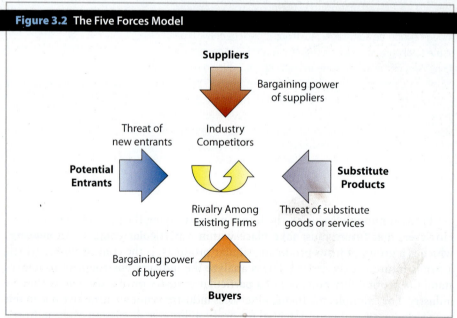

Table 3.2 Barriers to Entry into an Industry

Barrier	Description
Economies of scale	Without economies of scale, potential new entrants are likely to be at a cost disadvantage relative to established competitors with economies of scale.
Capital requirements	If the amount of financial capital needed isn't available, a firm may not be able to enter an industry at all or may lack the resources to compete against an established competitor.
Switching costs	A firm thinking of entering an industry would want to determine how costly it would be for an industry's customers to buy from a new firm compared with continuing to buy from an established competitor.
Differentiation	If customers decide that an established firm's product uniquely meets their needs, then it may be difficult for a new firm to enter that segment of the market.
Access to distribution channels	If established firms have developed relationships with the majority of distribution channels, potential entrants may find it difficult to gain access because a change may create switching costs for a distributor.
Government policy	Some industries are more regulated than others and require a government license or permit before business can be conducted; entry then becomes more difficult.

is no longer an immediate threat, American continues to face numerous challenges (such as rising fuel costs). American has trimmed its maintenance costs by finding new suppliers and by reducing the number of different aircraft in its fleet.[21] Despite the airline industry's significant barriers to entry by new firms, new market entrants have changed the nature of competition in the airline industry.

Entry barriers make it difficult for new firms to enter an industry and often place them at a competitive disadvantage even when they are able to enter. Therefore, existing competitors try to develop barriers that new firms must face when deciding whether to enter an industry. The barriers we will discuss next are briefly described in Table 3.2.

Economies of Scale
Economies of scale are the improvements in efficiency from incremental increases in the size of a firm's operations. Economies of scale can be realized through increased efficiencies in almost all business functions such as marketing, manufacturing, research and development, and purchasing. Importantly, economies of scale reduce the costs the firm incurs to produce additional units of its products. Often, new entrants do not have economies of scale and thus are at a cost disadvantage trying to compete against established competitors.

Capital Requirements
A significant amount of financial capital is often needed for a firm to establish operations in an industry. Financial capital enables the entering firm to build or lease physical facilities, purchase supplies, support marketing activities, and hire talented workers (human capital) who know how to compete in a particular industry. If the amount of financial capital needed isn't available, a firm may not be able to enter an industry or it may do so at a competitive disadvantage (because it lacked the capital to build or acquire what is needed to successfully compete against established competitors).

economies of scale
the improvements in efficiency a firm experiences as it incrementally increases its size

Switching Costs **Switching costs** are the one-time costs that customers incur when they decide to buy a product from a different supplier. Switching costs can be low, high, or anywhere in between. Think of the costs you would incur to fly with one airline instead of a competing airline. Assuming the ticket costs are about the same, it costs you essentially nothing to check in at a different ticket counter after arriving at the airport and to land at a different terminal or a different part of a terminal at your destination city. On the other hand, deciding to transfer as a last-semester senior from one college to another university or college could be quite costly because most educational institutions require students to complete the last 60 or so hours of course work on site. So the cost to switch to another university or college as a last-semester senior can be substantial. Existing competitors try to create switching costs for customers, such as airline frequent-flyer plans. A firm thinking of entering an industry should determine how costly it would be for an industry's customers to buy from a new firm compared with continuing to buy from an established competitor.

Differentiation Over time, customers may decide that an established firm's product uniquely meets their needs. Such perceptions of uniqueness are defined as *differentiation* (see Chapter 5 for a more formal definition). Even in a commodity-type business such as soft drinks, firms such as Coca-Cola and PepsiCo have been effective at establishing customer loyalty through strong marketing programs. In these circumstances, a potential entrant must invest significant resources to overcome existing customer loyalties. Often, this means entering with low-end products that compete on price rather than brand image. However, low-end products often require lower prices because of incumbent firms' economies of scale. New entrants may have difficulty in matching the low prices because it is difficult to achieve similar economies of scale. Thus, to match the low prices may require the firm to lose money on the products sold (until economies of scale are achieved).

Access to Distribution Channels Over time, established firms learn how to build and use effective distribution channels. Often, relationships develop between firms and their distributors, creating switching costs for the distributors. Thus, potential entrants frequently find it difficult to gain access to distribution channels. Price breaks and cooperative-advertising allowances might be proposed by a potential entrant. But if taken, these actions can be expected to reduce the new entrant's profit. However, most firms already competing in the industry likely will be able to match these actions.

Government Policy Entry can also be limited by government policy through licensing and permit requirements. Some industries are more regulated than others. Liquor retailing, banking, and trucking, for example, are highly regulated. Substantial regulations limit entry by new firms. The Federal Communications Commission (FCC) grants licenses to radio and television stations. In 1997, the FCC took bids on licenses for satellite radio, and only two licenses were granted to bidders. From these licenses, only two competing companies were formed: XM Radio and Sirius Radio. In early 2007, XM Radio and Sirius Radio announced a merger agreement between the two firms. However, they must obtain government approval. Government regulations in terms of antitrust policies will have a significant bearing on this possible transaction. In early 2008, the two firms applied with the FCC to operate under one license. They are awaiting the decisions on approval (or not) from the Antitrust division of the U.S. Department of Justice and the FCC.[22] It should be noted that even though regulations may protect established competitors from the challenges of new entrants, excessive regulations generate costs that reduce the industry's profitability potential.

switching costs

the one-time costs customers incur when they decide to buy a product from a different supplier

Substitute Products

Substitute products also have the potential to influence an industry's profitability potential. Substitute products are goods or services that perform functions similar to an existing product. For example, the music industry has experienced a number of substitute products over the years. Cassette tapes became substitutes for phonograph records, and compact discs (CDs) became substitutes for tapes. More recently, MP3 and other digital formats are being substituted for CDs. In general, product substitutes present a strong threat to an incumbent firm when the substitutes are more effective and sold at a lower price. Thus, the product performance relative to the price is the relevant concern, especially if the incumbent firms' products lack switching costs. However, if the incumbent firms can differentiate the existing product in ways that customers value (such as after-sales service), a substitute product's attractiveness will be lower.

Bargaining Power of Suppliers

Suppliers' actions can also reduce the ability of firms to earn profits while competing in an industry.[23] For example, if a supplier can either increase the price of its product or reduce the quality while selling it at the same price, the effect on established firms' profitability is negative. A supplier that can do one of these things is considered to be a powerful supplier. Suppliers tend to be powerful when

- There are a few large suppliers and the buying firms' industry is not concentrated.
- Substitute products are not available to the buying firms.
- The buying firms are not a significant customer for the suppliers.
- The suppliers' goods are essential to the buyers' marketplace success.
- The suppliers' products have high switching costs for the buyers.
- The suppliers pose a credible threat to integrate forward into the buyers' industry.

Interestingly, a number of new entrants came into the financial services industry to handle the subprime loans because demand for them was high (see Understanding Strategy: Learning from Failure). However, they did not have strong access to supplies of capital and many of the new entrants went out of business when problems were experienced with the subprime loans. The only firms receiving infusions of capital were the larger and more established firms (e.g., Citigroup, Bear Stearns).

Bargaining Power of Buyers

Firms selling a product want to enjoy high profitability, while their customers (buyers) want to buy high-quality products at a low price. These goals mean that buyers try to reduce their costs by bargaining with selling firms for lower prices, higher quality, and greater levels of service. In contrast, firms try to offer value to customers at prices that clearly exceed the costs of providing that value. Of course, powerful customers have the potential to reduce the profitability potential of an industry. Buyers or customers tend to be powerful when

- They buy a large portion of the selling firm's total output.
- The selling firm is dependent on the buyers for a significant portion of its sales revenue.
- They can switch to another seller's product with few switching costs.
- The selling industry's products are undifferentiated or similar to a commodity.
- They present a credible threat to integrate backward into the sellers' industry.

substitute products

goods or services that perform similar functions to an existing product

Certainly, firms want to provide significant value to their customers, value that exceeds that offered by competitors.[24] Yet, their owners (shareholders) also expect them to earn profits and create value as well. So firms must balance the value created for each group and contend with the buyers' power. For example, the average consumer does not have a strong preference to buy, for example, a Nokia phone instead of a Motorola phone. Phone service companies often lure customers with cell phone giveaway programs; customers' indifference to cell phone brand makes this possible. Unless cell phone manufacturers have sufficient market share to maintain the scale of their operation and keep costs low, their ability to earn profits likely will be reduced because of the power of their main customers.[25]

Rivalry Among Existing Firms

Competitive rivalry is the set of actions and reactions between competitors as they compete for an advantageous market position.[26] For example, competitive rivalry is highly visible and intense in the airline industry. When one airline lowers its prices in a market, that action is likely to affect a competitor's business in that market; so the tactical action of reducing prices by one airline invites a competitive response by one or more of its competitors. Competitive rivalry is likely to be based on dimensions such as price, quality, and innovation. Next, we discuss conditions that influence competitive rivalry in an industry.

Degree of Differentiation Industries with many companies that have successfully differentiated their products have fewer rivals, resulting in lower competition for individual firms and less of a negative effect on the industry's profitability potential. This stability usually happens when competing companies have established brand loyalty by offering differentiated products to their customers. Differentiated products to which customers are loyal cannot be easily imitated and often earn higher profits.[27] Yet, competitors will try to imitate successful competitors.[28] And when buyers view products as undifferentiated or as commodities, rivalry intensifies. Intense rivalry leads to buyers making purchasing decisions mainly on the basis of price. In turn, intense price competition negatively affects an industry's profitability potential.

Switching Costs The lower the buyers' switching costs, the easier it is for competitors to attract them. High switching costs partially protect firms from rivals' efforts to attract customers. Interestingly, the government has lowered the switching costs of cell phone carriers by reducing regulation of phone numbers. Consumers can now transport their old cell phone number to a new cell phone service provider, which reduces the switching cost for the customer. However, lower switching costs for customers increase rivalry among cell phone service providers.[29]

Numerous or Equally Balanced Competitors Intense rivalries are common in industries in which competing firms are of similar size and have similar competitive capabilities. An intense rivalry is evolving between SABMiller and Anheuser-Busch (AB).[30] These large competitors are battling to gain a dominant position in the global beer market. In China, one of the hotly contested markets, AB outbid SABMiller to acquire Harbin Brewery Group. This acquisition gives AB ownership of the fourth-largest Chinese brewer and serves as a platform for selling AB's own products in China.[31] SABMiller bought a 49 percent equity share in China Resources Breweries (CR Snow) and now claims to have the largest share of the Chinese market through CR Snow products.[32]

competitive rivalry

the set of actions and reactions between competitors as they compete for an advantageous market position

Slow Industry Growth Growing markets reduce the pressure to attract competitors' customers. However, when sales growth declines, the only way to increase sales for current products is to take market share from competitors. Therefore, rivalry usually increases in no-growth or slow-growth markets. The battle often intensifies as firms react to actions by competitors to protect their market shares. One of the worst downturns in the information and communication technology industry occurred between 2000 and 2003. In 2004, the industry began to recover, but firms vary in their financial conditions. Lucent Technologies, for instance, cut R&D deeply, while network giant Cisco invested considerable amounts in R&D to retool its product line.[33] In 2007 and 2008, the economic slowdown was particularly acute in financial services (as noted in Understanding Strategy: Learning from Failure) and home building. Even retailers suffered as noted in the Focusing on Strategy's discussion of Target. In these situations, firms with abundant resources often are able to take advantage of the weaker firms.

High Strategic Stakes Competitive rivalry tends to be high when it is important for competitors to perform well in their chosen market(s). For example, the competition for global market share between SABMiller and Anheuser-Busch represents high strategic stakes for both firms. Similarly, as airlines compete with lower demand for their services and with the growth of low-cost airlines, many larger carriers are not as competitive as they once were. Alitalia, the flagship Italian airline, has been struggling, and it lost 2.8 billion euros in the period 1999–2005. Besides mismanagement and political problems due to government involvement, Alitalia must compete against a number of low-cost carriers such as Ryanair.[34] Although several bidders sought to acquire the firm in 2007, government requirements and political interference caused all bidders to eventually drop out of the process.[35] Because of the importance of the Italian market to Alitalia and its competitors, continued significant competitive rivalry can be expected.

© Alessandro Garofalo/Reuters/Landov

High Fixed Costs or High Storage Costs When fixed or storage costs are a large part of total costs, companies try to spread costs across a larger volume of output. However, when many firms attempt to better utilize their capacity, excess capacity often results in the industry. Therefore, firms try to reduce their inventory by cutting the price of their product. Alternatively, they may offer rebates and other special discounts. This practice is quite common in the automobile industry and leads to more intense competition. This pattern is also often found in perishable goods industries; as perishable-goods inventory grows, intense competition follows, with price cutting used to sell products and avoid spoilage, further increasing rivalry.

High Exit Barriers Firms facing high exit barriers often continue competing in industries even when their performance is less than desirable. In such industries, intense competition often leads firms to make desperate choices to survive. Barriers to exiting from an industry include the following:

- Specialized assets (assets with values linked to a particular business or location)
- Fixed costs of exit (such as labor agreements)
- Strategic interrelationships (relationships of mutual dependence, such as those between one business and other parts of the company's operations, including shared facilities and access to financial markets)

- Emotional barriers (aversion to economically justified business decisions because of fear for one's career, loyalty to employees, and so forth)
- Government and social restrictions (more common outside the United States; often based on government concerns for job losses and regional economic effects)[36]

The airline industry has high exit barriers because of the specialized assets associated with air travel, agreements with airports and other partners, government restrictions, and unions. Satellite radio firms such as XM and Sirius have high exit barriers as well.

With an understanding of the potential of each of the five competitive forces to influence an industry's profitability, the firm can determine the attractiveness of competing in that industry. In general, the stronger the competitive forces, the less attractive the industry. An industry characterized by low barriers to entry, strong suppliers, strong buyers, the potential for product substitutes, and intense rivalry among competitors has low potential for firms to generate significant profits. On the other hand, an industry characterized by high entry barriers, suppliers and buyers with little bargaining power, few potential substitutes, and moderate rivalry suggests that the profitability potential of that industry is strong.

A competitor analysis is the final part of assessing the external environment that firms must undertake to fully recognize their opportunities and threats. The purpose of the competitor analysis is to fully understand the firm's competitors.

Competitor Analysis

Studying competitors is often the most important part of the external environment analysis (see Figure 3.1 on page 44). Answering the questions in Table 3.3 can help a firm recognize its most important current and future competitors.

Table 3.3 Basic Questions for Conducting an Industry Analysis to Screen Key Competitors

Threat of new entrants:
- Which firms have developed economies of scale, and how strong are they?
- How differentiated are the industry's products and services?
- Would buyers encounter switching costs to purchase from a new entrant?
- Which firms pose the most significant threat of potential new entry?

Substitute products:
- What product functionalities can be duplicated in some other fashion?
- Are there lower-cost alternatives to current products?

Bargaining power of suppliers:
- Is the supply chain dominated by only a few companies?
- How important is the industry to its suppliers?
- How differentiated are suppliers' products?
- Do suppliers pose a threat of forward integration into the industry?

Bargaining power of buyers:
- Are there large concentrations of buyers in the industry?
- Are products a high percentage of buyers' costs?
- Do buyers pose a threat of backward integration into the industry?

Rivalry among existing competitors:
- How many competitors are there?
- How differentiated are they?
- What are the exit barriers?
- Which competitors are most likely to respond to a specific competitive move?

Toyota: The King of Automakers

In 2007, Toyota almost became the world's largest automaker with the sale of 9.66 million vehicles compared to GM's 9.69 million sales. If Toyota had bested GM, it would have been the first time in 76 years that a company other than GM had the largest number of annual sales in the industry. Predictions suggest that Toyota will surpass GM in 2008.

In the same year, Toyota overtook Ford as the number two automaker in the U.S. market, which is the largest single market in the world. Toyota's sales in the United States increased by 3 percent in 2007 to 2.62 million vehicles. Alternatively, Ford's sales fell by 12 percent to 2.572 million vehicles. GM's sales in the U.S. market were 3.82 million vehicles, representing a decline of 6 percent from the previous year.

One of GM's best markets is in China. However, Toyota has targeted China with a goal of increasing its sales in this market by 20 percent in 2008. It appears that the two major automakers in the world are Toyota and GM. Although GM still holds the lead, it is losing its market share to Toyota and actually experiencing declining sales in the important U.S. market. The question is why has Toyota done so well and others have performed poorly?

Toyota has been described as having a fanatical attention to detail. Others use a famous Toyota tag line to describe the company: "the relentless pursuit of excellence." Toyota constantly seeks improvement. Toyota really believes that it can build an auto without flaws, and it nurtures the idea among its employees. In addition to the constant improvement, others compliment the company on its discipline. As an example, in 2007, Toyota launched a new initiative called "Everything Matters Exponentially." This effort involves a complete reexamination of product planning, customer service, sales, and marketing. In addition, Toyota is retraining all of its U.S. production employees. The intent described by one Toyota executive is to sustain the paranoia. A result of these efforts is that Toyotas is tops in quality studies.

Furthermore, Toyota leads in customer loyalty. In both 2006 and 2007, Toyota had the highest number of current owners buy another Toyota. For example, 65 percent of Toyota customers in 2007 were already Toyota owners. The industry average is 49 percent. The highest among U.S. names was Chevrolet at 56 percent, followed by Ford at 53 percent. The lowest score in customer retention was Pontiac at only 28 percent.

Toyota has done well with its gas-electric hybrid auto, the Prius. It was the tenth best-selling auto in the U.S. market during 2007. The CEO of Toyota predicts that the firm will sell 1 million hybrid cars by 2010. Certainly, its competitors will not sit on the sidelines and allow Toyota to take the world markets without a fight. GM, for example, has developed a hybrid electric concept car the Chevrolet Volt. It hopes to market the car by 2010 but is still trying to enlarge its mile range without the need to recharge.

Toyota's pursuit of excellence, targeting of emerging markets such as China and Russia, and strong sales among hybrid autos make it likely to be the leader in the global auto market for the foreseeable future.

Sources: 2008, Toyota's 2007 auto sales set new high, but 3,106 units short of GM, Trading Markets.com, www.ad.doubleclick.net/adiN3061.TradingMarkets, January 28; A. Taylor III, 2008, Toyota flexes its muscle, CNNMoney.com, www.cnnmoney.com, January 16; J. Reed, 2008, Toyota's answer to the green car, Ft.com, www.ft.com, January 15; J. Murphy, 2007, Toyota's expected sales could put it ahead of GM, *The Wall Street Journal Online*, www.wsj.com, December 26; 2007, Toyota aims to be no. 1 in 2008 vehicle sales, *New York Times*, www.nytimes.com, December 26; J. B. White, 2007, Big questions for car makers in '08: Recession, going green, boomers, *The Wall Street Journal Online*, www.wsj.com, December 19; D. Kiley, 2007, Toyota leads in customer loyalty, *BusinessWeek*, www.businessweek.com, December 6; D. Welch & I. Rowley, 2007, Toyota's all-out drive to stay Toyota, *BusinessWeek*, www.businessweek.com, November 21; D. Welch, 2007, Staying paranoid at Toyota, *BusinessWeek*, www.businessweek.com, July 2; D. Kiley, 2007, The Toyota way to no. 1, *BusinessWeek*, www.businessweek.com, April 26; B. Bremner, 2007, Toyota: A carmaker wired to win, *BusinessWeek*, www.businessweek.com, April 24.

Armed with a list of critical competitors, the firm is prepared to conduct a thorough analysis of each, focusing on the competitor's strategic intent, current strategy, and major strengths and weaknesses.

We describe the intense competition in the auto industry in Understanding Strategy: Learning from Success. As explained in the segment, Toyota has been winning the auto wars in the United States and many of the markets across the world. After reading about Toyota, decide whether you believe it will continue to be more successful over the next 10 years and what will happen to the U.S. competitors GM and Ford.

Competitor Strategic Intent

Strategic intent is the firm's motivation to leverage its resources and capabilities to reach its vision. Understanding a competitor's strategic intent increases a firm's ability to predict how that competitor will react to a competitive action.

strategic intent
the firm's motivation to leverage its resources and capabilities to reach its vision

The strength of strategic intent can be gauged by examining important competitor characteristics such as the competitor's market dependence. Market dependence is the extent to which a firm's revenues or profits are derived from a particular market. Competitors with high market dependence are likely to respond strongly to attacks threatening their market position.[37] Boeing is not as dependent on the commercial aircraft business as it once was; the firm has diversified into military aircraft and other defense-related equipment, as well as a space and satellite-launching business, to reduce its dependence on commercial aircraft production. Understanding Boeing's strategic intent in the commercial aircraft business can help Airbus formulate its strategy to compete with Boeing. Understanding the strategic intent and actions of competitors clearly contributes to the firm's ability to compete successfully.[38]

Current Competitor Strategy

Gathering data and information to understand a competitor's current strategy is critical to conducting an effective competitor analysis. Meaningful information about a competitor's current strategy helps the firm predict that competitor's behavior. Despite the importance of studying competitors, evidence suggests that only a relatively small percentage of firms uses formal processes to collect and disseminate such information. Some firms overlook analyzing competitors' future objectives as they try to understand their current strategies, thereby yielding incomplete insights about those competitors.[39] Even if research is inadequate, appropriate interpretation of that information is important. "Research found that how accurate senior executives are about their competitive environments is indeed less important for strategy and corresponding organizational changes than the way in which they interpret information about their environments."[40] Thus, although competitor scanning is important, investing money to appropriately interpret that information may be just as important as gathering and organizing it. Therefore, assessing whether a competitor represents an opportunity or a threat and evaluating that competitor's strengths and weaknesses are extremely important. This information is critical in the development of the firm's own strategy and its ability to respond to competitors' strategic actions.[41]

Strengths and Weaknesses of the Competitor

Assessing a competitor's strengths and weaknesses is the final component of a competitor analysis. Understanding a competitor's resources can help a firm formulate a strategy to gain a competitive advantage.[42] Firms with few or competitively unimportant strengths may not be able to successfully respond to a competitor's actions. Boeing has a number of strengths and resources that have enabled it to respond to Airbus's introduction of the A380 jumbo jet. But smaller jet producers such as Bombardier may be unable to respond to this action. Basic areas that firms study to understand where a competitor is strong and where it is weak are financial resources, marketing capability, human resource management, and innovation capability. A firm will want to avoid attacking a competitor where it is strong and instead attack where it is weak.

Complements to Competitive Interaction

When a product is sold, complementary products may be necessary to facilitate the sale or to increase the functionality of the product as it is used.[43] **Complementors** are the network of companies that sell goods or services that are complementary to another firm's good or service. If a complementor's good or service adds value to the sale of a firm's good or service, it is likely to create value for that firm. For example, a range of complements are necessary to sell automobiles, such as financial services to arrange credit and luxury options (stereo equipment, extended warranties, and so forth). Personal computers are complemented by peripheral

complementors

the network of companies that sell goods or services that are complementary to another firm's good or service

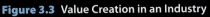

Figure 3.3 Value Creation in an Industry

Source: From *Co-opetition* by Adam M. Brandenburger and Barry J. Nalebuff, copyright © 1996 by Adam M. Brandenburger and Barry J. Nalebuff. Used by permission of Doubleday, a division of Random House, Inc., and Barry Nalebuff, Adam Brandenburger, and Helen Rees Literary Agency, Boston, Mass.

devices and services such as printers, scanners, personal digital assistants, operating systems, software and games, and Internet service providers. Digital cameras are complemented by digital storage disks, software that creates usable and storable digital images, and printers and services for printing digital photographs.

As illustrated in Figure 3.3, complementors are a part of understanding the nature of value creation in an industry. A firm can increase its chances of achieving value creation by paying attention to customers, suppliers, competitors, and complementors.

SUMMARY

The primary purpose of this chapter was to describe what firms do to analyze the three parts of their external environment: the general, industry, and competitor environments. In doing so, we examined the following topics:

- Although the firm's external environment is challenging and complex, examining it is important. Careful analysis of the external environment enables a firm to identify opportunities and threats. The firm cannot directly control its external environment; however, the firm can use information about the external environment in developing its strategies.
- The external environment has three major parts: (1) the general environment (trends in the broader society that affect industries and their firms), (2) the industry environment (forces that influence a firm in relationship to its buyers and suppliers and current and potential competitors), and (3) the competitor environment (in which the firm analyzes each major competitor's current and potential strategic actions).

- The general environment has seven categories of trends that need to be analyzed: demographic, economic, political/legal, sociocultural, technological, global, and physical.
- The five forces model of competition examines the threat of entry, the power of suppliers, the power of buyers, product substitutes, and the intensity of rivalry among competitors. By studying these forces, the firm can identify an attractive position in an industry. Compared to the general environment, the industry environment has a more direct effect on the firm's strategic actions.
- Competitor analysis informs the firm about the strategic intent, current strategies, and strengths and weaknesses of its major competitors. Competitor analysis helps the firm understand how its competitors likely will compete in its chosen industry.
- Understanding how complementors' products or services add value to the sale of the focal firm's product or service will help the focal firm improve its competitive position.

KEY TERMS

DISCUSSION QUESTIONS

1. Why is it important for a firm to study and understand the external environment?
2. What are the seven segments of the general environment that are important to study? Explain the relationships and differences among them.
3. How do the five forces of competition in an industry affect its attractiveness?
4. What three components are necessary to conduct a competitor analysis?
5. When would a competitor likely respond to a strategic competitive move?
6. How can complementors add value to a firm's competitive situation?

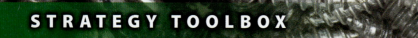

STRATEGY TOOLBOX

Introduction

Successful strategic management is based on the ability to navigate the turbulent waters of the macro environmental and competitor seas. Data to assist in the strategic management process are pentiful. In fact, the advent of the Internet and electronic databases makes available a plethora of data that can be used in ways never imaginable 20 years ago. This chapter's tool is designed to provide special guidance in searching for critical data to be used in analyzing external environments in a focused and efficient manner.

Business Intelligence

Competitor Data	Industry Data	Market Trends
• Factiva • General news • Detailed company reports • Daily newspapers • Mergent Online • Deep data on firms • Downloadable financials • Hoovers Online • Company profiles • Comprehensive reports	• Datamonitor • Consumer market reports • Quick hits on key trends within industries • S&P NetAdvantage • Outstanding industry data • Company comparisons and industry outlooks • Frost & Sullivan • Full industry reports • International coverage	• Reuters Business Insight • Global market reports • Includes healthcare, IT, transportation, and others • Investext Plus • Full text research reports • Prepared by industry research specialists • Government Data • Census.gov • Fedstats.gov • BLS.gov

Verizon and the Remaining Baby Bells Face Significant Competitive Challenges

Verizon and other local "baby bell" phone companies were formed in 1984 when the government required the breakup of AT&T. The original seven baby bells have merged into three giants: Verizon, AT&T, and Qwest. SBC bought AT&T and adopted the name of AT&T. Originally, each baby bell had a local monopoly, which meant that they didn't have to worry about customer defections to competitors; they kept customers locked in through the copper wires that ran through all homes and businesses in their region. Because of the monopoly positions, the baby bells were long regarded as the winners of the AT&T breakup. Verizon dominates the Northeast and competes directly with the new AT&T for dominance.

However, the government has deregulated different parts of the telecommunications industry. This deregulation allows all long-distance, local baby bell, and cell phone companies to compete in each different business. Because of this competition, Verizon, AT&T, and Quest have changed their businesses. For example, Verizon added new businesses such as wireless telecommunications. The newer businesses now account for more than half of Verizon's sales and are likely to account for an even higher percentage in the future. Verizon sales agents are trying to overcome the "monopoly mentality" by seeking to upgrade customers to newer services such as high-speed DSL Internet lines. Furthermore, Verizon now sells satellite TV service through a collaborative venture with DirecTV Group. In fact, Verizon Wireless, in a joint venture with Vodaphone Group, has provided significant growth to the company in recent times. For example, it added approximately 2 million subscribers in the fourth quarter of 2007 alone. It is positioned as the number two wireless carrier behind AT&T. In addition, Verizon added 17.9 percent more broadband subscribers in 2007.

In 2006, Verizon was provided significant flexibility over its rates charged to large companies using its broadband service. Essentially, this situation was the result of a deadlock in a vote by the FCC commissioners that allowed a deadline to expire. Verizon's competitors, especially Sprint Nextel and Qwest communications, filed suit to obtain the same opportunities; but to date, the courts have failed to find in their favor. Some see hope that the FCC will eventually grant

Qwest's request for relief or that Congress will pass a law providing equal opportunities for competitors in this market.

The future interface to the information services provided on the Internet will be cell phones and other wireless devices in place of personal computers. The demand for Internet services will continue to grow exponentially (e.g., e-mail, photo and video sharing, and social networking). For these reasons, in late 2007, Verizon announced that it will open its network to other applications and all devices. Yet, questions remain about how open Verizon will make its network. Several analysts predict that a truly open cellular phone network will occur, and the race is on to see who will provide it. If the current cellular carriers do not provide it, Google is likely to step in and do so.

To remain competitive in this industry in the years to come, Verizon and its competitors will need to carefully monitor all parts of their external environment—the general, industry, and competitor environments. Clearly, the external environment will continue to have a strong influence on these firms' performance.

Sources: L. M. Holson, 2008, Cellular unit and Internet stand out for Verizon, *New York Times*, www.nytimes.com, January 29; S. Ovide & D. Searcey, 2008, Verizon's profit gets wireless boost, *Wall Street Journal*, www.wsj.com, January 29; T. O'Reilly, 2007, Static on the dream phone, *New York Times*, www.nytimes.com, December 15; C. Boles, 2007, Verizon gets win in court over broadband, *Wall Street Journal*, www.wsj.com, December 10; A. Atour, 2004, Defensive linemen: After 20 years, baby bells face some grown-up competition, *Wall Street Journal*, May 28, A1, A5; J. Creswell, 2004, Verizon bets big on cable, *Fortune*, May 31: 120–128; S. Rosenbush, T. Lowery, R. O. Crockett, & B. Grow, 2004, Verizon: Take that, cable: It seeks to reclaim lost ground with a gutsy plunge into pay-TV services, *BusinessWeek*, May 24: 81.

Questions

1. What trends in the general environment have influenced Verizon's decisions as well as those of other baby bell companies?
2. Which of the five competitive forces seems to be having the most influence on Verizon's decisions? Justify your answer.
3. What competitive reactions do you expect Verizon to experience as a result of its entry wireless and broadband services?
4. What other actions would you recommend that Verizon take to remain competitive in the telecommunications industry?

EXPERIENTIAL EXERCISES

Exercise One: Competitor Analysis

Studying competitors is an important part of the external environment analysis and consists of a determination of the competitor's

strategic intent, the competitor's current strategy, and the main strengths and weaknesses of the competitor.

In Small Groups

The instructor will assign each group a pair of firms from the following list. Perform a competitor analysis for each firm in the pair by answering these questions:

1. What is the competitor's strategic intent? To answer this question, examine the competitor's market dependence. Competitors with high market dependence are likely to respond aggressively to threats to their market position.
2. What is the current competitor strategy? In answering this question, consider the competitor's future objectives.
3. What are the main strengths and weaknesses of the competitors? Firms with few or insignificant strengths will not be able to respond to a competitor's actions.
4. Which of the two firms in your competitor pair will be more successful in the near future? Give support for your choice.

Whole Class

Each group should present to the class its findings about strategic intent, current strategy, and main strengths and weaknesses. The groups should also present their choice for which firm will be more successful based on the competitor analysis.

Competitor Pairs

- CVS, Walgreens
- Delta Air Lines, AirTran Airways
- SABMiller, Anheuser-Busch
- Toyota, General Motors
- Wal-Mart, Target

BIZ FLIX

The Bourne Supremacy: Assessing Opportunities and Threats

This chapter emphasized the importance of accurately assessing a firm's external environment to identify opportunities and threats. The scene from *The Bourne Supremacy* shows Jason Bourne (Matt Damon) making such assessments but at a much faster pace than typical firms face.

Jason Bourne and Marie (Franka Potente) have taken assumed names and now live in a Goa, India, a seaside village. They hope to live normal lives, although Jason has repeated nightmares about his former life as a CIA agent.

Kirill (Karl Urban) arrives to kill them. Bourne quickly discovers that he must return to the life he left, that of a skilled CIA assassin. This exciting sequel to *The Bourne Identity* closes with a hint of its scheduled sequel, *The Bourne Ultimatum*.

This scene is an edited sequence from the "Blown" and "No Choice" segments that appear in the first 15 minutes of the film. The scene starts with Bourne calling to Marie from a jeeplike vehicle. He says, "Get in. We're blown." This sequence ends just before Marie is shot. The film continues with Bourne trying to avenge Marie's murder and clear his name.

What to Watch for and Ask Yourself

1. What threats does Jason Bourne assess before and during the chase?
2. What opportunities does Bourne assess during the chase?
3. Think of Kirill, who is pursuing Jason and Marie, as the competitor in a firm's environment. What is his strategic intent? Does Jason accurately assess Kirill's strategic threat?

ENDNOTES

1. M. H. Anderson & M. L. Nichols, 2007, Information gathering and changes in threat and opportunity perceptions, *Journal of Management Studies*, 44: 367–387.
2. D. Armstrong, 2004, Sale of Eckerd to CVS, Coutu appears close, *Wall Street Journal*, April 1: B1.
3. D. J. Hanford, 2004, Installation help is growing market for home retailers, *Wall Street Journal*, December 28: B6.
4. S. E. Page, 2007, Making the difference: Applying a logic of diversity, *Academy of Management Perspectives*, 21(4): 6–20.
5. G. Ip, 2007, Fed moves to curb risk of recession, *Wall Street Journal Online*, www.wsj.com, January 31.

6. A. J. Hillman, G. D. Keim, & D. Schuler, 2004, Corporate political activity: A review and research agenda, *Journal of Management*, 30: 837–857.
7. M. Delmas, M. V. Russo, & M. J. Montes-Sancho, 2007, Deregulation and environmental differentiation in the electric utility industry, *Strategic Management Journal*, 28: 189–209.
8. M. Peteraf & R. Reed, 2007, Managerial discretion and internal alignment under regulatory constraints and change, *Strategic Management Journal*, 28: 1089–1112.
9. *European Union v. Microsoft*, 2008, *Wikipedia*, http://en.wikipedia.org, February 2; J. Kanter, D. Clark, & J. R. Wilke, 2004, ED imposes sanctions on Microsoft, *Wall Street Journal*, March 25: A2.

10. Microsoft Corporation, 2008, *New York Times,* http://nytimes.com, February 2.

11. D. A. Ralston, D. H. Holt, R. H. Terpstra, & Y. Kai-Cheng, 2008, The impact of national culture and economic ideology on managerial work values: A study of the United States, Russia, Japan and China, *Journal of International Business Studies,* 39: 8–26.

12. E. Daneels, 2007, The process of technological leveraging, *Strategic Management Journal,* 28: 511–533.

13. C.-H Tseng, P. Tansuhaj, W. Hallagan, & J. McCullough, 2007, Effects of resources on growth in multinationality, *Journal of International Business Studies,* 38: 961–974; J. H. Dunning, M Fujita, & N. Yakova, 2007, Some macro-data on the regionalization/globalization debate: A comment on the Rugman/Verbeke analysis, *Journal of International Business Studies,* 38: 177–199.

14. D. E. Thomas, L. Eden, M. A. Hitt, & S. R. Miller, 2007, Experience of emerging market firms: The role of cognitive bias in developed market entry and survival, *Management International Review,* 47: 845–867; Y. Luo & R. L. Tung, 2007, International expansion of emerging market enterprises: A springboard perspective, *Journal of International Business Studies,* 38: 481–498.

15. O. Levy, S. Beechler, S. Taylor, & N. A. Boyacigiller, 2007, What we talk about when we talk about "global mindset": Managerial cognition in multinational corporations, *Journal of International Business Studies,* 38: 231–258.

16. L. Berchicci & A. King, 2008, Postcards from the edge: A review of the business and environment literature, in J. P. Walsh and A. P. Brief (Eds.), *Academy of Management Annals* (New York: Lawrence Erlbaum Associates), 513–547.

17. D. Browning, 2008, The melting point, *New York Times,* www.nytimes.com, February 2.

18. E. Rosenthal, 2008, Motivated by a tax, Irish spurn plastic bags, *New York Times,* www.nytimes.com, February 2.

19. Target Corporation: Our environmental philosophy, 2008, http://sites.target.com, January 19.

20. M. E. Porter, 1980, *Competitive Strategy,* New York: Free Press.

21. American Airlines, 2008, *Wikipedia,* http://en.wikipedia.org/wiki/American_Airlines, February 3; M. Maynard, 2004, No longer on the brink, American Air is still in peril, *New York Times,* www.nytimes.com, March 18.

22. XM/Sirus merger, 2008, *Wikipedia,* http://en.wikipedia.org/wiki/XM/Sirus_merger, February 4; FCC tunes in Sirius-XM Merger, 2007, *MediaWeek,* www.mediaweek.com, July 10.

23. A. Camuffo, A. Furlan, & E. Rettore, 2007, Risk sharing in supplier relations: An agency model for the Italian air-conditioning industry, *Strategic Management Journal,* 28: 1257–1266; G. T. Hult, D. J. Ketchen, Jr., & M. Arrfelt, 2007, Strategic supply chain management: Improving performance through a culture of competitiveness and knowledge development, *Strategic Management Journal,* 28: 1035–1052.

24. R. L. Priem, A consumer perspective on value creation, *Academy of Management Review,* 32: 219–235.

25. R. O. Crockett, A. Reinhardt, & M. Ihlwan, 2004, Cell phones: Who's calling the shots? *BusinessWeek,* April 26: 48–49.

26. M.-J. Chen, K.-H. Su, & W. Tsai, 2007, Competitive tension: The awareness-motivation-capability perspective, *Academy of Management Journal,* 50: 101–118.

27. D. M. De Carolis, 2003, Competencies and imitability in the pharmaceutical industry: An analysis of their relationship with firm performance, *Journal of Management,* 29: 27–50.

28. S. D. Dobrev, 2007, Competing in the looking-glass market: Imitation, resources, and crowding, *Strategic Management Journal,* 28: 1267–1289.

29. B. Stone, 2003, Cutting the (phone) cord, *Newsweek,* December 8: 103.

30. J. Ewing & J. Weber, 2004, The beer wars come to a head, *BusinessWeek,* May 24: 68.

31. C. Lawton, 2004, Anheuser, with Harbin in tow, sorts through China options, *Wall Street Journal Online,* www.wsj.com. October 12.

32. SAB Miller, 2008, www.sabmiller.com; SAB Miller China's biggest Brewer, 2006, Beer Forum, www.beertutor.com, October 10.

33. D. Pringle, 2004, Top tech firms to boost R&D spending, *Wall Street Journal,* January 29: B6.

34. J. Spencer, 2004, The discount jet-set: Europe's budget airlines, *Wall Street Journal,* April 27: D1.

35. Alitalia, 2008, *Wikipedia,* http://en.wikipedia.org, February 4.

36. C. Decker & T. Mellewigt, 2007, Thirty years after Michael E. Porter: What do we know about business exit? *Academy of Management Perspectives,* 21(2): 41–55.

37. K. G. Smith, W. J. Ferrier, & C. M. Grimm, 2001, King of the hill: Dethroning the industry leader, *Academy of Management Executive,* 15(2): 59–70.

38. G. McNamara, R. A. Luce, & G. H. Thompson, 2002, Examining the effect of complexity in strategic group knowledge structures on firm performance, *Strategic Management Journal,* 23: 153–170.

39. L. Fahey, 1999, Competitor scenarios: Projecting a rival's marketplace strategy, *Competitive Intelligence Review,* 10(2): 65–85.

40. K. M. Sutcliffe & K. Weber, 2003, The high cost of accurate knowledge, *Harvard Business Review,* 81(5): 74–82.

41. T. Yu & A. A. Cannella, 2007, Rivalry between multinational enterprises: An event history approach, *Academy of Management Journal,* 50: 665–686.

42. L. Capron & O. Chatain, 2008, Competitors' resource-oriented strategies: Acting on competitors' resources through interventions in factor markets and political markets, *Academy of Management Review,* 33: 97–121.

43. G. B. Dagnino, 2007, Coopetition strategy—Toward a new kind of interfirm dynamics, *International Studies of Management and Organization,* 37(2): 3–10; A. Brandenburger & B. Nalebuff, 1996, *Co-opetition,* New York, Currency Doubleday.

CHAPTER 4
Examining the Firm

Knowledge Objectives

Reading and studying this chapter should enable you to:

1. Explain how to identify the firm's strengths and weaknesses by using an internal analysis.

2. Define resources, capabilities, and core competencies and explain their relationships.

3. Describe the four characteristics that core competencies must have to be competitive advantages.

4. Explain the value chain and describe the differences between primary and support activities.

5. Define outsourcing and describe its advantages and disadvantages.

© BrandX Pictures

McDonald's: Where Being "Better" Is Proving Superior to Trying to Be "Bigger"

"We're listening to our customers and giving them what they expect from McDonald's—menu variety, enhanced convenience, and everyday value. This ongoing customer focus and execution through our Plan to Win is driving the sustained momentum of our global business." Jim Skinner, CEO, McDonald's

An extremely well-known and recognized global corporation, McDonald's is the world's largest restaurant company. As of mid-2008, the firm had locations in 119 countries, operated more than 31,000 units worldwide, employed more than 1.6 million people, and was serving 47 million customers daily. To understand the breadth and depth of McDonald's' market penetration, consider the fact that the firm served 1 billion more customers on a global basis in 2007 compared to 2006!

McDonald's financial performance over the last few years is quite positive. According to the firm's 2007 Annual Report, "Since 2004, the compound annual total return on our stock is 25 percent, more than double the Dow Jones Industrial Average and S&P 500 Index during the same period. Our cash dividend is a big contributor to this overall return, increasing more than 170 percent in the last three years." Positive financial results such as these demonstrate that a firm is creating value (defined later in this chapter) for customers. The firm claims that providing "great value" to customers has been a "hall-

© AP Photo/Kin Cheung

mark" of the McDonald's experience since its founding in 1955. As is true with all companies, McDonald's relies on its resources, capabilities, and core competencies to create value. (Although they were defined in Chapter 1, we fully describe these parts of the internal analysis—resources, capabilities, and core competencies—in this chapter.)

McDonald's claims to have several capabilities, including its employees and the training experiences provided to them. *Fortune* magazine's inclusion of McDonald's in its Top 20 Global Companies for Leaders in 2007 is some evidence of the importance the firm places on developing its employees' talents. Product innovation skills are another capability. A global food vision and a stable of full-time chefs in studios located in Hong Kong, Munich, and Chicago are examples of the resources that are combined to form the firm's product innovation capability.

Making all of this work is the firm's organizational structure (this structure may be a core competence and perhaps even a competitive advantage for the firm). McDonald's has never used a rigid hierarchical organizational structure. Instead, based on its "freedom within a framework" mantra, McDonald's uses a highly decentralized business model. This model gives local managers throughout the world a great deal of leeway to make their own decisions. This decision-making flexibility is at the core of the different menu items and different store layouts you see in various nations' McDonald's units. South Korea's Bulgogi Burger (a pork patty marinated in soy-based sauce), the Netherlands' McKroket (a deep-fried patty of beef ragout), and Taiwan's Rice burger (shredded beef between two rice patties) are examples of the locally oriented products resulting from McDonald's use of its decentralized organizational structure. The firm has a décor design studio in Grenoble, France. This group works with local units to choose a store layout design that will appeal to each unit's customers.

Collectively, McDonald's uses its resources, capabilities, and core competencies to focus on becoming "better" rather than to concentrate only on becoming "bigger." And it appears that one way McDonald's is becoming "better" is by creating value for customers by offering localized menu options and locally appealing store layouts and options.

Sources: P. Gumbel, 2008, Big Mac's local flavor, *Fortune*, May 5, 115–121; D. Kardos, 2008, McDonald's U.S. sales rebound, *The Wall Street Journal Online*, www.wsj.com, May 8; 2008, McDonald's reports rise in same-store sales, *The Wall Street Journal Online*, www.wjs.com, May 9; 2008, McDonald's momentum continues: Global comparable sales up 5.0% in April, *The Wall Street Journal Online*, www.wsj.com, May 8; 2008, McDonald's, Wikipedia, www.en.wikipedia.org/wiki/McDonald's, May 4; 2008, McDonald's sales increase 8.2%; Jump to record, *Bloomberg.com*, www.bloomberg.com, May 12; 2007, McDonald's annual report, www.mcdonalds.com, May 8.

In Chapter 3, we noted that a firm must be concerned with its competitors' actions as well as with other conditions in the external environment. At the same time, though, the firm must be concerned about its *internal environment*, which we defined in Chapter 1 as the set of conditions inside the firm affecting the choice and use of strategies. The reason managers must devote attention to understanding their firm's internal environment is that any strategy a firm chooses must be based on its resources. For example, McDonald's intention of creating more value for customers as a path to becoming "better" rather than focusing only on becoming "bigger" won't be fulfilled if the firm does not possess appropriate types and levels of resources. In Focusing on Strategy, we noted that McDonald's is using the skills of its human resources as the foundation for producing a number of new products to serve local customers' culinary interests and to design restaurants that are aesthetically appealing at the local level. New specialty coffees and the McSkillet breakfast burrito are examples of product innovations to which customers are responding positively.[1] Using the principles of feng shui to design a restaurant in Hacienda Heights, California, is an example of using the firm's design skills. (Feng shui is the ancient Chinese practice of arranging numbers and objects with the purpose of promoting health, prosperity, and harmony. Feng shui was used to design this restaurant because the majority of the unit's clientele are Asian.)[2]

In Chapter 1, we defined *resources* as the tangible and intangible assets held by a firm. To implement a strategy, managers integrate or combine different resources so the firm will be able to complete different work-related tasks. We also defined *capabilities* in Chapter 1. As we noted, *capabilities* result when the firm integrates several different resources so it will be able to complete a task or a series of related tasks. As we described in Focusing on Strategy, McDonald's integrates its training programs with its human capital to develop its employees' talents. Talented employees is a capability that contributes to product innovation and design as core competencies for McDonald's.

We described how to conduct an external analysis (analysis of the firm's external environment) in Chapter 3. In this chapter, we discuss how to complete an internal analysis of the firm. To discuss this topic, we first describe how resources are integrated to create capabilities and how some capabilities are then developed into core competencies. Core competencies that satisfy certain conditions are also competitive advantages for a firm. We describe these important conditions in this chapter as well. The chapter closes with discussions of two additional aspects of an internal analysis: the value chain and outsourcing.

Conducting an Internal Analysis

To develop and implement the best strategy, managers need to understand what the firm's resources, capabilities, and core competencies make possible. Indeed, as we noted earlier, a firm cannot successfully implement any strategy without being able to use the appropriate set of resources, capabilities, and core competencies. Think of it this way: A U.S.-based firm that wants to begin selling its products in Mexico won't be able to do so unless it has the resources needed to properly distribute its products in Mexico, the financial capital to support the new distribution channel, the manufacturing capacity to produce additional quantities of its products, the capability to sell its products in a market outside the United States, and so forth.

Therefore, because of the importance of resources, capabilities, and core competencies to the effectiveness of all strategies, managers complete an internal analysis to identify and understand them as a precursor to selecting a strategy.[3] Through an internal analysis, the firm discovers many things, including its strengths and weaknesses. As defined in Chapter 1, *strengths* are resources and capabilities that allow the firm to complete important tasks. **Weaknesses** are resource and capability deficiencies that make it difficult for the firm to complete important tasks. In general terms, *strengths* suggest possibilities while *weaknesses* suggest constraints. Think of a firm in your local community. What do you think its strengths and weaknesses are? Do you think the owners are aware of their firm's strengths and weaknesses? Do those owners rely on their firm's strengths to create value for you as a customer?

The analysis of a firm's internal environment focuses on resources, capabilities, and core competencies. We discuss these important concepts next.

Resources, Capabilities, and Core Competencies

Resources

Firms deal with two kinds of resources—tangible and intangible. **Tangible resources** are valuable assets that can be seen or quantified, such as manufacturing equipment and financial capital. **Intangible resources** are assets that contribute to creating value for customers but are not physically identifiable. Intangible resources often accumulate within a firm and become more useful over time. Reputation, brand name, know-how, and organizational culture are examples of intangible resources. Both tangible and intangible resources play important roles in creating value for customers. **Value** is judged in terms of the satisfaction a product creates for customers and is measured by the price customers are willing to pay to buy that product.[4]

Tangible resources such as financial capital are important for acquiring other physical assets (such as technology). Financial capital is also necessary to obtain human capital. Tangible resources alone, however, will not create value for customers. Intangible resources play a critical role in the value creation process. For example, manufacturing equipment must be operated by employees (human capital) or by computers programmed by and using software developed by human capital. In fact, human capital is likely the most valuable intangible resource for most firms,[5] largely because of the important role human knowledge plays in shaping capabilities and core competencies.[6]

Human capital at upper managerial levels can have a strong influence on a firm's performance, as demonstrated by Coca-Cola. Claiming that "refreshment is a language everyone understands, and no one speaks it better than Coca-Cola" and pursuing a mission "To Refresh the World . . . in body, mind, and spirit,"[7] this company owns a well-known global brand name with much potential to create value for customers. However, as evidenced by a languishing price of its stock, this potential was not being fully realized in the early 2000s. During this period of time, the poor performance was attributed largely to the firm's human capital in the form of its CEO and top management team. Analysts criticized the

weaknesses
resource and capability deficiencies that make it difficult for the firm to complete important tasks

tangible resources
valuable assets that can be seen or quantified, such as manufacturing equipment and financial capital

intangible resources
assets that contribute to creating value for customers but are not physically identifiable

value
the satisfaction a product creates for customers and is measured by the price customers are willing to pay to buy that product

© Jochen Tack/Alamy

two successive CEOs and management teams that governed the firm after the unfortunate death of former CEO Roberto Goizueta. Articles detailing the poor strategies, indecisiveness, and political infighting among Coca-Cola's top executives and board of directors left little doubt that the firm suffered from a weakness of strategic leadership for a number of years. However, Coca-Cola's fortunes improved almost immediately following the appointment in 2004 of E. Neville Isdell as CEO. Decisions to expand the firm's presence in global markets and to improve its distribution system are thought to be major contributors to the change in the firm's performance, which was very positive as of mid-2008.[8]

Managers constantly take action to acquire resources, including human capital. The full set of resources a firm holds is called a *resource portfolio*. McDonald's believes that the firm's success depends on the ability of its employees, affectionately known as those who work "under the arches." The firm's "people principles" (guidelines that validate individuals' importance and the value McDonald's places on their growth and development) and the firm's array of training programs are aspects of the McDonald's operations that help it manage resources as a part of the firm's resource portfolio.[9] In other cases, firms purchase other companies to add needed resources to their resource portfolio. Google's acquisition of DoubleClick is an example: Google bought DoubleClick to gain access to that firm's ability to deeply understand customers' needs.[10]

Firms such as McDonald's and Google hope that their actions will shape an effective resource portfolio—an important move, in that failing to do so can limit a firm's strategy or its ability to implement a particular strategy. For example, General Motors' inability to use its resources in ways that allow it to make more money producing small cars and sport utility vehicles is hampering the firm's attempt to "get its problems under control"[11] as it implements its strategies.

Intangible resources require constant attention to retain and extend their value. For example, employees' skills should be continuously updated so that the firm's human capital can perform at peak levels. Intangible resources such as brand names also must be reinforced with customers or their value will diminish. The need for reinforcement is why firms such as McDonald's and Coca-Cola continuously advertise their brands even though both of them have iconic status with customers throughout the world.

Additionally, managers must understand that negative events can harm a firm's reputation, another important intangible asset. For example, the banking crisis in general and the concerns about Citigroup's ability to continue growing given its size and complexity are damaging the firm's reputation as a global financial powerhouse. Also damaging the firm's reputation was the need for Citigroup to take billions of dollars in write-downs during the 2007–2008 credit crunch.[12] More effective management of Citigroup's resource portfolio might have prevented the firm's loss of reputation.

Although it may seem easy to identify strengths and weaknesses (which are products of the firm's resources and capabilities), it generally is somewhat difficult for several reasons. First, managers need full information about the firm's resources and capabilities to accurately evaluate them. Tangible resources (such as plants and equipment) aren't hard to identify, but intangible resources (such as organizational culture and brand name) are more challenging to identify and evaluate. Tangible resources—financial resources, for example—are usually identified in the firm's accounting system and audited and certified by an external accounting firm (however, given recent problems identified in some firms' financial reports, we recognize that they are not always accurate). Physical resources can be visually identified and values placed on them by standard (accepted) practices. Yet a firm's intangible resources, such as human capital, brand names, and reputation, are harder to evaluate. Ultimately, the judgment about the worth of a tangible or intangible resource is made in terms of that resource's ability to help the firm create value for customers.

Resources as Options Resources may be acquired or developed to use at a future time, in which case the resources are thought of as *options*. For example, a firm may purchase a piece of land and hold it for future expansion. The land can be used as a location for a facility such as a plant. In such an instance, the firm holds the purchased land as an *option* to expand. Some refer to these as *real options* because without the land, for example, the firm could not expand in that particular location if it decided to do so. Buying land in a current time period allows a firm the option to use it later to expand its operations. The thought is that the land will be more expensive later, which is why the firm took out an option on the land by buying it at a lower price today.

Real options create strategic flexibility for firms. When executed effectively, real options typically hold their value or may even increase in value. Therefore, if the firm decides not to use the resource being held as an option, the resource can be sold to recoup the original investment and possibly additional returns. In this way, real options represent investments having value and provide options to support future strategies.[13]

Resources acquired as real options can be especially useful for firms competing in highly uncertain environments, which is the case for pharmaceutical companies. These firms (such as Pfizer, Merck, and Johnson & Johnson) invest large sums of money in R&D and develop a number of new drug compounds, some of which are used as real options. In other words, they invest to develop a variety of drugs that are intended to treat different illnesses even though the firms know that many of the drugs won't succeed. These firms do not focus on only one drug or on a few drugs because of the uncertain success of new products (drugs) and the highly competitive nature of their industry. Each firm's competitors are also investing heavily to discover the next "blockbuster" drug. Investing to develop a variety of drugs provides the firm with a portfolio of potential drugs that can be developed and marketed.[14]

Many firms in high-technology industries also use their resources to create options. They invest in the development of a variety of technologies to provide flexibility to use if needed, given conditions in their highly competitive environments.[15]

Some firms that compete in highly uncertain industries even invest in resources that provide options to move into totally new industries. Firms take these actions to maintain flexibility in case the industry changes dramatically and they find themselves lacking the resources needed to adapt to those changes.[16] In the case of U.S. Steel, it was once only a steel manufacturer, but the firm now uses its resource portfolio to compete in a range of other businesses such as coal mining, transportation, real estate development, and mineral resource management. U.S. Steel initially took options in these different fields because of the intense competition it faced as a steel manufacturer. The same type of description can be given for Rolls Royce in that this firm has not produced high-end luxury automobiles since it sold its car unit to BMW in 1998. Today, Rolls Royce has four divisions—civil aerospace, defense aerospace, marine, and energy—and operates in 50 countries. The firm took options in these four businesses while still building and selling its luxury marquee cars.[17]

However, regardless of whether resources are held as options or are designed for current use only, simply having them is not enough to build a competitive advantage.[18] The true value of a firm's resources emerges when they are integrated to form capabilities.[19] Some capabilities are developed into core competencies, which are what the firm uses to create value for customers. We show the link among resources, capabilities, and core competencies in Figure 4.1.

Figure 4.1 Managing Resources to Develop Capabilities and Core Competencies

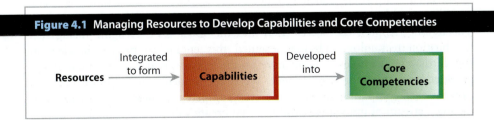

Capabilities

As we've said, capabilities result when the firm integrates several different resources to complete a task or a series of related tasks. Commonly, capabilities are part of organizational functions such as marketing, manufacturing, finance, and so forth. Apple Inc., for example, is thought to have a capability in the research and development function. People, work teams, equipment, and financial resources are some of the resources that Apple integrates to complete various research and development tasks. Similarly, as we explain in Understanding Strategy: Learning from Success about LG Electronics, this firm brings talented designers and engineers together (along with other resources such as organizational systems and equipment) to form a capability in the design of mobile phones. Honda uses its capabilities in product design, engineering, and manufacturing to build a wide variety of engines. In 2007 alone, Honda placed more than 24 million engines in products from "cars to weed whackers."[20] (In the next section, we'll describe core competencies for these three firms that flow from their capabilities.)

© Susan Van Etten

Several insights about capabilities are important to remember, and those trying to use a firm's resources to create value for customers must understand them. First, most capabilities are based on the knowledge held by the firm's employees (its human capital).[21] For example, Apple's new products are developed based on ideas from the software engineers and designers working in the firm's research and development function. Honda provides another example of human capital as the foundation for many capabilities. In this firm, engineers and others are given a great deal of free time to "tinker" with various aspects of product design and manufacturing to discover how things work. The discoveries they make while "tinkering" add to their stock of knowledge—knowledge that will facilitate their work on various projects. In this sense, Honda employees are encouraged to "dream" about what is possible in the future.

A second important insight about capabilities is that each of them is a product of deliberate attempts to integrate several resources with the purpose of completing one or more work tasks. In the vast majority of cases, capabilities do not spring to life on their own; rather, capabilities result when people (employees) think carefully about which combination of resources will allow the firm to create a capability with potential to become a core competence. Thus, while each core competence is grounded in a capability, not every capability becomes a core competence, and not every core competence leads to a competitive advantage.

Core Competencies

As defined in Chapter 1, *core competencies* are capabilities the firm emphasizes and performs especially well while pursuing its vision. When the firm's core competencies are different from those held by competitors, they may be referred to as *distinctive competencies,*[22] another term we defined in Chapter 1. When core competencies allow the firm to create value for customers by performing a key activity better than competitors, it has a *competitive advantage.*

Product innovation (called Product Leadership at LG Electronics) is a core competence and appears to be a distinctive competence for Apple, LG, and Honda. The iPhone (Apple), the Secret (LG) and the 1975 CVCC engine (using fuel-combustion technology, Honda designed this engine to meet U.S. clean-air standards) are examples of innovative products associated with each company's product innovation core competence. We've mentioned a single product innovation for each company; however, as a core competence, these firms are all introducing a stream of innovative products that create value for customers.

The Race in the Global Cell-Phone Business: Who's Gaining Market Share and Why?

If Motorola can't get its act together, "LG is poised to overtake the struggling company later this year [2008]." Thomas Kang, Strategy Analytics

Given Motorola's attractive position in the mobile-phone business only a few short years

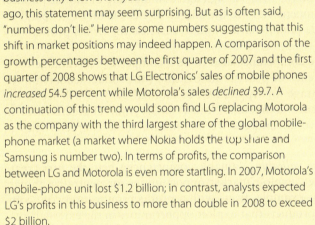

© Courtesy, LG Electronics

ago, this statement may seem surprising. But as is often said, "numbers don't lie." Here are some numbers suggesting that this shift in market positions may indeed happen. A comparison of the growth percentages between the first quarter of 2007 and the first quarter of 2008 shows that LG Electronics' sales of mobile phones *increased* 54.5 percent while Motorola's sales *declined* 39.7. A continuation of this trend would soon find LG replacing Motorola as the company with the third largest share of the global mobile-phone market (a market where Nokia holds the top share and Samsung is number two). In terms of profits, the comparison between LG and Motorola is even more startling. In 2007, Motorola's mobile-phone unit lost $1.2 billion; in contrast, analysts expected LG's profits in this business to more than double in 2008 to exceed $2 billion.

In response to these difficulties, Motorola announced on March 26, 2008, that it intended to spin off its mobile-phone unit as a tax-free distribution to shareholders. This transaction was to be completed by the end of 2009. Believing that the mobile-phone unit would perform much better as a stand-alone company, Motorola CEO Gregory Brown argued that the person who was chosen to head the soon-to-be-spun-off unit would have a "fantastic opportunity to restore and revitalize a proud franchise." Activist investor and Motorola shareholder Carl Icahn supported the decision to spin off the unit; however, he believed that the transaction should be completed more quickly than was intended.

What caused the reversal of fortunes for Motorola's mobile-phone business and the simultaneous march to success by LG Electronics in this business? Most agreed that product innovation is the key. Observers say that Motorola failed to continuously innovate in the rapidly changing mobile-phone business. Take, for example, the firm's decision to develop sequels (rather than new products) to its initially popular RAZR

phone. In contrast, Skott Ahn, the head of LG's mobile-phone business, "has relentlessly prodded his people to come up with distinctive new models." To support his desire to continuously develop distinctive and innovative new products, Ahn doubled the number of designers and engineers in the mobile-phone unit. One of the unit's new products (called Secret) was an immediate success when introduced in Europe. The Secret is made of carbon fiber and tempered glass and comes with a 5-megapixel camera as well as software that allows users to create their own music videos.

The types of success LG is having in the mobile-phone business results when a firm effectively uses its resources, capabilities, and core competencies. According to LG, product leadership, people leadership, and market leadership are core competencies on which its success is built. Product leadership "refers to the ability to develop creative, premium products through specialized new technologies." LG relies on systems it has in place to stimulate and support frequent product innovations by creatively using new technologies. The firm's commitment to "Fast Innovation" for example, involves a system of primary and support activities on which LG relies as it seeks to introduce 30 percent more innovations than do competitors. As a core competency, people leadership refers to "talented people who perform excellently by internalizing and practicing innovations." LG wants to hire individuals it considers to be "great people" and then to provide them education-focused opportunities to creatively use technologies as the foundation for continuously developing innovative products. Finally, the market leadership competency concerns the firm's "formidable market presence worldwide" and its ability to establish the LG brand as a major global force in electronics, information, and communications products that results from its significant presence in multiple markets throughout the world.

Sources: R. O. Crockett, 2008, Motorola sets its phone unit free, *BusinessWeek*, April 7, 36–37; L. M. Holson, 2008, Pressured, Motorola splits in two, *The New York Times Online*, www.nytimes.com, March 27; M. Ihlwan, 2008, LG closes in on Motorola, *BusinessWeek*, May 19, 30; 2008, Worldwide mobile phone market grows 14.3% amid economic jitters, *Cellular-News.com*, www.cellular-news.com, April 25; 2008, Mobile phones, LG Web site, www.lge.com, May 12.

Table 4.1 Characteristics of Core Competencies That Lead to a Competitive Advantage

Valuable	They contribute to value creation for customers by exploiting new opportunities or neutralizing threats.
Rare	They are held by few if any competitors.
Difficult to imitate	They are difficult to re-create because intangible resources or their specific contribution to the capability cannot be easily identified.
Nonsubstitutable	No resources/capabilities exist that can complete the tasks and provide the same value to customers.

In the previous Understanding Strategy, we discussed three core competencies—product leadership, people leadership, and market leadership—on which LG Electronics relies to create value for customers. We focused our analysis of this firm's core competencies on the firm's design and manufacture of mobile phones. As you will see, these competencies are the source of LG's ability to expand its share of the global mobile-phone market and to increase the firm's profitability while doing so.

So what causes a core competence also to be a competitive advantage for a firm? Is the core competence of product innovation (or product leadership for LG) a competitive advantage for Apple, LG, or Honda? As you will see in the following materials, a core competency must satisfy four characteristics in order to be a competitive advantage. We summarize these characteristics in Table 4.1.

1. Competencies must be *valuable.* Valuable competencies help the firm create value for the customer, exploit market opportunities, or neutralize threats from competitors. For example, firms with a product innovation core competency develop new products that exploit opportunities in the external environment. These opportunities represent customer needs that haven't been satisfied. Apple's iTunes digital music store provides a substantial selection of music at reasonable prices with easy access for customers, satisfying their need to listen to the music they prefer at a time that is convenient for them. Likewise, the sleek design of LG's Secret mobile phone, coupled with its capability for users to make their own music videos, offer a combination of functionalities that create more value for customers than did competitors' then-current offerings.

2. Competencies must be *rare.* Rarity means that few if any competitors have the competencies needed to complete a task or a set of tasks with the same quality as the focal firm. The firm holding a core competence that is valuable but not rare (i.e., the competence is held by at least some and perhaps many of the firm's competitors) has a competence that is a source of competitive parity rather than a source of competitive advantage.[23] Look, for example, at Coca-Cola and PepsiCo. Both of these firms have a core competence in terms of global distribution channels and practices. Even though this competence is valuable, it is not rare in that both firms are using capabilities in ways that yield a core competence when it comes to distributing products globally. In contrast, Honda's ability to produce an array of engines is certainly valuable and may also be rare. Because of its concentration on designing and producing multiple types of engines that are used in a variety of applications, Honda is often thought of as an engine company rather than as a car company.

3. Competencies must be *difficult to imitate*. Competitors want to imitate another firm's valuable and rare core competencies. However, doing so may be difficult. Think of product innovation as an example here. As we know, LG's product leadership (innovation) core competence is a function of the talents of its designers and engineers, the way those individuals work together as well as the systems and procedures they use to design and produce mobile phones. Being able to fully understand (and certainly to imitate) how LG is using its capabilities to create its core competencies is a challenge for competitors such as Motorola, Nokia, and Samsung. Similarly, Apple's product innovation core competence is a product of a number of capabilities, including the culture and environment that CEO Steve Jobs and other long-term employees established and continue to nurture as well as the way the firm organizes its R&D activities. Given the lack of full visibility of Apple's and LG's product innovation core competence to competitors and the difficulty competitors likely would have in attempting imitation, it is possible that the product innovation core competence for Apple and LG satisfy the first three criteria to become a competitive advantage.

4. Competencies must be *nonsubstitutable*. For a core competence to be a competitive advantage, a competitor that can perform the same function must not possess equivalent competencies. A core competence in customer service is an example of a core competence with no equivalent substitutes. When customers want service on the products they have purchased, the firm cannot use its design skills (for example) to satisfy the customer.

Firms selling products that are expensive relative to other offerings sometimes attempt to develop after-sales service competence. Lexus automobiles (which are made by Toyota) may be a product for which after-sales service is a core competence that lacks substitutes. The use of a free loaner automobile while the customer's car is being serviced and the ability to schedule an appointment to have a representative from the Lexus dealer come to a distant location to obtain a customer's car and then return it after it has been serviced are examples of a core competence that creates value and has no substitutes.

Competitive Advantages

Having a competitive advantage means that the firm is using its resources, capabilities, and core competencies in ways that create more value for customers compared to the value competitors' products create for those customers. In terms of the four criteria discussed earlier, firms with valuable and rare core competencies are able to achieve competitive advantages over their rivals, but likely for a relatively short period of time. Core competencies that are difficult to imitate and nonsubstitutable as well as valuable and rare often produce competitive advantages that last longer. No competitive advantage can be sustained forever; competitors eventually learn how to imitate another firm's core competencies or how to use their own capabilities to form competencies that allow them to produce products that create more value for customers.

Competitive advantages are important because they enable firms to capture larger shares of the market and to increase their returns. When they do so, they also create value for their owners and other stakeholders (having already created superior value for customers). As a result, managers are continuously searching for ways to develop core competencies that are valuable, rare, difficult to imitate, and nonsubstitutable. Managers must understand, though, that competitors will try to imitate their firm's competitive advantages or to create different advantages that create more value for customers. Firms can try to imitate a core competence that is also a competitive advantage in many ways. For example, even though a production innovation core competence is difficult to imitate, firms might acquire a company with an established R&D competence. Similarly, a firm could develop an alliance with companies having complementary capabilities that, when integrated with their own, form a core competence that is valuable and rare (and perhaps difficult to imitate and nonsubstitutable).

Next, we examine how firms use the value chain to understand the activities in which they can create value for customers. In actuality, capabilities and core competencies are combinations of activities that are required to complete one or more work tasks.

The Value Chain

The **value chain** is the structure of activities the firm uses to implement its business-level strategy. Firms analyze their value chain to better understand the activities that contribute most strongly to creating value for customers and the cost incurred to complete each activity. Of course, to succeed, the firm must create value that exceeds the costs incurred to produce, distribute, and service products for customers.[24]

Based on the firm's analysis of its value chain activities, it can compare them to those of competitors. One common means of making these comparisons is through benchmarking. **Benchmarking** is the process of identifying the best practices of competitors and other high-performing firms, analyzing them, and comparing them with the organization's own practices.[25] Through these comparisons, firms sometimes identify better ways to complete activities that create greater value for customers. For example, FedEx studied the activities and best practices of transportation companies to invent the overnight-delivery business. Other firms may develop means of handling the value chain activities differently from competitors because they could not complete the activity in a comparable way. For example, when founded, Dell decided to handle distribution activities differently from its competitors. As we know, Dell decided to sell its computers directly to customers rather than through retail outlets. It would have been highly difficult for Dell to obtain the needed retail agreements to sell its products. The growth and popularity of the Internet greatly enhanced Dell's ability to reach customers and sell its products using the direct-sales approach. Today however, virtually all PC manufacturers understand how to configure the value chain in order to deliver products directly to customers. In this sense, Dell's value chain innovations in terms of distribution have been imitated. (For a period of time, Dell's build-to-order distribution methods were a competitive advantage. The fact that competitors have imitated these methods demonstrates that no competitive advantage lasts permanently.)

The focus of value chain analysis is on primary and secondary activities. **Primary activities** include inbound logistics (such as sources of parts), operations (such as manufacturing if dealing with a physical product), sales and distribution of products, and after-sales service. Therefore, primary activities are directly involved in creating value for the customer. **Support activities** provide support to the primary activities so that they can be completed effectively. Support activities, then, are only indirectly involved in creating value for the customer as they support the primary activities. Next, we examine primary and support activities to more fully explain the value chain.

Focusing on the primary activities, the product moves from raw-material suppliers to operations, to finished-goods inventory, to marketing and distribution, and finally to after-sales service. These activities are shown in Figure 4.2. Each stage of the value chain's primary activities adds costs, but hopefully creates value as well.

Knowledge of the customer is a critical component of actions taken to use the value chain.[26] This knowledge must be injected into each stage of activities to increase the probability that activities are being used in ways to create value

---

value chain

the structure of activities the firm uses to implement its business-level strategy

benchmarking

the process of identifying the best practices of competitors and other high-performing firms, analyzing them, and comparing them with the organization's own practices

primary activities

inbound logistics (such as sources of parts), operations (such as manufacturing if dealing with a physical product), sales and distribution of products, and after-sales service

support activities

provide support to the primary activities so that they can be completed effectively for customers. For example, using knowledge about customers, the firm ensures that its raw materials are of appropriate quality to build a product that meets or exceeds customer needs. These materials should be delivered in a timely matter so that the firm can provide the finished product on the dates required by the customer. Of course, the firm must be able to transform the raw materials into a high-quality finished product. These products are then sent to inventory so that marketing can distribute them to the customer when needed at the lowest possible distribution cost. Marketing develops sales and promotion campaigns to attract customers and to ensure that they understand the value provided by the product. Finally, after-sales service helps customers use the product and makes certain that the product meets the customers' standards. The value provided is reflected in the size of the margin as shown in Figure 4.2.

Support activities are important even though their effect on creating customer value is indirect. As shown in Figure 4.2, purchasing, accounting, research and development, and human resource management are examples of support activities (information technology is yet another support activity). The human resource management function is responsible for recruiting the human capital needed to complete all primary and support activities. Research and development helps to create the new products that are produced and provided to customers through the primary activities. Shareholders and investors pay close attention to the reports provided by accounting to determine whether the firm is performing well and whether they want to make additional investments in the firm. This discussion emphasizes the necessity of the support functions and shows their effect on the creation of value for customers through the primary activities. With today's new technologies, some primary and support activities are being performed in new and more efficient ways. For example, firms can use the

Figure 4.2 The Value Chain

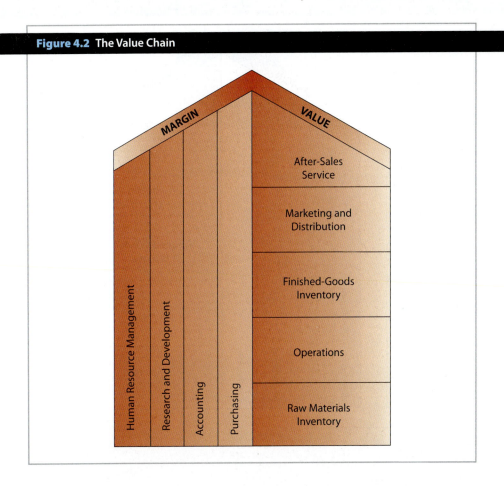

Internet to communicate with customers, track deliveries, and learn more about customers' needs.[27]

Firms analyze their value chain continuously to find ways to operate more efficiently as a means of creating more value for customers. Continuous analysis of the value chain is a prerequisite to developing a competitive advantage and sustaining it against substantial competition. In fact, analysis of the value chain has led to a significant amount of outsourcing of support activities and even some primary activities. When a firm identifies serious inefficiencies in how it completes one or more activities, those activities are candidates for outsourcing.

Outsourcing

Outsourcing involves acquiring a capability from an external supplier that contributes to the focal firm's ability to create value for customers.[28] Outsourcing is a popular strategic management tool that is being used by firms throughout the world, including a number of U.S. companies.

In Figure 4.3, we show hypothetically how a support activity—human resource management—might be outsourced. Of course, a firm could choose to outsource the entire human resource management activity or only certain parts of it. Information technology (IT) is another support activity that some firms choose to outsource. In mid-2008, for example, Royal Dutch Shell announced plans to outsource the majority of its IT activities to three companies—Electronic Data

outsourcing

acquiring a capability from an external supplier that contributes to the focal firm's ability to create value for customers

Figure 4.3 Outsourcing the HRM Function

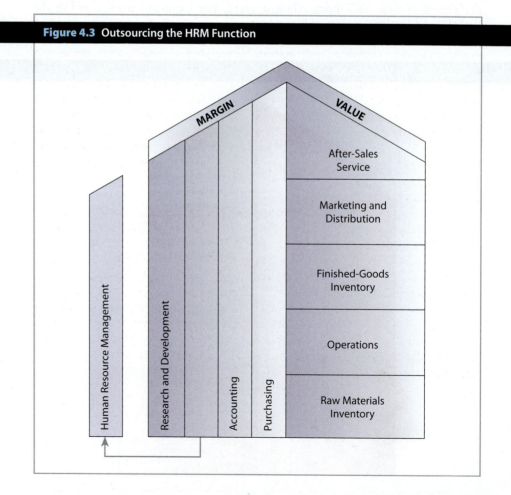

Systems (a firm that Hewlett-Packard announced in 2008 that it intended to acquire), AT&T and T-Systems.[29]

Firms seek one or more benefits when they decide to outsource the performance of an activity to an external supplier. Being able to create more value for its customers by using a company specializing in completing a particular activity is the key benefit that should drive a firm's decision to outsource. Royal Dutch Shell, for example, appears to believe that three companies specializing in IT can generate more value than the firm can create itself by developing and using its own IT operations. Being able to concentrate its resources on the activities for which the firm does have the potential to create core competencies is another important benefit of outsourcing. For example, for Royal Dutch Shell, outsourcing IT activities enables the firm to marshal its resources to concentrate on activities (perhaps exploration for natural resources) for which it has more potential to develop a core competence and, as a result, more potential to create value for customers. Other outsourcing benefits include reducing the risks the firm assumes when it allocates resources to activities for which it cannot create superior customer value and having the flexibility to more rapidly alter how activities are being used to implement its strategies.

The probability of achieving outsourcing's benefits increases significantly when the reasons for using outsourcing are strategic in nature rather than tactical. For the most part, the benefits of outsourcing that we just described accrue to a firm engaging in outsourcing for strategic reasons. Unfortunately, as mentioned in Understanding Strategy: Learning from Failure, only 27 percent of the executives Deloitte recently surveyed indicated that they hoped their firm would gain a competitive advantage as a result of their outsourcing decisions. In contrast, 64 percent of the surveyed executives cited cost reduction as the primary motive for their firm's outsourcing decisions. As a tactical decision, reducing costs is clearly an important objective. But cost reductions that are not part of a robust plan as to how the firm's entire resource portfolio is to be managed to create superior value for customers by developing and effectively using core competencies is not the path to long-term success. Another way of thinking about this is to say that tactical outsourcing decisions (such as cost reductions that are not sought within the context of a strategic set of decisions) typically prevent the firm from gaining access to the most important benefits associated with outsourcing (such as those discussed earlier). Thus, the challenge for managers is to make certain that their firm's outsourcing decisions are the product of deliberate analyses about how outsourcing certain activities will allow the firm to better manage its resources in order to develop value-creating core competencies.[30]

Additionally, though, managers need to understand that even strategic outsourcing decisions are not risk free. We explain the risks Boeing is encountering as a result of the strategic outsourcing decisions the firm made regarding the design and manufacture of its innovative 787 Dreamliner. For all managers, including those at Boeing involved with the 787 project, the challenge is to balance outsourcing's risks and costs with the anticipated benefits. The discussion of Boeing's strategic outsourcing decisions here sets the stage for an additional analysis of the advantages (benefits) and disadvantages (risks and costs) of Boeing's decision to outsource on a global basis a number of activities required to design and build the 787. This further discussion can be found in Understanding Strategy: Learning from Failure in Chapter 8.

Outsourcing: An Imperfect Strategic Management Tool

"Overall our survey shows that the emphasis on cost reduction and access to a vendor's skilled workers reveals a procurement-oriented mind-set that takes a narrow view of the potential benefits of an outsourcing relationship. In short, companies are aiming too low." Peter Moller, partner at Deloitte

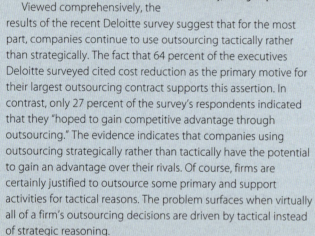

© Courtesy, Boeing Corporation

Viewed comprehensively, the results of the recent Deloitte survey suggest that for the most part, companies continue to use outsourcing tactically rather than strategically. The fact that 64 percent of the executives Deloitte surveyed cited cost reduction as the primary motive for their largest outsourcing contract supports this assertion. In contrast, only 27 percent of the survey's respondents indicated that they "hoped to gain competitive advantage through outsourcing." The evidence indicates that companies using outsourcing strategically rather than tactically have the potential to gain an advantage over their rivals. Of course, firms are certainly justified to outsource some primary and support activities for tactical reasons. The problem surfaces when virtually all of a firm's outsourcing decisions are driven by tactical instead of strategic reasoning.

In spite of their competitive potential though, outsourcing decisions that are made for strategic reasons are not without difficulties. The outsourcing decisions Boeing has made to manufacture its innovative 787 Dreamliner demonstrate this point. Partly because of the scale of the work they complete to design and manufacture aircraft, Boeing and competitor Airbus commonly outsource aspects of their operations. But the extent of Boeing's outsourcing with the 787 is quite unusual for the firm, which is the world's leading aerospace company and the largest manufacturer of commercial jetliners and military aircraft combined. Clearly, Boeing's outsourcing decisions concerning the 787 are strategic in nature and are intended to yield a competitive advantage for the firm relative to Airbus, its chief rival.

According to some analysts, "The 787 program is stretching technology to its outer edge, starting with the wing, the smart part of any airframe." Because of this, Boeing made a strategic decision to outsource the design of the 787's wing to three Japanese companies—Mitsubishi Heavy Industries, Fuji Heavy Industries, and Kawasaki Heavy Industries. Of course, in the process of outsourcing this work, Boeing must cooperate with these three companies. The problem in doing so though is that this collaboration is allowing the three Japanese companies to acquire some of Boeing's core competencies, "starting with wing technology and the new lightweight materials" that are being used to manufacture the 787's wing. The result of this situation is that "Over time, institutional learning and forgetting will put the suppliers in control of the critical body of knowledge, and Boeing will steadily lose touch with key technical expertise." Thus, through this strategic outsourcing decision, Boeing is risking the transfer of some of its core competencies to potential competitors.

Timing is another risk Boeing has accepted because of its strategic outsourcing decisions related to the 787. Largely because of the complexity and novelty of the 787 program, Boeing decided to outsource between 60 and 70 percent of the 787's overall construction to contractors. An unintended negative consequence of this decision was that many of the subcontractors found the scale and scope of the work that had been outsourced to them to be overwhelming, causing parts to run low and product quality to suffer. Collectively, these problems caused the initial launch of the 787 to be delayed by at least 14 months to late 2009.

The lessons about outsourcing as we are discussing this strategic management tool in this Understanding Strategy are clear: (1) tactical outsourcing decisions are less likely than strategic outsourcing decisions to lead to competitive advantage, but (2) strategic outsourcing decisions are simply not risk-free!

Sources: L. Krishnaswamy, 2008, Reverse outsourcing: India comes to the Midwest, *Medill Reports,* www.medill.northwestern.edu; May 6; C. Matlack, 2008, What Airbus learned from the Dreamliner, *BusinessWeek,* April 28; E. Vandore, 2008, Airbus announces new delays to A380, *Houston Chronicle Online,* www.chron.com, May 13; A. Van Der Luijt, 2008, Outsourcing is about more than just money, *Director of Finance Online,* www.dofonline.co.uk, February 15; J. Newhouse, 2007, Boeing versus Airbus: Flight risk, outsourcing challenges, *CIO,* www.cio.com, March L1.

The primary purpose of this chapter is to explain how a firm's resources can be managed to develop one or more core competencies that are also competitive advantages. In doing so, we examined the following topics:

- To develop and implement the most effective strategy, managers need to understand the firm's resources and capabilities. To reach this understanding, managers complete an internal analysis to identify the firm's strengths and weaknesses. Strengths are resources and capabilities that allow the firm to complete important tasks. **Weaknesses** are resource and capability deficiencies that make it difficult for the firm to complete important tasks.

- Firms have two types of resources—**tangible** and **intangible.** Tangible resources are valuable assets that can be seen or quantified, such as manufacturing equipment and financial capital. Intangible resources are assets that contribute to creating value for customers but are not physically identifiable.

- Resources may be acquired or developed to use in the future. These resources are considered *real options*. Resource options provide firms with strategic flexibility, or the ability to deal with issues as they surface. These options normally hold their value and may even increase in value.

- Capabilities are formed by integrating several resources with the intent of accomplishing a major task or series of related tasks. Capabilities are normally based on the knowledge held by the firm's employees (its human capital).

- Core competencies are capabilities the firm emphasizes and performs especially well while pursuing its vision. If these core competencies are different from those held by competitors, they may be referred to as distinctive competencies. When core competencies allow the firm to create value for customers by performing a key primary or support activity *better* than competitors, it has a competitive advantage. To be a competitive advantage, a core competence must be valuable, rare, difficult to imitate, and nonsubstitutable.

- The **value chain** is the structure of activities the firm uses to implement its business-level strategy. A firm analyzes its value chain to better understand the activities that contribute most strongly to creating value for customers and the costs of using each activity. This analysis yields information and insights the firm requires to wisely (i.e., efficiently) use its resources. The value chain includes both **primary and support activities. Value** can be created when using primary activities to produce, sell, distribute, and service a product and when using support activities to support wise use of the firm's resources.

- **Outsourcing** involves acquiring a capability from an external supplier that contributes to the focal firm's ability to create value for customers. Outsourcing is becoming more common because of increased capabilities in global markets by firms specializing in specific activities.

benchmarking, 74
intangible resources, 67
outsourcing, 76

primary activities, 74
support activities, 74
tangible resources, 67

value, 67
value chain, 74
weaknesses, 67

1. What are strengths and weaknesses, and how does the firm identify them?
2. What are resources, capabilities, and core competencies? How are these concepts related?
3. What four characteristics of core competencies are necessary for them to be a competitive advantage?
4. How would you explain the value chain to a classmate? What are primary and support activities?
5. What is outsourcing? How does outsourcing create value for the firm? What are the potential problems with outsourcing?

STRATEGY TOOLBOX

Introduction

After examining the external environment for opportunities to move a company forward, strategic leaders must carefully examine their firm's internal organization to identify capabilities. A vision that is disconnected with the reality of internal capabilities is doomed to failure. One of the most common elements of this analysis is a review of the industry value chain and an honest assessment of how the company compares to the competition. This chapter's tool summarizes how to systematically complete this review.

The Value Chain Assessor

ACTIVITY	IMPORTANCE (low, medium, or high)	SIGNIFICANTLY LOWER	SOMEWHAT LOWER	NEITHER HIGHER/LOWER	SOMEWHAT HIGHER	SIGNIFICANTLY HIGHER
		COMPARISON OF COMPANY'S COMPETENCY TO KEY COMPETITORS				
After-Sales Service						
Marketing and Distribution						
Finished-Goods Inventory						
Operations						
Raw Materials Inventory						
Human Resource Management						
Research and Development						
Accounting						
Purchasing						

MINI-CASE

Wm. Wrigley Jr. Company: Flexibly Using Its Resources to Increase Performance

"Wrigley has been feeling the heat from Cadbury," says a financial analyst. How would Wrigley use its resources to respond to this continuing competitive challenge? Surprisingly to many, CEO William Wrigley Jr., whose great-grandfather in 1891 founded the company bearing his name, announced on April 28, 2008, that the Wrigley Company was being sold to privately held Mars, Incorporated for $23 billion in cash. At a price of $80 per share, the purchase price was a 28 percent premium at the time the purchase was announced. According to

Wrigley's CEO, his firm, which was to become a division within Mars, was being sold at a "great price that provides value to Wrigley stock-holders." The intriguing issue is to understand how Wrigley and other top-level executives concluded that selling their firm to Mars would allow better use of its resources to create value for customers and superior returns for shareholders.

For many decades, Wrigley had used its resources wisely. Commit-ted to the "Spirit of Innovation" in all of its businesses, Wrigley grew to the point where it was selling its products in more than 180 countries. The company became "a recognized leader in confections and the world's largest manufacturer and marketer of chewing gum." In addi-tion to innovation, Wrigley Company believed that its merchandising skills, its ability to build brands globally, and its worldwide distribution system were core competencies on which its success was based. Over time, Wrigley relied on its core competencies (and the resources and capabilities on which they were based) to grow internally (primarily through product and process innovations) and through strategic acquisitions. The purchase of Altoids and Life Savers from Kraft Foods in 2005 for $1.48 billion was one of Wrigley's largest strategic acquisi-tions. This transaction was completed after Wrigley's failed 2002 attempt to buy Hershey Foods for $12 billion. The unrelenting need for scale and global reach in the global confectionary and gum mar-kets was the primary driver of Wrigley's acquisitions and efforts to grow internally.

In spite of what the firm was doing to use its resources to create additional value for customers through internal growth and strategic acquisitions, Wrigley was losing ground to competitors, particularly to British-based Cadbury Schweppes. A slightly different way to think about the situation is that Wrigley's core competencies in merchan-dising skills, the building of global brands, and its worldwide distribu-tion system were no longer able to be the foundation for continuous increases in customer value and shareholder returns. Indeed, today's competitive realities demanded that Wrigley find a way to use its resources to produce and distribute a larger number of products in a larger number of global territories or regions. The Mars/Wrigley com-bination appears to be the foundation for the scale of resources and their use that is required to meet this challenge. In fact, the combined Mars/Wrigley will control 14.5 percent of the world's confectionery market. Cadbury Schweppes is the next closest competitor with a

10 percent share of this market. Thus, although Cadbury had been gaining ground against Wrigley by introducing new gums (such as Trident Splash with a liquid center), this firm is at a manufacturing scale and global reach disadvantage relative to the combination of Mars and Wrigley.

Prior to selling the company, CEO William Wrigley Jr. had achieved some successes. Taking over the CEO position in 1999 and through 2006 (when he relinquished the CEO duties to William Perez but remained the board chairperson), Wrigley grew the firm's sales reve-nue from $2 billion to more than $5 billion. However, the inability of new product innovations (such as the 5 gum, a product for whom teenagers are the target) to reverse the loss of market share in the United States to Cadbury, coupled with the need for the firm to extend its global reach and increase its operational efficiency, convinced Wrigley that his company's resources would generate more value for customers and greater returns for shareholders when combined with Mars's resources and capabilities.

Sources: P. Gogoi, 2008, A bittersweet deal for Wrigley, *BusinessWeek*, May 12, 34; 2008, Cor-porate profile, Wrigley, www.investor.wrigey.com; D. Sterrett, 2008, Wrigley's juicy feud, *ChicagoBusiness.com*, www.chicagobusiness.com, May 5; D. Sterrett, 2008, Wrigley execs, family to snag sweet payouts in Mars merger, *ChicagoBusiness.com*, www.chicagobusiness .com, April 29; 2008, The Wrigley Company agrees to merger with Mars, Incorporated, *The Wall Street Journal Online*, www.wsj.com, April 28; 2008, Mars announces merger agreement with Wm. Wrigley, *The Wall Street Journal Online*, www.wsj.com, April 28.

Questions

1. Wrigley's core competencies are mentioned in the case. Go to Mars's Web site (www.mars.com) and use other materials available to you to identify Mars' core competencies. Do you believe the two firms' core competencies can be combined in ways to gain economies of scale and to expand the new firm's global reach?

2. Cadbury Schweppes will likely respond to Mars' purchase of the Wrigley Company. Use the Internet to find materials to help you identify the different options Cadbury might pursue in response to Mars's purchase of Wrigley.

3. Prior to its purchase, the Wrigley Company believed that its merchandising skills, an ability to build global brands, and a worldwide distribution system were its core competencies. On what tangible and intangible resources do you believe those competencies were based?

EXPERIENTIAL EXERCISES

Exercise One: Value Chains and Competencies

Organize into at least five groups (if you need more groups, have different groups do the same company), making sure that mem-bers in each group represent the different functional discipline majors (accounting, marketing, finance, management, information systems, and so forth).

Each group should draw the value chain of the following five companies:

- Disney
- General Motors
- Nike

- McDonald's
- Starbucks

Highlight any elements of each value chain that you think represent areas in which the firm has a core competence. Determine whether any of the firm's core competencies are valuable, rare, difficult to imitate and nonsubstitutable and as such are a competitive advan-tage. Also, identify any activities the firm has outsourced and explain the firm's decision to do so.

When the class reassembles, compare value chains and defend your choices.

BIZ FLIX

Ray: **Critique of Ray Charles: Strengths and Weaknesses**

Watch the scene from the film *Ray*. Think of Ray Charles as a recently bought resource of Atlantic Records. While watching this scene, recall this chapter's discussion about analyzing the firm.

Jamie Foxx gives an engaging 2004 Academy Award–winning portrayal of legendary American musician Ray Charles. This engaging film tells the story of how far Ray Charles rose in music despite almost impossible odds against his success. Great performances, music, cinematography, and film editing give unbeatable cinematic entertainment. If you do not already own Ray Charles's music before watching this film, you will after you see it.

The selected scene is an edited version of the "Messing Around" sequence that appears early in the film. This scene starts after Ahmet Ertugen (Curtis Armstrong) met Ray Charles in his Harlem apartment in 1952. He tells Charles that his company, Atlantic Records, bought Charles's contract from Swingtime. Charles has gone to an Atlantic Records studio to make some recordings. Ahmet and others in the control room have noted that Ray sounds like Nat King Cole or Charles Brown and does not have a unique sound.

The scene begins with Ahmet coming into the studio. Charles says, "Ahmet, what you think of that?" This scene ends with Charles starting his version of "The Mess Around." The film continues with its engaging chronicle of Ray Charles and his musical career.

What to Watch for and Ask Yourself

1. Is Ray Charles a tangible or intangible resource of Atlantic Records?
2. What are Ray Charles's strengths and weaknesses?
3. What capabilities and core competencies does Ray Charles bring to Atlantic Records?

ENDNOTES

1. D. Carpenter, 2008, Breakfast, Europe a winning combo, *Houston Chronicle Online*, www.chron.com, March 10.
2. 2008, McDonald's tries feng shui makeover, *AOL Money & Finance*, www.money .aco.com, February 25.
3. D. J. Collis & M. G. Rukstad, 2008, Can you say what your strategy is? *Harvard Business Review*, 86(4): 82–90.
4. D. G. Sirmon, M. A. Hitt, & R. D. Ireland, 2007, Managing firm resources in dynamic environments to create value: Looking inside the black box, *Academy of Management Review*, 32: 273–292.
5. C. O. Trevor & A. J. Nyberg, 2008, Keeping your headcount when all about you are losing theirs: Downsizing, voluntary turnover rates, and the moderating role of HR practices, *Academy of Management Journal*, 51: 259–276; Y. Liu, J. G. Combs, D. A. Ketchen, Jr., & R. D. Ireland, 2007, The value of human resource management for organizational performance, *Business Horizons*, 50: 503–511; M. A. Hitt, L. Bierman, K. Shimizu, & R. Kochhar, 2001, Direct and moderating effects of human capital on strategy and firm performance in professional service firms, *Academy of Management Journal*, 44: 13–28.
6. D. J. Miller, M. J. Fern, & L. B. Cardinal, 2007, The use of knowledge for technological innovation within diversified firms, *Academy of Management Journal*, 50: 308–326; S. K. McEvily & B. Chakravarthy, 2002, The persistence of a knowledge-based advantage: An empirical test for product performance and technological knowledge, *Strategic Management Journal*, 23: 285–305.
7. 2008, Behind the brand, Coca-Cola, www.thecoca-colacompany.com, May 12.
8. 2008, The Coca-Cola company reports first quarter 2008 results, *The Wall Street Journal Online*, www.wsj.com, April 16.
9. 2008, McDonald's Corporation, McDonald's, www.mcdonalds.com/cor/values/ people/opportunity.html, May 12.
10. 2008, Google's strength grows as it completes DoubleClick deal, *Houston Chronicle Online*, www.chron.com, March 11.
11. D. Welch, 2008, GM's good news: A $3 billion loss, *BusinessWeek*, May 12, 31.
12. C. J. Loomis, 2008, Can anyone run Citigroup? *Fortune*, May 5, 80–91.

13. R. E. Hoskisson, M. A. Hitt, R. D. Ireland, & J. S. Harrison, 2008, *Competing for Advantage*, 2nd ed., Mason, OH: Thomson South-Western, Chapter 13; R. G. McGrath & A. Nerkar, 2004, Real options reasoning and a new look at R&D investment strategies of pharmaceutical firms, *Strategic Management Journal*, 25: 1–21.
14. V. Gurin, 2007, BioTech & Pharma consulting, www.gurinpharma.com, October 16.
15. R. Oriani & M. Sobrero, 2008, Uncertainty and the market valuation of R&D within a real options logic, *Strategic Management Journal*, 29: 343–361; C. M. Scherpereel, 2008, The option-creating institution: A real options perspective on economic organization, *Strategic Management Journal*, 29: 455–470; K. D. Miller & A. T. Arikan, 2004, Technology search investments: Evolutionary, option reasoning, and option pricing approaches, *Strategic Management Journal*, 25: 473–485.
16. M. S. Olson, D. van Bever, & S. Verry, 2008, When growth stalls, *Harvard Business Review*, 86(3): 51–61; T. B. Folta & J. P. O'Brien, 2004, Entry in the presence of dueling options, *Strategic Management Journal*, 25: 121–138.
17. B. Clanton, 2008, Rolls-Royce name lives on—as supplier, *Houston Chronicle Online*, www.chron.com, May 8.
18. R. D. Ireland & J. W. Webb, 2007, Strategic entrepreneurship: Creating competitive advantage through streams of innovation, *Business Horizons*, 50: 49–59; Sirmon, Hitt, & Ireland, Managing firm resources.
19. H. Lee & D. Kelley, 2008, Building dynamic capabilities for innovation: An exploratory study of key management practices, *R&D Management*, 38: 155–168; M. Blyler & R. W. Coff, 2003, Dynamic capabilities, social capital and rent appropriation: Ties that split pies, *Strategic Management Journal*, 24: 677–686.
20. A. Taylor, III, 2008, Inside Honda's brain, *Fortune*, March 17, 100–106.
21. T. Felin & W. S. Hesterly, 2007, The knowledge-based view, nested heterogeneity, and new value creation: Philosophical considerations on the locus of knowledge, *Academy of Management Review*, 32: 195–218; S. E. Jackson, M. A. Hitt, & A. DeNisi, 2003, *Managing Knowledge for Sustained Competitive Advantage*, San Francisco: Jossey-Bass.

22. C. Quintana-Garcia & C. A. Benavides-Velasco, 2008, Innovative competence, exploration and exploitation: The influence of technological diversification, *Research Policy*, 37: 492–507; M. A. Hitt & R. D. Ireland, 1985, Corporate distinctive competence, strategy, industry and performance, *Strategic Management Journal*, 6: 273–293.

23. J. Barney, 2001, Is the resource-based view a useful perspective for strategic management research? Yes, *Academy of Management Review, 26*: 41–56.

24. M. A. Hitt, R. D. Ireland, & R. E. Hoskisson, 2008, *Strategic Management: Competitiveness and Globalization*, 8th ed., Mason, OH: Thomson South-Western; D. P. Lepak, K. G. Smith, & M. S. Taylor, 2007, Value creation and value capture: A multilevel perspective, *Academy of Management Review, 32*: 180–194; M. Porter, 1985, *Competitive Advantage*, New York: Free Press.

25. M. A. Hitt, J. S. Black, & L. W. Porter, 2009, *Management*, 2nd ed., Upper Saddle River, NJ: Pearson Prentice Hall; T. Kollat, 2008, *Strategy*, Atlasbooks.com.

26. R. J. Harrington & A. K. Tjan, 2008, Transforming strategy one customer at a time, *Harvard Business Review*, 86(3): 62–72.

27. S. Nambisan & P. Nambisan, 2008, How to profit from a better "virtual customer environment," *MIT Sloan Management Review*, 49(3): 53–61; R. Amit & C. Zott, 2001, Value creation in e-business, *Strategic Management Journal*, Volume 22(6/7): 493–520.

28. O. E. Williamson, 2008, Outsourcing: Transaction cost economics and supply chain management, *The Journal of Supply Chain Management*, 44(2): 5–16; F. T. Rothaermel, M. A. Hitt, & L. Jobe, 2006, Balancing vertical integration and strategic outsourcing: Effects on product portfolio, product success, and firm performance, *Strategic Management Journal*, 27: 1033–1056.

29. R. Marshall, 2008, Shell could miss out in new outsourcing deal, *Accountancy Age*, www.accountancy.age.com, January 4.

30. S. D. Vivek, D. K. Banwet, & R. Shankar, 2008, Analysis of interactions among core, transaction, and relationship-specific investments: The case of offshoring, *Journal of Operations Management*, 26: 180–197; M. J. Leiblein, J. J. Reuer, & F. Dalsace, 2002, Do make or buy decisions matter? The influence of organizational governance and technological performance, *Strategic Management Journal*, 23: 817–833.

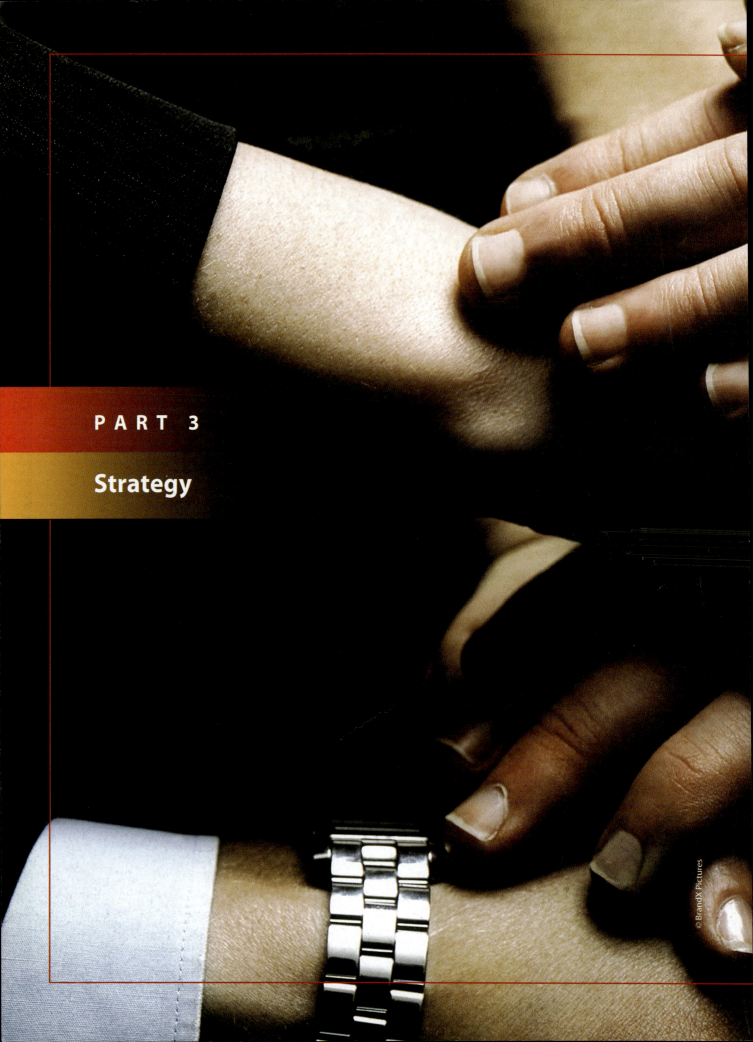

PART 3

Strategy

CHAPTER 5
Strategy at the Business-Level

Knowledge Objectives

Reading and studying this chapter should enable you to:

1. Define business-level strategy.

2. Define and explain the differences among the five business-level strategies.

3. Describe how to successfully use each business-level strategy.

4. Identify the risks of each business-level strategy.

5. Explain the structures to best implement each business-level strategy.

© BrandX Pictures

FOCUSING ON STRATEGY

The Times, They Are A'Changin': The Evolution of Wal-Mart

In 2007, Wal-Mart became the largest corporation on the *Fortune* 500 list with sales of almost $379 billion. Wal-Mart has more than 6,800 stores worldwide, and they are expected to add about 10 percent more stores in 2008. Wal-Mart has 1.9 million associates, with 1.3 million of them in the United States. It has operations in 13 other countries and is expanding its supplier network globally. Wal-Mart's scale of operations is unrivaled by any competitor. Its market is observable with suppliers as they do almost whatever Wal-Mart asks because of the exceptionally large quantities of goods the firm purchases. In 2007, it reaffirmed its intent to offer its customers the lowest price available. This strategy was exemplified by its holiday actions planned almost one year earlier in which it opened stores one hour earlier than competitors and provided special holiday discounts in the early morning hours to attract customers. This strategy was effective because its December 2007 sales increased by 2.7 percent over one year earlier while Target, Wal-Mart's chief rival experienced sales declines of 5 percent. Wal-Mart clearly has employed a cost leadership strategy.

© Shaul Swartz/Getty Images

Yet even with its market power and reaffirmation of its cost leadership strategy, Wal-Mart has been slowly making changes in its product offerings and approach to customers. For example, it developed and implemented a "Store of the Community" concept in which store designs and merchandise were tailored to each community. As such, they customize stores to the affluence of the community and the types of merchandise desired. To customize the stores and merchandise, staff conducts in-depth marketing research.

Wal-Mart has announced that it plans to open 400 in-store health care clinics by 2010. These clinics are to be staffed largely by nurse practitioners and will provide basic services to handle normal medical problems at low costs. In the early clinics opened in Wal-Mart stores, approximately 55 percent of the patients had no health insurance. With approximately 47 million citizens without health care insurance, these clinics may offer an opportunity for medical care unavailable to many in other ways. Wal-Mart also announced a plan to help companies more effectively manage their prescription drug costs. Wal-Mart currently offers generic drugs at lower prices than competitors.

Wal-Mart has also instituted a number of "green" policies designed to have a more positive impact on the physical environment. The company intends to measure and reduce its greenhouse gas emissions and to encourage all of its suppliers to do the same. For example, Wal-Mart improved the efficiency of its fleet of trucks by 15 percent. Wal-Mart is promoting energy efficiency by advertising and selling long-life low-energy lightbulbs. It sold more than 100 million of these lightbulbs in 2007. Wal-Mart also published a comprehensive report on its social and environmental practices, which required considerable effort because of its many stores and global operations.

Even though Wal-Mart has not abandoned its low-cost strategy, it is making other changes that allow it to compete even more effectively with its rivals.

Sources: Corporate facts, 2008, www.walmart.com, February 23; Out in front, 2008, www.walmart.com, February 23; A. Gonzales, 2008, Wal-Mart to open 400 health clinics nationally by year 2010, *Phoenix Business Journal*, www.bizjournals.com, February 22; M. Kabel, 2008, Wal-Mart says it likely will profit off hard times, *Houston Chronicle*, www.chron.com, February 19; M. Freudenheim, 2008, Wal-Mart will expand in-store medical clinics, *New York Times*, www.nytimes.com, February 7; M. Barbaro, 2008, Wal-Mart: The new Washington, *New York Times*, www.nytimes.com, February 3; M. Barbaro, 2008, Wal-Mart's holiday strategy proved a timely one, *New York Times*, www.nytimes.com. January 11; M. Gunther, 2007, Wal-Mart's mixed green bag, CNNMoney.com, http//:money.com, November 16.

87

In Chapter 1, we defined strategy as an action plan designed to move an organization toward achievement of its vision. The different types of strategies firms use to meet this goal are shown in Figure 1.1 in Chapter 1.

Business-level strategy, the topic of this chapter, is one of the types of strategies firms develop to achieve their vision. A **business-level strategy** is an action plan the firm develops to describe how it will compete in its chosen industry or market segment. A business-level strategy describes how the firm will compete in the marketplace on a day-by-day basis and how it intends to "do things right."[1] Wal-Mart's primary strategy has been one of cost leadership. However, in recent times, Wal-Mart has been adding services and approaches that differentiate it from its primary competitors. For example, customizing stores to the community through store design and merchandise stocked allows it to broaden the set of rivals with which it competes. None of its primary rivals currently provides health care services for customers either. Thus, while its primary strategy is that of cost leadership, it has integrated some elements of a differentiation strategy as well.

A firm's main objective in using a business-level strategy is to consistently provide a good or service to customers that they will buy because it creates more value (in the form of performance characteristics or price) for them than does a competitor's good or service. This approach is illustrated in the opening Focusing on Strategy in this chapter, which describes Wal-Mart's cost leadership strategy. In fact, Wal-Mart's market research suggests that about 90 percent of citizens in the United States shop at Wal-Mart (an extremely high percentage) and that 91 percent of these shoppers give the firm positive favorability ratings.[2] A business-level strategy is most successful when everybody in the firm fully understands the chosen strategy[3] and when it is implemented with zeal and efficiency.[4] In other words, firms must be precise in describing what they seek to accomplish with their strategy. The strategy must "connect" with the target customers as well. For example, the goal of BMW North America's business-level strategy is clear: "to be the leader in every premium segment of the international automotive industry."[5] Of course, as is the case with all of the firm's strategies, ethical practices should guide how the business-level strategy is used.[6] Often, a firm's intended ethical practices are made public by recording them in written documents such as a code of ethics, a code of conduct, and a corporate creed. The statements in these documents signal to stakeholders how the firm intends to interact with them. They also set the expectation that a firm's employees adhere to the behaviors specified in these documents.

A business-level strategy is intended to help the firm focus its efforts so it can satisfy a group of customers.[7] An effective business-level strategy has a clear statement of the value to be created for customers. This point is illustrated by the founding of Wal-Mart. Through the strategic leadership of Sam Walton, its founder, Wal-Mart initially formed a business-level strategy that was intended to offer a large assortment of many different products at low prices to consumers living in towns with a population no greater than 25,000.[8] Thus, for early Wal-Mart customers, the value this firm provided to them was the opportunity to buy goods at prices that were always lower than the prices of those goods from locally owned stores. Everyone working at Wal-Mart understood the value the firm was creating for its customers, which helped the firm effectively implement its chosen business-level strategy. In addition, by comparison shopping and then buying from Wal-Mart, customers quickly understood the value the firm was providing to them in the form of lower prices on a wide assortment of items. Interestingly, Wal-Mart still follows this strategy and has achieved considerable success with it.

We fully discuss five business-level strategies in this chapter. These five strategies are sometimes referred to as generic because they are used in all industries and by all types of firms. A properly chosen business-level strategy favorably positions the firm relative to the competitive forces we discussed in Chapter 3. Being effectively positioned enables the firm to simultaneously create value for customers

business-level strategy

an action plan the firm develops to describe how it will compete in its chosen industry or market segment

and returns for shareholders.[9] We also use the value chain (see Chapter 4) to show the primary and support activities that are required to successfully use each business-level strategy. Not surprisingly, the firm accepts some risks when it decides to use a particular business-level strategy. We also discuss the risks of each type of strategy. Strategic leaders monitor these risks and make the appropriate strategic decisions (e.g., regarding changes in strategy or in implementing the strategy).[10] In formulating the firm's business-level strategy, strategic leaders must ensure that the strategy fits well with the business model in order to achieve the highest performance.[11] In this chapter, we also describe the particular organizational structure (defined later in the chapter) that should be used to effectively implement each generic strategy. Because it affects the behavior of individual employees, the responsibilities assigned to them, and the leadership style they experience, organizational structure is an important aspect of how business-level strategies are implemented.

As the Wal-Mart example shows, a firm's business-level strategy is never set in stone. As an action plan, a business-level strategy is a living document that is constantly subject to changes based on opportunities and threats emerging in the firm's external environment as well as changes in the competitive advantages that are a product of the resources, capabilities, and core competencies in the firm's internal environment.

Types of Business-Level Strategies

Firms choose from five business-level strategies: cost leadership, differentiation, focused cost leadership, focused differentiation, and integrated cost leadership/differentiation (see Figure 5.1). As shown in this figure, the firm's business-level strategy has two key dimensions: competitive advantage and competitive scope. The business-level strategy the firm chooses is a function of the basis for the competitive advantage (either cost or uniqueness) that it seeks to achieve or maintain (if it already

Figure 5.1 Five Business-Level Strategies

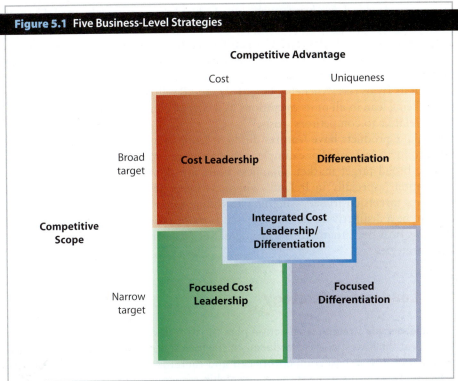

has an advantage over competitors)[12] and the breadth (either broad or narrow) of the target market it wishes to serve. When using the cost leadership or differentiation strategy, the firm seeks to apply its competitive advantage in many customer segments. When using either focused cost leadership or focused differentiation, the firm uses its cost advantage or its uniqueness advantage in narrower market segments. Specifically, with focus strategies, the firm "selects a segment or group of segments in the industry and tailors its strategy to serving them to the exclusion of others."[13]

Procter & Gamble's Tide soap is an example of a product that has a broad target market, while Porsche's 911 Carrera is designed to serve the needs of a narrow group of customers. Each firm's decision about competitive scope (broad or narrow) is influenced by opportunities and threats in its external environment. A market segment is a group of people with similar needs with respect to certain variables such as price, quality, and product features. Segmenting markets into smaller groups with similar needs can be a threat to firms with a relatively standardized product serving the needs of multiple customer segments. Tide, for example, is designed to fit a broad target market. Simultaneously, though, being able to identify people with a specific need that isn't being satisfied by the product aimed at a broad target market creates opportunities for other firms. A number of smaller companies develop specialty laundry detergent and soaps for market segments (e.g., hypoallergenic cleansing products for people who want to avoid the types of chemicals in products such as Tide).

© AP Photo/Str/Porche

In general, a firm's capabilities and core competencies enable it either to produce standardized products at lower costs than those of their competitors or to produce unique products that differ from competitors' products in ways that create superior value for customers. In the first instance, the firm has a competitive advantage based on costs; in the second instance, it has a competitive advantage based on uniqueness (see Figure 5.1).

By standardized products, we mean products that are widely available and have a large customer demand. Think of automobile tires as an example. We all need tires for our vehicles, and Cooper Tire & Rubber is known for producing relatively inexpensive (yet reliable) tires for cars and trucks. Cooper can charge lower prices because its production, distribution, and service costs are lower than those of its rivals (i.e., Michelin, Goodyear, and Pirelli). Cooper remains committed to being lean in all of its operations as a way of continuously holding its costs down relative to competitors' costs.[14]

Unique products have features different from or in addition to the standardized product's features. For example, although more expensive than beers designed for the broad target market, Guinness beers are popular with segments of the population (especially in Ireland). Guinness beers are more expensive because Guinness targets customers who may be willing to pay more for what some perceive to be a distinctive taste—a taste that is more expensive to produce.[15]

Let's turn our attention to learning about each of the five generic business-level strategies.

Cost Leadership Strategy

A **cost leadership strategy** is an action plan the firm develops to produce goods or services at the lowest cost.[16] Producing at the lowest cost enables the firm to price its product lower than competitors can and therefore gain a larger share of its target market. Firms using the cost leadership strategy typically sell standardized products to the industry's "average" customers because they are usually the largest target segment. Thus, Cooper Tire & Rubber intends to sell its tires to the

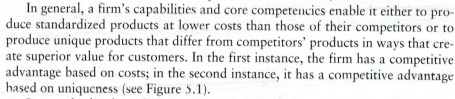

cost leadership strategy

an action plan the firm develops to produce goods or services at the lowest cost

customer with "average" or "typical" needs. Successful use of the cost leadership strategy across time results when the firm continuously finds ways to reduce its costs relative to competitors' costs by constantly examining how the costs of its primary activities and support activities can be lowered without damaging the functionality of its products. Firms using a cost leadership strategy commonly have economies of scale because of the large quantities of standardized products produced.[17] Firms implementing the cost leadership strategy have strong process engineering skills, emphasize manufacturing processes that permit efficient production of products, have performance evaluation systems that reward employees on the quantity of their output, and know how to buy raw materials needed to produce their products at low costs. For example, some firms are able to achieve low costs by manufacturing modular products in which parts may fit several different product variations.[18]

In Chapter 4, we described how firms use value-chain analysis to identify the primary activities and support activities in which they are able to create value. A firm's value chain can be managed to achieve low costs.[19] In Figure 5.2, we show how the cost leader could create value in each primary activity and in each support activity. A firm does not need to outperform competitors in every one of these activities to successfully use the cost leadership strategy; however, the more primary and support activities in which the firm can outperform its competitors, the more likely that its costs will be lower than its competitors' costs.

Figure 5.2 Examples of Value-Creating Activities Associated with the Cost Leadership Strategy

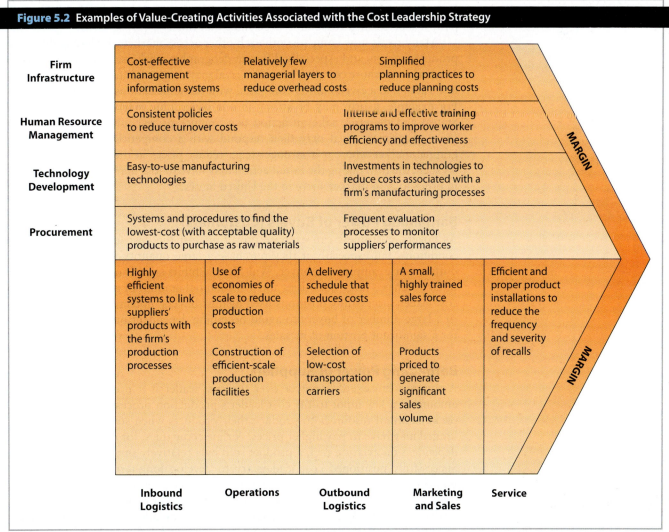

Source: Adapted with the permission of The Free Press, an imprint of Simon & Schuster Adult Publishing Group, from *Competitive Advantage: Creating and Sustaining Superior Performance* by Michael E. Porter, p. 47. Copyright © 1985, 1988 by Michael E. Porter. All rights reserved.

Effective use of the cost leadership strategy positions the firm in the marketplace in a way that enables it to create value for customers, especially through lower prices. In recent years, such a strategy has been effective for reaching unique markets with low income levels not previously considered by many firms.[20] Also, as we describe in the next five subsections, effectively implementing the cost leadership strategy enables a firm to establish a strong market position relative to the five competitive forces we introduced in Chapter 3.

Rivalry with Existing Competitors

Competitors find it extremely difficult to compete against the cost leader on the basis of price. To meet the cost leader's sales price, a competing firm must reduce its profit margins when selling its products. In turn, lower margins leave that firm with less capital to invest to improve its operational efficiency. Therefore, competing on the basis of price against the cost leader places a competitor in a cycle of falling farther behind in terms of efficiency and cost reductions. Kmart encountered this competitive circumstance when trying to compete against cost leader Wal-Mart on the basis of price. Kmart's cost structure, compared to Wal-Mart's, was higher. The higher cost structure prevented Kmart from being able to offer products at prices as low as Wal-Mart's. Having emerged from bankruptcy, Kmart no longer attempts to compete against Wal-Mart on the basis of costs and product prices. Instead, the firm changed its product mix to reduce the degree to which it competes directly with cost leader Wal-Mart. In fact, after it was acquired by Sears in 2004, Kmart's strategy changed further and the Sears holding company has performed reasonably well since that time.[21]

Many rivals now compete with each other across markets, including different product markets and especially different geographic markets.[22] This multimarket competition is more complex because a rival may respond differently to a competitor's action in a given market compared with the same actions in another market. For example, a firm may be strong in one geographic market (e.g., the United States) and therefore take an action (e.g., reduce prices) to increase its market share. A primary rival may then respond with a competitive action in a geographic market where it is stronger (e.g., reduce prices in the European Union). As such, the firm taking the initial action may have to lose market share in Europe in order to gain market share in the United States.[23]

Bargaining Power of Buyers (Customers)

As buyers, customers can exercise power against the cost leader under several conditions, but especially if they purchase a large quantity of the cost leader's output. For example, as a buyer, Wal-Mart exhibits significant power because it often purchases large quantities and a substantial amount of a firm's output. The cost leader successfully positions itself against buyers' potential power by selling to a large number of buyers to avoid becoming dependent on any one customer for a significant portion of its sales.

Bargaining Power of Suppliers

A supplier can exercise power over the cost leader if it provides a significant amount of a key input to the cost leader's production process. Firms dependent on key natural resources to produce their products when sources of supply are limited may have to pay higher prices. Airline companies, for example, are highly dependent on aviation fuel, a product sold by a relatively small number of firms. Successfully positioned cost leaders try to develop long-term contracts with a number of suppliers at favorable rates to reduce the potential of suppliers raising their prices, which would affect the cost leader's position in terms of costs. Cost leader Southwest Airlines is quite savvy about forming long-term contracts with fuel suppliers. These contracts often keep Southwest's fuel costs lower than those of its competitors.

Potential Entrants

The favorably positioned cost leader operates at a level of efficiency that can't be matched by firms thinking of entering the industry in which the cost leader is well established. The cost leader's ability to continuously drive its costs lower and lower while still satisfying customers' needs makes it difficult for potential entrants to the market to compete against the cost leader.

Product Substitutes

A product substitute is a product that can replace the focal product because it has essentially the same functionality. For example, NutraSweet is a replacement or substitute for sugar. To compete against a cost leader, though, a substitute must offer something in addition to the same functionality. This "something different" could be a lower purchase price (which is unlikely when competing against the cost leader) or a feature that customers value that isn't a part of the cost leader's product. (As you know, NutraSweet's "something different" is a taste similar to that of sugar but without sugar's calories.) The successfully positioned cost leader commonly responds to product substitutes by reducing the purchase price of its product, which makes it difficult for a substitute to attract the attention of the cost leader's customers.

Competitive Risks of the Cost Leadership Strategy

The cost leadership strategy has two major risks. First, competitors' innovations may enable them to produce their good or service at a cost that is lower than that of the cost leader. For the price-conscious "typical" consumer, the lower cost is attractive. Second, concentrating too much on reducing costs may eventually find the cost leader offering a product at low prices to customers who are less inclined to purchase it. Even though the cost leader must keep its costs down, it can't lose contact with its customers to the point that it fails to fully understand changes in customers' expectations relative to the product in terms of price and features. At some point, for example, customers wanting to buy low-cost products may become willing to pay more for additional features such as increased product safety and extended product warranties. The cost leader must stay in close touch with its customers so it will be able to detect changes in their needs.

As explained in Understanding Strategy: Learning from Failure, JetBlue was initially quite successful in its use of the cost leadership strategy. Yet, when it tried to expand its services, it experienced significant cost increases (e.g., new airplanes, increased training costs). Worse, it was unable to manage the more complex operations effectively, and its service suffered. As a result, the airline's financial performance suffered and it continues in its attempts to overcome these problems with a new leadership team at the helm.

Differentiation Strategy

A **differentiation strategy** is an action plan the firm develops to produce goods or services that customers perceive as being unique in ways that are important to them. The "uniqueness" a firm provides when using the differentiation strategy may be physical or psychological. It can be created by the way in which the firm uses one or more of either the primary activities or the support activities. Product durability, ease of repair, and superior installation services are examples of physical sources of differentiation. Perceptions of the quality of service after the sale and of the courtesy of salespeople are examples of sources of psychological differentiation. Interestingly, JetBlue followed a cost leadership strategy but also provided small differences in service to differentiate it from other low-cost airlines such as Southwest. This strategy worked until Southwest tried to implement major differentiation strategies in addition to its low prices.

differentiation strategy
an action plan the firm develops to produce goods or services that customers perceive as being unique in ways that are important to them

How to Lose While Holding a Winning Hand: JetBlue's Stumble

© Greg Mathieson/MAI/Landov

JetBlue began with high expectations, and most of them were fulfilled in the first few years of operations. JetBlue operated with a cost leadership strategy but also offered a few special amenities to passengers (e.g., leather seats and individual monitors for viewing in-flight programs). JetBlue received a number of awards for excellent service in the first several years of its operation and earned profits as well (unusual for start-ups and for airlines in general). JetBlue did a number of things well. In addition to imitating many of the positive attributes of Southwest Airlines, it employed a significant amount of information technology to largely eliminate paper (tickets and reports were handled online). The firm started with a strong leadership team, agreed on a set of positive values, and were able to hire employees without the interference (and costs) of unions. Because of the initial capital, it also started with a new fleet of airplanes, which reduced its maintenance costs. It received the highest rating among airlines on the University of Nebraska's national airline quality rating for four years in a row (2003–2006). In the early years, its stock price remained reasonably high.

Despite its unusual success in the early venture years, especially for the airline industry, and its large cemetery of failed airlines, the leaders at JetBlue decided to change the firm's strategy. Decisions were made to expand service to international routes and to compete more directly with many of the larger full-service airlines. To do so required that the airline buy other and different airplanes (to handle longer flights, for example), develop new training programs to operate the new airplanes, and hire more employees to operate and maintain them. The stock market reacted negatively to the announced changes, and the stock price did not recover thereafter.

In addition to these problems, JetBlue had a major debacle in its service. Due to extremely poor weather at its major hub in New York, JetBlue had many passengers trapped on its planes (on runways for many hours) and then canceled more than 1,000 flights in the next six days. This dramatic change in service levels caused a substantial amount of criticism, and the stock price fell even further. Three months after this debacle, the CEO moved to the board chair position and a new CEO was named. Later in the same year, 2007, the CFO unexpectedly resigned. Thus, 2007 was not a good year for JetBlue.

Most observers believe that the strategy change was inappropriate. It caused management confusion, and the firm lacked the capabilities to implement it effectively. Although JetBlue announced a loss early in 2008, analysts think it is in line for a good year. It made changes and is focusing on managing its costs and providing quality service. Furthermore, with the economy sinking, it is gaining more business passengers looking for lower-cost fares.

Sources: A. Keeton, 2008, Northwest, JetBlue post losses, *Wall Street Journal*, online.wsj.com, January 30; C. Gutierrez, 2008, JetBlue shares surprisingly strong, *Forbes*, www.forbes.com, January 29; M. Linder, 2007, Skies are gray for JetBlue, *Forbes*, www.forbes.com, November 9; J. Bailey, 2007, Five days; New pilot at JetBlue, *New York Times*, www.nytimes.com, May 12; 2007, A change in the cockpit at JetBlue, *BusinessWeek*, www.businessweek.com, May; J. McGregor, 2007, An extraordinary stumble at JetBlue, *BusinessWeek*, www.businessweek.com, March 5; S. McCartney, 2007, Unusual route: Discount airlines woo business set, *Wall Street Journal*, online.wsj.com, February 19.

The cost leader commonly serves an industry's typical customer. In contrast, the firm using the differentiation strategy serves customers who want to buy a good or service that is different from the good or service purchased by an industry's average customer. The goods offered by Ralph Lauren provide examples of differentiated items. The logo appearing on many of the firm's clothing products is used to differentiate these goods from those made for the clothing industry's typical customer. In addition to the logo, the firm's dress shirts for men are made of high-quality raw materials and lack a pocket. The logo, the materials, and the absence of a pocket are differentiated features that create value for customers desiring to wear something other than a "typical" dress shirt.

Think about goods and services (e.g., cars and clothes) that you believe are different from those serving the typical customers in an industry. Doing so suggests that the ways goods and services can differ from one another are virtually endless. Different tastes, responsive customer service, product design, alternative distribution methods, and customer loyalty programs are but a few examples of how goods or services can offer unique value to customers.

Many firms offer unique products by emphasizing innovation in their organization.[24] In doing so, they continuously introduce new and unique products that provide value to customers. Some firms offer a special service or identity with a segment of the market. For example, banks from Latin America have established subsidiaries in Miami, Florida, and focus on serving the large Hispanic community in the area.[25] Other firms try to differentiate the value provided to customers through the after-sales service. In fact, recent research shows that firms can closely monitor their customers' satisfaction after the sale and any returns of products in order to develop information to improve their products and gain a competitive advantage.[26]

The value chain can be used to highlight the primary and support activities where value should be created to use the differentiation strategy. Through this approach, the firm emphasizes the primary and support activities shown in Figure 5.3 to create more value than competitors can create for customers. The firm using the differentiation strategy wants to develop core competencies in one or more of the primary and support activities. The more unique value the firm can create for customers, the more likely the firm will be able to successfully use the differentiation strategy.

Next, we explain how the firm effectively using the differentiation strategy is able to position itself in the marketplace. In the next five subsections, we explain how an effective differentiation strategy results in a strong market position for the firm by countering each of the five competitive forces discussed in Chapter 3.

Figure 5.3 Examples of Value-Creating Activities Associated with the Differentiation Strategy

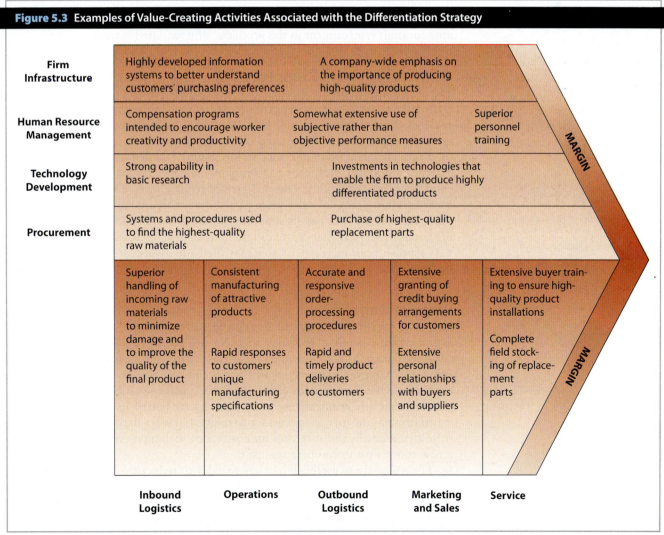

Source: Adapted with the permission of The Free Press, an imprint of Simon & Schuster Adult Publishing Group, from *Competitive Advantage: Creating and Sustaining Superior Performance* by Michael E. Porter, p. 47. Copyright © 1985, 1988 by Michael E. Porter. All rights reserved.

Rivalry with Existing Competitors

Customers tend to be loyal buyers of products that create unique value for them. For this reason, firms using the differentiation strategy do everything they can to increase the loyalty of their customers by providing them greater benefits than do rivals.[27] With increasing loyalty, customer sensitivity to the price of the product they are buying is reduced. Reducing price sensitivity is important because the firm using the differentiation strategy needs to establish large profit margins on its products to earn the resources required to continuously reinvest in its products so that the valued sources of difference can be maintained. Think of it this way: providing differentiated goods and services can be expensive. The firm needs to earn high returns on what it sells to be able to pay for the costs of creating differentiated features while producing its products.

Bargaining Power of Buyers (Customers)

The uniqueness of a differentiated good or service reduces customers' sensitivity to the product's price. Firms using the differentiation strategy continuously stress the uniqueness of their products to customers (often through advertising campaigns) to reduce customers' sensitivity to price. For example, the Lexus slogan of "The Relentless Pursuit of Perfection" by Toyota, the manufacturer of Lexus products, signals to the customer that even though the product's price is higher than that of cars aimed at the typical customer, the Lexus is a superior product because it is made by people seeking perfection in their work. When a firm's effort to emphasize product uniqueness is successful, customers' sensitivity to price is reduced, thus enabling the firm to continue selling its products at a price that permits constant reinvestment in the products' differentiated features.

Bargaining Power of Suppliers

The firm using the differentiation strategy typically pays a premium price for the raw materials used to make its product. For a good, a premium price means that some of the raw materials will be expensive (e.g., high-quality cotton used to make expensive, yet differentiated clothing items). Alternatively, for a service, the firm may pay a premium price to hire highly talented employees. For example, the consultants McKinsey & Company must hire skilled and knowledgeable employees to provide differentiated service to its clients. However, the returns earned from a premium sales price of a differentiated good or service yield the funds the firm needs to pay its suppliers' higher prices. In addition, a firm providing goods or services that create differentiated value to customers may be able to pass supplier price increases on to its satisfied and loyal customers in the form of higher prices.

Potential Entrants

Customer loyalty and the need to provide customers with more value than an existing firm's product provides to them are strong challenges for potential rivals that are considering competing against a firm successfully using the differentiation strategy. Customer loyalty is difficult to earn (doesn't a firm have to consistently meet your needs for quite a while before you become loyal to it?), meaning that a new entrant typically faces a long battle. In addition, the established firm has the margins necessary to reinvest in ways that will further enhance the differentiated value it creates for customers, making it even more difficult for a new competitor to compete against it.

Firms also try to establish barriers to entry to reduce the number of potential entrants. For example, in some industries, firms use patents on their unique products to stop potential rivals from imitating them.[28] Yet patents are sometimes difficult to defend, and smart competitors make enough changes in their products to avoid legal patent violations.

Product Substitutes

It is difficult for competitors to create substitute products that will satisfy loyal customers of a firm that provides them differentiated value from a good or service. Perceived unique value is difficult to replace, even when a product substitute has a better performance-to-price ratio that favors substitution. For most of us, it would take a lot to get us to switch to a substitute when we are satisfied with the product we've been buying for a long time. Thus, firms with loyal customers tend to be largely insulated from competitors' substitute products that are intended to provide different value to the focal firm's customers.

Competitive Risks of the Differentiation Strategy

The differentiation strategy is not risk-free. The first risk is that customers may decide that the price they are paying for a product's differentiated features is too high. This situation can happen especially when a cost leader learns how to add some differentiated features to its product without significantly raising the product's price, as JetBlue did in its early years in the industry. The customers buying the differentiated product may decide that the value received is too expensive relative to the combination of some differentiation and low price of the cost leader's good or service. A second risk is that the source of differentiation being provided by the firm may cease to create value for the target customers. For example, men buying Ralph Lauren dress shirts might conclude that the logo, lack of a pocket, and high-quality cotton no longer provide value for which they are willing to pay. For this reason, some firms go to great lengths to continuously innovate and bring new and improved products to the market (to stay ahead of competition). As part of their efforts, these firms may form joint ventures with other firms to obtain access to unique knowledge and skills, thereby enriching their innovations.[29]

Customer experiences are the third risk; by using a differentiated product and comparing its performance with lower-cost alternatives, the customer may conclude that the cost of the differentiation isn't acceptable. When first introduced, the IBM brand name enabled the firm to charge premium prices for its personal computers (PCs). However, through experience, many customers learned that the performance of competitors' lower-priced products was virtually equivalent to that of the IBM PC. Finally, differentiated products run the risk of being somewhat effectively counterfeited. Although of much lower quality, the counterfeit product that looks like "the real thing" can be appealing, even for the customer capable of buying the true differentiated product. Here, the customer thinks about why he or she should pay the higher price for "the real thing" when the counterfeit product looks about as good.

Whole Foods Market implements a differentiation strategy explained in Understanding Strategy: Learning from Success. As the world's largest retailer of natural and organic foods, it emphasizes the unique products and services it provides to customers. These are described in the five values presented in the firm's Declaration of Interdependence. With more than 200 stores and $5.6 billion-plus in sales, its success is unequaled in the natural and organic foods market.

Focus Strategies

A **focus strategy** is an action plan the firm develops to produce goods or services that serve the needs of a specific market segment. Therefore, focus strategies serve a more narrow segment within a broader market.[30] Firms using the focus strategy intend to serve the needs of a narrow customer segment better than their needs can be met by the firm targeting its products to the broad market (see Figure 5.1). A particular buyer group (such as teenagers, senior citizens, or working women), a specific segment of a product line (such as professional painters rather than "do-it-yourself" painters), and particular geographic markets (such as the West Coast

focus strategy

an action plan the firm develops to produce goods or services to serve the needs of a specific market segment

Whole Foods Market: Differentiation the Organic Way

The Whole Foods Market is the largest natural foods retailer in the world. Whole Foods sells natural and organic food products in all types of food categories, such as meat, produce, and baked and prepared foods. The company now has more than 200 stores, employs about 45,000 associates, and generates annual sales exceeding $5.6 billion. It is the most successful natural and organic food retailer. Although competitors existed, Whole Foods was the first to build a larger supermarket that carried all natural and organic foods. So it gained first mover advantages.

Whole Foods now has a number of competitors who try to imitate its products and services. As such, Whole Foods encourages its managers and associates to be innovative in the development of new products and services it can provide customers. Each store is organized into self-directed work teams with each team responsible for a category of products (e.g., prepared foods, meats and poultry, and customer service). Team members go through a rigorous selection process and are highly trained to do their jobs. These actions are necessary for Whole Foods to continue to command a premium price for its products. Because compensation is partly based on individual, team, and store results, associates are motivated to ensure that customers are highly satisfied with the products and service they receive.

© AP Photo/Harry Cabluck

Whole Foods implements its differentiation strategy through its "Declaration of Interdependence." This declaration explains Whole Foods' five primary values:

- Providing only high-quality foods
- Satisfying and delighting customers
- Promoting team member excellence and happiness
- Creating wealth through profits and growth
- Caring about communities and the environment

The values are designed to show the interdependence among Whole Foods' stakeholders (e.g., customers, associates, shareholders, and communities) and the intent to work with all of them in an effective manner.

Whole Foods carefully monitors its competitors even though it is much larger than most of them. In fact, Whole Foods has acquired several of its competitors including the recent purchase of its largest competitor Wild Oats. Many of its competitors serve only regional markets similar to FreshDirect, an online marketer of quality foods in the New York City market. Thus, Whole Foods benefits from its national reputation and name recognition.

Sources: 2007, Whole Foods Market. *Wikipedia*, www.wikipedia.com, September 2; 2007, Whole Foods closes buyout of Wild Oats, *New York Times*, www.nytimes.com, August 29; 2007, Our core values, Whole Foods Market Web site, www.wholefoodsmarket.com, April 29; M. Hogan, 2007, Whole Foods: A little too rich? *BusinessWeek*, www.businessweek.com, July 21; 2007, Declaration of interdependence, Whole Foods Market, www.wholefoodsmarket.com, April 29.

or the East Coast of the United States) are examples of different target market segments on which a firm might focus. As noted in Understanding Strategy: Learning from Success, many of Whole Foods' competitors follow a focus differentiation strategy by serving a specific geographic region (e.g., FreshDirect's focus on the New York City market). Firm's can use either the focused cost leadership strategy or the focused differentiation strategy to successfully serve the needs of a narrow market segment.

Focused Cost Leadership Strategy

The **focused cost leadership strategy** is an action plan the firm develops to produce goods or services for a narrow market segment at the lowest cost. Based in Sweden, IKEA uses the focused cost leadership strategy.

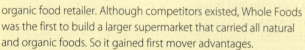

focused cost leadership strategy

an action plan the firm develops to produce goods or services for a narrow market segment at the lowest cost

IKEA is a global furniture retailer with locations in more than 30 countries. IKEA targets younger customers desiring style at a low cost.[31] IKEA offers home furnishings with good design and function and acceptable quality at low prices to young buyers who, according to IKEA's research, aren't wealthy, work for a living, and want to shop at hours beyond those typically available from firms serving the broad furniture market.

To successfully use its focused cost leadership strategy, IKEA concentrates on lowering its costs and understanding its customers' needs. To keep the firm's costs low, IKEA's engineers design low-cost modular furniture that customers can easily assemble. To appeal to young buyers who often are short of time and are inexperienced when it comes to buying furniture, IKEA arranges its products by rooms instead of by products. These configurations enable customers to see different living combinations (complete with sofas, chairs, tables, and so forth) in a single setting.[32]

Focused Differentiation Strategy

The **focused differentiation strategy** is an action plan the firm develops to produce goods or services that a narrow group of customers perceive as being unique in ways that are important to them. Thomas Pink is a business unit of LVMH Moet Hennessy Louis Vuitton, which produces clothing and apparel.

All of LVMH's business units, including Thomas Pink, use the focused differentiation strategy. For example, Thomas Pink introduced men's shirts made of 170-count cotton. This count of cotton is quite high and is the main way the product is differentiated in the marketplace (in comparison, a T-shirt from Old Navy is made of 18-count cotton). When introduced, these shirts were priced at $195 each. Thus, this shirt is targeted to a narrow target market: men who have achieved a great deal of success in corporate settings and who want to feel comfortable about the shirt they are wearing.[33]

To successfully use either focus strategy, a firm must perform many of the value chain's primary and support activities in ways that enable it to create more value than competitors can create for a narrow group of target customers. The specific activities required to successfully use the focused cost leadership strategy are identical to those shown in Figure 5.2, while the activities needed to be successful with the focused differentiation strategy parallel those shown in Figure 5.3. The difference in the value chains shown in these two figures is that each activity is performed with a narrow market instead of a broad market segment in mind. Therefore, Figures 5.2 and 5.3 and the text regarding the five competitive forces describe how a firm successfully using one of the focus strategies is favorably positioned against the five competitive forces. However, to maintain its favorable position, when using the focused cost leadership strategy, the firm must continually drive its costs lower compared to competitors. In addition, when using the focused differentiation strategy, the firm must continue to differentiate its product in ways that are meaningful to the target customers.

Competitive Risks of Focus Strategies

Using a focus strategy carries several risks. First, a competitor may learn how to "outfocus" the focusing firm. For example, Charles Tyrwhitt Shirts is using its skills to try to outfocus Thomas Pink in men's high-quality dress shirts. Tyrwhitt introduced a 180-count cotton shirt priced at $160, creating significant competition for Thomas Pink.[34] Second, a company serving the broad target market may decide that the target market being served by the focusing firm is attractive. Ralph Lauren, for instance, could introduce a dress shirt with a cotton count lower than that used by Thomas Pink and Charles Tyrwhitt and a slightly lower price. Ralph Lauren could rely on its brand image to entice its competitors' customers to try its dress shirt. Finally, the needs of the narrow target customer may change and become similar to those of the broad market. For example, increases in their disposable income and

focused differentiation strategy

an action plan the firm develops to produce goods or services that a narrow group of customers perceive as being unique in ways that are important to them

experience with buying furniture might change some of IKEA's young buyers' needs to those that can be satisfied by a firm serving the broad market.

Integrated Cost Leadership/Differentiation Strategy

The **integrated cost leadership/differentiation strategy** is an action plan the firm develops to produce goods or services, with strong emphasis on both differentiation and low cost. With this strategy, firms produce products that have some differentiated features (but not as many as offered by firms using the differentiation strategy) and that are produced at a low cost (but not at a cost as low as those of the firm using the cost leadership strategy). This strategy can be used to serve the needs of a broad target market or a narrow target market. McDonald's uses this strategy to serve the needs of a broad market, while Anon uses it to focus on the needs of a narrow target market. (Anon makes semicustomized rooftop air-conditioning systems for large customers such as The Home Depot, Wal-Mart, and Target.) Because the integrated cost leadership/differentiation strategy requires firms to be somewhat differentiated while producing at relatively low costs, firms must develop the flexibility needed to serve both of these objectives. They have to achieve a balance between the two objectives.[35]

Lenovo, which acquired IBM's personal computer business, must attempt to maintain this balance as well. It must invest in R&D to continuously develop new technology and designs such as its newest ultrathin ThinkPad laptop computer. Yet because personal computers have become a commodity, Lenova must also keep its costs low in order to compete effectively in the PC market worldwide.[36]

The possibility of being "neither fish nor fowl" is the main risk of using the integrated cost leadership/differentiation strategy. In other words, when a firm fails to produce somewhat differentiated products at relatively low costs, it becomes stuck in the middle.[37] The risk of this strategy and the problem of being stuck in the middle is highlighted in the discussions of JetBlue's changing strategy earlier in this chapter. JetBlue began largely following a cost leadership strategy and was successful. However, as it changed its strategy, it experienced problems of trying to provide differentiated services and maintain the service quality while also keeping costs down. Thus, it appears that JetBlue has become stuck in the middle.

Implementing Business-Level Strategies

To be successful, business-level strategies must not only match the needs of the marketplace, they also need to be implemented effectively. Organizational structure is an important dimension of implementing strategies. An **organizational structure** specifies the firm's formal reporting relationships, procedures, controls, and authority and decision-making processes.[38] Matching the right structure with the chosen strategy enhances firm performance.

Three major types of organizational structure are used to implement strategies: a simple structure, a functional structure, and a multidivisional structure.[39] Only the simple structure and the functional structure can be used to implement business-level strategies. A **simple structure** is an organizational structure in which the owner/manager makes all of the major decisions and oversees all of the staff's activities. This structure calls for few rules, a dependence on informal relationships, and limited task specialization. The work is coordinated through frequent informal communications between the owner/manager and staff. This type of structure is best suited for use in a small business. The **functional structure** is an organizational structure consisting of a CEO and a small corporate staff. Here, the managers of major functional areas usually report to the CEO or a member of the corporate staff. This structure emphasizes functional specialization and facilitates active information sharing within each function. However, the functional orientation sometimes makes it difficult to communicate and coordinate across functions.

integrated cost leadership/ differentiation strategy

an action plan the firm develops to produce goods or services with a strong emphasis on both differentiation and low cost

organizational structure

specifies the firm's formal reporting relationships, procedures, controls, and authority and decision-making processes

simple structure

an organizational structure in which the owner/manager makes all of the major decisions and oversees all of the staff's activities

functional structure

an organizational structure consisting of a CEO and a small corporate staff

Figure 5.4 Functional Structure for Implementing the Cost Leadership Strategy

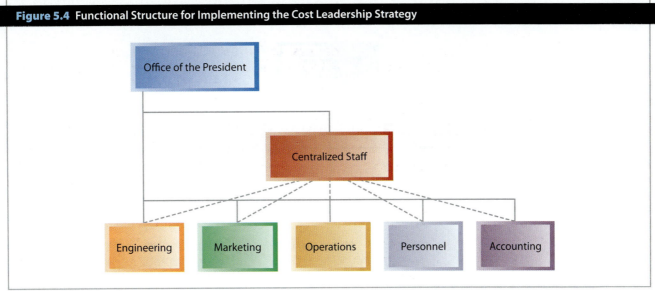

Notes: • Operations is the main function.
          • Process engineering is emphasized rather than new product R&D.
          • Relatively large centralized staff coordinates functions.
          • Formalized procedures allow for emergence of a low-cost culture.
          • Overall structure is somewhat rigid, causing job roles to be relatively structured.

Implementing the Cost Leadership Strategy

Firms implementing the cost leadership strategy use a functional structure with highly centralized authority in the corporate staff (see Figure 5.4). Recall that with a cost leadership strategy, the firm produces a relatively standardized product that is sold to the industry's average customer. To ensure that the product is produced at low costs and with standard features, the firm's structure calls for a high degree of centralized authority. To create efficiency, jobs are highly specialized and organized into homogenous subgroups and highly formalized rules and procedures are established. The substantial efficiency resulting from this structure helps firms keep their costs low. The operations function is emphasized in this structure to ensure that the firm's product is being produced at low costs.

Implementing the Differentiation Strategy

The functional structure used by firms implementing the differentiation strategy differs from the one used by firms implementing the cost leadership strategy. In this version of the functional organizational structure, the R&D and marketing functions are more important. R&D is emphasized so the firm can continuously differentiate through innovations in products and designs that create value for customers, and marketing is emphasized so customers will be aware of the unique value being created by the firm's products (see Figure 5.5). Authority is decentralized in this structure so employees closest to the customer can decide how to appropriately differentiate the firm's products. Jobs in this structure have low specialization, and employees work without a large number of formal rules and processes. The characteristics of this form of the functional structure enable employees to frequently communicate and to coordinate their work. Communication and coordination are vital parts of being able to understand customers' unique needs in order to produce unique products to satisfy those needs.

Implementing the Focus Strategies

When firms following a focus strategy have only a single product line and operate in a single geographic market, a simple structure is effective for implementing the strategy. These firms are often small, and the focus is direct. However, in firms that are larger and more complex (i.e., those with several product lines or that operate in multiple geographic markets), a functional structure usually is

Figure 5.5 Functional Structure for Implementing the Differentiation Strategy

Figure 5.5 Functional Structure for Implementing the Differentiation Strategy

Notes:
- Marketing is the main function (to track new product ideas).
- New product R&D is emphasized.
- Most functions are decentralized, but R&D and marketing may have centralized staffs that work closely with each other.
- Formalization is limited so that new product ideas can easily emerge and change is more readily accomplished.
- Overall structure is relatively flexible, causing job roles to be less structured.

more effective. The type of functional structure used is matched to the type of strategy. Firms using a focused cost leadership strategy should use a centralized functional structure that emphasizes efficiency. However, firms using a focused differentiation strategy should use a functional structure that is decentralized and encourages interaction across functions to create innovation that continuously differentiates the firm's products.

Implementing the Integrated Cost Leadership/Differentiation Strategy

Because of the competing demands of the cost leadership strategy's concern with efficiency and the differentiation strategy's concern with innovation, an integrated cost leadership/differentiation strategy is difficult to implement. To satisfy these competing demands, a firm using this strategy needs a structure in which decisions are partly centralized and partly decentralized. Jobs are semispecialized, and some formal rules and procedures are needed, as well as some informal behavior. In short, flexibility is required. This strategy requires efficient processes to maintain lower costs. Yet the ability to change is also important in order to develop and maintain differentiated goods or services. Flexible manufacturing systems, quality-control systems, and sophisticated information systems can all contribute to simultaneous efficiency and flexibility. For example, Target, a major competitor of Wal-Mart, uses an integrated strategy. It buys in volume, and with its many outlets, it builds economies of scale. Additionally, it tries to maintain nice but efficient stores to keep costs at manageable levels. To differentiate its product, it has developed alliances with brand-name companies such as Eddie Bauer (camping and outdoor equipment) and Mossimo (apparel), among others. Of course, Wal-Mart's recent changes to customize stores and merchandise to local communities is an attempt to compete more directly with Target's differentiation strategy.

Business-Level Strategy Success Across Time

As we've described in this chapter, a business-level strategy is based on the firm's capabilities and competencies and designed to achieve competitive advantages. This strategy is used to position the firm favorably in the marketplace relative to its rivals. Once formed, though, the firm must continuously evaluate its business-level strategy and change it as needed to create more value for customers or bring the firm back on course. Being "on course" means that the strategy is helping the firm reach its vision as well as the mission that is a core part of the vision, as explained in Chapters 1 and 2. Sometimes, major changes in strategy or the implementation of major strategic actions are needed to turn around a firm's performance when its business-level strategy is unsuccessful.[40]

For many years, Hershey depended on the quality of its products and its reputation for producing excellent candies (especially chocolate) to differentiate its products from those of rivals. This strategy was effective for a long time. However, other firms began developing new chocolate candies and eroding Hershey's market share. Rather than develop new candies, top executives at the firm depended on acquisitions to add new product lines (e.g., Reese's Peanut Butter Cups). In 2008, the Hershey company experienced declines in its financial performance and thus considered potential options such as a merger with another major company such as Cadbury Schweppes. Yet it has also taken other strategic actions to turnaround its performance. For example, it has introduced some new candy products to compete more effectively with its major rival, Mars, and entered new international markets such as China.[41] Recent research suggests that both innovation and internationalization have potential to turn around a firm's performance.[42]

© Susan Van Etten

One way the firm can learn how to create more value for customers by using its business-level strategy is to ask them how it can do so. Sam Walton was known for recommending that firms trust their customers and frequently talk to them to find out what they want.

Diversified firms, ones with multiple businesses competing in many industries and market segments, develop business-level strategies for each of their business units. For example, GE has more than a dozen business units, each of which develops a business-level strategy to describe how it intends to compete in its industry or market segments. In the next chapter, we describe the multiproduct strategies that firms such as GE use.

Unlike GE, nondiversified firms that compete in a single product market develop only one business-level strategy. A neighborhood dry-cleaning store and favorite locally owned restaurant are examples of firms with a single business-level strategy. Every firm needs a business-level strategy, and diversified firms need multiple business-level strategies plus a multiproduct strategy (see Chapter 6) as well as an international strategy (see Chapter 8) if they compete in more than a single country's markets.

SUMMARY

The primary purpose of this chapter is to explain the different business-level strategies firms can use to compete in the marketplace. In doing so, we examined the following topics:

- Business-level strategy is an action plan the firm develops to compete in its chosen industry or market segment. A business-level strategy details how the firm intends to compete in the marketplace on a continuous basis to satisfy customers' needs.
- The five generic business-level strategies are referred to as *generic* because they can be used by any firm regardless of the industry. Opportunities and threats in the external environment and the firm's capabilities and core competencies suggest the

business-level strategy the firm should implement to achieve a competitive advantage.

- Each business-level strategy has two dimensions: competitive advantage (either a cost advantage or a uniqueness advantage) and competitive scope (either broad or narrow). The cost leadership and differentiation strategies are used to serve a broad market, while the focused cost leadership and focused differentiation strategies serve the specialized needs of a narrow market. The integrated cost leadership/differentiation strategy strikes a balance between the competitive advantage and competitive scope dimensions.

- When using the cost leadership strategy, a firm produces standardized products that are intended to satisfy the needs of the typical or "average" customer, which is usually the largest market segment. These products are produced at costs lower than those of competitors. To use this strategy successfully across time, the firm must continuously drive its costs lower than competitors' costs so it can sell its products at lower prices.

- Firms use the differentiation strategy to produce products that customers consider unique in ways that are important to them. Target customers for this strategy are willing to pay for product uniqueness that creates value for them. Uniqueness can be physical (e.g., superior reliability) or psychological (e.g., perceived status). Earning margins that are sufficient to support continuous reinvestment in sources of differentiation that customers value is the key to long-term success with this strategy.

- Focus strategies (cost leadership and differentiation) rely on either the cost or uniqueness advantage to better serve the specialized needs of a narrow target market, as compared to serving a broad target market.

- Firms use the integrated cost leadership/differentiation strategy to produce products that have some differentiation at a relatively low price. Because low cost and differentiation are sought simultaneously, the firm must be flexible to successfully use this strategy to avoid becoming stuck in the middle. The main risk of the integrated cost leadership/differentiation strategy is being outperformed by firms successfully using either the cost leadership or differentiation strategy.

- Two versions of the functional structure are best suited to implement the cost leadership strategy and the differentiation strategy. These two versions differ in their degree of centralization, specialization, and formalization. To promote efficiency, the functional structure for the cost leadership strategy holds decision-making authority in centralized staff functions, is highly specialized, and uses formal rules and procedures. In contrast, the functional structure used to implement the differentiation strategy is decentralized to different organizational functions. The emphasis here is on R&D and marketing to promote innovation. This structure requires less specialization, greater use of cross-functional teams, and fewer formal rules and procedures. Structures for the focus strategies largely match the structures used to implement the cost leadership or differentiation strategy. However, if a firm using a focus strategy is small, a simple structure is used. The structure for the integrated cost leadership/differentiation strategy is more complex. It must be flexible, with some centralization and some decentralization in order to promote efficiency and innovation simultaneously. Use of flexible manufacturing systems, quality-control systems, and sophisticated information systems aid the flexibility.

KEY TERMS

business-level strategy, 88
cost leadership strategy, 90
differentiation strategy, 93
focus strategy, 97

focused cost leadership strategy, 98
focused differentiation strategy, 99
functional structure, 100

integrated cost leadership/differentiation
    strategy, 100
organizational structure, 100
simple structure, 100

DISCUSSION QUESTIONS

1. What is a business-level strategy? Why is a business-level strategy important to a firm's success?
2. What are the definitions of the five business-level strategies discussed in this chapter? What are the differences among the five business-level strategies?

3. What specific actions should a firm take to effectively use each business-level strategy?
4. What risks are associated with using each business-level strategy?
5. What organizational structures should be used to implement each of the business-level strategies?

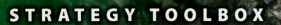

STRATEGY TOOLBOX

Introduction

A company's business-level strategy must be based upon a clear understanding of the company's customers. The Pareto principle, or the 80/20 rule, can be applied to the analysis of customers targeted and served by a company. At a given point in time, many companies find that 80% of the profit is derived from 20% of the customers. This chapter's tool builds on this possibility and provides a lens through which strategists can examine their customer base, with a particular focus on identifying the profit per customer or customer segment. This knowledge can help inform the viability of a particular business-level strategy for each particular segment.

Customer Value Analysis

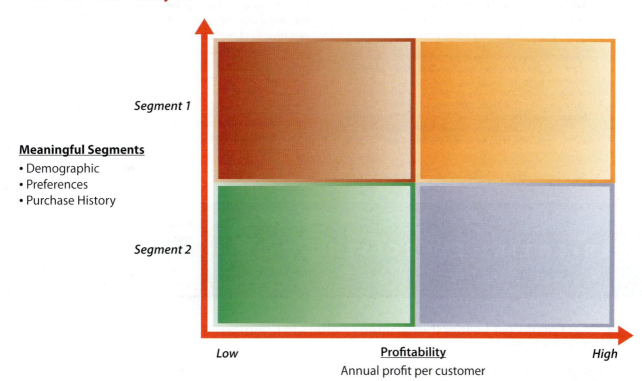

Meaningful Segments
- Demographic
- Preferences
- Purchase History

Segment 1

Segment 2

Low   <u>Profitability</u>   *High*
Annual profit per customer

MINI-CASE

Krispy Kreme: Will Dough Continue to Flow to Shareholders?

Launched in 1937, Krispy Kreme Doughnuts is a branded specialty retailer of premium doughnuts. Its Original Glazed doughnut is the firm's most recognizable product. However, Krispy Kreme's commitment to innovation results in frequent tests of potential new doughnuts such as its whole wheat 180-calorie doughnut introduced in 2007. New products that are well received by customers are then added to the stores' inventory of doughnuts. The variety of flavors Krispy Kreme can incorporate into its doughnuts is virtually endless.

As this brief discussion suggests, Krispy Kreme uses a differentiation strategy. It seeks to sell its premium doughnuts to customers who value the doughnuts' uniqueness. The firm's Doughnut Theatre is a source of differentiation between Krispy Kreme and its competitors. The Doughnut Theatre is the in-store manufacturing process customers can watch to see employees make doughnuts.

Are Krispy Kreme doughnuts really significantly different from competitors' offerings? As we noted earlier in this chapter, some differentiation is tangible, while other differentiation may be more psychological in nature. Some believe that Krispy Kreme's uniqueness is more psychological than tangible. One analyst even suggested, "It isn't what's inside a Krispy Kreme doughnut that creates the demand. It's what's inside the customer's head that makes a Krispy Kreme a Krispy Kreme." Regardless of the nature of the differentiation, Krispy Kreme achieved great success with its differentiation strategy for many decades.

However, the situation began to change for Krispy Kreme in 2004. Essentially, Krispy Kreme overexpanded, taking on significant debt in the process. One indicator of the seriousness of the change is the firm's stock price. After hitting a high of more than $50 in March 2003, it fell to roughly $7.50 per share in February 2005.

We noted in Chapter 3 that firms can't control events in the external environment, but those events can significantly affect a firm's performance. The low-carb diet is a trend in the general environment that is having a major effect on Krispy Kreme. Stated simply, the firm's doughnuts are high in fat, high in carbohydrates, and high in sugar. In addition, at the end of 2004 and continuing into 2005, Krispy Kreme was investigated for alleged accounting irregularities. The firm has tried to respond to the problems with appropriate actions. It brought in a turnaround specialist for a stint as CEO, and a new permanent CEO, Daryl Brewster, was named in 2006. Additionally, the whole wheat doughnut was a response to concerns about high calories. Finally, the company removed all grams of trans fat from its products. Yet its sales continued to decline. After the stock price fell to a new all-time low of under $3 per share, the CEO resigned in January 2008. Some investors suggested that Krispy Kreme should expand further into international markets. Yet it already has stores in 10 foreign countries outside the United States. Analysts believe that the brand remains valuable but the firm has not found a successful business model. The new CEO has significant challenges to decide what strategic actions can be taken to turn around the once highly successful company.

Sources: 2008, Krispy Kreme's CEO resigns, *Wall Street Journal,* online.wsj.com, January 8; 2008, Krispy Kreme's Chief Executive Officer quits amid turnaround, *New York Times,* www.nytimes.com, January 8; M. Linder, 2007, Krispy Kreme fills its hole, for now, *Forbes,* www.forbes.com, September 9; M. Umy, 2007, The way we live now; the hole is healthy, *Financial Times,* www.ft.com, February 27; F. Norris, 2006, Krispy Kreme names a chief executive, and its shares jump nearly 21%, *New York Times,* www.nytimes.com, March 8; 2004, Krispy Kreme to close Ravenna plant, blames low-carb fad, *Wall Street Journal,* www.wsj.com. October 5; D. Stires, 2004, Krispy Kreme is in the hole—again, *Fortune,* November 1, 42–44.

Questions

1. Go to the Krispy Kreme Web site (www.krispykreme.com) and read about how the firm operates. Based on what you read, prepare a list of each source of differentiation the firm is using to make its doughnuts and the way the firm sells them that is unique relative to its competitors.
2. Using the information collected in responding to the first question, determine the sustainability of Krispy Kreme's differentiation strategy. Are the firm's sources of differentiation sustainable over the next 10 years? Why or why not?
3. If you were appointed CEO of Krispy Kreme, what actions would you take and why?

EXPERIENTIAL EXERCISES

Exercise One: Focus Cost Leadership Strategy Falters in Countering Forces in the U.S. Airline Industry

In March and April 2008, four discount carriers—ATA Airlines, Champion Air, Skybus Airlines, and Frontier Airlines—declared Chapter 11 bankruptcy, ceased operations, or announced plans to do so. Frontier Airlines, unlike the others, declared bankruptcy but planned to continue service for the near future. These small carriers used the focus-cost leadership strategy, competing in a limited market segment with a low-cost strategy. In contrast, discount carriers Southwest Airlines, JetBlue, and AirTran have continued to perform strongly. Of the most recent new entrants, Skybus (started May 2007) was the first to fail. In contrast, another recent low-cost new entrant, Virgin America Inc. (started in August 2007) continues to operate and plans to add 30 planes in 2008 and 20 more in 2009. U.S. and British investors plan to inject $100 million of additional funds into Virgin America to keep it operating.

Were these failures a result of the inability of the airlines' strategies to counter the forces in the industry? Your assignment is to choose one failing discount airline (or any other recently failed discount carrier) such as Skybus and one successful airline such as JetBlue to determine why one strategy was successful against the industry forces while the other was not. Was the airline failure a result of poor strategy formulation? If so, what could have been done differently?

Sources: Susan Carey, 2008, Low-cost carrier Skybus closes down business, *Wall Street Journal*, April 5; Susan Carey, 2008, Champion Air plans to shut down, *Wall Street Journal*, March 31; Susan Carey & Melanie Trottman, 2008, ATA shutdown signals discount carrier woes," *Wall Street Journal*, April 4; Paulo Prada, 2008, Virgin America investors to inject $100 million," *Wall Street Journal*, April 12; Melanie Trottman, 2008, Frontier to fly amid bankruptcy filing," *Wall Street Journal*, April 12.

BIZ FLIX

About a Boy: Focused Differentiation of the Will Lightman Product

This chapter discussed differentiation strategies that firms can use to their competitive advantage. Watch this scene from *About a Boy* and assess Will Lightman's (Hugh Grant's) strategy to attract eligible women to him.

Will Lightman lives on the royalties of his father's hit song "Santa's Super Sleigh." A self-absorbed bachelor, Will has mastered getting through a day with no responsibilities. In his constant search for guilt-free short-term relationships, he stumbles on the idea of dating single mothers. He successfully presents himself as a single father at a Single Parents Alone Together (SPAT) meeting that leads to his meeting a boy named Marcus (Nicholas Hoult). Marcus is an outcast at school, so Will teaches him how to be cool. Marcus, in turn, teaches Will about the value of long-term relationships.

The scene comes from the SPAT sequence about 15 minutes after the film starts. Will attends his first meeting after seeing a SPAT advertisement in a magazine. The scene starts with Will describing his (fictional) son Ned. It ends as Will compliments himself for his performance. The film continues with Will's enthusiastic involvement in the meeting and the group's activities.

What to Watch for and Ask Yourself

1. Does Will use a focused differentiation strategy to distinguish himself from other men for this target group? What does he emphasize that appears important to SPAT members?
2. Does he emphasize physiological or psychological differences? What are they?
3. Does he create "perceived unique value" as discussed earlier in this chapter? Could a competitor easily replace what Will offers to SPAT members? Why or why not?

ENDNOTES

1. M. E. Porter & E. Olmstead-Teisberg, 2004, Redefining competition in health care, *Harvard Business Review*, 82(6): 64–76.
2. M. Barbaro, 2008, Wal-Mart: The new Washington, *New York Times*, www.nytimes.com, February 3.
3. M. Beer & R. A. Eisentat, 2004, How to have an honest conversation about your business strategy, *Harvard Business Review*, 82(2): 82–89.
4. G. Stalk Jr. & R. Lachenauer, 2004, Hardball: Five killer strategies for trouncing the competition, *Harvard Business Review*, 82(4): 62–71.
5. B. Breen, 2002, BMW: Driven by design, *Fast Company*, September, 123–127.
6. L. K. Trevino & M. E. Brown, 2004, Managing to be ethical: Debunking five business ethics myths, *Academy of Management Executive*, 18(2): 69–81.
7. B. C. Skaggs & M. Youndt, 2004, Strategic positioning, human capital, and performance in service organizations: A customer interaction approach, *Strategic Management Journal*, 25: 85–99.
8. 2004, Becoming the best: What you can learn from the 25 most influential leaders of our times, Knowledge @ Wharton, www.knowledge.wharron.upenn.edu, February 11.
9. K. Z. Zhou, J. R. Brown, C. S. Dev, & A. Agarwal, 2007, The effects of customer and competitor orientations on performance in global markets: A contingency analysis, *Journal of International Business Studies*, 38: 303–319.
10. S. Elbanna & J. Child, 2007, The influence of decision, environmental, and firm characteristics on the rationality of strategic decision making, *Journal of Management Studies*, 44: 561–583.
11. C. Zott & R. Amit, 2008, The fit between product market strategy and business model: Implications for firm performance, *Strategic Management Journal*, 29: 1–26; S. Elbanna & J. Child, 2007, Influences on strategic decision effectiveness: Development and test of an integrative model, *Strategic Management Journal*, 29: 431–453.
12. F. F. Suarez & G. Lanzolla, 2007, The role of environmental dynamics in building first mover advantage theory, *Academy of Management Review*, 32: 377–392.
13. M. E. Porter, 1985, *Competitive Advantage*, New York: Free Press, 15; S. D. Dobrev, 2007, Competing in the looking-glass market: Imitation, resources, and crowding, *Strategic Management Journal*, 28: 1267–1289.
14. 2008, About Us, Cooper Tire & Rubber, www.coopertire.com. March 9.
15. 2008, Guinness, Wikipedia, http://en.wikipedia.org, March 9.
16. M. E. Porter, 1980, *Competitive Strategy*, New York: Free Press, 35–40.
17. J. Bercovitz & W. Mitchell, 2007, When is more better? The impact of business scale and scope on long-term business survival, while controlling for profitability, *Strategic Management Journal*, 28: 61–79.
18. M. Kotabe, R. Parente, & J. Y. Murray, 2007, Antecedents and outcomes of modular production in the Brazilian automobile industry: A grounded theory approach, *Journal of International Business Studies*, 38: 84–108.
19. T. Shervani, G. Frazier, & G. Challagalla, 2007, The moderating influence of firm market power on the transaction cost economics model: An empirical test in a forward channel integration context, *Strategic Management Journal*, 28: 635–652.
20. C. Seelos & J. Mair, 2007, Profitable business models and market creation in the context of deep poverty: A strategic view, *Academy of Management Perspectives*, 21(4): 49–63.
21. 2008, Message from the chairman, Sears Holdings, www.searsholdings.com, March 9.
22. H. R. Greve, 2008, Multimarket contact and sales growth: Evidence from insurance, *Strategic Management Journal*, 29: 229–249.
23. T. Yu & A. A. Cannella, 2007, Rivalry between multinational enterprises: An event history approach, *Academy of Management Journal*, 50: 665–686.
24. A. M. Kleinbaum & M. L. Tushman, 2007, Building bridges: The social structure of interdependent innovation, *Strategic Entrepreneurship Journal*, 1: 103–122; D. J. Miller, M. J. Fern, & L. B. Cardinal, 2007, The use of knowledge for technological innovation within diversified firms, *Academy of Management Journal*, 50: 308–326.
25. S. R. Miller, D. E. Thomas, L. Eden, & M. A. Hitt, 2008, Knee deep in the big muddy: The survival of emerging market firms in developed markets, *Management International Review*, in press.
26. V. Jayaraman & Y. Luo, 2007, Creating competitive advantages through new value creation: A reverse logistics perspective, *Academy of Management Perspectives*, 21(2): 56–73.
27. R. L. Priem, 2007, A consumer perspective on value creation, *Academy of Management Review*, 32: 219–235.
28. B. B. Allred & W. C. Park, 2007, Patent rights and innovative activity: Evidence from national and firm-level data, *Journal of International Business Studies*, 38: 879 900.
29. D. Li, L. Eden, M. A. Hitt, & R. D. Ireland, 2008, Friends, acquaintances, or strangers? Partner selection in R&D alliances, *Academy of Management Journal*, 51, in press.
30. G. Leask & D. Parker, 2007, Strategic groups, competitive groups and performance within the U.K. pharmaceutical industry: Improving our understanding of the competitive process, *Strategic Management Journal*, 28: 723–745.
31. K. Kling & I. Goteman, 2003, IKEA CEO Andres Dahlvig on international growth and IKEA's unique corporate culture and brand identity, *Academy of Management Executive*, 17(1): 31–37.
32. 2008, IKEA, *Wikipedia*, http://en.wikipedia.org, March 10.
33. 2008, Thomas Pink, LVMH Moet Hennessy Louis Vuitton, www.lvmh.com, March 10.
34. 2008, Charles Tyrwhitt Shirts, www.ctshirts.co.uk, March 10.
35. F. T. Rothaermel, M. A. Hitt, & L. A. Jobe, 2006, Balancing vertical integration and strategic outsourcing: Effects on product portfolio, product success, and firm performance, *Strategic Management Journal*, 27: 1033–1056.
36. C. Z. Lui, 2007, Lenova: An example of globalization of Chinese enterprises, *Journal of International Business Studies*, 38: 573–577.
37. Porter, *Competitive Advantage*, 16.
38. B. Keats & H. O'Neill, 2001, Organizational structure: Looking through a strategy lens, in M. A. Hitt, R. E. Freeman, & J. S. Harrison (Eds.), *Handbook of Strategic Management*, Oxford, UK: Blackwell, 520–542.
39. R. E. Hoskisson, M. A. Hitt, R. D. Ireland, & J. S. Harrison, 2008, *Competing for Advantage*, Mason, Ohio: Thomson South-Western.
40. J. L. Morrow, D. G. Sirmon, M. A. Hitt, & T. R. Holcomb, 2007, Creating value in the face of declining performance: Firm strategies and organizational recovery, *Strategic Management Journal*, 28: 271–283.
41. J. Jargon, M. Karnitschnig, & J. S. Lublin, 2008, How Hershey went sour, *Wall Street Journal*, online.wsj.com, February 23; J. Fishbein, 2008, Chocolatiers look to Asia for growth, *BusinessWeek*, www.businessweek.com, January 17.
42. Morrow et al., 2007, Creating value in the face of declining performance.

CHAPTER 6
Multiple Product Strategies

Knowledge Objectives

Reading and studying this chapter should enable you to:

1. Define a multiproduct strategy.

2. Understand the differences between the levels of diversification.

3. Discuss the related diversification multiproduct strategy.

4. Explain the unrelated diversification multiproduct strategy.

5. Understand two motives that top-level managers have to diversify the firms they lead.

6. Describe the organizational structures used to implement the different multiproduct strategies.

© BrandX Pictures

Adding Electronic Data Systems to the Mix: Does This Make Sense for Hewlett-Packard?

"You could have bought a smaller, faster-growing company . . ." (Toni Sacconaghi, Sanford C. Bernstein analyst)

The comment from a Sanford Bernstein analyst concerned Hewlett-Packard's (HP) decision to acquire Electronic Data Systems (EDS) for $13.9 billion. (Announced in May 2008, this deal was expected to be finalized by the end of 2008.) At $25 per share, HP paid roughly a 33 percent premium for EDS at the time the deal was announced. Why was HP willing to pay 33 percent more for EDS than the firm was worth? To answer that question, we need to know more about HP and its multiproduct strategy.

HP is a global technology company employing more than 172,000 employees and operating in more than 170 countries. The fact that 67 percent of sales revenue in 2007 was generated outside the United States (where HP is headquartered) demonstrates the breadth of HP's customer base. According to company information, HP "provides computers and printers and a wide range of related products, technologies, solutions and services to individual and enterprise customers worldwide."

The array of products and services HP offers indicates that the firm uses a multiproduct strategy. Because less than 70 percent of the firm's sales revenue comes from any one of its businesses and because some resources and activities that are needed to produce and sell prod-

© Susan Van Etten

ucts and services in different markets are shared across the businesses, we conclude that HP uses the related constrained multiproduct strategy (a type of strategy discussed in this chapter).

When EDS was acquired, HP had three divisions that were sharing some resources and activities: (1) Imaging and Printing Systems (27 percent of 2007 sales revenue), (2) Personal Systems (personal computers and handheld devices—34 percent of 2007 revenue), and (3) Technology Solutions (36 percent of 2007 revenue). (HP Financial Services, which is a support function, generated the remaining 3 percent of 2007 revenue.) The total sales revenue generated by HP's Personal Systems increased significantly as a result of the firm's $19 billion acquisition of Compaq Computer Corporation in 2002.

HP Services is one of three product segments of the Technology Solutions' division. Accounting for 16 percent of the division's total revenue, HP Services has been identified by CEO Mark Hurd as an area in which growth is highly desirable. Just as Compaq was acquired to facilitate expansion of HP's Personal Systems unit, EDS was acquired to support the firm's intention of increasing its share of the lucrative but fiercely competitive technology services business—a business in which IBM is dominant. With revenue of $38 billion, the HP/EDS combination still lagged behind the $54 billion in revenue IBM generated in 2007. As an area of business activities, technology services includes handling information technology operations for companies and consulting with firms to facilitate their efforts to best configure and network the complex array of servers, storage, and network gear they purchase to support producing the goods or services they provide to their customers. Founded in 1962, EDS launched the business model through which other firms outsourced their technology services operations to a provider specializing in those activities.

Having learned a bit about HP, let's return to the comment from the Sanford Bernstein analyst. Why did this person criticize HP's acquisition of EDS? Digging deeper into the matter, we discover that seeking to expand HP's presence in the technology services area is not the issue in that handling outsourced information technology activities for other companies is lucrative. Some believe though that EDS is not the best company for HP to buy to reach its expansion objective. The reason is that "the top-tier (technology) services companies need large, low-cost, global work-forces, and their operations need to be tightly integrated so employees with diverse skills collaborate smoothly." It seems that IBM and India's Tata Consultancy Services are two technology services providers that have reached those objectives while EDS has not. In fact, at the time of the acquisition, EDS "had only a smattering of employees in low-cost locations" while efforts to integrate employees were less successful compared to those undertaken at IBM and Tata. Instead of EDS, some observers believed that a smaller, yet faster-growing firm such as India's Satyam Computer Services might have been a better match for HP than was EDS. However, HP officials believed that the then-current array of loyal EDS customers was a sufficient base on which to build and that those customers justified paying a 33 percent purchase premium. As our discussion suggests, the degree of success HP will attain as a result of acquiring a firm to boost its capabilities in one product segment of one of its business units is an unanswered question.

Sources: S. Hamm, 2008, Why HP's deal is a head-scratcher, *BusinessWeek*, May 26, 30; M. Liedtke, 2008, HP has eye on IBM as it discusses EDS acquisition, *Houston Chronicle Online*, www.chron.com, May 13; L. Steffy, 2008, 8 years later, HP does it Fiorina's way, *Houston Chronicle Online*, www.chron.com, May 13; 2008, Hewlett-Packard Company, *Yahoo! Finance*, www.biz.yahoo.com, May 25.

In Chapter 1's Mini-Case, we examined some of the actions CEO Mark Hurd is taking as a strategic leader at Hewlett-Packard (HP). In this chapter's Focusing on Strategy, we explain HP's use of a multiproduct strategy. Effective use of a multiproduct strategy is certainly part of Hurd's vision for HP.

A **multiproduct strategy** is an action plan the firm uses to compete in different product markets. Using a multiproduct strategy causes a firm to become more diversified. In this chapter, our focus is on how firms diversify by competing in different product markets; in Chapter 8, our focus is on how firms diversify by competing in different geographic locations.

The primary reason firms use multiproduct strategies is to improve their performance.[1] Multiproduct strategies result in performance improvements when their use allows firms to create operational relatedness, corporate relatedness, or financial economies. We define and discuss these terms later in the chapter. HP's acquisition of EDS demonstrates an attempt to improve the firm's performance in a product segment (HP Services) of one of its divisions (Technology Solutions) by creating operational relatedness. In Table 6.1, we present other reasons firms use multiproduct strategies to diversify into additional product markets.

Firms such as HP deal with two issues when choosing a multiproduct strategy: What products or services will the firm produce and sell? How will the firm manage the different units it creates to produce and sell its products and services?[2] As indicated in Focusing on Strategy, the products and services HP offers are organized into three divisions: Imaging and Printing Systems (inkjet, LaserJet, and commercial printing; printing supplies; and digital photography), Personal Systems (business and consumer personal computers, workstations, and mobile computing devices), and Technology Solutions (storage and servers, software,

multiproduct strategy

an action plan the firm uses to compete in different product markets

Table 6.1 Reasons Firms Use Multiproduct Strategies to Diversify
• Achieve profitable growth
• Reduce the risk of being involved with a single product line
• Learn how to apply core competencies in other value-creating ways
• Gain exposure to different technologies
• Develop economies of scope
• Extend the firm's brand into additional product areas

and managed services). Because these divisions share some resources and activities to produce and sell their respective products and services, HP is using a related constrained multiproduct strategy. Later in the chapter, we'll discuss this strategy as well as the organizational structure firms such as HP use to support their implementation.

To explain multiproduct strategies, we first describe how diversified a firm becomes (from low to high) when it selects a multiproduct strategy. We then examine two levels of product diversification (related and unrelated) in some detail. Firms frequently use these multiproduct strategies. Following these discussions, we describe two motives that top-level managers have to diversify the firm in ways that may or may not create value for stakeholders. Closing this chapter are discussions of the different organizational structures firms use to implement the different multiproduct strategies.

Levels of Diversification

We show five levels of diversification (from low to high) in Figure 6.1. Firms using the single business multiproduct strategy are least diversified, while companies using the unrelated diversification multiproduct strategy are most diversified. A firm with a low level of diversification has a smaller total number of different products and generates a larger percentage of its sales from its dominant business. A firm with a high level of diversification has a larger number of different products and generates a smaller percentage of its sales revenue from its dominant business.

Low Levels of Diversification

As shown in Figure 6.1, the sources of a firm's sales revenue are used to determine its level of product diversification. This technique of determining a firm's degree of product diversification is based on a classic work completed by Richard Rumelt.[3]

Figure 6.1 Levels of Diversification

Low Levels of Diversification

Single business:	More than 95 percent of revenue comes from a single business.	A
Dominant business:	Between 70 and 95 percent of revenue comes from a single business.	A B

Moderate to High Levels of Diversification

Related constrained:	Less than 70 percent of revenue comes from the dominant business, and all businesses share product, technological, and distribution linkages.	A B C
Related linked (mixed related and unrelated):	Less than 70 percent of revenue comes from the dominant business, and only limited links exist between businesses.	A B C

Very High Levels of Diversification

Unrelated:	Less than 70 percent of revenue comes from the dominant business, and no common links exist between businesses.	A B C

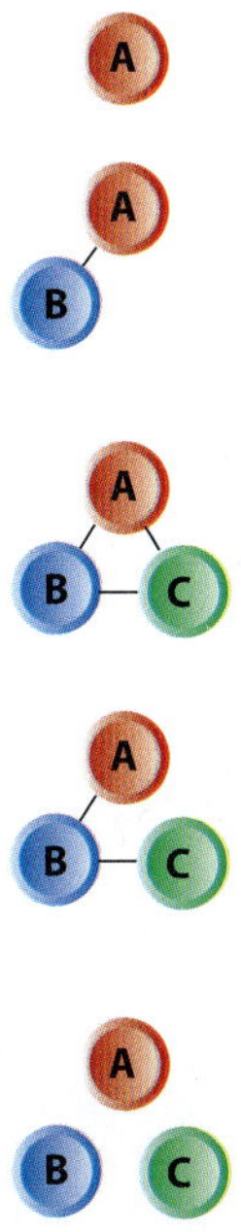

Source: Adapted from R. P. Rumelt, 1974, *Strategy, Structure, and Economic Performance*, Boston: Harvard Business School.

Single Business Multiproduct Strategy A firm pursuing low levels of diversification uses the single or a dominant business multiproduct strategy. With the single business strategy, the firm generates at least 95 percent of its sales revenue from a single business. A *single business* is one in which the firm makes and sells a single product or service or a variety of that product or service.

JetBlue and Whole Foods are examples of companies using the single business multiproduct strategy. JetBlue concentrates on air travel for individuals, but the firm also offers air cargo services for corporations. Thus, this firm sells two types of air services, with the service for individual travelers accounting for more than 95 percent of its sales revenue. Similarly, Whole Foods Market is involved with several aspects of what it sees as the "food chain." In addition to being the world's leading retailer of natural and organic foods, the company also owns and operates three seafood processing and distribution facilities. Whole Foods does this to provide customers with "the highest quality seafood from the freshest catches available from dock to door."[4] Because the seafood facilities support the firm's retail food outlets, we conclude that the degree of Whole Foods' product diversification is minor, meaning the firm is using the single business multiproduct strategy.

Kohl's Corporation, initially launched in Wisconsin in 1946 as a traditional grocery store, also uses the single business strategy. With a mission of being "the leading value-oriented, family-focused, specialty department store," Kohl's operates more than 1,000 stores in the United States and is the nation's twenty-third largest retailer. We discuss Kohl's continuing success in Understanding Strategy: Learning from Success. Given its success using the single business multiproduct strategy, can you imagine this firm choosing to become more diversified to the point of using the dominant business strategy? If so, what additional product markets do you think Kohl's might choose to enter and why?

Dominant Business Multiproduct Strategy A firm using the dominant business multiproduct strategy generates between 70 and 95 percent of its sales revenue from a single product group. Historically, United Parcel Service (UPS) used this strategy while competing in three business areas: U.S. Package Delivery, International Package, and Supply Chain Solutions. In 2005, the firm generated 74 percent, 17 percent, and 9 percent of its revenue, respectively, from those three product markets. Thus, the firm was using the dominant business strategy at the close of 2005.

The sources of the firm's sales revenue from 2007, however, show a change in UPS's multiproduct strategy in that U.S. Package Delivery accounted for 62 percent of revenue, International Package accounted for 21 percent of revenue, and Supply Chain Solutions accounted for 17 percent of revenue.[5] Those numbers mean that UPS changed to a related multiproduct strategy. Contributing to this change in multiproduct strategies were the number of shipping-related opportunities in international markets relative to those in the firm's domestic U.S. market and its stronger focus on using technology to provide other companies with logistics and distribution services. Because of those opportunities, UPS was serving a larger number of international markets and providing additional logistics services to an increasingly diverse customer base. In essence then, UPS was becoming more diversified geographically by serving additional international markets and more diversified in terms of product offerings by providing additional types of logistics services.

UPS's experience with multiproduct strategies highlights two points. First, achieving additional successes in different product markets may cause a firm to become more diversified. Second, changing the multiproduct strategy a firm is using signals a need to change the organizational structure in place to support implementing that strategy.

Kohl's Corporation: Where Concentrating on a Single Business Area Is the Foundation to Success

"Our 125,000 associates bring talent, inspiration and leadership to Kohl's to ensure we consistently deliver great brands, value, convenience and customer service in each of our locations." (Larry Montgomery, CEO of Kohl's Corporation)

© Vicki Beaver

Telling them that they should "Expect Great Things," Kohl's wants to be the preferred shopping destination for busy women. Traditionally, these busy women are married and between 25 and 54 years of age. As suggested by the CEO's statement, great brands, value, convenience, and strong customer service are the key benefits customers can expect from their shopping experience at one of Kohl's 1,000-plus locations.

Recall from Chapter 4 that the integrated cost leadership/differentiation strategy is one of the business-level strategies firms use to compete in their chosen industry or market. Kohl's uses this strategy as it seeks to differentiate itself from competitors by offering mid-priced name-brand and private-label apparel, shoes, and accessories. In more specific language, Kohl's sees itself as a "family-focused, value-oriented specialty department store offering (products) in an exciting shopping environment."

Selling an array of products that includes clothing, shoes, and accessories finds Kohl's competing in a single business as it implements the integrated strategy in that business. But Kohl's decision to organize its products into six major lines of business (men's clothing, women's clothing, children's clothing, footwear, home, and accessories) demonstrates the different types of products (all of which are highly related to each other) the firm offers through a specialty department store format. To precisely serve customers' needs, Kohl's uses price and quality to batch its products into three categories—good, better, and best. Three distinct customer styles are served within each of the three categories: "the 'classic' customer who wants a coordinated look without bending the rules; the 'updated' customer who likes classic styles with a twist; and the more fashion-forward 'contemporary' customer."

One of the keys to Kohl's success while using the single business diversification multiproduct strategy is its ability to offer recognizable brands at affordable prices. KitchenAid, Dockers, and Chaps by Ralph Lauren are examples. Kohl's sometimes forms partnerships with suppliers such as Ralph Lauren Company to offer exclusive versions of their products to Kohl's customers at affordable prices. For example, Kohl's is to be the exclusive U.S. retailer for Dana Buchman women's apparel, intimates, accessories, and footwear when the collection is introduced in the spring of 2009. Kohl's also has a multiyear contract with Vera Wang to create an exclusive premium fashion and lifestyle brand for the firm. Called Simply Vera Vera Wang, the collection that is exclusive to Kohl's includes sportswear, intimate apparel, and handbags, among other items.

Sources: 2008, Kohl's Corp, *Standard & Poor's Stock Report*, www.standardandpoors.com, May 24; 2008, Financial news, Kohl's Corporation, www.kohlscorporation.com, April 30; 2008, Kohl's, http://en.wikipedia.org, May 30; R. Fuhrmann, 2007, Fool on the street: The secret of Kohl's success, *The Motley Fool.com*, www.motleyfool.com, September 25.

Moderate to High Levels of Diversification—Related Diversification Multiproduct Strategies

Related Diversification Multiproduct Strategy A firm generating less than 70 percent of sales revenue from its dominant business is using either the related or the unrelated diversification multiproduct strategy (see Figure 6.1). Let's look at the differences between these strategies.

Firms using a related diversification multiproduct strategy try to create economies of scope. **Economies of scope** are cost savings the firm accrues when it successfully shares some of its resources and activities between its businesses or transfers corporate-level core competencies into its businesses.

economies of scope

cost savings the firm accrues when it successfully shares some of its resources and activities between its businesses or transfers corporate-level core competencies into its businesses

The differences between the two forms of the related diversification multiproduct strategy are subtle but important. With the *related constrained* multiproduct strategy, the firms' businesses are related to each other.[6] The relatedness between the groups occurs as they share some resources and activities to produce and sell products.[7] As shown in Figure 6.1, the hypothetical firm using the related constrained strategy has three businesses (A, B, and C). The lines connecting all three businesses show hypothetically that they are somewhat constrained in the activities used to produce their goods or services because they share some resources (e.g., raw materials as inputs to the manufacturing processes used to make the business's final product) and activities (e.g., capabilities that are used to develop advertising campaigns). Consumer product giant Procter & Gamble (P&G) uses the related constrained strategy as does UPS. (We describe an example of how P&G's businesses are related to one another in the upcoming paragraphs.)

In the *related linked* diversification strategy, only limited links or relationships exist between the firm's businesses. As shown in Figure 6.1, the hypothetical firm using the related linked strategy has three businesses (A, B, and C). The line connecting business A and business B reflects a hypothetical relationship, as does the line between business B and business C. Notice, however, that business A and business C are not related.

Resources and activities may be shared between some of the businesses that are a part of a firm using the related linked strategy. However, the focus in these firms is on transferring corporate-level core competencies into different businesses. **Corporate-level core competencies** are complex sets of resources and capabilities that link different businesses, primarily through managerial and technological knowledge, experience, and expertise. Typically, personnel in the diversified firm's corporate headquarters take the actions required to transfer core competencies into the firm's different businesses. An ability to price the firm's products and services effectively is an example of a corporate-level core competency that can create economies of scope when transferred from one of the firm's businesses to its other businesses.[8]

Unrelated Diversification Multiproduct Strategy

A firm that does *not* try to transfer resources and activities between its businesses or core competencies into its businesses is using an unrelated diversification multiproduct strategy. Commonly, firms using this strategy are called *conglomerates*. The unrelated diversification multiproduct strategy is frequently used in both developed markets (e.g., the United Kingdom and the United States) and emerging markets. In fact, firms using this strategy dominate the private sector in Latin American countries and in China, Korea, and India.[9] Conglomerates account for the largest percentage of private firms in India.[10] Similarly, the largest business firms in Brazil, Mexico, Argentina, and Colombia are family-owned, highly diversified enterprises.[11]

We now turn our attention to discussing the related and unrelated diversification multiproduct strategies in detail and the way firms use them to generate economies of scope by achieving either operational relatedness or corporate relatedness. **Operational relatedness** is achieved when the firm's businesses successfully share resources and activities to produce and sell their products. **Corporate relatedness** is achieved when corporate-level core competencies are successfully transferred into some of the firm's businesses. Most commonly, these transfers involve core competencies that are based on intangible assets such as marketing knowledge, design skills, and brand name.

Looking at Figure 6.2, notice that firms using the related constrained multiproduct strategy create economies of scope *primarily* by achieving operational relatedness (see cell 1 in Figure 6.2), while firms using the related linked multiproduct strategy create economies of scope *primarily* by achieving corporate relatedness (see cell 2 in Figure 6.2). Even though the firm using the related constrained strategy emphasizes the sharing of resources and activities between its businesses as a means of creating economies of scope, it also tries to create

corporate-level core competencies

complex sets of resources and capabilities that link different businesses, primarily through managerial and technological knowledge, experience, and expertise

operational relatedness

achieved when the firm's businesses successfully share resources and activities to produce and sell their products

corporate relatedness

achieved when corporate-level core competencies are successfully transferred into some of the firm's businesses

Figure 6.2 Value-Creating Strategies of Diversification:
Operational and Corporate Relatedness

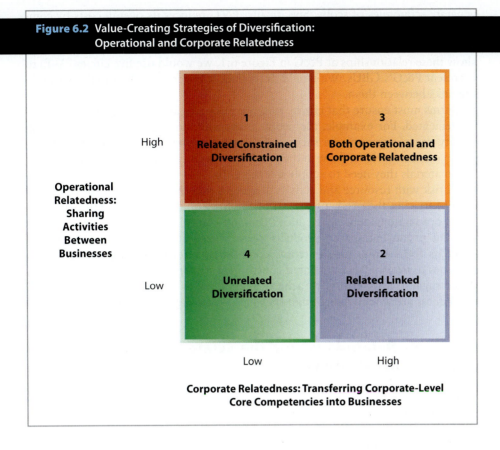

economies of scope by transferring corporate-level core competencies between its businesses when it can do so. Similarly, although the firm using the related linked strategy emphasizes transferring corporate-level core competencies into its businesses as a means of creating economies of scope, it also tries to create economies of scope through the sharing of resources and activities between its businesses when it can do so.

Operational Relatedness and the Related Constrained Multiproduct Strategy

Economies of scope are created through operational relatedness when the firm successfully shares primarily tangible resources (such as plant and equipment) and/or when a primary activity (such as inventory delivery systems) or a support activity (such as purchasing procedures) is successfully used in more than one of its businesses. We'll use Procter & Gamble (P&G) to describe how this operational relatedness is accomplished.

Currently, P&G has five global business units (GBUs)—Baby Care/Family Care, Beauty Care/Feminine Care, Fabric & Home Care, Snacks & Beverage, and Health Care—that share some resources and activities. Consider, for example, that in some form or fashion, paper is an important raw material input for products produced by several of the GBUs. Accordingly, P&G operates a paper production facility that provides paper-based raw materials (in some form) to the GBUs; the paper-based raw material inputs (a tangible resource) that are needed by the GBUs are similar enough that one facility can produce many if not most of those items. Because many of the GBUs' products are sold in some of the same outlets (grocery stores, for example), these products also share distribution channels (a primary activity) and networks of sales representatives.[12] The sharing of these resources (raw materials) and activities (distribution) enables P&G to generate economies of scope. Specifically, P&G reduces its overall costs by combining assets to produce similar raw materials in a single facility and then using similar channels to distribute the products produced with those materials. To show these relationships at P&G in Figure 6.1, we would use five circles (A–E) to represent P&G's GBUs. We would draw lines between the GBUs to demonstrate the links between them.

Firms must ensure that efforts to share resources and activities are effectively implemented. For example, the people responsible for P&G's paper production facility must communicate successfully with personnel in the GBUs. Through these communications, those in the production facility learn about the quantity of raw materials they need to supply to each GBU.

A risk with resource and activity sharing is that the demand for the output of a unit servicing the needs of several of the firm's businesses may fall below the unit's production capacity. Reduced demand could lead to a situation in which the unit producing shared products doesn't generate enough sales revenue to cover its fixed costs. This outcome complicates efforts to share resources and activities in firms using the related constrained strategy.[13] However, research evidence suggests that efforts to achieve economies of scope through operational relatedness are worthwhile in that they help create value for stakeholders.[14]

Corporate Relatedness and the Related Linked Multiproduct Strategy

Economies of scope are generated through corporate relatedness when the firm successfully transfers corporate-level core competencies into its different businesses. Let's see how GE uses corporate relatedness.

GE has six strategic business units, each with a number of divisions.[15] A **strategic business unit (SBU)** is a semi-autonomous unit of a diversified firm with a collection of related businesses. One of GE's SBUs, GE Healthcare, has five divisions while GE Industrial has two divisions, each of which has separately identifiable product groups. Innovation is a corporate-level core competency that is transferred to each of GE's SBUs. In fact, GE allocated $6 billion to its research and development budget in 2007. The 2,350 patents the firm filed in various parts of the world in 2007 are an indication of the success the company achieves by transferring its innovation corporate-level core competency across its SBUs.

The knowledge individuals acquire by participating in managerial and leadership training programs is one way GE transfers corporate-level core competencies. In fact, one of the objectives of GE's executive education programs is for participating managers to develop knowledge that is imported into the firm's businesses. The importance of knowledge at GE is shown by the fact that "worldwide, (the firm) invests about $1 billion annually on training and education programs to develop some of the best leaders and some of the most widely practiced business techniques."[16]

Here's an example of how knowledge is transferred at GE. GE's NBC Universal SBU was recently formed through the merger of NBC and Vivendi Universal Entertainment. Managers from Universal are participating in executive education programs to work on the "integration" of its businesses with other parts of the newly created business unit, while "GE is shipping company-trained CFOs west to scope out the Hollywood units."[17]

strategic business unit (SBU)

a semi-autonomous unit of a diversified firm with a collection of related businesses

© Susan Van Etten

Simultaneously Seeking Operational Relatedness and Corporate Relatedness

As shown in cell 3 in Figure 6.2, firms can develop economies of scope by simultaneously seeking high levels of operational relatedness and corporate relatedness.[18] Essentially, then, the firm's multiproduct strategy is a hybrid with characteristics of both the related constrained and related linked multiproduct strategies.

Experience shows that it is difficult for firms to achieve operational and corporate relatedness simultaneously.[19] Although sharing is difficult with tangible resources when primary and support activities are combined to achieve operational relatedness, transferring intangible resources that are the foundation for corporate-level core competencies is more challenging. Transferring intangible resources (such as knowledge about how to interpret market trends) between businesses to generate economies of scope by achieving corporate relatedness is more difficult because the potential outcome is less visible. (That is, it is difficult to know that an intangible resource is being transferred unless that resource is an individual manager.) So you can imagine how difficult it is for a firm to focus simultaneously on *sharing* tangible resources and activities while simultaneously concentrating on *transferring* intangible core competencies.

Although it is challenging to attain operational relatedness and corporate relatedness simultaneously, evidence suggests that firms able to do so have developed a competitive advantage that is difficult for competitors to imitate.[20] Walt Disney Studios, one of Walt Disney Company's business units, can share resources and activities as it creates, produces, and promotes movies in its different studios (such as Touchstone Pictures and Miramax Films). If Disney were to identify product promotion as one of its skills, it could share the activity with another part of Walt Disney Studies (e.g., Disney Theatrical Productions) to create operational relatedness and transfer the knowledge about how the skill was developed into other business units (e.g., Parks and Resorts)[21] to create corporate relatedness.

Unrelated Diversification Multiproduct Strategy

As indicated by cell 4 in Figure 6.2, firms using the unrelated diversification multiproduct strategy do not emphasize operational relatedness or corporate relatedness as a means of creating economies of scope. Instead, firms using the unrelated strategy emphasize financial economies to create economies of scope.

Financial economies are cost savings or higher returns generated when the firm effectively allocates its financial resources based on investments inside or outside the firm.[22] With respect to internal investments, the firm creates financial economies when it allocates its resources efficiently through the efforts of corporate headquarters personnel who represent a capital market for the entire organization. In terms of investments outside the firm, the company using the unrelated diversification strategy creates financial economies when it is able to buy another firm, restructure that firm's assets in value-creating ways, and then (when and if appropriate) sell that company at a price exceeding its investment (price paid plus amount invested to increase the quality of the purchased company's assets). We consider each type of financial economy in greater detail in the next two sections.

Efficient Internal Capital Market Allocation

As you'll recall from your study of economics and finance in particular, capital markets are assumed to be efficient in allocating capital among competing investment opportunities. Efficiency results as investors take an equity position in firms by purchasing shares of stock in companies they believe have high future cash

financial economies

cost savings or higher returns generated when the firm effectively allocates its financial resources based on investments inside or outside the firm

flow value. Efficient markets also allocate capital in the form of debt as share-holders and debt holders seek to improve the value of their investments by taking stakes in firms they believe have high growth and profitability prospects.

In companies using the unrelated strategy, corporate headquarters personnel allocate the firm's capital across its portfolio of divisions, each of which sells a variety of products. At United Technologies Corporation (UTC), for example, corporate headquarters personnel allocate capital across the firm's six divisions—Carrier, Otis, Pratt & Whitney, UTC Fire & Security, Hamilton Sundstrand, and Sikorsky. (Carrier accounts for the largest amount of UTC's sales revenue—28 percent in 2007.)[23]

At UTC and other firms using the unrelated diversification strategy, capital is allocated on the basis of what headquarters personnel believe will generate the greatest amount of financial economies. At Japan Tobacco, for example, additional capital is being allocated to the firm's cigarette manufacturing division so it can acquire other firms. The purpose of the acquisitions is for Japan Tobacco's cigarette manufacturing division to increase the breadth and depth of its cigarette product lines. Financial capital is allocated to the firm's cigarette division because headquarters personnel believe that its growth and profitability prospects are greater than those of the firm's other divisions (foods, pharmaceuticals, agribusiness, engineering, and real estate).[24] At Japan Tobacco and UTC, as well as in other firms using the unrelated strategy, financial capital is allocated only after extensive in-depth analyses of each division's prospects for revenue and profitability growth.

Internal capital market allocations in firms using the unrelated diversification strategy may be the basis for superior returns to shareholders compared to returns shareholders would receive as a result of allocations by the external capital market.[25] Access to information is the main reason for this possibility. Indeed, while managing the firm's portfolio of divisions, headquarters personnel may gain access to detailed information that isn't available to the external capital market about the ability of one or more of the firm's divisions to create value by growing its revenue and profitability streams. For example, at Japan Tobacco, headquarters personnel may know more about the growth prospects in the firm's tobacco division than is known by investors.

Another potential benefit of internal capital market allocations is that those evaluating the performance of all of a firm's divisions can internally discipline poorly performing units by allocating fewer or different types of resources to them.[26] Disciplined divisional managers are likely to respond favorably by working hard to improve their units' performance as the first step to receiving a larger percentage of the entire firm's financial capital.

The external capital market relies on information produced by the firm to estimate the organization's ability to generate attractive future revenue and earnings streams. Annual reports, press conferences, and filings mandated by various regulatory bodies are the most common sources of information available to the external capital market. In these communication media, firms may overemphasize positive news while ignoring or deemphasizing negative news about one or more divisions. Firms may not want to divulge additional information when using these media because it might help competitors better understand and imitate the competitive advantages of product divisions within divisions. Therefore, in-depth knowledge about the positive and negative performance prospects for all of the firm's divisions creates a potential informational advantage for the firm relative to the external capital market.

Restructuring

A firm using the unrelated diversification multiproduct strategy can also produce financial economies by buying some or all of another company's assets. This process works two ways.[27] (These processes are called restructuring to denote that changes are made regarding the assets in question.) In one instance, a firm buys another's assets because it believes those assets would create more value if they were operated under its ownership. Prestige Brands Holdings, Inc., uses this restructuring approach to create financial economies. Recognized as "a lifesaver in the business of resuscitating offloaded consumer product brands,"[28] Prestige buys branded products from other companies such as Procter & Gamble, Colgate-Palmolive, and Unilever. These products (such as Spic and Span, Right Guard deodorant, and Clear Eyes) are cast off because their former owner has lost faith in them or because they no longer fit with its portfolio of products. Prestige revitalizes them by devoting full attention to each product to enhance its market position, expand its distribution, and successfully launch product extensions.

The second way restructuring can create financial economies is when a firm buys another company's assets with the intention of selling them as soon as it finds ways to make the assets more productive. Private equity firms such as the Carlyle Group, the world's largest firm of this type, use this multiproduct strategy. Some criticize private equity firms, seeing them as entities that focus on cutting costs without showing an appropriate amount of concern for those affected by the cost reductions.[29]

In general, it is easier to create financial economies by restructuring the assets of firms competing in relatively low-technology businesses because of the uncertain future demand for high-technology products. Moreover, firms seeking to create financial economies by buying and selling restructured assets must be able to restructure those assets at a cost below their expected future market value when they are sold to another company.

© Vicki Beaver

Managerial Motives to Diversify

In addition to the reasons for diversification that are shown in Table 6.1, top-level managers may have two additional motives to use a multiproduct diversification strategy. These motives may or may not be in the best interests of the firm's stakeholders.

Reducing the risk of losing their job is the first motive for top-level executives.[30] If a firm has multiple businesses and one business fails, the firm is unlikely to experience total failure if the other businesses are doing well. Therefore, additional diversification reduces the chance that top-level executives of a diversified firm will lose their jobs.

However, the managerial/leadership challenge increases greatly when a firm diversifies beyond the level of the single-business multiproduct strategy. The risk here is that managers who believe that keeping their top-level positions depends on greater levels of product diversification may overdiversify the firm. Similar to business-level strategies, the multiproduct strategy used by the firm should be a function of opportunities in the firm's external environment. That strategy also should take into account the degree to which the firm has resources and activities that businesses can share or corporate-level core competencies that, when transferred from one business to another one in the firm's portfolio, can create value in product markets beyond its core product market. A firm's board of directors must ensure that the level of diversification top-level managers pursue is based on a match between opportunities in the external environment and the company's resources, activities, and corporate-level core competencies.

The relationship between firm size and executive compensation is the second managerial diversification motive. Research shows that as a firm's size increases, so does the compensation for top-level managers.[31] Of course, increasing a firm's level of diversification increases the firm's overall size. The relationship between firm size and managerial compensation is perhaps not surprising in that larger, more diversified organizations are more difficult to manage than smaller, less diversified firms.[32] Common sense suggests that more complex and difficult work should be more highly compensated. Nonetheless, a board of directors should compensate managers in ways that will cause them to engage in value-creating diversification rather than compensate them simply on the basis of the firm's size.

In Chapter 5, we noted that organizational structure plays a major role in implementing a business-level strategy once it is chosen. Because of their importance, we next discuss the appropriate organizational structures for implementing the different multiproduct strategies.

Implementing Multiproduct Strategies

The **multidivisional (M-form) structure** is an organizational structure in which the firm is organized to generate economies of scope or financial economies. Thus, the M-form is the structure of choice for firms with moderate to high levels of product diversification. Firms using the single business and dominant business multiproduct strategies still rely on the different forms of the functional structure used to implement the business-level strategies we examined in Chapter 5. Each of the three versions of the M-form (see Figure 6.3) is used to support a different multiproduct strategy.

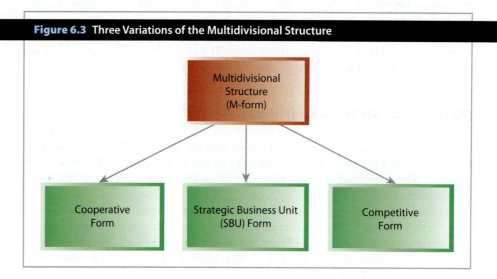

Figure 6.3 Three Variations of the Multidivisional Structure

The Cooperative M-Form and the Related Constrained Multiproduct Strategy

The **cooperative M-form** is an organizational structure in which horizontal integration is used so that divisions can share resources and activities. Firms using the related constrained multiproduct strategy (such as P&G) adopt the cooperative M-form (see Figure 6.4). The divisions in a firm's M-form structure must cooperate with one another to share resources and activities and generate economies of scope by achieving operational relatedness.[33] Earlier, we explained how P&G's global business units cooperate to share the outputs of the firm's paper production facility and distribution channels.

Success with the cooperative M-form is significantly affected by how well divisions process information about the resources and activities they intend to share and how they intend to share them. *Horizontal linkages* are the mechanisms used to facilitate information sharing in these instances. One obvious

multidivisional (M-form) structure

an organizational structure in which the firm is organized to generate economies of scope or financial economies

cooperative M-form

an organizational structure in which horizontal integration is used so that divisions can share resources and activities

Figure 6.4 Cooperative Form of the Multidivisional Structure for Implementing the Related Constrained Strategy

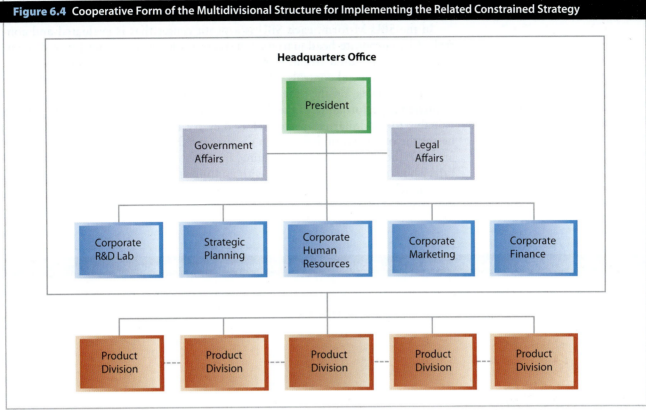

Notes:
- Structural integration devices create tight links among all divisions.
- Corporate office emphasizes centralized strategic planning, human resources, and marketing to foster cooperation between divisions.
- R&D is likely to be centralized.
- Rewards are subjective and tend to emphasize overall corporate performance in additon to divisional performance.
- Culture emphasizes cooperative sharing.

horizontal linkage is holding frequent meetings with division managers to discuss the products or services they produce and sell. In addition, managers can describe what resources are available in their division and how those resources are used to form capabilities as the foundation for completing different activities in the value chain. A key objective of these discussions is to determine whether the different divisions' resources can be combined to create a new capability that can be shared among the divisions.

Temporary teams (sometimes called task forces) are a second horizontal integrating mechanism. Teams are typically formed for a project that requires sharing the resources and activities of two or more businesses. Developing a new product and finding a way to create more value by completing one or more activities in the value chain are the objectives sought by temporary teams.

An operational reality of the cooperative form of the multidivisional structure is that individual managers are held accountable for the performance of their division. For this reason, headquarters personnel should use compensation systems that reward sharing. As a result, for example, each manager's compensation might be based on a composite of his or her unit's performance as well as that of the other units, especially those that are cooperating on joint product development and management. This type of compensation signals that each manager's success is at least partly a function of the success of cooperation.

The SBU M-Form and the Related Linked Multiproduct Strategy

The **strategic business unit (SBU) M-form** is an organizational structure in which corporate headquarters personnel try to transfer corporate-level core competencies

strategic business unit (SBU) M-form

an organizational structure in which corporate headquarters personnel try to transfer corporate-level core competencies into the firm's businesses

into the firm's businesses. Firms using the related linked multiproduct strategy (such as GE) adopt the SBU M-form (see Figure 6.5).

In the SBU M-form, each SBU is a profit center that is evaluated and controlled by corporate headquarters. Although both strategic controls and financial controls are used (recall our discussion of these two types of controls in Chapter 2), financial controls are vital to headquarters' evaluation of each SBU. Strategic controls, on the other hand, are critical when those leading each SBU evaluate the performance of the divisions in their SBU. Strategic controls are also valuable to headquarters personnel as they try to determine whether the businesses the organization has chosen to enter (as shown by its collection of SBUs) are the right ones. As you can imagine, the SBU M-form can be a complex structure. Think of GE's size (six SBUs with multiple divisions in each SBU). It doesn't take much imagination to conclude that GE's organizational structure is immensely complicated.

Figure 6.5 SBU Form of the Multidivisional Structure for Implementing the Related Linked Strategy

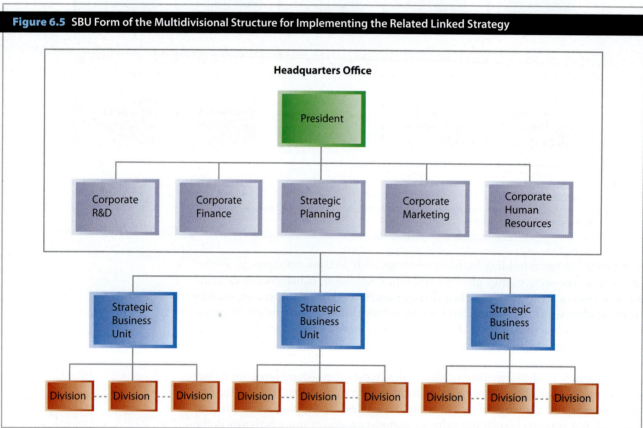

Notes: • Structural integration among divisions within SBUs, but independence across SBUs.
        • Strategic planning may be the most prominent function in headquarters for managing the strategic planning approval process of SBUs for the president.
        • Each SBU may have its own budget for staff to foster integration.
        • Corporate headquarters staff serve as consultants to SBUs and divisions, rather than having direct input to product strategy, as in the cooperative form.

The Competitive M-Form and the Unrelated Diversification Multiproduct Strategy

The **competitive M-form** is an organizational structure characterized by complete independence between the firm's divisions. Firms using the unrelated diversification multiproduct strategy adopt the competitive M-form structure (see Figure 6.6). Recall that with the unrelated diversification strategy, the firm seeks to generate financial economies rather than develop economies of scope through either operational relatedness or corporate relatedness.

competitive M-form

an organizational structure characterized by complete independence between the firm's divisions

Figure 6.6 Competitive Form of the Multidivisional Structure for Implementing the Unrelated Diversification Strategy

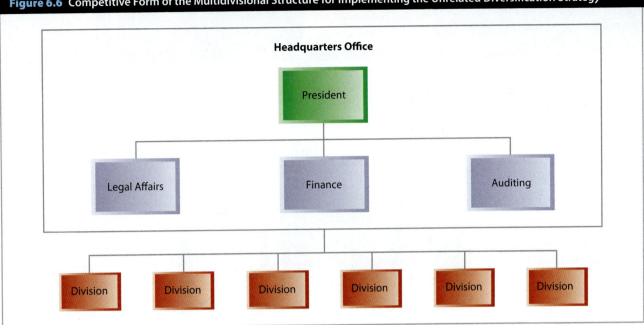

Notes:
- Corporate headquarters has a small staff.
- Finance and auditing are the most prominent functions in the headquarters office to manage cash flow and ensure the accuracy of performance data.
- The legal affairs function becomes important when the firm acquires or divests assets.
- Divisions are independent and separate for financial evaluation purposes.
- Divisions retain strategic control, but cash is managed by the corporate office.
- Divisions compete for corporate resources.

Divisions operating in a competitive M-form structure actually compete against one another for the firm's resources. Indeed, an efficient internal capital market allocates resources to the divisions with the greatest probability of generating excess returns on the firm's financial capital. Because of this focus, corporate headquarters personnel make no effort to find ways for resources and activities to be shared between divisions or for corporate headquarters personnel to transfer corporate-level core competencies into different divisions. Instead, the focus of the headquarters office is on specifying criteria that will be used to evaluate the performance of all divisions. As we discuss in this chapter's Mini-Case, return on invested capital is the primary performance criterion used by corporate headquarters personnel at Textron, a large conglomerate.[34]

With the competitive M-form, headquarters personnel rely on strategic controls to establish financial performance criteria; financial controls are then used to monitor divisional performance relative to those criteria. So the focus of headquarters is on performance appraisal, resource allocations, and long-range planning to ensure that the firm's financial capital is being used to maximize financial success.[35]

Regardless of the multiproduct strategy chosen and the multidivisional structure selected to support use of that strategy, performance declines suggest the need for change. Sears Holdings Corporation experienced such declines. Formed in 2005 and following Kmart's announcement that it intended to acquire Sears Roebuck & Company, Sears Holdings' financial performance was deteriorating in mid-2008. As explained in Understanding Strategy: Learning from Failure, decisions being made by strategic leaders suggested that the firm was going to use a different multidivisional structure to help reverse its fortunes. As you read the Understanding Strategy that describes these changes, try to determine the degree of success you think the proposed changes will bring to Sears Holdings as well as the reasons the changes were being made.

The Marriage of Kmart and Sears: What Lessons Can We Learn?

© Vicki Beaver

"Sears Holdings Corp. swung to a loss on weak sales, and many of its customers appeared to have fled to discounters such as Costco Wholesale Corp., whose results told a quite different tale." (Karen Talley and Donna Kardos, *Wall Street Journal* reporters)

Both Sears Roebuck & Company and Kmart Corporation experienced declining performance during the 1990s and into the early years of the twenty-first century. Both firms were competing as full-line department stores as customers' sensitivity to price became the primary decision criterion when purchasing products and services. Neither company possessed the capabilities needed to effectively compete against the likes of Wal-Mart, Sam's, and Costco when dealing with price-sensitive customers.

Seeing underlying value in their brands though, Edward S. Lampert's ESL Investments Inc. (a hedge fund) acquired Kmart in 2003 and Sears in 2005. Lampert then combined the two firms into Sears Holdings Corporation, a company in which ESL Investments has a 49.6 percent ownership stake. When formed, Sears Holdings was grouped into three business segments (or divisions) that operated independently: Kmart, Sears Domestic, and Sears Canada. Thus, the competitive form of the multidivisional structure (see Figure 6.6) was in place and was intended to support Lampert's strategy of maintaining respectable sales growth while limiting capital expenditures in order to "generate prodigious cash flow."

It seems then that initially, Lampert sought to create financial economies by using a form of the multidivisional structure that is designed to facilitate implementation of the unrelated diversification strategy. Evidence suggests though that the decisions made initially with Sears Holdings as a means of creating financial economies were perhaps not as effective as they might have been. More specifically, it may be that strategy and structure were not matched in this instance. (Remember that in Chapter 5, we noted that a firm's performance will decline when strategy and structure are not matched.) Let's consider this possibility further.

Combining Kmart and Sears resulted in a large firm that was essentially offering similar products and services. In fact, some observers said that the structurally independent units were all trying to sell the same or similar major appliances (refrigerators, dishwashers, and so forth), home improvement/home repair

services, auto repair services and groceries, often to the same customer groups. The issue here is that the competitive form of the multidivisional structure is used to support the unrelated strategy—one in which the firm is highly diversified in terms of products it offers and customers it serves. It is difficult to generate financial economies by asking units offering essentially the same products and services to the same or similar customers to compete against one another for capital allocations.

In mid-2008 though, structural change was taking place at Sears Holdings. Specifically, the firm was being divided into five strategic business units (with multiple divisions as part of each SBU): brands, real estate, support, online, and store operations. Commenting about this structural change, Lampert said that it was time "to empower individual businesses and teams to focus on the customer experience and performance. Stronger business units will be better able to support each other, build a stronger company, and be more attractive to partners and talent." Thus, Sears Holdings was changing to the SBU form of the multidivisional structure—a structure that is designed to support use of the related linked diversification multiproduct strategy. Given that some indirect but relatively few direct relationships across the firm's newly formed business units are likely, it seems that strategy and structure may now be matched. Because of this match, the probability that the firm will be able to improve its performance by creating corporate relatedness is increased.

What lesson can we learn from the description of Sears Holdings? The importance of matching strategy and structure is a core lesson here. Additionally, it may be that a related linked multiproduct strategy was effectively in place (remember that Kmart and Sears were selling similar products and services to the same or similar customer groups) when Sears Holdings was created. If that is true, the firm's performance decline (as reported in mid-2008) may have been, at least in part, a function of a mismatch between multiproduct strategy and the multidivisional structure in place to support its use.

Sources: P. Eavis, 2008, The pain at Sears grows, *The Wall Street Journal Online*, www.wsj.com, May 30; J. Eisinger, 2008, The marriage from hell, *Conde Nast Portfolio*, February, 86–88, 130–132; K. Talley & D. Kardos, 2008, Sears turns in loss as sales drop 5.8%, *The Wall Street Journal Online*, www.wsj.com, May 30; 2008, Report: Sears to reorganize into units, *Houston Chronicle Online*, www.chron.com, January 20; 2008, Report: Sears Holdings to break into separate units, *Dallas Morning News Online*, www.dallasnews.com, January 19.

SUMMARY

The primary purpose of this chapter is to discuss the different multiproduct strategies that firms can use to enter new product markets. We examined the following topics:

- We noted that a **multiproduct strategy** is an action plan that the firm uses to compete in different product markets. When using multiproduct strategies, firms become more diversified in terms of the number and types of products they produce and sell to customers.
- Five multiproduct strategies range from low levels of diversification (the single business and dominant business strategies) to moderate to high levels of diversification (the related constrained, related linked, and unrelated diversification strategies). As a firm becomes more diversified, the number of products it offers and the number of product markets in which it competes increase.
- A firm using the single-business multiproduct strategy makes and sells a single product or a variety of a single product line and generates at least 95 percent of its sales revenue from its dominant business or product line. As firms continue to develop the ways in which their resources and activities can be used to create additional products or to compete in different product markets, they may begin to pursue the dominant business strategy—a multiproduct strategy through which the firm generates between 70 and 95 percent of its sales revenue from a single business.
- Firms using a related diversification multiproduct strategy try to create **economies of scope**, which are cost savings that result from the successful sharing of some resources and activities between the firm's businesses or from the transfer of corporate-level core competencies into its different businesses. In each of the two types of related diversification multiproduct strategies, the firm earns less than 70 percent of sales revenue from its dominant business.
- With the related constrained strategy, most or all of the firm's businesses share some resources (usually tangible resources) and activities (that are a part of the value chain) to generate economies of scope. Firms sharing resources and activities between their businesses achieve **operational relatedness.**
- With the related linked strategy, few relationships exist between the firm's businesses. The focus with this strategy is on transferring corporate-level core competencies into the firm's different

businesses to generate economies of scope. **Corporate-level core competencies** are complex sets of resources and capabilities that link different businesses, primarily through managerial and technological knowledge, experience, and expertise. Firms generating economies of scope by transferring corporate-level core competencies achieve **corporate relatedness.**

- In the unrelated diversification multiproduct strategy, resources, activities, and corporate-level core competencies are not shared between the firm's divisions. Commonly, firms using this strategy are called conglomerates. With this strategy, the firm tries to create financial economies instead of economies of scope. **Financial economies** are cost savings or higher returns generated when the firm effectively allocates its financial resources based on investments inside or outside the firm. The firm's divisions compete against one another to gain access to a larger share of the entire organization's financial capital. Firms generate financial economies when they successfully allocate their own financial capital across their divisions or when they buy other companies, restructure those firms' assets, and then sell the acquisitions in the marketplace at a profit.
- Managers often have personal motives for increasing the diversification of their firm. For example, increasing the number of product markets in which the firm competes reduces managers' risk of losing their jobs (and balances firm performance across markets). Additionally, executive compensation is often related to firm size. Thus, growing the size of the firm through diversification may increase executives' pay. Engaging in a multiproduct strategy for these reasons may or may not create value for the firm's shareholders.
- It is important to match each multiproduct strategy with the proper organizational structure. Firms using the single business and dominant business strategies continue to use one of the functional structures we discussed in Chapter 5. However, the related and unrelated diversification strategies are effectively used only when supported by a version of the **multidivisional structure** (in which the firm is organized to generate economies of scope or financial economies). The **cooperative M-form** supports the related constrained strategy, the **SBU M-form** supports the related linked strategy, and the **competitive M-form** supports the unrelated strategy.

KEY TERMS

DISCUSSION QUESTIONS

1. What is a multiproduct strategy? Why do some firms use this strategy?
2. What are the different levels of diversification (from low to high) that firms experience when using a multiproduct strategy?
3. What is the related diversification multiproduct strategy? How can the firm create value by using this strategy?
4. What is the unrelated diversification multiproduct strategy? What are the ways that a firm can create value by using this strategy?
5. What are the two additional motives that top-level managers have to diversify their firms?
6. What organizational structure is used to implement each of the different multiproduct strategies?

STRATEGY TOOLBOX

Introduction

Competitive analysis is a critical part of the strategic management process that firms use when selecting a multiproduct strategy. A competitive analysis includes the identification, profiling, and comparison of the entire competitor set. All too often, those involved with a firm's strategic management process focus only on the *immediate* competitors, as they have been announced and are already under study. This chapter's tool takes this analysis two steps further and considers *impending* and *invisible* competitors as well. Analyzing the three types of competitors facilitates a firm's efforts to carefully examine all types of competitors (current and potential) when selecting a multiproduct strategy.

3 I's Competitive Radar Screen

Invisible	• Large players considering an unanticipated move from other (unrelated) industrial segments into your market—in secret • Low knowledge base
Impending	• Small players making a move for growth and market share capture • Major players from other (related) industrial segments announcing entry into your market • Medium knowledge base
Immediate	• Existing major players in your particular industrial segment(s) • Public admission of competitive position and market share • High knowledge base

MINI-CASE

Textron, Inc.: Achieving Success Using the Unrelated Diversification Multiproduct Strategy

"Textron's earnings release on Thursday proved that the multi-industrial player is feeling few ill effects from the slowing U.S. economy. Continuing an impressive string of quarterly results, Textron posted a 19.2 percent jump in earnings as sales flew ahead 18.7 percent."
(*The Motley Fool*)

Those comments from financial analysts describe results Textron Inc. achieved during the first quarter of 2008. Given the quality of the firm's performance while facing difficult global economic conditions, Textron's shareholders were likely pleased by the results. This firm's vision and the multiproduct strategy it uses in efforts to reach that vision are intriguing.

Recall from Chapter 1 that a *vision* presents a picture of the firm as it hopes to exist in the future, while a *strategy* is an action plan designed to move a firm toward achieving its vision. "Textron's vision is to become *the* [italics in the original document] premier multi-industry company, recognized for our network of powerful brands, world-class enterprise processes and talented people." A widely diversified conglomerate, Textron uses the unrelated diversification multiproduct strategy as its action plan for becoming the premier multi-industry company.

Choosing to use the unrelated strategy means that Textron seeks to generate financial economies rather than operational relatedness or corporate relatedness to create value for customers and wealth (in the form of strong financial returns) for shareholders. Thus, Textron allocates its financial capital to pursue investment opportunities available inside the units it currently owns or to acquire assets from other companies that it can effectively restructure. As noted earlier in the chapter, Textron uses return on invested capital "as both a compass to guide every investment decision and a measure of Textron's success."

Currently, Textron has five divisions—Bell, Cessna, Defense and Intelligence, Industrial, and Finance. During 2007, Cessna accounted for the largest percentage of the firm's sales revenue (38 percent) while Finance accounted for the smallest percentage (7 percent). In terms of organizational structure, Textron uses the competitive form of the multidivisional structure. Looking at Figure 6.6, visualize Textron's five divisions with different product segments being associated with those divisions. For example, E-Z-Go, Greenlee, Jacobsen, Kautex, and Fluid and Power Group are product segments comprising the Industrial division.

At the beginning of this chapter, we noted that companies using multiproduct strategies deal with two core issues: What products or services will the company produce and sell? How will the firm manage the units it creates to produce and sell its products and services? According to company documents, Textron's corporate-level personnel spend a great deal of their time dealing with the first of those two questions as they go about "identifying, selecting, acquiring and integrating the right mix of businesses that will drive higher performance." With respect to the second issue, we have noted that Textron uses the competitive form of the multidivisional structure to manage its five divisions. As of mid-2008, it seems that Textron was dealing successfully with these two core issues while using the unrelated multiproduct strategy.

Sources: 2008, Textron businesses, Textron, www.textron.com, May 30; 2008, Textron vision and strategy, Textron, www.textron.com, May 30; 2008, Textron flies high, *The Motley Fool*, www.fool.com, April 18; 2008, Textron Inc., *Standard and Poor's Stock Report*, www.standardandpoors.com, May 28; 2008, Textron Systems unit gets Air Force contract, *The Wall Street Journal Online*, www.wsj.com, May 22.

Questions

1. Go to Textron's Web site (www.textron.com) to see whether the firm still operates with five divisions. While at the Web site, determine whether the Industrial division has the same product segments that are mentioned in the Mini-Case. If you find differences, what do you think influenced the decisions to make changes to one division's product segments or to the firm's set of divisions?

2. Use the Internet to find sources describing Textron's financial performance during the most recent quarter of the most recent year. Did sales revenue and earnings increase during the time period you examined relative to the same period the prior year? What do you think influenced the financial results you found?

3. What performance-related risks does Textron face while using the unrelated diversification multiproduct strategy? In your view, is the firm effectively managing those risks? Why or why not?

EXPERIENTIAL EXERCISES

Exercise One: Multiproduct Strategies at Novartis and in the Pharmaceutical Industry

Novartis AG, the Swiss pharmaceutical company, recently bought a 77 percent share in the eye care company Alcon Inc. from Nestlé SA for about $39 billion. The Alcon acquisition increases Novartis's presence in eye care by adding Alcon's glaucoma drugs and cataract surgery products. Novartis already had a presence in eye care through its Ciba Vision contact lens brand. Novartis is the world's fourth largest drug maker (2007 total sales of $49 billion) with products such as Diovan for blood pressure, Gleevec for certain kinds of cancer, and Trileptal for epilepsy. Novartis had previously diversified into other areas of the pharmaceutical industry. For example, in 2005, it acquired two generic drug makers, and in 2006, it acquired Chiron Corp., a company in the vaccine business. Despite these diversifications, prescription drugs still made up 60 percent of its total sales in 2007.

Questions

1. What kind of multiproduct strategy (related constrained, related linked, or unrelated) is Novartis following? Explain.

2. Why did Novartis diversify into the eye care business? Relate the reasons to those given in Table 6-1. (You will need to do some research to answer this question.)

3. How does the pattern of product diversification by Novartis compare to other major firms in the pharmaceutical industry? Choose at least one major firm (e.g., Pfizer, GlaxoSmithKline, Sanofi-Aventis, or Roche Holdings) and investigate recent patterns of diversification. Classify the kinds of diversification according to whether they are related constrained, related linked, or unrelated. Look at sources such as *The Wall Street Journal*, *BusinessWeek*, *Fortune*, and *Forbes*.

Sources: R. Langreth, 2008, Why Novartis bought Alcon stake, *Forbes.com*, April 7; J. Whalen, 2008, Novartis picks up eye-care unit, *The Wall Street Journal*, April 8.

BIZ FLIX

Josie and the Pussycats: Related or Unrelated Multiproduct Strategy?

Recall this chapter's discussion of multiproduct strategies and especially the Procter & Gamble case. Assume while watching this scene that a single firm produces and markets all products and services shown in the scene.

Riverdale's little-known rock-and-roll trio The Pussycats gets an unexpected career boost following the mysterious disappearance of renowned rock group Dujour. Wyatt Frame (Alan Cumming), a MegaRecords executive, discovers the group on a city street. His scheming mind combines with the maniacal scheming mind of Fiona (Parker Posey), MegaRecords chief executive officer, to propel the newly named Josie and the Pussycats to national success. Unknown to this talented group, Fiona plans to use subliminal advertising embedded in their recordings to control the minds and spending habits of the nation's teenagers.

This scene is an edited composite from different parts of the film. The scene does not appear exactly as shown in the film. If you have seen *Josie and the Pussycats,* you may recall some of these moments.

What to Watch for and Ask Yourself

1. How many products and services does this hypothetical company produce and market? You may need to view the scene more than once to get a good count. You can also pause the scene to study any part of it more closely.
2. What level of diversification does the scene imply for the firm—low or high?
3. Assess the multiproduct strategy implied by the scene. Could any firm successfully carry out this strategy? Why or why not?

ENDNOTES

1. M. F. Wiersema & H. P. Bowen, 2008, Corporate diversification: The impact of foreign competition, industry globalization, and product diversification, *Strategic Management Journal* 29: 115–132; H. Kim, R. E. Hoskisson, & W. P. Wan, 2004, Power dependence, diversification strategy, and performance in Keiretsu member firms, *Strategic Management Journal* 25: 613–636.
2. R. E. Hoskisson, M. A. Hitt, R. D. Ireland, & J. S. Harrison, 2008, *Competing for Advantage*, 2nd ed., Mason, OH: Thomson South-Western; M. E. Porter, 1987, From competitive advantage to corporate strategy, *Harvard Business Review* 65(3): 43–59.
3. R. Rumelt, 1974, *Strategy, Structure, and Economic Performance,* Boston: Harvard Business School.
4. 2008, Whole Foods Market: Products/Seafood, Whole Foods, www.wholefoods. com, May 30.
5. 2008, United Parcel Service, Inc., *Standard and Poor's Stock Report,* www.standardandpoors.com, May 28.
6. M. A. Hitt, L. Tihanyi, T. Miller, & B. Connelly, 2006, International diversification: Antecedents, outcomes, and moderators, *Journal of Management* 32: 831–867; R. A. Bettis & C. K. Prahalad, 1995, The dominant logic: Retrospective and extension, *Strategic Management Journal* 16: 5–14; R. A. Bettis, 1986, The dominant logic: A new linkage between diversity and performance, *Strategic Management Journal* 7: 485–501.
7. D. J. Miller, M. J. Fern, & L. B. Cardinal, 2007, The use of knowledge for technological innovation within diversified firms, *Academy of Management Journal*, 50: 308–326; Rumelt, *Strategy, Structure, and Economic Performance.*
8. S. Dutta, M. J. Zbaracki, & M. Bergen, 2003, Pricing process as a capability: A resource-based perspective, *Strategic Management Journal* 24: 615–630.
9. O. Beisheim & F. Guenther, 2008, Performance effects of firms' expansion paths within and across industries and nations, *Strategic Organization* 6: 47–81.
10. 2008, Chinese and Russian retailers break into world's top 250, according to Deloitte study, *Deloitte,* www.deloitte.com, January 19.
11. J. Santiso, 2007, The emergence of Latin multinationals, *Deutsche Bank Research*, www.dbresearch.com, March 27.
12. 2008, P&G corporate information, Procter & Gamble, www.procterandgamble. com, May 25.
13. M. A. Hitt, J. S. Harrison, & R. D. Ireland, 2001, *Mergers and Acquisitions: A Guide to Creating Value for Stakeholders,* New York: Oxford University Press.
14. V. Swaminathan, F. Murshed, & J. Hulland, 2008, Value creation following merger and acquisition announcements: The role of strategic emphasis alignment, *Journal of Marketing Research* 45: 33–47; H. Tanriverdi & N. Venkatraman, 2005, Knowledge relatedness and the performance of multibusiness firms, *Strategic Management Journal* 26: 97–119.
15. 2008, Our company, GE, www.ge.com, May 30.
16. 2008, GE fact sheet, GE, www.ge.com, May 30.
17. R. Grover, D. Brady, & T. Lowry, 2004, Lights! Camera! Bean Counters! NBC is set to get its Hollywood studio. Can the GE unit handle the culture clash? *BusinessWeek,* May 17: 82.
18. A. Kachra & R. E. White, 2008, Know-how transfer: The role of social, economic/ competitive, and firm boundary factors, *Strategic Management Journal* 29: 425–445; K. M. Eisenhardt & D. C. Galunic, 2000, Coevolving: At last, a way to make synergies work, *Harvard Business Review* 78(1): 91–111.
19. A. Tuppura, S. Saarenketo, K. Puumaiainen, A. Jantunen, & K. Kylaheiko, 2008, Linking knowledge, entry timing and internationalization strategy, *International Business Review*, in press.
20. M. R. Haas & M. T. Hansen, 2007, Different knowledge, different benefits: Toward a productivity perspective on knowledge sharing in organizations, *Strategic Management Journal* 28: 1133–1153; Eisenhardt & Galunic, Coevolving, 94.
21. 2008, The Walt Disney Company and Affiliated Companies, Walt Disney, http://corporate.disney.go.com, May 25.
22. L. Capron & J.-C. Shen, 2007, Acquisitions of private vs. public firms: Private information, target selection, and acquirer returns. *Strategic Management Journal*

28: 891–911; D. D. Bergh, 1997, Predicting divestiture of unrelated acquisitions: An integrative model of ex ante conditions, *Strategic Management Journal* 18: 715–731.

23. 2008, United Technologies Corporation, *Standard and Poor's Stock Report*, www.standardandpoors.com, May 24.

24. H. Kachi, 2008, Japan Tobacco posts rise in net, tells recall's toll, *Wall Street Journal—Eastern Edition*, February 8, B3.

25. O. E. Williamson, 1975, *Markets and Hierarchies: Analysis and Antitrust Implications*, New York: Macmillan.

26. S.-S. Chen, 2008, Organizational form and the economic impact of corporate new product strategies, *Journal of Business Finance & Accounting* 35: 71–101.

27. T. P. Moliterno & M. F. Wiersema, 2007, Firm performance, rent appropriation, and the strategic resource divestment capability, *Strategic Management Journal* 28: 1065–1087; R. E. Hoskisson, R. A. Johnson, D. Yiu, & W. P. Wan, 2001, Restructuring strategies and diversified business groups: Differences associated with country institutional environments, in M. A. Hitt, R. E. Freeman, & J. S. Harrison (eds.), *Handbook of Strategic Management*, Oxford, U.K.: Blackwell, 433–463.

28. 2008, Prestige Brands Holdings, Inc., *Yahoo! Finance*, www.yahoo.com, June 1.

29. G. Morgenson, 2008, Questions of rent tactics by private equity, *The New York Times Online*, www.nytimes.com, May 9.

30. M. Larraza-Kintana, R. M. Wiseman, L. R. Gomez-Mejia, & T. M. Welbourne, 2007, Disentangling compensation and employment risks using the behavioral agency model, *Strategic Management Journal* 28: 1001–1019; W. Shen & A. A. Cannella, 2002, Power dynamics within top management and their impacts on CEO dismissal followed by inside succession, *Academy of Management Journal* 45: 717–733.

31. P. M. Guest, 2008, The impact of mergers and acquisitions on executive pay in the United Kingdom, *Economica*, in press; J. J. Cordeiro & R. Veliyath, 2003, Beyond pay for performance: A panel study of the determinants of CEO compensation, *American Business Review* 21(1): 56–66.

32. D. A. Garvin & L. C. Levesque, 2008, The multiunit enterprise, *Harvard Business Review* 86(6): 106–117; J. G. Combs & M. S. Skill, 2003, Managerialist and human capital explanation for key executive pay premiums: A contingency perspective, *Academy of Management Journal* 46: 63–73.

33. C. C. Markides & P. J. Williamson, 1996, Corporate diversification and organizational structure: A resource-based view, *Academy of Management Journal* 39: 340–367.

34. 2008, Textron profile, Textron, www.textron.com, June 1.

35. T. R. Eisenmann & J. L. Bower, 2000, The entrepreneurial M-form: Strategic integration in global media firms, *Organization Science* 11: 348–355.

CHAPTER 7
Acquisition and Integration Strategies

Knowledge Objectives

Reading and studying this chapter should enable you to:

1. Define acquisitions, takeovers, mergers, and acquisition strategy.

2. Discuss the five basic reasons that firms complete acquisitions.

3. Describe target screening, target selection, target negotiating, and due diligence.

4. Explain the importance and process of successful postacquisition business integration.

5. Discuss the four major pitfalls of acquisitions and remedies for their prevention.

6. Describe the major restructuring strategies for failed acquisitions.

© BrandX Pictures

M&A Deals in the Air

The airline industry has been in a chaotic state ever since the events of September 11, 2001. In 2007–2008, the problems began to increase because of the rising fuel prices and the declining performance in major economies, especially in the United States. In fact, several smaller U.S. airlines went bankrupt and closed their operations in 2008. Other larger airlines are experiencing major losses primarily because of the high fuel prices. Continental estimated that its fuel costs in 2008 would be $1.5 billion greater than those in 2007.

Because of these problems, airlines are searching for a way to survive and compete effectively. As a result, several of them are seeking consolidation to grow larger and obtain economies of scale.

Consolidation in the industry began a few years ago when the airlines continued to experience financial problems that were exacerbated by 9/11. The merger between America West and US Airways occurred during this time period. Consolidation among airlines is a global activity; in 2008, the Board of Alitalia accepted the acquisition offer from Air France-KLM, the result of a merger itself. Alitalia had been losing significant amounts of money and needed a financial injection in order to survive. Air France-KLM agreed to invest €1 billion (euros) after completing the acquisition. The Italian government had invested about €4.3 billion euros since 2003, trying to help Alitalia survive.

Delta and Northwest airlines largely agreed to a merger as well. However, they have been unable to gain

© Segar/Reuters/Landov

the approval of the separate pilot unions for each company. Between them, they have 11,000 pilots. The deal will be a complicated one if achieved. An equity stake was acquired by Air France-KLM as well. It is an alliance partner of Northwest at present. Delta is the third largest airline, while Northwest is the sixth largest. Because of this potential deal, other U.S. airlines have been engaging in talks about a potential merger. For example, Continental has had discussions about potential mergers with United and with American Airlines. If the Delta and Northwest merger is finalized and approved by regulatory authorities, other consolidations in the airline industry are possible.

The major issues seem to revolve around costs, a gain in economies of scale, and an ability to remain competitive. Problems in the U.S. economy and in other economies in the worlds (e.g., countries in Europe) increase the pressure on airlines to merge to increase their efficiencies. Also, consolidation reduces competition, making it a little easier to achieve competitive parity or possibly a competitive advantage. But merger success is not guaranteed.

Sources: J. Baer, 2008, Pilot standoff clouds Delta deal chances, *Financial Times*, www.ft.com, March 18; Alitalia accepts Air France-KLM's takeover bid, 2008, *USA Today*, www.usatoday.com, March 17; C. Barry, 2008, Alitalia board accepts bid from Air France, *Washington Post*, www.washingtonpost.com, March 17; B. Hensel, 2008, Continental warns of "tough" decisions, *Houston Chronicle*, www.chron.com, March 14; S. Carey & P. Prada, 2008, Delta-Northwest deal looks near, *Wall Street Journal*, http://online.wsj.com, February 19; C. Paris, 2008, Air France lays plans for Alitalia, *Wall Street Journal*, http://online.wsj.com, February 19; J. Baer, 2008, Deals in the air: Rising costs force U.S. carriers to seek mergers, *Financial Times*, www.ft.com, February 18.

An **acquisition** is a transaction in which a firm buys a controlling interest in another firm with the intention of either making it a subsidiary business or combining it with its current business or businesses. It is important to understand that for some firms, an acquisition is a "one-time only" event. For example, a firm using a differentiation business-level strategy might decide to acquire only one other company because it has truly specialized skills that the focal firm requires to create unique value for its customers. It is rare, though, for a firm to complete only a single acquisition. Most firms involved with acquisitions form an acquisition strategy. An **acquisition strategy** is an action plan that the firm develops to successfully acquire other companies. An effective acquisition strategy enables significant firm growth.[1] Firms pursue acquisitions for a number of other reasons. In fact, 2007 was a record year for acquisitions with a value of $4.5 trillion.[2] Many of the airlines described in Focusing on Strategy are using an acquisition strategy to increase their efficiencies, reduce costs, and reduce their competition. These reasons clearly describe the rationale for the proposed Delta-Northwest merger.

A **takeover** is a specialized type of acquisition in which the target firm does not solicit the acquiring firm's offer. For instance, in 2007, US Airways made an unsolicited offer to buy (take over) Delta. The CEO of Delta reacted negatively to US Airways' bid. He proclaimed to senators and others that the proposed takeover would threaten the nation's transportation industry and lead to higher ticket prices and fewer flights from which customers could choose.[3] Even though these claims are likely an overstatement, Delta rejected the offer. When a target firm reacts negatively to a proposal, the proposed transaction is called a hostile takeover.

A **merger** is a transaction in which firms agree to combine their operations on a relatively equal basis. For example, DaimlerChrysler was created by the merger between Daimler-Benz and Chrysler and was originally described as a merger. However, as it turned out, Daimler actually acquired Chrysler and installed its own managerial team. Mergers are more common than takeovers, while acquisitions are more common than mergers. Our emphasis in this chapter is on acquisitions and the acquisition strategy because of their frequency of use.

It is interesting to note that the number of acquisitions involving firms from different countries (called cross-border acquisitions) continues to increase (see Chapter 8). Relaxed regulations and improved trade relations among various countries are contributing to the growth of cross-border acquisitions such as the one between Daimler-Benz and Chrysler. In the European Union, as more countries have been added, the number of regulations and restrictions between firms in these countries has been reduced. As home markets mature, governments are more motivated to facilitate the efforts of firms in their country to seek growth in other countries' markets. Yet these transactions are challenging as well. Among the challenges are the difficulties of screening firms, selecting a target firm, and then negotiating with target firm managers. Differences in languages and cultures require understanding and sensitivity from both sides of the transaction.

We use Figure 7.1 as the framework for discussion of acquisitions and the acquisition strategy. First, we describe the five major reasons that firms complete acquisitions. We then examine target screening and selection, target negotiating, and due diligence. In this discussion, we examine four questions firms should answer when engaging in due diligence. Our attention then turns to what should be done to successfully integrate the target firm into the acquiring firm. We discuss four major pitfalls to successful integration and the steps firms can take to avoid them. In spite of good intentions, acquisitions sometimes fail. We close the chapter with a discussion of what firms do when firms face this failure.

Reasons for Acquisitions

Firms complete acquisitions and use an acquisition strategy for many reasons. We discuss five major reasons in the following sections.

acquisition

a transaction in which a firm buys a controlling interest in another firm with the intention of either making it a subsidiary business or combining it with its current business or businesses

acquisition strategy

an action plan that the firm develops to successfully acquire other companies

takeover

a specialized type of acquisition in which the target firm does not solicit the acquiring firm's offer

merger

a transaction in which firms agree to combine their operations on a relatively equal basis

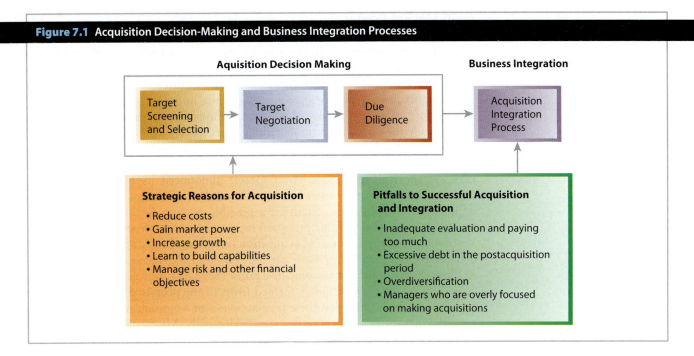

Figure 7.1 Acquisition Decision-Making and Business Integration Processes

Reduce Costs

Firms often use horizontal acquisitions to reduce costs. A **horizontal acquisition** is the purchase of a competitor competing in the same market or markets as the acquiring firm. An airline buying another airline (e.g., Delta acquiring Northwest) is an example of a horizontal acquisition.

Firms gain scale economies through horizontal acquisitions, which is one reason so many horizontal acquisitions take place in the pharmaceuticals industry. As you might imagine, the ability to combine two firms' R&D skills often drives horizontal acquisitions between pharmaceuticals firms. The economies-of-scale increases from mergers are highly important in the airline industry.[4]

Horizontal acquisitions can also lead to increases in productivity, especially where firms have similar but some different resources that complement one another.[5] In addition, some firms acquire others to reduce the competition. Reducing the competition is part of the reason for the consolidation in the airline industry.[6] Additionally, the merger of XM and Sirius is clearly a desire on the part of each to reduce the competition. In fact, both were experiencing problems surviving when competing with each other.[7]

A **vertical acquisition** is the purchase of a supplier or distributor of one or more of a firm's goods or services.[8] Vertical acquisitions can also be used to increase scale and to gain market power, which is discussed in the next section. Rupert Murdoch built News Corporation and continues to manage it today. He began acquiring British newspapers in the 1970s and then began an acquisition program in the United States in 1976 when he acquired the *New York Post*. Books (HarperCollins), magazines (*TV Guide*), television networks (FOX), and movie studios (Twentieth Century Fox) have been added to create News Corporation. Murdoch acquired a controlling interest in DirecTV by offering $6.6 billion to buy General Motors' 20 percent stake in Hughes Electronics. The acquisition of DirecTV by News Corporation is a vertical acquisition, as DirecTV is a satellite TV company through which News Corporation can distribute more of its media content: news, movies, and television shows. In 2007, Murdoch capped his acquisitions by purchasing *The Wall Street Journal*.[9]

horizontal acquisition

the purchase of a competitor competing in the same market or markets as the acquiring firm

vertical acquisition

the purchase of a supplier or distributor of one or more of a firm's goods or services

© AP Photo/Brian Charlton

Gain Market Power

Market power exists when the firm sells its products above competitive prices or when its costs are lower than those of its primary competitors. Firms commonly use horizontal and vertical acquisitions to gain market power. Horizontal acquisitions have been used in the business software industry. Declines in corporate spending because of the global economic malaise in the early part of the twenty-first century influenced the use of horizontal acquisitions in this industry. Acquisitions enable the acquiring firm to reduce overcapacity in the industry (reducing competition) by eliminating duplicate operations during the integration process.

An opportunity to reduce overcapacity may have influenced Oracle's hostile takeover of rival PeopleSoft. After Oracle announced its bid for PeopleSoft, Microsoft and SAP, two other large players in the technology infrastructure and application software area, discussed a possible merger. Antitrust concerns prevented serious pursuit of this proposed merger, however. Nonetheless, the highly visible nature of the announced acquisition (involving Oracle and PeopleSoft) and possible merger (involving Microsoft and SAP) signaled the need for smaller firms in this industry to be able to compete against the market power these transactions would create for the two newly formed firms (if the proposed transactions were completed). Some think that these transactions sent a message to smaller competitors that they needed to "eat or be eaten."[10] Recently, Microsoft changed its focus to acquiring Internet businesses exemplified by its bid to acquire Yahoo![11]

However, pursuing market power can be problematic as well. Firms can pay too much for an acquisition as they compete to gain market power and the larger share of a market. When firms pay more than the current market value of a firm, it is referred to as a **premium**. Firms paying a premium assume that they can create synergy by merging the two firms, thereby increasing the value of the assets of the firm acquired. However, a number of firms do not create adequate synergy to earn returns beyond a premium. In these cases, executives of the acquiring firm often take more drastic steps to make the acquisition pay, such as selling off productive assets, laying off valuable employees to reduce costs, or buying additional businesses to integrate as they try to build synergy.[12]

Increase Growth

Some industries have significant fragmentation, with many small competitors of equal size. In these instances, some firms use an acquisition strategy to increase their growth rate relative to competitors. This strategy can be especially valuable if the acquiring firm is the first or one of the first to make such acquisitions in the industry. If they do so, it gives them an advantage in market power and position.[13]

Understanding Strategy: Learning from Success explains how Tata Motors is using acquisitions to grow. In particular, it is growing its reach into international markets with the acquisition of Jaguar and Land Rover from Ford. So adding these businesses not only increases Tata's sales revenue but also provides access to international markets, especially in the United States. The reason it is listed as a successful acquisition is because Tata acquired the businesses for approximately one-third the price that Ford paid when it acquired them. Of course, examining it from Ford's point of view might suggest a failure, largely for the same reasons. Ford lost considerable money on the sales of the two businesses. In fact, Ford has experienced such major losses that it needed to sell the businesses to obtain cash. Thus, Tata took advantage of Ford's ineptness to acquire the two businesses.

Learn to Build Capabilities

Learning from a target firm and building new capabilities are more reasons that firms acquire other companies. Target companies often have unique employee skills, organizational technologies, or superior knowledge that are available to the acquiring firm only through acquisitions. Learning from acquired firms is common in cross-border acquisitions. Although acquiring firms may gain new knowledge

---

market power

power that exists when the firm sells its products above competitive prices or when its costs are lower than those of its primary competitors

premium

occurs when firms pay more than the current market value to acquire another firm

Growth by Acquisition at a Discount

Tata Motors acquired the Jaguar and Land Rover businesses from Ford Motor Company in 2008. Ford originally paid $2.5 billion to acquire Jaguar (1989) and $2.75 billion to acquire Land Rover (2000). Tata acquired both businesses from Ford for $1.7 billion. Essentially, Ford has been losing money ($12.6 billion in 2006) and needed cash to finance its plan to turn around the business. Thus, it sold these businesses at a discount. Ford also needed to focus on its core business, Ford automobiles, and these two businesses represented a distraction for the executives.

Land Rover performed well in recent years, but Jaguar experienced sales declines. Given that Jaguar was acquired in 1989, the $2.5 billion would represent considerably more in today's dollars. And given that Land Rover was performing well, it was certainly worth more than when it was acquired for $2.75 billion. Therefore, it is rather simple to conclude that Tata Motors acquired these businesses at a discount. Furthermore, both businesses represent well-known and respected brands. As a result, Tata Motors appears to have made an excellent deal.

© AP Photo/StevenSenne

© Fabrice Coffini/AFP/GettyImages

These acquisitions allow Tata to grow quickly, to access luxury markets, and to extend its global reach in autos, especially in the U.S. auto market, which remains the largest in the world. Tata plans to use these two businesses to enter new international markets. Tata can learn from the engineering and design expertise in these businesses to enrich its capabilities to build high-quality autos and luxury brands for the Indian markets and others globally. These brands also add other value to Tata. It does not have the pricing power of most of its direct competitors such as Toyota and Maruti, but the addition of these businesses can enhances the firm's reputation.

Clearly, these acquisitions will help Tata build its car business over time with the new capabilities, access to new international markets, and the growth potential.

Sources: India eNews, 2008, Jaguar, Land Rover in the black soon, says Tata Motors, www.indiaenews.com, March 27; M. Spector & E. Bellman, 2008, Tata and Ford reach deal for Land Rover, Jaguar, *Wall Street Journal*, http://online.wsj.com, March 27; Ford sells luxury brands for $1.7 billion, 2008, *New York Times*, www.nytimes.com, March 26; R. David, 2008, Tata Motors: Ready to take on the world? *Forbes*, www.forbes.com, January 8.

in several areas from the acquisition, they usually learn market-specific knowledge (e.g., about customers, distributors, suppliers, and government regulations).[14] Additionally, pooling the companies' combined resources and capabilities may enable development of new "centers of excellence" for specialized products in new markets.[15] Cisco Systems, Microsoft, and Intel are examples of firms completing technology-driven acquisitions to build their capabilities.[16] Furthermore, Tata Motors' acquisition of Jaguar and Land Rover (see Understanding Strategy: Learning from Success) should help the firm develop new capabilities. Tata has generally developed and marketed autos for the low end of the market. It can gain knowledge from the design and engineering skills of Jaguar and Land Rover. Tata can learn how to build higher-quality autos and how to market to customers in the luxury car market.

Building capabilities through acquisitions is a future-oriented reason to complete acquisitions compared to the reasons of reducing costs, gaining market power, and increasing growth.

The first three reasons for acquisitions are about exploiting current advantages, while learning how to build the firm's capabilities is about exploring to create tomorrow's advantages. In general, exploitation was the base for many acquisitions in the 1980s and 1990s, while financial reasons (discussed next) influenced acquisitions in the 1970s. It appears that capability-building acquisitions are a dominant reason for many acquisitions in the first decade of the twenty-first century.[17]

Manage Risk and Other Financial Objectives

Facing stiff competition, some firms choose to use acquisitions to diversify their operations, thereby reducing their dependence on performance in an intensely competitive market. Many years ago, GE diversified away from the consumer electronics market into financial services to reduce its dependence on the consumer electronics area. Furthermore, GE has diversified into other service areas rather than base its revenue solely on industrial products.[18] At times, firms also make acquisitions to gain access to tax advantages or to reduce business or financial risk. Of course, such acquisitions need to be done in a way that cannot be replicated by shareholders through portfolio diversification. In recent times, private equity firms amass financial capital from multiple investors and use this capital to make acquisitions. They usually acquire firms that they believe can provide significant and rapid returns on their investment. In particular, they search for undervalued assets.[19]

Screening, Selecting, and Negotiating with Target Firms

Research suggests that financial acquirers (such as Kohlberg Kravis Roberts [KKR]) experience higher valuations in their acquisitions than do corporate acquisitions.[20]

Financial acquirers such as leveraged buyout (defined later in the chapter) firms often complete two or three acquisitions per year. However, these firms may explore as many as 400 or 500 possibilities and examine closely perhaps 25 targets before selecting the four or five target firms they'll attempt to acquire. Acquisition opportunities can come without warning and usually need to be evaluated quickly. Accordingly, it is important for firms to balance the need to think strategically with the need to react to an acquisition opportunity in a timely way. Firms whose stock is publicly traded have a great deal of data available to examine because regulations require that they make much of their financial data public. However, private firms whose stock is not traded on the stock exchange do not have to reveal much information. Therefore, while some private firms may be attractive, it is challenging for acquiring firms to obtain adequate information to evaluate the viability of the private firms as acquisition targets.[21] Cisco Systems has completed a large number of acquisitions; it may examine three potential markets and decide to enter only one of them and may evaluate five to ten candidates for each deal that it closes. This extra screening enables the acquiring party to identify the acquisition opportunities that exist while at the same time determining the appropriate price. Although this process takes time, it helps managers develop experience in screening, allowing them to increase the speed and effectiveness of the screening process over time.

To focus too strongly on an "exciting" opportunity and set aside the firm's basic strategy can be a major mistake. After the screening process is completed in a rational and strategic way, negotiations are initiated.

Key issues requiring careful analysis should be identified early in the negotiating process. For instance, it is important to clarify what role the top executives will play in the newly combined organization. Determining the executive positions

Table 7.1 Considerations in Successful Acquisition (Including Cross-Border) Negotiation Processes

1. Be very clear about the strategic logic behind the proposed acquisition.

2. Be patient, acting decisively when needed but in a way that does not create emotion. Take a long-term view, which often runs counter to the strategic objective among participants in the negotiation process.

3. Seek to develop government, industry, and company contacts well before the transaction takes place.

4. Identify the potential players in the proposed deal-making process, including government administrators. Understand who will be for the deal and differentiate between those who will be unconditionally opposed and those whose objectives can be met in the negotiation process.

5. Understand who will defer to which group and sequence the negotiation process in a way that will maximize the chance of success.

6. Think about how you will negotiate with potential deal blockers and how you can give them a vision that meets your needs while enabling them to persuade others among their constituents of the transaction's value for their particular group's interests.

7. Act to ensure the sustainability of the deal. Remember that once the transaction is completed, negotiations are not finished. Integration between deal participants can be facilitated by taking a long-term view of the participants involved.

Sources: Adapted from J. K. Sebenius, 2002, The hidden challenge of cross-border negotiations, *Harvard Business Review*, 80(3): 76–85; J. K. Sebenius, 1998, Negotiating cross-border acquisitions, *Sloan Management Review*, 39(2): 27–41.

needed in the newly created firm and the people who will fill those positions is an important topic for negotiations.

Because most proposed transactions are greeted with skepticism by managers and employees in the target firm, acquirers with experience often try to develop a spirit of cooperation to negotiate a mutually beneficial agreement. A cooperative relationship between personnel in the acquiring and acquired firms is the foundation on which the most serious issues can be successfully negotiated. Table 7.1 provides a list of suggestions that are helpful in the negotiation process. In particular, government officials may also need to be included in order to successfully negotiate a deal, especially in cross-border transactions.

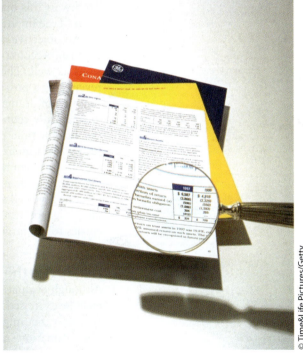

© Time&Life Pictures/Getty

Due Diligence

Due diligence is the rational process by which acquiring firms evaluate target firms. Due diligence is concerned with verifying that the reason for the proposed transaction is sound strategically and financially. To understand how to improve due diligence, Bain and Company, a strategy consulting firm, studied 20 companies, both private and public, known for the quality of their due diligence processes. We summarize the results of their research into four basic questions around which an acquiring firm's due diligence efforts should be framed.[22]

What Is the Acquiring Firm Really Buying?

Acquiring firms frequently form a team to conduct due diligence. Rather than relying on potentially biased secondary sources for information, the due diligence team should build its own bottom-up view of the target firm and the industry. In this process, the team collects information from multiple parties, including customers, suppliers, and competitors as well as the target firm. This information helps the team carefully examine each assumption made by the acquiring firm regarding the target firm and its value.

Studying customers and suppliers enables the due diligence team to answer important questions about the target firm such as: Is the target customer group growing? Has the target firm fully explored the needs of its target customers? What

due diligence

the rational process by which acquiring firms evaluate target firms

distribution channels is the target firm using to serve customers? Are superior channels available? Has the target firm negotiated favorable deals with its suppliers? If not, why hasn't it done so?

Analyzing competitors is another important source of information when it comes to understanding the target firm. Important questions in evaluating the target firm's competitors include the following: Is the target firm more profitable than its competitors? In what part of the value chain are most of the profits made? Is the target firm underperforming or outperforming its competitors in the key parts of the value chain? How will the target firm's competitors react to an acquisition, and how might this influence competition between the target and its competitors?

Finally, the due diligence team should assess the target firm's capabilities by considering a host of questions: Does the target have cost advantages relative to its competitors? How could the target's cost position help the acquiring firm's cost position? Could the target's capabilities be integrated with those of the acquiring firm to create sources of differentiation? If so, how valuable would those be and how long would it take to develop those new capabilities?

The due diligence team's evaluation of the target firm is studied to ensure that no "deal breakers" exist and to verify that the proposed transaction is appropriate strategically. This evaluation likely provides information regarding the target firm's value.

What Is the Target Firm's Value?

Acquisitions can seem glamorous—a fact that sometimes biases decision makers to quickly conclude that a proposed acquisition is virtually without potential flaws. To thwart this bias, the due diligence team must assess the target's true financial value. True financial value is determined through an objective, unbiased process.

An objective analysis verifies the absence of accounting anomalies at the target firm. Accounting anomalies may signal problems and possibly unethical decisions as well. The team should consider rapid and significant increases in sales revenue as a possible accounting anomaly. For example, such changes may be a function of dramatically lower sales prices rather than true growth. Even though dramatically reducing prices to sell more products makes revenue look good in the current time period, such sales can't be sustained. Of course, the acquiring firm is most interested in future sales of a target firm. Another accounting anomaly occurs when the firm treats recurring items as extraordinary costs, thus keeping them off the profit and loss statement. These and other accounting anomalies must be revealed to understand the historical and projected cash flows. Thus, the due diligence team must extensively interact with target firm personnel about entries to the target's financial statements.

Where Are the Synergies Between the Combined Firms?

Although evaluating the target firm to determine its actual value is wise, caution must be exercised when doing so. The due diligence team should also consider the synergies that might be created by integrating the target with the acquiring firm. This evaluation should identify potential synergies, the probability of realizing the synergies, and the time and investment required to do so. Acquisitions often fail because of an inability to obtain expected synergies, an outcome that highlights the importance of carefully studying proposed synergies and their costs.

What Is the Acquiring Firm's Walk-Away Offer Price?

The emotional pressure to make an acquisition can be significant. Think of the pressure that acquiring firm executives may encounter after a proposed acquisition is announced to the press. Extensive coverage highlights a transaction's visibility and can make it harder for the acquiring firm to walk away from the possible deal. However, successful acquisitions result from logical, unemotional decisions.

To increase the probability that a rational decision will be made, the acquiring firm should decide on a purchase price it will not exceed. To do this, the acquiring firm must determine who makes the top-price decision and the decision criteria he or she will use. These determinations should be made before final negotiations begin. Additionally, creating incentive systems for those negotiating transactions can be fruitful. For example, Clear Channel Communications, an international radio, billboard, and live entertainment company, has an incentive system that is focused on an acquisition's results. Thus, Clear Channel's integration teams' compensation is partly based on the profitability of the completed acquisitions. Interestingly, Clear Channel decided to take the firm private by partnering with two private equity groups, Bain Capital and Thomas H. Lee partners. Yet the financing of the acquisition remains in question because of the subprime financing crisis that occurred in 2007 and 2008.[23]

Based on the results of its due diligence process, the acquiring firm decides whether it will acquire the target firm. If the acquisition is completed, the focus shifts to what must be done to integrate the acquired firm into the acquiring firm's operations.

Integrating the Newly Acquired Business

The activities leading to an acquisition decision (target screening, target selection, target negotiating, and due diligence) influence the success of individual acquisitions along with the acquisition strategies. However, in the final analysis, a particular acquisition will succeed or fail on the basis of how well the target firm and acquiring firm integrate their operations.[24] Integration success is more likely when an integration team, including employees from the acquiring firm and the acquired firm, is formed and charged with full responsibility to integrate the two companies to create value.

Although implementing acquisitions involves many challenges, as acquiring and target firms begin to integrate their operations, unanticipated opportunities for creating new value may be discovered. When firms are intent on learning from each other or where complementary assets are brought together in ways that enable such value creation, these value-creating opportunities are more likely to arise.[25] Other research suggests that creating a culture of a merger of "equals" is likely to reinforce existing organizational identities and create expectations for strict equality.[26] If the integration process is carried out thoroughly and appropriately, opportunities are likely for increased growth as learning occurs.[27] Effective integration often allows the merged firm to leverage the capabilities (e.g., technological capabilities) of both firms to create enhanced value. Alternatively, poor integration of the two firms hinders the ability to leverage the special capabilities of the two firms, thereby producing lower value.[28] Effective integration is especially important when the acquiring firm pays a significant premium to buy the target firm. In this case, it must achieve the potential synergies of combining the businesses in order to create new value that will return the premium paid.[29]

Pitfalls in Pursuing Acquisitions and Their Prevention

The importance of successful integration in the postacquisition period cannot be overestimated.[30] Because combined firms often lose target firm managers through turnover, it is important to retain key executives and other valuable human capital, especially if the acquiring firm wants to gain new skills from the acquired firm.[31] In addition, because much of an organization's knowledge is contained in its human capital,[32] turnover of key personnel from the acquired firm should be avoided.[33] Involving these employees in the integration process reduces the likelihood that they will leave the newly combined firm.

The Wake-Up Call That Caused Ringing in Sprint's Ears

Prior to the merger of Sprint and Nextel, both had been considered good-performing firms. However, they were much smaller than their primary rivals AT&T and Verizon Wireless. In fact, the merger of the two firms was partially designed to create a firm that could compete effectively with these two firms. Yet despite

© AP Photo/Douglas C. Pizac

its logic and the potential synergy to be gained, the merger has not paid off. After the merger in 2005, the new combined firm, Sprint, began to experience problems. Those problems culminated in a massive $29.7 billion loss in fourth quarter of 2007 (announced in early 2008). In 2008, Sprint took approximately $31 billion in charges against its assets, eliminating almost all of the merger's original value.

Sprint experienced several problems after the merger, particularly in merging the two companies' assets and capabilities. As such, it did not capture the synergies that were expected. Additionally, Sprint's top executives implemented a financial and quantitative metrics approach to management, which placed top priority on increasing efficiency and reducing costs. Because of a strong emphasis on costs, customer service suffered. Because of the poor service that customers received, Sprint began to lose customers, a problem that continued for some time. In fact, the CEO was replaced, and the new CEO's plan to turn around the

company's performance acknowledged an expected loss of another 1.2 million premium customers in 2008.

Management's emphasis on cost efficiencies and incentives to capture new business caused some employees to cut ethical corners. This problem was enhanced by the fact that management also punished employees who did not adhere to strict policies. For example, one employee who worked in a call center was fired when she took a few days off because her father died. Combined, the actions by management encouraged managers to extend service contracts to customers without their approval and to ignore customer complaints (because of the costs required to correct problems). Managers did not pay attention to data on lost customers or the quality of service.

In 2008, the company faced a highly competitive environment, a declining customer base, and high debt costs with significant short-term payoff requirements. Some predicted that it may be facing bankruptcy if it is unable to meet the debt payments. It also has been rumored as a target for an acquisition because its stock value has declined significantly.

Sources: L. M. Holson, 2008, Sprint Nextel posts $29.5 billion loss, *New York Times*, www.nytimes.com, February 29; S. E. Ante, 2008, Sprint's world of pain, *BusinessWeek*, www.businessweek.com, February 28; C. Gutierrez, 2008, Sprint can't get a signal, *Forbes*, www.forbes.com, February 28; Sprint's massive loss, 2008, *Financial Times*, www.ft.com, February 28; S. E. Ante, 2008, Sprint's wake-up call, *BusinessWeek*, www.businessweek.com, February 21.

As noted in Understanding Strategy: Learning from Failure, Sprint was unable to achieve an effective integration of Nextel into its operations after the acquisition. The approach used by Sprint's management to implement the acquisition caused many problems and led to a major decline in customer service. As a result, the company lost many customers and began to experience financial losses. The firm has lost almost all of the value obtained in the acquisition and may decline further. Thus, the poor integration resulted in a substantial challenge for Sprint managers.

History suggests that acquisitions are risky. However, learning how to deal effectively with prominent pitfalls increases the chance of acquisition success. Next, we discuss four major pitfalls.

Inadequate Evaluation and Paying Too Much

As we've discussed, effective due diligence is important in ensuring that a rational approach is used after negotiations begin. We also highlighted the importance of the acquiring firm's establishing a price above which it will not go. Notwithstanding due diligence and the use of investment bankers to help with this process, many firms still act too irrationally in acquiring the target, and as a result, they pay too much for it (the premium is too high). Research suggests that "a combination of cognitive biases and organizational pressures often causes managers to make overly optimistic forecasts in analyzing proposals for major investments" such as acquisitions.[34] Anchoring (quickly becoming committed to a position and being highly resistant to changing it) and overconfidence in one's opinion are two examples of cognitive biases that may surface during an acquisition process. Regardless of the causes, those evaluating a target firm as an acquisition candidate must ensure that the acquiring firm's evaluation of that target is complete and that the acquiring firm doesn't overpay to acquire the target.

Excessive Debt in the Postacquisition Period

As illustrated in Understanding Strategy: Learning from Failure, many companies that make acquisitions have significant debt levels. In fact, Sprint is experiencing significant problems making its payments on a total of about $20 billion in debt. When credit rating agencies such as Moody's & Standard and Poor's reduce a firm's credit rating, the firm likely incurs higher costs to obtain additional financial capital. For example several rating agencies reduced the rating of Sprint to "junk" status.[35] This reduction is logical because firms with lower credit ratings are thought to be riskier investments. And investors expect higher returns from risky investments. An acquiring firm should also remember that if its debt load becomes too high, it will have less cash to invest in R&D, human resources, and marketing.[36] Investments in these organizational functions are important parts of what the firm does to be successful in the long term.

Overdiversification

Frequent acquisitions help meet capital markets' expectations for the firm to grow and have the potential to increase top-level managers' salaries. Top-level managers' salaries tend to increase with growth in the firm's overall size. Therefore, capital markets and the relationship between organizational size and salaries for top-level managers may influence top-level managers to make frequent acquisitions. This behavior can be problematic, though, in that firms can become overdiversified. In the late 1990s and early 2000s, a number of media companies such as AOL Time Warner, Vivendi, and Bertelsmann completed several acquisitions that did not turn out well. A number of analysts concluded that these firms had become overdiversified, a condition that makes it difficult for the firm to effectively manage each successive acquisition. The response to overdiversification is for the firm to divest acquisitions that it can't successfully manage.[37]

Managers Who Are Overly Focused on Making Acquisitions

Acquisitions require significant managerial time and energy. Managers have opportunity costs for the time and energy spent searching for viable acquisitions, completing due diligence, preparing for and participating in negotiations, and managing the integration process after an acquisition is completed. Time and energy spent dealing with potential acquisitions obviously can't be invested in managing other aspects of the firm's operations. Furthermore, when acquisition negotiations are initiated, target firm managers often operate in "suspended animation" until the acquisition and integration processes are completed.[38] Therefore, it is important for managers to encourage dissent when evaluating an acquisition target. If failure occurs, leaders are tempted to blame it on others or on unforeseen circumstances. Rather, it is important that managers recognize when they are overly involved in the acquisition process. "The urge to merge is still like an addiction in many companies: doing deals is much more fun and interesting than fixing fundamental problems. So, as in dealing with any other addictions or temptations maybe it is best to just say no."[39]

Table 7.2 Major Pitfalls of Acquisitions and Their Prevention

Pitfall	Prevention
Paying too much	Establish rational due diligence processes with a walk-away offer price and make certain that when this price is reached, managers involved do walk away.
Taking on too much debt	Ensure that the firm has adequate cash as well as debt capacity to complete the transaction at or below the walk-away offer price.
Becoming overdiversified	Understand fully the nature of synergy in the acquisition and the integration processes necessary to achieve it. Also, ensure that any unrelated transactions are justified based on strong financial rationales. However, even when such justification is in place, the deal may not be positive for strategic-fit reasons because it may lead to overdiversification. Therefore, make certain that strategic fit does not lead to overdiversification.
Managers who are overly focused on acquisitions	Establish checks and balances so that top managers are challenged by the board and other stakeholders regarding proposed acquisitions. These actions are especially important in firms making frequent acquisitions.

In Table 7.2, we summarize the four major pitfalls of acquisitions and present possible preventive actions firms can take to avoid a pitfall or to reduce the negative consequences experienced because of a pitfall. As suggested in the table and as we've discussed, it is important for the firm to establish a rational due diligence process and to make certain that the walk-away offer price is fixed in order to thwart the temptation to surpass the rational price to pay for a target firm. Paying too much often happens when many bidders are involved; this tendency is called the "winner's curse" in the research literature.[40] Similarly, managers must ensure that the firm has enough cash on hand and debt capacity to complete the transaction at or below the established walk-away offer price. When faced with the possibility of becoming overdiversified, managers must fully understand the nature of synergy and the actions necessary to create it in the integration stage. Even with potential synergies and a transaction justified by its expected financial outcomes, a deal may not be good to execute due to lack of strategic fit with the acquiring firm's core strengths. Finally, it is important to establish a checks-and-balances system in which managers are challenged to support the acquisition decision, especially when a firm regularly uses an acquisition strategy. If these checks and balances can be established with integrity, they will likely protect managers from becoming overly focused on completing acquisitions to the detriment of other issues warranting managerial attention. When managers overcome the pitfalls and manage the process effectively, successful acquisitions result. Unfortunately, only a small number of firms appear to manage the acquisition process effectively.[41]

Acquisition Failure and Restructuring

Regardless of the effort invested, acquisitions sometimes fail. When they do, divestiture may be the best course of action. A **divestiture** is a transaction in which businesses are sold to other firms or spun off as independent enterprises. Some divestitures occur because the firm wants to restructure its set of businesses to take advantage of new opportunities.[42] Commonly, though, divestitures are made to deal with failed acquisitions. Sears, Roebuck is a famous example of a firm that failed with its acquisitions. In 1981, Sears acquired Dean Witter Reynolds to diversify into financial services and Coldwell Banker to diversify into real estate. At first, the results of these acquisitions seemed positive. Quickly, though, it became obvious that the synergies Sears expected among its retail, financial services, and real estate businesses would not materialize. The inability to rapidly create synergies caused Sears executives to focus too much time on trying to develop those synergies. The net

divestiture
a transaction in which businesses are sold to other firms or spun off as independent enterprises

result of these efforts was that Sears' core retail business received little managerial attention, causing it to lose market share and perform poorly. Pressured by institutional investors to correct the problems, Sears announced the divestiture of its financial services and real estate businesses so that it could concentrate on its retail business. Research suggests that despite initial gains over the period when Sears was diversified, the firm's shareholders suffered significant opportunity losses when compared to a portfolio of firms that maintained a focus on their core retailing sector.[43] Unfortunately, Sears is again in trouble; it is experiencing declining sales and an inability to compete against such firms as Wal-Mart, Target, and JCPenney. Sears must find a way to differentiate itself from the major competitors and attract new customers. Currently, it appears that Sears may allow each of its primary units to operate independently, suggesting a possible break-up of the firm.[44]

Leveraged buyouts are commonly used as a restructuring strategy to correct for managerial mistakes. A **leveraged buyout (LBO)** is a restructuring strategy in which a party buys all or part of a firm's assets in order to take the firm or a part of the firm private. After the transaction is completed, the company's stock is no longer traded publicly. Usually, significant amounts of debt are incurred to finance a buyout; hence the term *leveraged* buyout. To support debt payments, the new owners may immediately sell a number of assets in order to focus on the firm's core businesses.[45] Because leveraged buyout organizations (such as KKR) often control these firms, the intent is to restructure the firm to the point that it can be sold at a profit within five to eight years. However, besides improving efficiencies, such buyouts can also represent a form of firm rebirth to facilitate entrepreneurial efforts and stimulate strategic growth. Equity firms such as those acquiring some of the equity in Clear Channel Communications have become more common in recent years.[46] Regardless, firms that engage in unsuccessful revisions often have to take actions to reverse the negative results. Some refer to this process as *merger repair*.[47]

leveraged buyout (LBO)

a restructuring strategy in which a party buys all or part of a firm's assets in order to take the firm or a part of the firm private

SUMMARY

The primary purpose of this chapter is to describe the actions necessary to provide the foundation for an effective acquisition strategy. In doing so, we examined the following topics:

- An acquisition occurs when one firm buys controlling interest in another firm with the intention of either making the acquired firm a subsidiary business or combining it with a current business. An acquisition strategy is an action plan that the firm develops to successfully complete acquisitions. A takeover is a specialized acquisition strategy in which a target firm does not solicit the acquiring firm's offer. Takeovers are often hostile transactions. A merger is a transaction in which firms agree to combine their operations on a relatively equal basis.

- Companies complete acquisitions for five basic reasons: (1) to reduce costs; (2) to gain market power; (3) to increase growth; (4) to learn and to build new capabilities; and (5) to manage managerial, financial, and risk-reduction objectives.

- Target screening, target selection, and target firm negotiations are activities firms complete to make an acquisition. Effective screening enables the acquiring firm to gain an overall sense of the acquisition opportunities that exist and helps to establish the appropriate price. After the screening and selection are completed, negotiating with target firm leaders begins. In negotiating, it is important to clarify the roles top executives of the acquiring and target firms will play in the new firm. Also, government officials may need to be consulted to conclude negotiations, especially in cross-border deals.

- Effective due diligence is critical to making the best decision about a possible acquisition. Four basic questions are answered when engaging in due diligence: (1) What is the acquiring firm really buying? (2) What is the target firm's true financial value? (3) Where are the potential synergies between the acquiring and acquired firms? (4) What is the acquiring firm's walk-away offer price?

- Efforts to integrate the acquired firm into the acquiring firm after the transaction is completed may be the strongest predictor of acquisition success or failure. After a transaction is completed, it is critical to assess and improve, as required, the morale of all employees, but especially target firm employees. Building bridges between personnel in the target firm and personnel in the acquiring firm increases the likelihood that the firms will be effectively integrated.

- In addition to integration difficulties, acquisitions face other potential pitfalls: (1) inadequately evaluating the target firm and paying too much for the target, (2) taking on excessive debt in the postacquisition period, (3) overdiversifying, and (4) having managers who are overly focused on making acquisitions.

- Acquisitions sometimes fail. When they do, firms divest businesses that are causing performance problems so that they might again focus on their core businesses. Leveraged buyouts are also used to restructure firms when particular acquisitions have failed or when a firm's whole acquisition strategy has failed.

KEY TERMS

acquisition 132
acquisition strategy 132
divestiture 142
due diligence 137

horizontal acquisition 133
leveraged buyout (LBO) 143
market power 134
merger 132

premium 134
takeover 132
vertical acquisition 133

DISCUSSION QUESTIONS

1. What are the definitions of an acquisition, takeover, merger, and acquisition strategy? Why are acquisitions important to understand?
2. What are the five basic reasons that firms make acquisitions? Over the next 10 years or so, do you think any of these reasons will become more important than the others? If so, why?
3. What are target screening, target selection, target negotiating, and due diligence? In your opinion, why do some firms fail to perform these activities effectively?

4. What process should be used to successfully integrate acquisitions, and why is integration important?
5. What are the four major pitfalls of acquisitions? How can these pitfalls be prevented?
6. What major restructuring strategies do firms use to deal with a failed acquisition? What are the trade-offs among the restructuring strategies?

STRATEGY TOOLBOX

Introduction

Acquisitions are one of the most common and most important strategic management tools in use today. The bad news is that most fail (the general rule of thumb is that up to 80%–85% do not achieve estimated synergies). Many times, acquisitions are not well thought out ahead of time or are the personal mission of CEOs. This chapter addresses many of the pitfalls and remedies, and this chapter's tool—The Acquisition Stoplight—is a guide for making an informed decision.

The Acquisition Stoplight

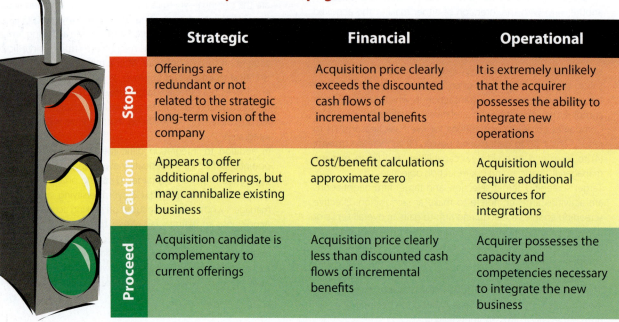

	Strategic	Financial	Operational
Stop	Offerings are redundant or not related to the strategic long-term vision of the company	Acquisition price clearly exceeds the discounted cash flows of incremental benefits	It is extremely unlikely that the acquirer possesses the ability to integrate new operations
Caution	Appears to offer additional offerings, but may cannibalize existing business	Cost/benefit calculations approximate zero	Acquisition would require additional resources for integrations
Proceed	Acquisition candidate is complementary to current offerings	Acquisition price clearly less than discounted cash flows of incremental benefits	Acquirer possesses the capacity and competencies necessary to integrate the new business

MINI-CASE

Credit Agricole Became the World's Third Largest Bank in 2004 But Sold Off Some Assets in 2008

Agricole started a long-anticipated consolidation of European banks by acquiring Credit Lyonnais SA. Becoming the third largest bank in the world, it was believed that Credit Agricole's actions might force a response from large European rivals such as Barclays Bank of the United Kingdom and Deutsche Bank. With the expansion of the European Union to include many new Eastern European countries, the scale of banking has become larger.

Because of limited growth opportunities in their mature home markets, each large European bank desires to expand by entering other countries. Furthermore, many of these banks' largest clients operate across borders in the European Union. Thus, banks want to follow and continue to serve their clients as they expand to new geographic areas. In 2003, Credit Agricole, with its 16 percent holding in Bancalntesa SpA, Italy's largest bank, was the only large European bank to own a position in a fairly large European rival.

Consolidation of European banks proceeded much more slowly in Europe than in the United States, where the banking industry continued to consolidate through acquisitions. Each European country's desire to have its own major bank has influenced decisions about acquisitions. Yet potential consolidation in the European banking sector picked up steam in 2007 and 2008 with the financial crises emanating from the United States. In fact, the largest acquisition in banking history was announced in 2007. A consortium of European banks, Royal Bank of Scotland, Banco Santander Central Hispano (Spain), and Fortis (Belgium-Dutch) acquired ABN Amro (Dutch) for $99.8 billion. The three-bank consortium outbid Barclays (U.K.) for the Dutch bank. The sales price was 25 times its annual earnings. The three banks agreed to split the ABN assets among themselves.

The losing bidder, Barclays, in turn decided to acquire Expobank, a private commercial bank in Russia to expand its reach in the global banking sector. Barclays paid $745 million for the Russian bank. Alternatively, Agricole announced a fourth-quarter 2007 loss of $1.3 billion and decided in early 2008 not to make further acquisitions at the time. In fact, it sold some assets (e.g., its stake in a utility, Suez) for $1.6 billion to shore up its balance sheet.

Sources: Laferty Ltd., 2004, Europe's banks commence mating season, *European Banker*, February: 1; J. Wrighton, 2004, France's Credit Agricole is making its move; Carron faces challenge of turning bank into European powerhouse; regional holders may pose hurdle, *Wall Street Journal*, June 3: C1; V. Ram, 2007, Sum of ABN's parts worth more than the whole, *Forbes*, www.forbes.com, October 5; D. Larner & A. Lagorce, 2008, Agricole sells Suez stake as banks bolster capital, *Wall Street Journal*, http://online.wsj.com, January 15; V. Ram, 2008, Barclays banks on Russia, *Forbes*, www.forbes.com, March 3; L. Laurent, 2008, Credit Agricole rises on bid rule-out, *Forbes*, www.forbes.com, March 5.

Questions

1. What would be the strategic motivations for a consolidation of large banks in the European Union? (*Hint*: Examine this chapter's Focusing on Strategy.)
2. What other issues in addition to strategic concerns are hindering or motivating banks that are considering acquiring other banks in the European Union?
3. What competitive reactions do you expect from the Credit Agricole in response to the ABN acquisition and Barclays' acquisition of the Russian bank?
4. If you were the CEO of Agricole, would you pursue an acquisition target in the near future? Why or why not?

EXPERIENTIAL EXERCISES

Exercise One: 2008's Biggest Mergers and Acquisitions

The following list gives the top 10 mergers and/or acquisitions for 2008 taken from *CNNMoney.com* (http://money.cnn.com/news/deals/mergers/biggest.html). Select two of these firms and determine (a) whether the deal was a merger or an acquisition, (b) whether it

occurred across borders and what the nationality of the target and acquirer were, (c) whether the deal was friendly or a takeover, and (d) how many of the five strategic reasons in Figure 7.1 were applicable to the deal. Provide supporting arguments for your conclusions.

Target Name	Acquirer Name	Deal Date	Value of Deal ($ millions)
Yahoo! Inc.	Microsoft Corp.	Feb. 1, 2008	43,711.60
Inmobiliaria Colonial SA	Investment Corp. of Dubai	Jan. 31, 2008	15,213.20

(Continued)

Target Name	Acquirer Name	Deal Date	Value of Deal ($ millions)
Rio Tinto PLC	Shining Prospect Pte Ltd	Feb. 1, 2008	14,284.20
Alcon Inc.	Novartis AG	Apr. 7, 2008	10,547.50
Bolsa de Valores de Sao Paulo	Bolsa Brasileira de Mercadorias	Feb. 20, 2008	10,309.10
Millennium Pharmaceuticals Inc.	Mahogany Acquisition Corp	Apr. 10, 2008	8,734.10
Citigroup Inc	Government of Singapore Investment Corp Pte Ltd	Jan. 15, 2008	6,880.00
Weyerhaeuser Co. (Containerboard Packaging and Recycling Business)	International Paper Co.	Mar. 17, 2008	6,000.00
MMX Mineracao e Metalicos SA (Certain Assets)	Anglo American PLC	Jan. 17, 2008	5,500.00
Scania AB	Volkswagen AG	Mar. 3, 2008	4,377.50

BIZ FLIX

Meet the Parents: Assessing the Greg Focker Acquisition

Business acquisitions have a striking parallel to a major acquisition in people's lives—marrying into another family. Think of this scene from *Meet the Parents* as a metaphorical look at business acquisitions. Carefully consider the following questions while viewing the scene.

Greg Focker (Ben Stiller) hopes his weekend visit to his girlfriend Pam's (Teri Polo's) home will leave a positive impression on her parents. Unfortunately, Jack Byrnes (Robert De Niro), Pam's father, immediately dislikes him. Jack's fondness does not improve after Greg accidentally breaks the urn holding the ashes of Jack's mother. Other factors do not help the developing relationship: Greg is Jewish, while Jack is a WASP ex-CIA psychological professor. These factors blend well to cause the continuous development of stress and stress-related responses of all parties involved.

This scene comes from the "No More Lies" segment near the film's end. Jack says, "Is your name Gaylord Focker?" Jack holds Greg's wrists to feel his pulse. This scene ends after Jack says, "Will you be my son-in-law?" while holding the engagement ring. The film continues to its end after this scene with Jack suggesting to his wife Dina (Blythe Danner) that they meet the Fockers, Greg's parents.

What to Watch for and Ask Yourself
1. Does Jack Byrnes carefully screen Greg Focker, the potential acquisition?
2. Does Jack Byrnes apply due diligence as described in this chapter while assessing Greg Focker?
3. Are there any pitfalls in this acquisition? Recall this chapter's discussion of pitfalls and apply them to this scene.

ENDNOTES

1. J. E. Ashton, F. X. Cook Jr., & P. Schmitz, 2003, Uncovering hidden value in a midsize manufacturing company, *Harvard Business Review*, 81(6): 4–12.
2. M. Karnitschnig, 2008, For deal makers, tale of two halves, *Wall Street Journal*, http://online.wsj.com, January 2.
3. J. Baer, 2008, Deals in the air: Rising costs force U.S. carriers to seek mergers, *Financial Times*, www.ft.com, February 18.
4. X. Yin & M. Shanley, 2008, Industry determinants of the "merger versus alliance" decision, *Academy of Management Review*, 33: 473–491.
5. R. Kapoor & K. Lim, 2007, The impact of acquisitions on the productivity of inventors at semiconductor firms: A synthesis of knowledge-based and incentive-based perspectives, *Academy of Management Journal*, 50: 1133–1155.
6. C. Marquis & M. Lounsbury, 2007, Vive la resistance: Competing logics and the consolidation of U.S. community banking, *Academy of Management Journal*, 50: 799–820.
7. A. R. Sorkin, 2007, When unequals try to merge as equals, *New York Times*, www.nytimes.com, February 25.

8. T. S. Gabrielsen, 2003, Conglomerate mergers: Vertical mergers in disguise? *International Journal of the Economics of Business,* 10(1): 1–16.

9. S. Ellison & M. Karnitschnig, 2007, Murdoch wins his bid for Dow Jones, *Wall Street Journal,* http://online.wsj.com, August 1; A. Lashinsky, 2004, Murdoch's air war, *Fortune,* December 13: 131–138.

10. D. Bank & D. Clark, 2004, Microsoft, SAP teach a lesson: Eat or be eaten, *Wall Street Journal,* June 9: C1, C4.

11. M. Karnitschnig, 2008, Microsoft pitches merger vision to Yahoo at meeting, *Wall Street Journal,* http://online.wsj.com, March 14.

12. H. A. Krishnan, M. A. Hitt, & D. Park, 2007, Acquisition premiums, subsequent workforce reductions and postacquisition performance, *Journal of Management Studies,* 44: 709–732.

13. G. M. McNamara, J. Haleblian, & B. J. Dykes, 2008, The performance implications of participating in an acquisition wave: Early mover advantages, bandwagon effects, and the moderating influence of industry characteristics and acquirer tactics, *Academy of Management Journal,* 51: 113–130; B. Mascarenhas, A. Kumaraswam, D. Day, & A. Baveja, 2002, Five strategies for rapid firm growth and how to implement them, *Managerial and Decision Economics,* 23: 317–330.

14. S.-F. Chen, 2008, The motives for international acquisitions: Capability procurements, strategic considerations, and the role of ownership structures, *Journal of International Business Studies,* 39: 454–471.

15. L. Wang & E. J. Zajac, 2007, Alliance or acquisition? A dyadic perspective on interfirm resource combinations, *Strategic Management Journal,* 28: 1291–1317.

16. A. L. Ranft & M. D. Lord, 2002, Acquiring new technologies and capabilities: A grounded model of acquisition implementation, *Organization Science,* 13: 420–441.

17. J. Gammelgaard, 2004, Access to competence: An emerging acquisition motive, *European Business Forum,* Spring: 44–48.

18. M. Warner, 2002, Can GE light up the market again? *Fortune,* November 11: 108–117.

19. D. R. Dalton, M. A. Hitt, S. T. Certo, & C. M. Dalton, 2008, The fundamental agency problem and its mitigation: Independence, equity and the market for corporate control, in J. P. Walsh & A. P. Brief (Eds.), *The Academy of Management Annals,* New York: Lawrence Erlbaum Associates, 1–64.

20. R. J. Aiello & M. D. Watkins, 2000, The fine art of friendly acquisition, *Harvard Business Review,* 78(6): 100–107.

21. L. Capron & J.-C. Shen, 2007, Acquisitions of private vs. public firms: Private information, target selection, and acquirer returns, *Strategic Management Journal,* 28: 891–911.

22. G. Cullinan, J.-M. Le Roux, & R.-M. Weddigen, 2004, When to walk away from a deal, *Harvard Business Review,* 82(4): 96–104.

23. D. Lieberman, 2008, Clear Channel's plan to go private stumbles, *USA Today,* March 27: 1B.

24. T. Vestring, T. Rouse, & S. Rovit, 2004, Integrate where it matters, *MIT Sloan Management Review,* 46(1): 15–18.

25. M. Blyler & R. W. Coff, 2003, Dynamic capabilities, social capital, and rent appropriation: Ties that split pies, *Strategic Management Journal,* 24: 677–697.

26. R. A. Weber & C. F. Camerer, 2003, Cultural conflict and merger failure: An experimental approach, *Management Science,* 49: 400–415.

27. T. Saxton & M. Dollinger, 2004, Target reputation and appropriability: Picking and deploying resources in acquisitions, *Journal of Management,* 30: 123–147.

28. P. Puranam & K. Srikanth, 2007, What they know vs. what they do: How acquirers leverage technology acquisitions, *Strategic Management Journal,* 28: 805–825.

29. T. Laamanen, 2007, On the role of acquisition premium in acquisition research, *Strategic Management Journal,* 28: 1359–1369.

30. Y. Weber & E. Menipaz, 2003, Measuring cultural fit in mergers and acquisitions, *International Journal of Business Performance Management,* 5(1): 54–72.

31. A. K. Bucholtz, B. A. Ribbens, & I. T. Houle, 2003, The role of human capital in post-acquisition CEO departure, *Academy of Management Journal,* 46: 506–514.

32. M. A. Hitt, L. Bierman, K. Uhlenbruck, & K. Shimizu, 2006, The importance of resources in the internationalization of professional service firms: The good, the bad and the ugly, *Academy of Management Journal,* 49: 1137–1157; M. A. Hitt, L. Bierman, K. Shimizu, & R. Kochhar, 2001, Direct and moderating effects of human capital on strategy and performance in professional service firms, *Academy of Management Journal,* 44: 13–28.

33. J. A. Krug, 2003, Why do they keep leaving? *Harvard Business Review,* 81(2): 14–15; H. A. Krishnan & D. Park, 2002, The impact of workforce reduction on subsequent performance in major mergers and acquisitions: An exploratory study, *Journal of Business Research,* 55(4): 285–292.

34. D. Lovallo & D. Kahneman, 2003, Delusions of success: How optimism undermines executives' decisions, *Harvard Business Review,* 87(5): 56–64.

35. S. E. Ante, 2008, Sprint's world of pain, *BusinessWeek,* www.businessweek.com, February 28; Sprint's massive loss, 2008, *Financial Times,* www.ft.com, February 28.

36. M. A. Hitt & D. L. Smart, 1994, Debt: A disciplining force for managers or a debilitating force for organizations? *Journal of Management Inquiry,* 3: 144–152.

37. K. Shimizu, 2007, Prospect theory, behavioral theory, and the threat-rigidity hypothesis: Combinative effects on organizational decisions to divest formerly acquired units, *Academy of Management Journal,* 50: 1495–1514.

38. M. L. A. Hayward, 2002, When do firms learn from their acquisition experience? Evidence from 1990–1995, *Strategic Management Journal,* 23: 21–39; M. A. Hitt, J. S. Harrison, & R. D. Ireland, 2001, *Mergers and Acquisitions: A Guide to Creating Value for Stakeholders,* New York: Oxford University Press

39. J. Pfeffer, 2003, The human factor: Curbing the urge to merge, *Business 2.0,* July: 58.

40. N. P. Varaiya, 1988, The "winner's curse" hypothesis and corporate takeovers, *Managerial and Decision Economics,* 9: 209–219.

41. J. L. Morrow, D. G. Sirmon, M. A. Hitt, & T. R. Holcomb, 2007, Creating value in the face of declining performance: Firm strategies and organizational recovery, *Strategic Management Journal,* 28: 271–283.

42. O. Furer, J. R. Pandian, & H. Thomas, 2007, Corporate strategy and shareholder value during decline and turnaround, *Management Decision,* 45: 372–392; K. E. Meyer & E. Lieb-Doczy, 2003, Post-acquisition restructuring as evolutionary process, *Journal of Management Studies,* 40: 459–483; L. Capron, W. Mitchell, & A. Waminathan, 2001, Asset divestiture following horizontal acquisitions: A dynamic view, *Strategic Management Journal,* 22: 817–844.

43. S. L. Gillan, J. W. Kensinger, & J. D. Martin, 2000, Value creation and corporate diversification: The case of Sears, Roebuck & Co., *Journal of Financial Economics,* 55: 103–138.

44. G. McWilliams, 2008, Why Sears must engineer its own makeover, *Wall Street Journal,* http://online.wsj.com, January 15.

45. M. F. Wiersema & J. P. Liebeskind, 1995, The effects of leveraged buyouts on corporate growth and diversification in large firms, *Strategic Management Journal,* 16: 447–460.

46. M. Wright, R. E. Hoskisson, & L. W. Busenitz, 2001, Firm rebirth: Buyouts as facilitators of strategic growth and entrepreneurship, *Academy of Management Executive,* 15(1): 111–125.

47. T. Galpin & M. Herndon, 2008, Merger repair: When M&As go wrong, *Journal of Business Strategy,* 29: 4–12.

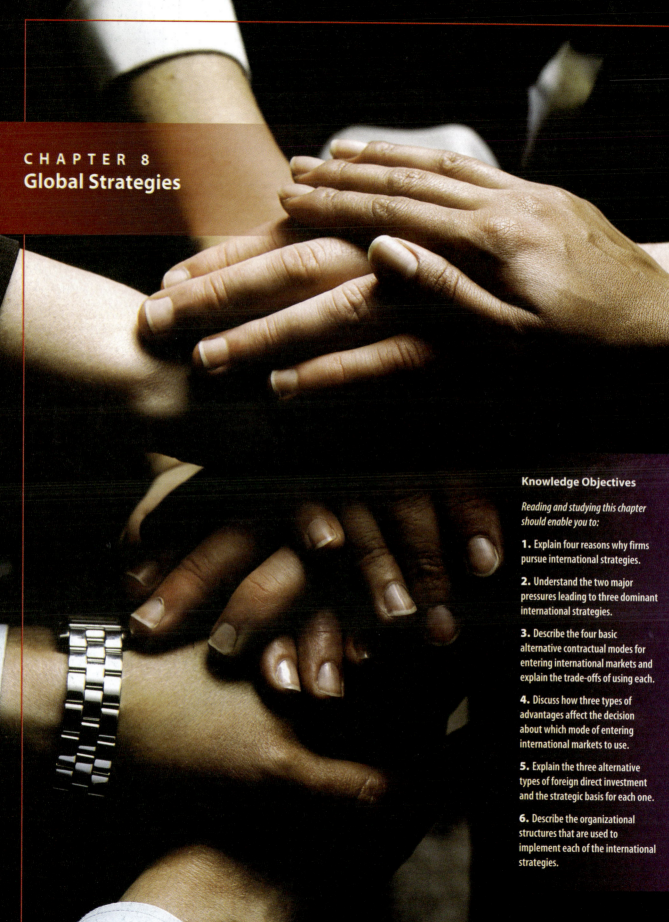

CHAPTER 8
Global Strategies

Knowledge Objectives

Reading and studying this chapter should enable you to:

1. Explain four reasons why firms pursue international strategies.

2. Understand the two major pressures leading to three dominant international strategies.

3. Describe the four basic alternative contractual modes for entering international markets and explain the trade-offs of using each.

4. Discuss how three types of advantages affect the decision about which mode of entering international markets to use.

5. Explain the three alternative types of foreign direct investment and the strategic basis for each one.

6. Describe the organizational structures that are used to implement each of the international strategies.

© BrandX Pictures

Sara Lee Is Creating a Global Buzz

Sara Lee made a number of changes in recent years and is now reaping the benefits of them. First, it decided to sell or spin off its noncore businesses to focus on core and faster-growth businesses. As such, it spun off its well-known Hanes Playtex and Wonderbra apparel units. These actions were taken to focus on its food, beverage, and household products units. Currently, Sara Lee has approximately $12 billion in annual sales with 52,000 employees across 200 countries.

Second, Sara Lee decided to increase its presence in international markets. Because of this change, in 2008, 75 percent of Sara Lee's operating income is from international (non-U.S.) markets. For example, Sara Lee's international beverage unit experienced increases in sales of 23 percent in the first half of 2008 over 2007. A Sara Lee spokesperson stated, "Our international businesses play a major role in Sara Lee's success." The company's presence is growing in major emerging markets, especially Brazil, China, India, and Russia. Because of this new emphasis, some perceive Sara Lee as a European company. For example, its coffee brands sell exceptionally well in France and the Netherlands. In contrast, Sara Lee's North American food business units have single-digit sales growth ranging from 2 percent to slightly less than 7 percent.

© Susan Van Etten

Sara Lee's international expansion has enhanced its growth and financial performance. It now has a 40 percent market share in the single-serve coffee market with the Senseo coffee brand. Its international beverage business has been exceptionally strong and is well-positioned for the market trend of consuming beverages outside the home. Simultaneously, Sara Lee has been expanding its global sourcing for ingredients in its products. It searches for high quality and lower price. Through its centralized global ingredient purchasing, the company obtains about one-third of the ingredients for its new whole grain white bread from foreign suppliers. Finally, the international emphasis has helped the firm to enhance its innovation. For example, it recently announced a partnership with Henkel from the Netherlands to launch a U.S. version of the successful 3Volution air freshener. The U.S. version, Renuzit Tri Scents, releases different fragrances on a regular basis.

These changes and the increasing success of Sara Lee spurred the selection of the firm's CEO, Brenda Barnes, one of *Fortune's* 50 most powerful women. In fact, in 2006, she ranked sixth on this list behind such luminaries as Ann Mulcahy (CEO of Xerox) and Indra Nooyi (CEO of PepsiCo).

Sources: K. Richardson, 2008, Sara Lee's coffee sales create buzz, *Wall Street Journal*, online.wsj.com, April 24; Sara Lee Corporation declares 249th consecutive quarterly dividend, 2008, *Forbes*, www.forbes.com, April 24; Sara Lee highlights strategy for growth at CAGNY's annual conference, *Forbes*, www.forbes.com, February 29; Sara Lee and Henkel partner to launch innovation in the U.S., 2008, *Forbes*, www.forbes.com, February 4; A. Barrionuevo, 2007, Globalization in every loaf, *New York Times*, www.nytimes.com, June 16; A. Schoenfeld, 2007, A multinational loaf, *New York Times*, www.nytimes.com, June 16; Sara Lee's Brenda Barnes named one of *Fortune's* 50 most powerful women, 2006, *CNNMoney*, www.cnnmoney.com, October 12; Sara Lee reports on spinoff plan, 2006, *New York Times*, www.nytimes.com, May 25.

As Focusing on Strategy indicates, expanding international operations is increasingly important to Sara Lee's strategic and financial performance as it enhances the brands it sells throughout the world. The increase in globalization mentioned in Chapter 3 is based on several historical changes in the global business environment. In the first half of the twentieth century, firms wanting to enter new markets were frustrated because of barriers against foreign trade and investments imposed by national governments. After World War I, many countries imposed tariffs and quotas on imported goods that favored local firms; as a result, international trade declined throughout the 1930s. These tariffs and quotas contributed to the severity of the U.S. depression.

However, after World War II, these policies were reversed as major trading powers negotiated reductions in tariffs and quotas and eliminated many barriers to foreign direct investment (FDI). **Foreign direct investment** is a process through which a firm directly invests (beyond exporting and licensing) in a market outside its home country.[1] These negotiations were embodied in the General Agreement on Tariffs and Trade (GATT) and its successor organization the World Trade Organization (WTO). Furthermore, regional trading agreements such as the European Union and the North American Free Trade Agreement (NAFTA) have also relaxed trade and investment barriers among member countries. Thus, globalization has become highly important in the world economy, but equally important has been the development of new technologies and the enhanced skills and capabilities they have facilitated.[2]

Investments in technology, particularly communications and transportation technologies, are making international transactions more feasible and more profitable by reducing the costs of transactions. Similarly, the rapidly growing use of the Internet has affected international transactions by facilitating trade in services such as banking, consulting, and retailing, by making competition between large and smaller firms more reasonable regardless of the product sold, and by creating a more efficient networking capability among businesses. This facilitation of trade is evident in Sara Lee's development of a global purchasing system whereby as much as 40 percent of ingredients for some of its products are provided by foreign suppliers.

These changes are producing a new global competitive landscape where emerging market countries are playing an increasingly important role. Countries such as Brazil, Russia, India, and China (BRIC) are having a greater impact on the global economy and provide opportunities for multinational firms to market their products and to obtain resources (e.g., quality but cheaper labor). In fact, recent predictions suggest that the BRIC countries are likely to be among the top 10 in the size of their economies within the next 30 years.[3] As a result of these changes, managers must develop a global mind-set. A **global mind-set** is a cognitive model that motivates a manager to search for opportunities in foreign markets; to develop strategies that exploit those opportunities; and to coordinate units, tasks, and people in multiple geographic locations throughout the world.[4] Brenda Barnes, CEO of Sara Lee, displays a global mind-set and is obviously building such a mind-set among Sara Lee managers.

Even though significant trends have fostered growth in international business, the costs and risks of doing business outside a firm's domestic market can be significant.[5] The research literature labels these costs the **liability of foreignness**.[6] As Chapter 4 indicated, a firm must have resources that enable it to overcome these additional costs. In this chapter, we discuss firm-specific resources as well as location advantages that help to overcome these costs.

In summary, international strategies are becoming more widespread because of the environmental and technological changes taking place in the twenty-first century.[7] However, firms must still have the resources necessary to formulate and implement a strategy to overcome the continuing costs of the liability of foreign entry. In this chapter, as illustrated in Figure 8.1, we explore the reasons for and types of international strategies that firms use. We begin this important exploration by outlining the motives for using an international strategy. Next,

foreign direct investment

a process through which a firm directly invests (beyond exporting and licensing) in a market outside its home country

global mind-set

a cognitive model that motivates a manager to search for opportunities in foreign markets; to develop strategies that exploit those opportunities; and to coordinate units, tasks, and people in multiple geographic locations throughout the world

liability of foreignness

the costs and risks of doing business outside a firm's domestic market

Figure 8.1 International Strategy: Motives, Strategic Approach, Mode of Entry, and Structural Implementation

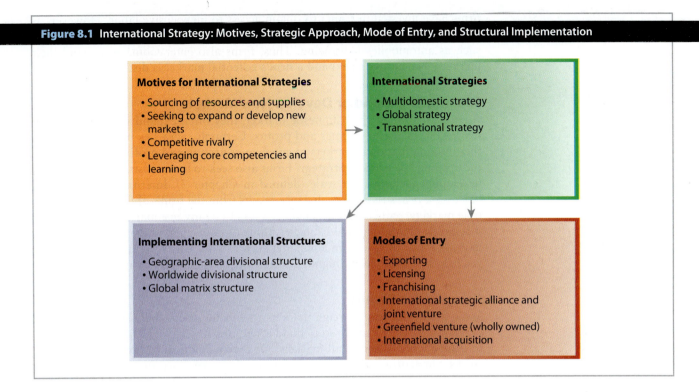

we explore the basic international strategies employed by firms. After a strategy is chosen, managers must choose a mode of international entry. Finally, the firm must choose an organizational structure and accompanying processes to implement the chosen strategy.

Motives for International Strategies

A number of motives drive the use of international strategies. Next, we describe four of the most prominent motives.

Use of Current Resources and Access to New Resources

Commonly, companies seek to gain economies of scale and scope in the use of their current resources by expanding into new markets, increasingly foreign markets.[8] Firms may use their well-known product brands, such as those held by Sara Lee, to enter new international markets. Firms commonly use what is referred to as social capital—that is, partners in alliances and networks—to help them enter and compete effectively in international markets.[9] At times, some firms enter international markets to access new resources. For example, they may obtain access to valuable raw materials, specialized knowledge, or low-cost labor.[10] One resource commonly sought over the years has been valuable sources of supply.

During the Middle Ages, for example, Italy used its political and military strength in Venice, Genoa, and Florence as the foundation for its ability to be a major center of international commerce and banking. During this time, Italy was the major trading link between Europe and Asia. However, after these trade routes were severed by the Turks in 1453, European governments sought new ocean routes to the Far East. This situation is one of the reasons the Spanish government backed Christopher Columbus's expedition to sail west from Europe, looking for such routes. Inadvertently, as we know, Columbus found new sources of supply in the Americas, a discovery that ultimately led to the colonization of the Americas by European countries. As we explained in Focusing on Strategy, Sara Lee obtains a number of its product ingredients from foreign sources. Many firms have invested in China to obtain access to inexpensive labor. However, as China's markets continue to provide a source of supply, demand for products such as automobiles is growing. Thus, firms also enter China to expand their markets. The motive to expand a firm's potential market is discussed next.

Seeking to Expand or Develop New Markets

As firms mature in their domestic market, they often expand into international markets to increase revenues and profits. Certainly, Sara Lee has expanded further into international markets to enhance its growth and profits, as described in the opening Focusing on Strategy. Firms also seek to lower costs of production by developing economies of scale (defined in Chapter 3). International expansion balances a firm's risk.[11] This balance results from the firm's ability to sell in multiple markets, reducing its dependency on sales in any one market.[12] To show the magnitude of international strategies, think of how many of the products you use that are made by a foreign company, such as your car, your stereo system, and your clothes. This clearly highlights the global nature of the world's economy.

Competitive Rivalry

Some businesses enter foreign markets to enhance their ability to compete with major rivals. They may do so to build economies of scale or scope, allowing them to compete better across all markets. Or they may do so to prevent or reduce a rival's competitive advantage.[13] For example, Coca-Cola and PepsiCo are both aggressively expanding their international operations. Of course, each firm is trying to prevent the other from gaining a competitive advantage in global markets.[14] Think about this outcome. If Pepsi or Coke gained a significant advantage in global markets, the additional profitability earned as a result of that advantage could be used to damage the competitor in the all-important U.S. market. About 40 percent of PepsiCo's revenues come from international markets.[15] The relationship between earth-moving equipment firms Caterpillar and Komatsu are similar as each firm actively competes against its rival in global markets.[16] This competitive rivalry exists to prevent a competitor from gaining a significant advantage in any one country or region.

Interestingly, other firms pursue international ventures to avoid domestic competition. In the local Japanese automobile market, competition is very intense because of the number of large firms competing in the local market, including Toyota, Honda, Nissan, Mazda, Mitsubishi, Suzuki, Subaru, Isuzu, and Daihatsu. Part of the reason for moving into the international market was the nature of domestic competition.[17] Japanese automakers have largely been successful in their international ventures. In fact, the "big two" in the United States, Ford and General Motors, have been losing money in their domestic market primarily because of Japanese competitors.[18]

Leveraging Core Competencies and Learning

As we discussed in Chapter 4, firms invest heavily to develop core competencies. After a firm has developed a core competence that is a competitive advantage in its domestic market, the firm may be able to use that competitive advantage in international markets as well. Research has shown that competitive advantages based on knowledge-based resources often contained in core competencies produce faster and larger international expansion than do physical asset-based advantages (e.g., property).[19] When the competitive advantage is in R&D, the firm may have the foundation needed to rely on innovation as the source of entry to international markets. We speak further on the use of innovation to enter new markets in Chapter 10.

Learning is also an important reason for international expansion. Firms often invest in countries that have centers of excellence in industries such as semiconductors. These firms enter international markets to gain access to product and manufacturing process knowledge. For example, large pharmaceuticals firms have formed alliances with foreign partners in order to learn about new drug

Boeing's Global Sourcing Bites Back

Boeing's development of the new Dreamliner aircraft allowed it to retake its global market share lead from Airbus. Orders for more than 900 of these aircraft were obtained by Boeing after it announced this new lighter, quieter, and more fuel-efficient airplane. Yet it has experienced difficulties in making its first deliveries, setting it 1.5 years behind schedule. These delays harmed Boeing in a number of ways.

Boeing's ability to be competitive in recent years has been partly based on its global alliances with a number of parts suppliers. In fact, approximately 60 percent of the components of Boeings commercial aircraft are provided by foreign firms. Even more important is the fact that almost 70 percent of the new Dreamliner's parts come from foreign suppliers. The Dreamliner was specifically designed to include manufacturing processes by a large number of foreign suppliers because the manufacturing space required to manufacture it was estimated to be 3 million square feet, which would have been too costly to build. Also, using many suppliers for different parts allows them to be manufactured simultaneously rather than sequentially. In theory, this approach should allow an aircraft to be manufactured more quickly.

While Boeing experiences some clear benefits from using a series for foreign suppliers, its global supply network must be managed effectively. For example, the major delays in delivery of its Dreamliner orders are largely the result of delays in the

© AP Photos/Boeing

completion of major components by its foreign suppliers. Thus, problems with the Dreamliner's global supply chain are harming Boeing's reputation with customers.

In addition to the harm done to Boeing's revenue stream, the airline recently lost a major U.S. government defense contract to a consortium of companies from Europe to build refueling tankers. Although many reasons were given for the decision, some analysts believe that Boeing's delays because of problems with its global supply chain contributed to the decision. For example, it won contracts to build tankers for Japan and Italy but was a year late in making its first delivery on the contracts.

Boeing's management is now feverishly trying to resolve these problems to avoid any further embarrassment and loss of contracts. Thus, global activities have advantages and disadvantages. Clearly, global operations present challenges of coordination and management that go well beyond those experienced in domestic operations.

Sources: J. L. Lunsford, 2008, Boeing CEO fights headwind, *Wall Street Journal*, http://online.wsj.com, April 25; J. Crown, 2008, Boeing's McNerney digging out of a hole, *BusinessWeek*, www.businessweek.com, April 23; M. V. Copeland, 2008, Boeing's big dream, CNN Money, http://cnnmoney.com, April 24; H. Weitzman, 2008, Dreamliner lays burden on Boeing, *Financial times*, www.ft.com, April 9; K. Epstein & J. Crown, 2008, Globalization bites Boeing, *BusinessWeek*, March 24, 32; C. Mallack, 2008, Boeing's trouble with tankers, *BusinessWeek*, www.businessweek.com, March 11.

research that could lead to developing and introducing new products into their domestic market.[20]

As explained in Understanding Strategy: Learning from Failure, not all global operations are effective for the firm. The Boeing example of global sourcing shows the benefits and costs of such activity. Clearly, Boeing's global supply chain has helped it to be competitive with Airbus in global markets. Yet the complexities of a global supply chain and coordination difficulties are shown by its major delays in fulfilling contracts to produce aircraft. Research supports the notion that international expansion causes difficulties for firms and sometimes is not profitable because of these challenges.[21]

We've discussed motives influencing firms to use strategies to compete in international markets, learning that costs of international expansion also exist. As you would expect, firms can choose from several different strategies to compete in international markets. We discuss these strategies in the next few sections.

International Strategies

Firms consider two important and potentially competing issues when choosing an international strategy: the need for global efficiencies and the need to customize a good or service for a particular host country market.[22] Generally, efficiency increases when the firm can sell its current good or service in multiple international markets. In contrast, the need for customization to serve international markets increases when the firm sells a good or service that must be adapted specifically to a particular local market.

Firms seeking global efficiency may decide to locate in countries where their production and distribution costs will be low. For example, a firm may locate in a country with low labor costs. It might also obtain economies of scale by building factories that can serve customers in more than a single country. Alternatively, by broadening their product line in countries they enter, firms can achieve economies of scope and thereby reduce their production and marketing costs for related products.

In some international settings, firms can be more successful by customizing their products to meet local market tastes and interests. For instance, KFC adapted its restaurant foods to fit the culture and taste preferences of local markets. KFC offers more fish dishes in Asian countries and less chicken, for example. Language can also present challenges as the following indicates: "Pepsi-Cola went into Taiwan and carefully translated its slogan, 'Come alive with the Pepsi generation.' However, the translation came out as 'Pepsi will bring your ancestors back from the dead.' And, KFC's slogan 'Finger licking good,' in Chinese translates to, 'Eat your fingers off.'"[23]

As shown in Figure 8.2, the need for global efficiency and the need to satisfy a local host country market's unique needs result in a two-dimensional matrix that illustrates the different global strategies. We next describe the three international strategies shown in Figure 8.2.

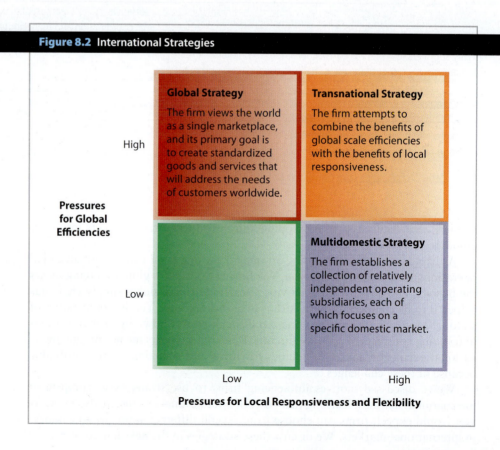

Figure 8.2 International Strategies

Global Strategy

The firm views the world as a single marketplace, and its primary goal is to create standardized goods and services that will address the needs of customers worldwide.

Transnational Strategy

The firm attempts to combine the benefits of global scale efficiencies with the benefits of local responsiveness.

Multidomestic Strategy

The firm establishes a collection of relatively independent operating subsidiaries, each of which focuses on a specific domestic market.

Pressures for Global Efficiencies — High / Low

Pressures for Local Responsiveness and Flexibility — Low / High

The Multidomestic Strategy

The **multidomestic strategy** is an action plan that the firm develops to produce and sell unique products in different markets. To use this strategy, a firm establishes a relatively independent set of operating subsidiaries in which each subsidiary develops specific products for a particular domestic market. Each subsidiary is free to customize its products' marketing campaign and operating techniques to best meet the needs of local customers. The multidomestic strategy is particularly effective when clear differences between national markets exist; potential economies of scale for production, distribution, and marketing are low; and the cost of coordination between the parent and foreign subsidiaries is high. Because each subsidiary must be responsive to the local market, the parent usually delegates considerable power and authority to managers of host country subsidiaries. Many multinational corporations used the multidomestic strategy during World War II because it was difficult to communicate and transfer technologies. Many European firms also adopted this strategy because of the cultural and language differences they needed to overcome in order to conduct business in each European country.

In the early part of the twenty-first century, the French defense contractor French Thomson-CSF transformed into a global defense and aerospace electronics group called Thales SA. Thales won contracts worldwide by using a multidomestic strategy. It has become a local supplier in six countries outside France to include Britain, the Netherlands, Australia, South Africa, South Korea, and Singapore. However, it continues to expand its network through acquisitions and joint ventures. For example, it acquired Alcatel in 2006 and recently formed a joint venture with the Samtel Group to manufacture and sell avionics systems in India.[24]

© AFP/Getty Images

The Global Strategy

The **global strategy** is an action plan that the firm develops to produce and sell standardized products in different markets. With this strategy, a firm uses a central divisional office to develop, produce, and sell its standardized products throughout the world. A firm using a global strategy seeks to capture economies of scale in production and marketing, as well as economies of scope and location advantage. Because the global strategy requires worldwide coordination, the production and marketing strategies are usually centralized with decisions made at a division headquarters. Mercedes-Benz, a unit of Daimler, uses the global strategy to sell its products in many global markets. This strategy is successful for Mercedes-Benz because its products are known for their quality and reliability.[25] However, because of the importance of a particular location for access to critical customers and markets or access to financial resources, a firm may move its headquarters to a foreign setting.[26] It is important to note that at times, the global strategy presents difficulties in marketing the firm's standardized products to local consumer markets. For example, both Microsoft and Nintendo encountered difficulty using a global strategy to sell their platforms (Xbox for Microsoft; GameCube for Nintendo) outside their home markets.

The Transnational Strategy

The **transnational strategy** is an action plan the firm develops to produce and sell somewhat unique, yet somewhat standardized, products in different markets. With this strategy, the firm attempts to combine the benefits of global scale efficiencies with the advantages of being locally responsive in a country or geographic region; it requires both centralization and decentralization simultaneously. IKEA, a worldwide furniture producer, employs the transnational strategy. In using this strategy, IKEA relies on standardization of products with global production and

multidomestic strategy
an action plan that the firm develops to produce and sell unique products in different markets

global strategy
an action plan that the firm develops to produce and sell standardized products in different markets

transnational strategy
an action plan that the firm develops to produce and sell somewhat unique, yet somewhat standardized, products in different markets

Schlumberger, the Stealth Transnational

Schlumberger is the largest firm in the oil service industry. It is considered to have the best technology among its rivals and has been highly successful. In 2007, its sales reached $21 billion and its operating earnings increased by 38 percent to almost $7 billion. Its nearest rival, Halliburton, achieved annual sales of $15 billion with operating

© AFP/Getty Images

earnings totaling about $3.5 billion. Schlumberger has more than 80,000 employees across operations in 80 countries.

Schlumberger's success is exemplified by its 21 percent growth in revenues in 2007. It accomplished its success using a unique strategy that may transform the global oil industry and spell trouble for the large global oil companies. Schlumberger increased its market share of the oil services market by stealthily moving into new markets. It uses "stealth" by acquiring local firms (or sometimes setting up local subsidiaries), injecting its technology and knowledge of managing projects, while simultaneously keeping the local culture and company names. Using this approach, Schlumberger has been highly successful in Russia in recent years. In fact, the firm has almost 14,000 employees in Russia and expects its operations there to rival those in the United States in a few years.

Schlumberger has also been a primary service provider to government-owned oil companies; thus, it competes with many of the major oil companies (e.g., ExxonMobil and Royal Dutch Shell). It does not ask for an equity position in the oil as do many of the majors and keeps the local culture in its operations, thereby making them more compatible with local companies.

Schlumberger developed a new business called Integrated Project Management (IPM), which often competes directly with the major oil companies. IPM offers almost any service to local companies, including managing and operating drilling programs and production. It will take some of the risk to enjoy greater rewards (if the well is successful) but does not want a stake in the oil reserves.

Schlumberger has also enjoyed significant success in Saudi Arabia and Mexico. A former executive with Saudi Aramco suggested that Schlumberger played a major role in the development of Saudi's oil fields. Likewise, some of IPM's largest contracts have been in Mexico. Schlumberger is continuously searching for new opportunities as well. For example, it has partnered in joint ventures with Saxon Energy sources in Mexico and Columbia. In fact, Schlumberger has recently been negotiating a possible acquisition of Saxon, which has major oil well–drilling operations in North and South America.

Schlumberger is also innovative, exemplified by its recent introduction of the world's first wireless broadband service for offshore and remote oil drilling rigs and productions operations. It allows a more seamless communication between central units and remote operations and enables employees at these facilities to maintain regular communications with family and friends.

Sources: Wireless world first for offshore workers, 2008, Schlumberger, www.slb.com, April 25; Saxon, Schlumberger in takeover talks, 2008, *The Canadian Press*, www.reportonbusiness.com, April 21; L. Motta, 2008, Schlumberger expects strong year, *Forbes*, www.forbes.com, April 18; Nibbling big oil's lunch, 2008, *Financial times*, www.ft.com, April 16; S. Reed, 2008, The stealth oil giant, *BusinessWeek*, www.businessweek.com, January 3.

distribution, but it also has a system (called "democratic design") through which new designs for local markets are developed and introduced. Democratic design is helping IKEA produce products that meet the tastes of local customers. IKEA is a world leader in furniture production and distribution and is now one of the top furniture retailers in the United States. In fact, 10 percent of American homes have at least one IKEA item.[27] Although the transnational strategy is more difficult to manage and expensive to implement, it is often the most effective international strategy for facilitating learning. The balance of centralization and decentralization usually results in a corporate culture that promotes transfer of knowledge among subsidiaries and a transnational diffusion of organizational practices.[28] The multidomestic strategy uses a decentralized authority structure.

This structure makes it difficult to transfer knowledge across subsidiaries. The global strategy, on the other hand, centralizes decision making, which hampers new knowledge development. When using the global strategy, the firm learns less from different host country markets because of its focus on exploiting the firm's current knowledge in each of the markets rather than learning from each market to adapt the products.

As suggested in Understanding Strategy: Learning from Success, Schlumberger has been highly successful using the transnational strategy. It acquires, forms joint ventures, or develops new subsidiaries for local markets, injecting its technology and knowledge of oil services but tries to maintain the local culture and "flavor" of the operation. As result, Schlumberger is the largest and most successful oil services firm in the world.

Modes of International Market Entry

After a firm decides to pursue an international strategy, it must choose a mode for entering new foreign markets. Factors affecting the choice of an entry mode are presented in Figure 8.3.[29] These factors include firm-specific resource advantages, country-specific or location advantages, internal coordination or administrative advantages, need for control, and resource availability. We begin with an explanation of each mode of entry followed by a discussion of how each potential advantage affects the choice of entry mode.

Entry Modes

Exporting Perhaps the simplest and most common mode of entry is exporting domestic products to a foreign country. **Exporting** is the process of sending goods and services from one country to another for distribution, sale, and service. The advantage of exporting is that the firm can gradually enter an international market without taking too many risks. Exporting also has the advantage of helping the firm to acquire knowledge about a local market before making large investments.

exporting
the process of sending goods and services from one country to another for distribution, sale, and service

---

Figure 8.3 International Modes of Entry and Decision Factors

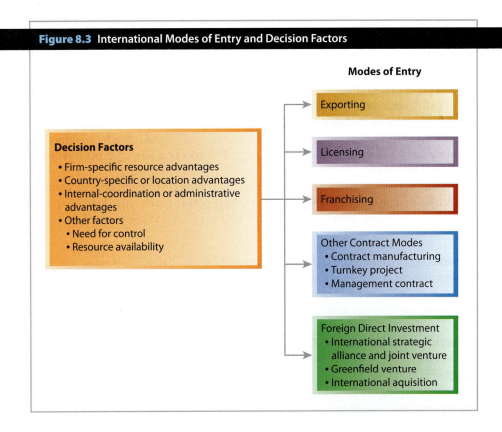

But exporting isn't without problems. Firms exporting their products are vulnerable to tariffs and often encounter logistical challenges in getting products to an international market and especially to the ultimate consumer in those markets. Exporting firms also are likely to be in conflict with local distributors who may want to distribute the firm's products instead.

Licensing   **Licensing** is the process of entering an international market by leasing the right to use the firm's intellectual property—technology, work methods, patents, copyrights, brand names, or trademarks—to a firm doing business in the targeted international market. The firm doing the leasing is the licensor, and the firm receiving the license is the licensee. Licensing is popular because it involves little direct cost or risk for the licensor. Electronic Arts successfully uses this strategy as it licenses games worldwide to game platform or hardware producers such as Sony (PlayStation), Nintendo (GameCube), and Microsoft (Xbox). These firms are willing to pay a license fee to Electronic Arts to have rights to the firm's innovative games and titles. Through licensing, Electronic Arts generates revenues and develops new video games, thereby stimulating further demand for its games and other products. The firm had sales revenue of approximately $3.1 billion in 2007.[30] Although licensing has low financial risks, it provides few opportunities for profit growth. Licensing may provide a low-cost means to assess market potential, but it also creates dependence on the licensee for exploiting that potential. Another risk is that the licensee can learn the technology and become a competitor of the licensor. Microsoft, for instance, is a software producer and has produced its own video games.

Franchising   Franchising is a special form of licensing and is discussed further in Chapter 9 as a cooperative strategy. **Franchising** is the licensing of a good or service and business model to partners for specified fees (usually a signing fee and a percentage of the franchisee's revenues or profits). The franchisor provides trademarks, operating systems, and well-known products as well as service support such as advertising, specialized training, and quality-assurance programs. McDonald's has developed a successful global franchising system. Pizza Hut, KFC, and Taco Bell have also franchised restaurants worldwide. Benetton uses franchised retail stores to distribute stylish clothing in more than 120 countries.

Other Contracting Modes   Contract manufacturing is another popular contractual mode of entry. Large firms in Asia, such as Taiwan Semiconductor Manufacturing Company (TSMC), manufacture chips for large clients such as Hewlett-Packard (HP). TSMC and other big Asian contract manufacturers are expected to do better than smaller U.S. firms because their cost advantage in Asia has attracted large clients, such as HP, that can invest significant amounts of capital, thereby enabling the manufacturers to keep their competitive edge. The cost of a new chip plant requires more than $2 billion.

Similarly, turnkey projects, often construction projects to build large infrastructure facilities such as coal- or gas-fired electrical power plants, are done on a contractual basis. Management agreements to run such facilities are done on a contractual basis as well.

Approaches to Foreign Direct Investment   With FDI entry modes, the firm has greater control of its destiny in the international market it enters, but FDI investments are not insulated from risk. Next, we discuss three approaches to FDI: strategic alliances and joint ventures, greenfield ventures, and acquisitions.

International Strategic Alliances and Joint Ventures

International strategic alliances represent a cooperative agreement in which home and host country firms work closely together. In the case of a joint venture, "working together" results in creating a separate company to promote the partners' mutual interests (joint ventures and strategic alliances are discussed further in

---

licensing

the process of entering an international market by leasing the right to use the firm's intellectual property, technology, work methods, patents, copyrights, brand names, or trademarks to a firm doing business in the targeted international market

franchising

the licensing of a good or service and business model to partners for specified fees (usually a signing fee and a percentage of the franchisee's revenues or profits)

Chapter 9). Firms in emerging economies often want to form international alliances and ventures to gain access to sophisticated technologies that are new to them (learning from their partner).[31] This type of arrangement can benefit the foreign firm as well, providing access to a new market without the firm paying tariffs to do so (because of its local partner). However, the firm with the valuable technology needs to ensure that its partner doesn't copy it.[32] Therefore, in the selection of a partner, it is important to choose one that is reliable and trustworthy.[33]

Greenfield Venture

In a **greenfield venture**, a firm buys or leases land, constructs a new facility and hires or transfers managers and employees, and then independently launches a new operation (commonly called a *wholly owned subsidiary*) without involvement of a partner. The firm maintains full control of its operations with a greenfield venture. More control is especially advantageous if the firm has proprietary technology. Research also suggests that "wholly owned subsidiaries and expatriate staff are preferred" in service industries where "close contacts with end customers" and "high levels of professional skills, specialized know-how, and customization" are required.[34] The major disadvantage with a greenfield venture launched in an international market is that it takes time to implement and gain acceptance in the market.[35] A lack of experience with and knowledge about the international local market makes it hard for the greenfield venture to have rapid success. Therefore, firms establishing greenfield ventures in international markets need to be patient in order to achieve success with the venture.

International Acquisition

The final FDI entry mode is one in which a firm acquires an existing host country firm. By acquiring a current business, the purchaser gains control over the acquired firm's assets, employees, technology, brand names, and distribution. Therefore, entry is much faster than by other modes. Wal-Mart entered Germany and the United Kingdom by acquiring local firms.

Using the acquisition entry mode is not without risk. The main risk centers on the fact that the acquiring firm often assumes all of the acquired firm's liabilities.[36] Complicating cross-border acquisitions is the fact that the firms are commonly from countries with different cultures and institutional frameworks. Thus, integrating the two firms can be more difficult.[37] This factor was one of the problems leading to the failure of the merger between Daimler (German firm) and Chrysler (U.S. firm). The risk in these acquisitions is also illustrated by Wal-Mart's withdrawal from the German market only a few years after it entered.

We've explored the entry modes available to firms that want to enter international markets. Next, we consider the factors influencing the firm's choice of an entry mode, as illustrated in Figure 8.3.

Factors Affecting the Selection of Entry Mode

Firm-Specific Resource Advantages

Firm-specific resource advantages are the core competencies that provide a competitive advantage over a firm's rivals.[38] As we recall from our discussions in Chapter 4, core competencies are often based largely on intangible resources. When the success of a firm's entry into an international market relies on transferring core competencies, an entry mode involving an equity stake should be used. Therefore, a joint venture, an acquisition, and a greenfield venture represent the best entry mode choices in these cases because the firm retains more control over its competencies. However, if the firm-specific advantage is a brand name, which is protected by law, a licensing or franchising entry mode may also be a good choice.

greenfield venture

a venture in which a firm buys or leases land, constructs a new facility and hires or transfers managers and employees, and then independently launches a new operation (commonly called a *wholly owned subsidiary*) without involvement of a partner

Country-Specific or Location Advantages

Country-specific or location advantages are concerned with the desirability of producing in the home country versus locating production and distribution assets in the host country. If country-specific advantages for production are stronger in the

home country, exporting is likely the best choice for entering an international market. Such location advantages can be influenced by costs of production and transportation requirements as well as the needs of the intended customers. Many firms, for instance, have located their assets in Turkey because its geographic, religious, linguistic, and cultural ties provide opportunities to enter Central Asian markets of the former Soviet Union as well as markets in the Middle East.[39]

However, political risks such as the likelihood of terror or war, unstable governments, and government corruption may discourage direct investments in a host country. Government policies can also influence the mode of entry. For example, high tariffs discourage exporting and encourage local production through direct investments. Similarly, economic risks such as currency fluctuations may create problems for international investment. If a currency is devalued, so are the assets invested through FDI in that country. Currently the dollar has a lower value than other currencies, such as the euro, which supports U.S. exports. However, the lower value of the dollar hurts foreign exporters coming into the United States from countries with a higher-valued currency. Cultural influences may also affect location advantages and disadvantages. A strong match between the cultures in which international transactions are carried out lowers the liability of foreignness in cases of greater cultural distance.[40]

Internal Coordination or Administrative Advantages

Internal coordination or administrative advantages make it desirable for a firm to produce the good or service rather than contracting with another firm to produce or distribute it.[41] When a firm outsources the manufacture and distribution of a product, it experiences transaction costs, or the costs of negotiating, monitoring, and enforcing the contract. If these costs are high, a firm may rely on some form of FDI rather than using exporting or contracting (such as licensing or franchising) as an entry mode. Toyota has two advantages that must be maintained internally: efficient manufacturing techniques using a team approach and a reputation for producing high-quality automobiles.[42] These advantages for Toyota are based on effective management; if Toyota outsourced manufacturing, it would likely lose these advantages. Therefore, Toyota uses some form of FDI (such as greenfield and joint ventures) rather than franchising and licensing for its foreign manufacture of automobiles.

After choosing an appropriate entry mode, the firm must implement its international strategy. Next, we discuss the different organizational structures firms use to implement the multidomestic, global, and transnational international strategies.

Implementing the Multidomestic Strategy

The geographic-area divisional structure is used to implement the multidomestic strategy (see Figure 8.4). The **geographic-area divisional structure** is a decentralized organizational structure that enables each division to focus on a geographic area, region, or country.[43] This structure is particularly useful for firms selling products with characteristics that frequently change (such as clothing). The geographic-area structure facilitates managers' actions that tailor the product mix to meet the cultural or special tastes of local customers. However, cost efficiencies are often sacrificed when using the geographic-area structure. Indeed, economies of scale are difficult to achieve using this structure because each country has unique products. The disadvantage of this structure, then, is duplication of resources across each

country-specific or location advantages

advantages that are concerned with the desirability of producing in the home country versus locating production and distribution assets in the host country

internal coordination or administrative advantages

advantages that make it desirable for a firm to produce the good or service rather than contracting with another firm to produce or distribute it

geographic-area divisional structure

a decentralized organizational structure that enables each division to focus on a geographic area, region, or country

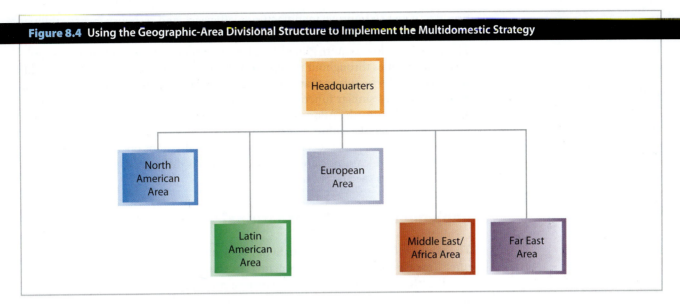

Figure 8.4 Using the Geographic-Area Divisional Structure to Implement the Multidomestic Strategy

division; for example, each division has its own functional marketing specialists and production facilities. Coordination across divisions is also difficult and expensive due to the decentralization.[44]

Implementing the Global Strategy

The worldwide divisional structure is used to implement the global strategy (see Figure 8.5). The **worldwide divisional structure** is a centralized organizational structure in which each product group is housed in a globally focused worldwide division or worldwide profit center.[45] In this structure, the first organizational level below corporate headquarters is that of worldwide product divisions. The development and commercialization of new products for global markets is the responsibility of the worldwide division. Because a specific division focuses on a single product or product group, division managers are exposed to all aspects of managing products on a global basis. This experience helps managers learn how to integrate the

worldwide divisional structure

a centralized organizational structure in which each product group is housed in a globally focused worldwide division or worldwide profit center

Figure 8.5 Using the Worldwide Divisional Structure to Implement the Global Strategy

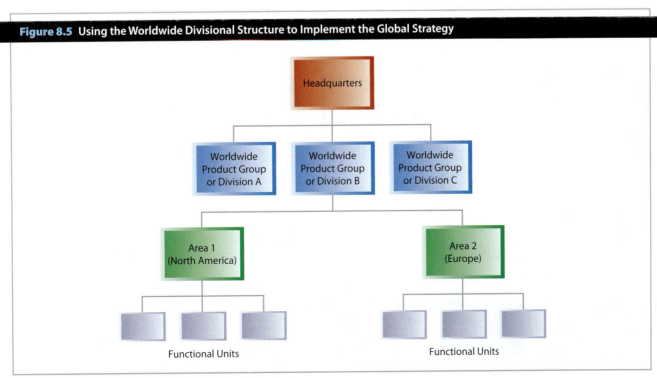

firm's activities to improve manufacturing efficiency and responsiveness—abilities that help the firm adjust production requirements to fluctuating global demand. This approach does require global standardization in management practices, policies, and activities throughout the division.[46] The major disadvantage of the worldwide divisional structure is that it allows extensive duplication of activities because each division has similar functional skills in marketing, finance, information management, and so forth. Additionally, each product group must develop its own knowledge about the cultural, legal, and political environments of the various regional and national markets in which the various divisions operate. Furthermore, coordination and learning across product groups is difficult. It also results in low responsiveness to specific country needs.

Implementing the Transnational Strategy

The transnational strategy is usually implemented through a global matrix structure[47] (see Figure 8.6). The **global matrix structure** is an organizational structure in which both functional and product expertise are integrated into teams so the teams will be able to respond quickly to requirements in the global marketplace. The global matrix structure promotes flexibility in designing products and responding to customer needs from different geographical areas. However, it places employees in a position of being accountable to more than one manager. In fact, at any given time, an employee may be a member of several cross-functional or product or crossgeographical teams and may find it difficult to be loyal to all of them. Although the global matrix structure gives authority to managers who are most able to use it, the corporate reporting relationships are so complex and vague that it often takes longer to approve major decisions. This type of structure requires considerable coordination to ensure the sharing of knowledge within and across global teams.[48]

Most firms now operate in international markets. Therefore, international strategies and the organizational structures used to implement them are highly relevant to you.

global matrix structure

an organizational structure in which both functional and product expertise are integrated into teams so the teams will be able to respond quickly to requirements in the global marketplace

Figure 8.6 Using the Global Matrix Structure to Implement the Transnational Strategy

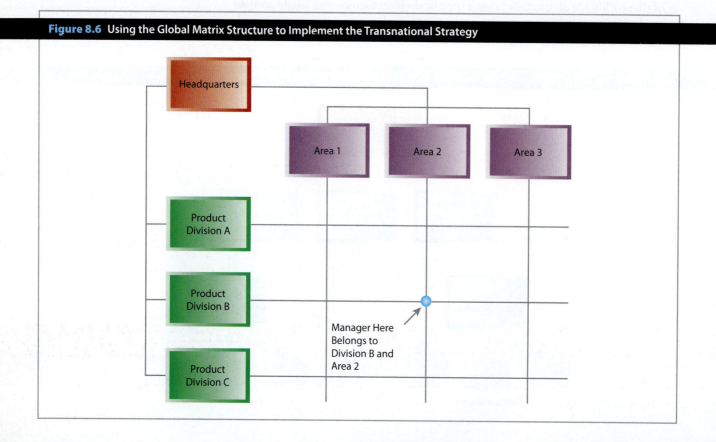

Headquarters

Area 1   Area 2   Area 3

Product Division A

Product Division B

Product Division C

Manager Here Belongs to Division B and Area 2

SUMMARY

The primary purpose of this chapter is to examine firm strategies that extend across national borders. In doing so, we examined the following topics:

- The use of international strategies is increasing as firms seek to gain access to new markets and to valuable resources or to reduce their labor costs. The Internet and other technological innovations, such as those in logistics, facilitate global business transactions. Reduced regulations and tariffs also foster greater opportunities for the use of international strategies. These changes are producing a new global competitive landscape where emerging market countries are playing an increasingly important role. Countries such as Brazil, Russia, India, and China (BRIC countries) are having a greater impact on the global economy. This changing global competitive landscape creates a need for managers to develop a global mind-set. A global mind-set is a cognitive model that motivates a manager to search for opportunities in foreign markets; to develop strategies that exploit those opportunities; and to coordinate units, tasks, and people in different geographic locations throughout the world.

- International strategies are driven by four major motives: (1) to reduce costs and secure resources, (2) to increase economies of scale and scope and to capitalize on opportunities to secure desirable locations, (3) to respond to pressure by rivals who have moved into regions untapped by others, and (4) to seek learning and other advantages that provide new knowledge from international markets.

- Firms going abroad usually select one of three international strategies. Firms use a multidomestic strategy to sell products that are customized to the needs of individual host country markets. This international strategy works best when decision-making authority is decentralized to each business so it can operate freely in separate regions or countries. The decentralized authority allows the business to adapt its goods and services to the local geographic market. When global markets demand similar characteristics in a good or service, the firm uses a global strategy to sell standardized products to global customers with similar needs. Being able to operate efficiently is critical to the success of a global strategy. Finally, a transnational strategy combines characteristics of both multidomestic and global strategies in order to respond to pressures for local responsiveness and the need to globally integrate and coordinate operations for efficiency purposes.

- Firms can use several different modes to enter an international market. Entry modes requiring lower asset commitment include international exporting, licensing, and franchising. These entry modes have less financial risk but also provide less control over operations. They also reduce potential profits because they are shared with the licensee or franchisee. Other contract approaches include contract manufacturers, turnkey projects, and management contracts. These approaches require more investment by the licensee but also have similar advantages of reduced financial investment relative to the previously discussed contract approaches.

- FDI modes include joint ventures or strategic alliances, greenfield ventures, and acquisitions. Each FDI entry mode requires more up-front investment but allows for more control of the venture. A joint venture includes a separate entity in which control is shared with a local partner. A greenfield venture (new wholly owned subsidiary) allows more control and is most appropriate when proprietary technology needs to be protected. An acquisition is more appropriate when speedy entry is important. However, acquisitions often have significant challenges, including the difficulty of conducting due diligence in international settings and the complexities of integrating businesses from two different cultures and institutional environments.

- FDI strategies may encounter significant political and economic risks. Political risks include terrorism, wars, and nationalization of a private firm's assets by the host country. Economic risks include currency fluctuations and devaluations. Commonly, economic risks are accentuated in transition or emerging economies where the economy is less stable. Of course, political and economic risks are often interrelated.

- Implementing international strategies is often complex and can limit international expansion opportunities. The multidomestic strategy requires decentralization and therefore is implemented with a geographic-area divisional structure. The global strategy is implemented with a worldwide divisional structure. The transnational strategy requires both centralization and decentralization and is commonly implemented with a global matrix structure.

KEY TERMS

country-specific or location
    advantages, 160
exporting, 157
foreign direct investment, 150
franchising, 158
geographic-area divisional structure, 160

global matrix structure, 162
global mind-set, 150
global strategy, 155
greenfield venture, 159
internal coordination or administrative
    advantages, 160

liability of foreignness, 150
licensing, 158
multidomestic strategy, 155
transnational strategy, 155
worldwide divisional structure, 161

DISCUSSION QUESTIONS

1. What are the basic reasons firms choose to expand their operations internationally by employing international strategies?

2. What are the two primary pressures leading to three main international strategies?

3. What are the four contract-based international entry modes?

4. What major advantages influence the type of entry mode firms choose to enter international markets?

5. What are the three types of foreign direct investment (FDI), and what rationale supports the use of each one?

6. What structures are used to implement the multidomestic, global, and transnational strategies?

STRATEGY TOOLBOX

Introduction

When devising cross-border strategies, many business leaders fall into predictable, biased patterns of behavior known as blind spots. In the case of global expansion, for example, companies often base their strategies on what has worked in their own countries, without adequate consideration of the expansion territory context. This chapter's tool is designed to help executives break through the blind spots and avoid costly strategic mistakes.

Defending Against Blind Spots

Blind Spots	Remedies
■ Overconfidence	■ Checks and balances
■ Invalid assumptions	■ Extensive data analysis
■ "Sending good news" bias	■ External perspectives

MINI-CASE

The Olympic Games: An Opportunity for Growing International Businesses

The Games provide a way for outstanding national athletes to compete on an international stage. However, for global firms, the Olympics are a significant opportunity to increase global brand awareness. Firms such as Coca-Cola, Panasonic, Lenovo, and Samsung have the opportunity to market their products worldwide and in specific markets during the Olympic period by using a number of local and regional outlets to establish their global identities.

Likewise, large media firms seek to benefit from the potential advertising revenue associated with the Olympics. NBC, for example, commits significant sums of money to obtain the broadcast rights for the Olympic Games in North America. The network paid $1.27 billion for the broadcast rights of the 2000 Sydney Summer Games and the 2002 Salt Lake City Winter Games. Additionally, NBC paid $2.3 billion for the broadcast rights of the 2004, 2006, and 2008 Games and agreed to pay an additional $2.2 billion for the 2010 and 2012 Games even though the sites for these Games hadn't been determined at the time of the agreement. Additional broadcast rights for Europe, Australia, Asia, and the rest of the Americas go for smaller amounts but are still quite large for the local broadcasters in these areas. NBC and other local broadcasters pay so much for the broadcast rights to these Games because of the importance of international marketing and global mind-sets.

The Olympics are managed by the International Olympic Committee (IOC), based in Switzerland. Because of the high cost of running the Olympics, the IOC and national Olympic committees continually search for ways to offset the costs. Revenues received from firms for the rights to broadcast the Games are a great help in covering the Games' costs. In addition, the IOC uses the prestige and the marketing capability of the Games to sell high-profile corporate sponsorships. These sponsorships enable global corporations to capture the status and visibility of being associated with the Games. A worldwide partnership, the most expensive designation, costs $70 million or more. For the 2008 Olympic Games in Beijing, 12 companies have paid to be worldwide sponsors: Coca-Cola, Samsung, Johnson & Johnson, GE, Atos Origin, Kodak, Manulife, McDonald's, Omega Watch Company, Panasonic, and Visa.

The primary advantage of a worldwide partnership with the IOC is that it provides advertising space during Olympic event broadcasts. For instance, Coca-Cola paid an additional $15 million to be one of the three sponsors for the running of the Olympic torch. It is estimated that Coca-Cola will spend approximately three times its front-end $90 million investment to advertise at the Olympics. In fact, the games provide a specific opportunity for Coca-Cola to market directly to the 1.3 billion Chinese consumers.

In summary, the Olympic Games represent an opportunity for firms whose markets have become more global to advertise to the world during the two-week period of the Games. People across the world watch these games and global firms seek to advertise their products in increasingly international markets. Lenova is using the Olympic Games to announce to the world that it is a global company selling to global markets. In fact, Lenova designed the 2008 Olympic torch to provide special visibility for the firm and its products. The 2008 Olympic Games are expected to reach a cumulative audience of 40 billion people, so it represents a significant opportunity for truly global marketing.

Sources: Advertising of 2007: Coke, Lenova, and others have launched original campaigns that have engaged and entertained consumers, WSMV.com, www.wsmv.com, April 29; Beijing 2008, 2008, Beijing Olympic Broadcasting, www.en.beijing2008.com, April 29; Navigating Olympic sponsorship: Marketing your brand without alienating the world, Knowledge@Wharton, www.knowledge.wharton.upenn.edu, April 16; J. G. Collier, 2008, Coke takes neutral stance on Olympic protests, *Atlanta Journal-Constitution*, www.ajc.com, April 13; J. M. Higgins & S. McClellan, 2004, Welcome to the Olympics, *Broadcasting & Cable*, June 7, 1; J. Lafayette, 2004, Peacock crowing about Olympics, *TelevisionWeek*, August 30, 4; A. Romano, 2004, NBC plans to give local cable ads an Olympian push, *Broadcasting & Cable*, January 19, 35–36; P. McClintock, 2003, Ebersol's got games: NBC Sports chair's pact covers next 5 Olympics, *Daily Variety*, December 17, 7–9; B. Steinberg & Stefan Fatsis, 2003, NBC Olympics bid easily clears bar—GE agrees to pay $2 billion for rights to broadcasts, soaring past competition, *Wall Street Journal*, June 9, B5.

Questions

1. If you wanted to build your firm's brand image at the Olympics and you were pursuing a global strategy, how would you market your products? Would you market your products differently if you were pursuing a multidomestic strategy? Describe the marketing approaches that you might use in advertising as well as local promotion at the Games.

2. What international strategy (multidomestic, global, or transnational) is NBC using to market in its region in North America (including the United States, Canada, and Mexico)? What are the characteristics of its international strategy?

3. What structure should be used to implement the particular strategy chosen in Question 2? Explain why the structure you chose was most appropriate.

EXPERIENTIAL EXERCISES

Exercise One: Top Foreign Direct Investment and Trade Partners

The chapter discussed both foreign direct investment (a process through which a firm invests in a market outside the United States) and trade (exporting and importing). To complete this exercise, collect data on foreign direct investment and trade by looking at sources such as the *Survey of Current Business* and the U.S. Department of Commerce Web site. Then determine the top five countries that are recipients of U.S. foreign direct investment and the top five countries that invest in the United States. In addition, determine the top five trading partners of the United States, the top five recipients of U.S. exports, and the top five countries from which the United States imports. For the trade part of the exercise, consider only goods (not services). What conclusions do you draw from this exercise?

BIZ FLIX

Mr. Baseball: Lessons in Reducing the Liability of Foreignness

This chapter emphasized the *liability of foreignness* as an important obstacle to successful entry into foreign markets. Firms that pursue international strategies need to have cultural sensitivity and cultural awareness for successful, smooth entry. Watch this *Mr. Baseball* scene carefully while considering the following questions.

The New York Yankees trade aging baseball player Jack Elliot (Tom Selleck) to the Chunichi Dragons, a Japanese team. This lighthearted comedy traces Elliot's bungling entry into Japanese culture and exposes his cultural misconceptions, which almost cost him everything—including his new girlfriend Hiroko Uchiyama (Aya Takanashi). After Elliot slowly begins to understand Japanese culture and Japanese baseball, his teammates finally accept him. This film shows many examples of Japanese culture, especially its love for baseball.

This scene is an edited version of the "Welcome to Japan" sequence that appears early in the film. Jack Elliot arrives at Nogoya International Airport, Tokyo, Japan. Yoji Nishimura (Toshi Shioya) meets him and acts as Jack's interpreter and guide. The film continues after this scene with the unfolding adventure of Jack Elliot playing for the Chunichi Dragons.

What to Watch for and Ask Yourself
1. Is Jack Elliot culturally sensitive or culturally insensitive?
2. What cross-cultural errors does he appear to make on his arrival in Japan?
3. What could have been done to decrease Jack Elliot's "liability of foreignness"?

ENDNOTES

1. S. Mani, K. D. Antia, & A. Rindfleisch, 2007, Entry mode and equity level: A multilevel examination of foreign direct investment ownership structure, *Strategic Management Journal,* 28: 857–866.
2. D. Brooks, 2008, The cognitive age, *New York Times,* www.nytimes.com, May 2; A. S. Tsui, 2007, From homogenization to pluralism: International management research in the academy and beyond, *Academy of Management Journal,* 50: 1353–1364.
3. M. A. Hitt & X. He, 2008, Firm strategies in a changing global competitive landscape, *Business Horizons,* in press.
4. M. Javidan, R. M. Steers, & M. A. Hitt (eds.), 2007, *The Global Mindset,* Amsterdam: Elsevier Ltd.; O. Levy, S. Beechler, S. Taylor, & N. A. Boyacigiller, 2007, What we talk about when we talk about "global mindset": Managerial cognition in multinational corporations, *Journal of International Business Studies,* 38: 231–258.
5. T. Hutzschenreuter & J. C. Voll, 2008, Performance effects of "added cultural distance" in the path of international expansion: The case of German multinational enterprises, *Journal of International Business Studies,* 39: 53–70; R. Mudambi & S. A. Zahra, 2007, The survival of international new ventures, *Journal of International Business Studies,* 38: 333–352.
6. E. W. K. Tsang & P. S. L. Yip, 2007, Economic distance and the survival of foreign direct investments, *Academy of Management Journal,* 50: 1156–1168; J. Mezias, 2002, How to identify liabilities of foreignness and assess their effects on multinational corporations, *Journal of International Management,* 8: 265–282.
7. J. W. Spencer, 2008, The impact of multinational enterprise strategy on indigenous enterprises: Horizontal spillovers and crowding out in developing countries, *Academy of Management Review,* 33: 341–361; M. A. Hitt, L. Tihanyi, T. Miller, & B. Connelly, 2006, International diversification: Antecedents, outcomes, and moderators, *Journal of Management,* 32: 831–867.
8. M. A. Hitt, L. Bierman, K. Uhlenbruck, & K. Shimizu, 2006, The importance of resources in the internationalization of professional service firms: The good, the bad, and the ugly, *Academy of Management Journal,* 49: 1137–1157.
9. L. Li, Z. Lim, & B. Arya, 2008, The turtle–hare race story revisited: Social capital and resource accumulation for firms from emerging economies, *Asia Pacific Journal of Management,* 25: 251–275; G. K. Lee, 2007, The significance of network resources in the race to enter emerging product markets: The convergence of communications and computer networking, 1989–2201, *Strategic Management Journal,* 28: 17–37.
10. S. Fernhaber, B. A. Gilbert, & P. P. McDougall, 2008, International entrepreneurship and geographic location: An empirical examination of new venture internationalization, *Journal of International Business Studies,* 39: 267–290; H. Berry, 2007, Leaders, laggards, and the pursuit of foreign knowledge, *Strategic Management Journal,* 27: 151–168.
11. F. T. Rothaermel, S. Kotha, & H. K. Steensma, 2006, International market entry by U.S. Internet firms: An empirical analysis of country risk, national culture, and market size, *Journal of Management,* 32: 56–82.
12. T. W. Tong & J. J. Reuer, 2007, Real options in multinational corporations: Organizational challenges and risk implications, *Journal of International Business Studies,* 38: 215–230.
13. T. Yu & A. A. Cannella, 2007, Rivalry between multinational enterprises: An event history approach, *Academy of Management Journal,* 50: 665–686.
14. D. Luhnow & C. Terhune, 2003, Latin pop: A low-budget cola shakes up markets south of the border; Peru's Kola Real takes on Coke and Pepsi by cutting frills, targeting bodegas; how plastic leveled the field, *Wall Street Journal,* October 27: A1.
15. J. Birchall, 2008, Pepsi in deal with Russia juice group, *Financial Times,* www.ft.com, March 20.
16. I. Brat, 2008, Overseas business boosts Caterpillar profit, *Wall Street Journal,* online.wsj.com, April 19.
17. A. Delios, A. S. Gaur, & S. Makino, 2008, The timing of international expansion: Information, rivalry, and imitation among Japanese firms, *Journal of Management Studies,* 45: 169–195.
18. J. Reed, 2008, GM loses top sales slot to Toyota, *Financial Times,* www.ft.com, April 23.
19. C.-H. Tseng, P. Tansuhaj, W. Hallagan, & J. McCullough, 2007, Effects of firm resources on growth in multinationality, *Journal of International Business Studies,* 38: 961–974.
20. K. T. Yeo, 2003, Factors motivating MNCs to set up local R&D facilities: The case of Singapore, *International Journal of Technology Transfer & Commercialization,* 2(2): 128–138.
21. A. Cuervo-Cazurra, M. M. Maloney, & S. Manrakhan, 2007, Causes of the difficulties in internationalization, *Journal of International Business Studies,* 38: 709–725.
22. P. Ghemawat, 2004, Global standardization vs. localization: A case study and model, in J. A. Quelch & R. Deshpande (eds.), *The Global Market: Developing a Strategy to Manage across Borders,* New York: Jossey-Bass, Chapter 8.
23. G. Hoffman, 1996, On foreign expansion, *Progressive Grocer,* September, 156.
24. Thales, Samtel form joint venture for avionics, 2008, *Thaindian News,* www.thaindian.com, May 8; D. Michaels, 2003, World business (a special report); Victory at sea: How did a French company capture several British naval contracts? Think "multidomestic," *Wall Street Journal Europe,* September 26, R5.
25. Corporate profile, 2008, Daimler AG, www.daimler.com, May, 8; P. Wonacott & L. Hawkins Jr., 2003, A global journal report: Saying "beamer" in Chinese; Western luxury car makers see sales boom in China as newly rich seek status, *Wall Street Journal,* November 6, B1.
26. J. Birkenshaw, P. Braunerhjelm, U. Holm, & S. Terjesen, 2006, Why do some firms relocate their headquarters overseas? *Strategic Management Journal,* 27: 681–700.
27. 2008, IKEA, *Wikipedia,* en.wikipedia.org, March 10; C. Daniels, 2004, Create IKEA, make billions, take bus, *Fortune,* May 3, 44; E. Brown, 2002, Putting EAMES within reach, *Fortune,* October 30, 98–100.
28. W. G. Sanders & A. Tuschke, 2007, The adoption of institutionally contested organizational practices: The emergence of stock option pay in German, *Academy of Management Journal,* 50: 33–56.

29. X. Yin & M. Shanley, 2008, Industry determinants of the "merger versus alliance" decision, *Academy of Management Review*, 33: 473–491; D. E. Miller, L. Eden, M. A. Hitt, & S. R. Miller, 2007, Experience of emerging market firms: The role of cognitive bias in developed market entry, *Management International Review*, 47: 845–867; P. Herrmann & D. K. Datta, 2006, *Journal of Management Studies*, 43: 755–778.

30. Electronic Arts, 2008, *Wikipedia*, en.wikipedia.org, May 8; C. Edward, 2004, Keeping you glued to the couch; In video games, top developer Electronic Arts zaps the competition, *BusinessWeek*, May 27, 58–59.

31. C. Lakshman & R. C. Parente, 2008, Supplier-focused knowledge management in the automobile industry and its implications for product performance, *Journal of Management Studies*, 45: 317–342.

32. Y. Luo, 2007, Are joint venture partners more opportunistic in a more volatile environment? *Strategic Management Journal*, 28: 39–60.

33. D. Li, L. Eden, M. A. Hitt, & R. D. Ireland, 2008, Friends, acquaintances, or strangers? Partner selection in R&D alliances, *Academy of Management Journal*, 51: 315–334.

34. C. Bouquet, L. Hebert, & A. Delios, 2004, Foreign expansion in service industries: Separability and human capital intensity, *Journal of Business Research*, 57: 35–46.

35. J. Li, J. Y. Yang, & D. R. Yue, 2007, Identity, community, and audience: How wholly owned foreign subsidiaries gain legitimacy in China, *Academy of Management Journal*, 50: 175–190.

36. K. Shimizu, M. A. Hitt, D. Vaidyanath, & V. Pisano, 2004, Theoretical foundations of cross-border mergers and acquisitions: A review of current research and recommendations for the future, *Journal of International Management*, 10: 307–353; M. A. Hitt & V. Pisano, 2003, The cross-border merger and acquisition strategy: A research perspective, *Management Research*, 1: 133–144.

37. I. Bjorkman, G. K. Stahl, & E. Vaara, 2007, Cultural differences and capability transfer in cross-border acquisitions: The mediating roles of capability complementarity, absorptive capacity and social integration, *Journal of International Business Studies*, 38: 658–672.

38. M. Nippa, S. Beechler, & A. Klossek, 2007, Success factors for managing international joint ventures: A review and an integrative framework, *Management and Organization Review*, 3: 277–310; B. Lev, 2004, Sharpening the intangible edge, *Harvard Business Review*, 82(6): 109–116.

39. E. Tatoglu, K. W. Glaister, & F. Erdal, 2003, Determinants of foreign ownership in Turkish manufacturing, *Eastern European Economics*, 41(2): 5–41.

40. S. H. L. Slangen, 2006, National cultural distance and initial foreign acquisition performance: The moderating effect of integration, *Journal of World Business*, 41: 161–170.

41. W. Malone, 2004, Bringing the market inside, *Harvard Business Review*, 82(4): 107–114.

42. S. J. Spear, 2004, Learning to lead at Toyota, *Harvard Business Review*, 82(5): 78–86.

43. A. Ferner, P. Almond, I. Clark, T. Colling, & T. Edwards, 2004, The dynamics of central control and subsidiary anatomy in the management of human resources: Case study evidence from US MNCs in the UK, *Organization Studies*, 25: 363–392.

44. B. Ambos & B. B. Schlegelmilch, 2007, Innovation and control in the multinational firm: A comparison of political and contingency approaches, *Strategic Management Journal*, 28: 473–486.

45. J. Wolf & W. G. Egelhoff, 2002, A reexamination and extension of international strategy–structure theory, *Strategic Management Journal*, 23: 181–189.

46. A. Tempel & P. Walgenbach, 2007, Global standardization of organizational forms and management practices? What new institutionalism and business-systems approach can learn from each other, *Journal of Management Studies*, 44: 1–24.

47. G. Letto-Gillies, 2002, *Transnational Corporations: Fragmentation Amidst Integration*, New York: Routledge.

48. S. Li & H. Scullion, 2006, Bridging the distance: Managing cross-border knowledge holders, *Asia Pacific Journal of Management*, 23: 71–92.

CHAPTER 9
Alliance Strategies

Knowledge Objectives

Reading and studying this chapter should enable you to:

1. Define strategic alliances and explain the difference between equity and nonequity alliances.

2. Explain why firms develop strategic alliances.

3. Identify business-level strategic alliances and explain vertical and horizontal alliances.

4. Describe how strategic alliances are used to implement corporate-level strategies.

5. Explain why strategic alliances represent a common means of entering international markets.

6. Identify the major risks of strategic alliances. Explain how strategic alliances can be managed to increase their success.

Foreign Firms Seek Joint Ventures to Enter China's Emerging Market While Chinese Firms Seek Joint Ventures to Expand Internationally

Traditional joint ventures in China have been quite compelling for foreign firms. The foreign partners from more developed countries would usually provide capital, knowledge, and access to international markets and high-technology capabilities. Alternatively, the Chinese partners provided access to cheap labor, local regulatory and market knowledge, and improved access to increasing demand by the emerging middle class for branded as well as other products. Furthermore, the Chinese government often provided land, tax breaks, and an attractive welcome to encourage foreign direct investment into China. Although China protects many important industries such as financial services and automobile manufacturing through restrictive entry requirements, the future potential of the market as well as the availability of lower-cost production has created attractive market entry potential for companies.

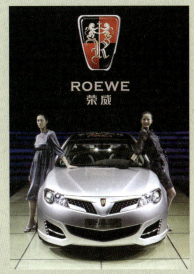

© Mark Ralston/AFP/Getty Images

For example, Medtronics, a Minneapolis-based medical-device maker, is forming a partnership with Weigao, a similar company in mainland China. Medtronics is seeking to expand its market because of the demand it perceives to exist for spinal injury patients and for the potential demand by patients who use cardiac pacemaker products. Medtronics expects that China's demand for its products will surpass Japan's demand (its largest market in Asia currently) within 10 years. Alternatively, Weigao seeks to further its expansion into artificial knees and hips through its partnership with Medtronics. It also desires help in improving its product quality and increasing the array of products it can offer in its home market.

Interestingly, although many joint ventures and partnerships in China have been successful, Chinese firms are not as hungry as they once were for capital; and many are implementing improved technology that they have learned to develop from international partners or from their own experience abroad. Moreover, demand for foreign branded products has fallen as local competitor's products have improved and the availability of cheap labor has fallen; as such, Chinese firms are less interested in providing access to foreign partners.

Also, many of the rules for foreign partners have led to difficulties. For instance, Peugeot (cars), Rémy Martin (spirits), Foster's (beer), Fletcher Challenge (steel), News Corporation (media), and a number of telecommunication firms have found their joint ventures to be problematic because of complex and contradictory rules, and difficulty in appropriating profits and controlling their investments. Even firms with 51 percent ownership, such as Danone, a large French food producer, are not able to control their ventures given the local rules in China. However, Wahaha, a local Chinese partner with Danone, has been able to wrestle control of the joint venture with Danone.

Additionally, local Chinese firms have been pursuing partnerships domestically and internationally to improve their own competitive market share in world markets outside China. For example, China's SAIC Motorcorp and Nanjing Automobile Corp. created a joint venture to develop a "national car company" to challenge foreign automakers in China and produce cars for export.

Therefore, they decided to pull out of the joint venture with Fiat Automobile SpA. This local joint venture between two Chinese firms will allow them to pursue a strategy to build branded cars through the acquisition of Rover and its use of the MG brand.

Sources: A. K. Bhattacharya & D. C. Michael, 2008, How local companies keep multinationals at bay, *Harvard Business Review*, 86(3): 84–95; A. Harman, 2008, SAIC, Nanjing to form car company; Fiat quits JV, *Ward's AutoWorld*, January, 9; J. Xia, J. Tan, & D. Tan, 2008, Mimetic entry and bandwagon affect: The rise and decline of international equity joint ventures in China, *Strategic Management Journal*, 29: 195–217; J. T. Areddy & L. Chao, 2007, Groupe Danone gets a cool response in peace offering to partner in China, *Wall Street Journal*, December 17, B2; G. Fairclough, 2007, Passing lane: GM's Chinese partner loses as a new rival; Learning from Detroit, Shanghai Automotive pushes its own cars, *Wall Street Journal*, April 20, A1; L. Santini, 2007, Medtronic moves to widen China foot print: Partnership with Weigao is part of growth strategy in medical-device market, *Wall Street Journal*, December 18, 82; 2007, Business: Wahaha-haha!; Joint ventures in China, *The Economist*, April 27, 85.

The popularity of Chinese markets is shown in Focusing on Strategy. Because of its size and subsequent sales potential as well as low-cost labor, firms from many parts of the world want to enter Chinese markets. Focusing on Strategy describes a recent joint venture by Medtronics, a medical equipment device maker, with Weigao to further access the Chinese market as well as reduce its labor costs. It also illustrates how Chinese firms are accessing needed resources from foreign partners and how Chinese firms are teaming with other local firms as well as creating their own joint ventures abroad to learn and expand their product lines and market access. Combined, these actions emphasize the importance of strategic alliances to firms throughout the world, not only in China.

A **strategic alliance** is a relationship between firms in which the partners agree to cooperate in ways that provide benefits to each firm. A strategic alliance is a type of cooperative strategy. A **cooperative strategy** is an action plan a firm develops to form cooperative relationships with other firms. Although firms choose to cooperate with one another rather than compete when using a cooperative strategy, such as a strategic alliance, the purpose of doing so is the same in both instances: namely, to develop a competitive advantage.[1] Thus, a cooperative strategy adds to the repertoire of strategies firms use to build competitive advantages that can help them successfully compete in one or more markets.

Two types of strategic alliances are equity alliances and nonequity alliances. In an **equity alliance,** each partner owns a percentage of the equity in a venture that the firms have jointly formed. If a separate business is created by this alliance, it is often referred to as a **joint venture.** A **nonequity alliance** is a contractual relationship between two or more firms in which each partner agrees to share some of its resources or capabilities.[2]

In previous chapters, we discussed business-level strategies, corporate-level (product diversification) strategies, and international strategies, which all concern actions the firm takes to compete in markets against other firms operating in the same markets. In this chapter, we explore the use of strategic alliances, the reasons for them, and their different types. We also examine alliances at the business and corporate levels along with international alliances. Finally, we explore the means of managing alliances, including balancing the risks of using such strategies. We begin with the reasons to develop strategic alliances.

Reasons for Developing Strategic Alliances

As suggested in Focusing on Strategy, strategic alliances are a highly popular strategy used by firms throughout the world. Strategic alliances represent a major trend in global business primarily because of the potential value they provide to partnering firms. They can help firms grow and likewise have a major effect on the performance of partner firms.[3] They are an important strategy for many reasons. We present some of these reasons in Table 9.1. Before examining Table 9.1, think of reasons you believe would cause firms to form alliances. You likely identified some of the reasons listed in the table and may have included a few others as well.

strategic alliance

a relationship between firms in which the partners agree to cooperate in ways that provide benefits to each firm

cooperative strategy

an action plan a firm develops to form cooperative relationships with other firms

equity alliance

an alliance in which each partner owns a percentage of the equity in a venture that the firms have jointly formed

joint venture

a separate business that is created by an equity alliance

nonequity alliance

a contractual relationship between two or more firms in which each partner agrees to share some of its resources or capabilities

---

Table 9.1 Reasons for Strategic Alliances

- Gain access to a restricted market
- Develop new goods or services
- Facilitate new market entry
- Share significant R&D investments
- Share risks and buffer against uncertainty
- Develop market power
- Gain access to complementary resources
- Build economies of scale
- Meet competitive challenges
- Learn new skills and capabilities
- Outsource for lower costs and higher-quality output

A major reason for firms to engage in strategic alliances is to allow them to enter restricted markets. China provides a prime example; the Chinese government requires foreign firms to form joint ventures with Chinese partners in order to enter many Chinese industries. For example, automobile firms and airlines had to form alliances with Chinese firms to enter and serve Chinese markets. Alliances also can allow a firm to overcome trade barriers to enter a market. In other words, a firm may form a joint venture in a country to produce and market products so it would not have to pay major tariffs on those same products if they were imported.

R&D alliances to facilitate development of new goods and services have become increasingly common. R&D alliances help firms share the costs and risks associated with developing new products. The success of new products in the marketplace is low. Therefore, sharing the costs and risks allows individual firms either to invest less in R&D or to invest the same amount and increase the number of successes in the market (by introducing more new products, for example). Additionally, partner firms may develop better new-product ideas by cooperating to integrate resources from each to create new and different capabilities.[4]

As we noted previously, risks arise because success with new products is highly uncertain. Other forms of uncertainty exist as well. For example, entering new international markets presents uncertainty in the form of market demand, government actions, and competitor reactions. Therefore, firms may develop strategic alliances such as R&D alliances to overcome uncertainty and share the risks. Besides overcoming risk, such alliances also help international firms build their knowledge base.[5] Nokia's actions illustrate this type of benefit.

Nokia is in every country of the world and has reinvented itself a number of times, mostly through alliances with competitors and through buyer-supplier arrangements. It has entered into R&C consortia (large alliances with competitors) to help form a new industry standard. For instance, Nokia formed a large equity joint venture with Ericsson, Motorola, Psion, Siemens, and Matsui, creating a company called Symbian. This joint venture was aimed at creating a common operating system for wireless information. In 2007, Symbian held 76 percent of the operating system used in smartphones compared to the next most dominant competitors, Microsoft and Research in Motion, with 13 and 10 percent, respectively. Over time, Nokia used alliances more frequently because of the large investments required and the short product cycles necessary to compete in this quick-changing industry.[6]

As suggested by the Nokia example, competitors may combine their resources and skills, and as such, alliances can provide access to complementary resources. **Complementary resources** are resources that each partner brings to the partnership that, when combined, allow for new resources or capabilities that neither firm could readily create alone. By integrating their complementary resources, partners

complementary resources

resources that each partner brings to the partnership that, when combined, allow for new resources or capabilities that neither firm could readily create alone

can take actions that they could not take separately. So gaining access to complementary resources is a major reason for engaging in strategic alliances.[7] Nokia expects that the complementary resources held by its partners and within its firm can help it create better designs and access to other skills (such as manufacturing) for the products it sells in global markets.

Firms can also use alliances to gain market power. For example, the German airline Lufthansa is forming a partnership with JetBlue in order to create an opportunity to gain landing spots in the United States, especially at the John F. Kennedy (JFK) airport. It plans on investing a 19 percent ownership stake in JetBlue, thereby creating a quasi-hub in JFK. Recently, Lufthansa also took a 30 percent ownership stake in British Midland Airways (BMI), which made Lufthansa the second largest slot holder in London's Heathrow airport. With these landing opportunities in London and New York, Lufthansa as well as its partners can begin to challenge British Airways' (BA) lucrative routes between Europe and the United States. BA earns a significant amount of its profits on transatlantic flights between Europe and the United States. These alliances would not only expand Lufthansa's ability to compete with BA in this lucrative market, but also provide opportunities for JetBlue as well as BMI to expand their opportunities more fully into international markets.[8] Market power can be achieved when partners combine their resources to create synergy and when their market share increases as a result of doing so.

At times, firms form alliances to meet competitive challenges. In fact, they may need to gain access to partners' resources to compete effectively. For example, Sematech was formed in Austin, Texas, during the 1980s by a group of U.S. semiconductor firms with the blessing of the U.S. government. It was developed to conduct joint R&D to meet the competitive challenges of foreign semiconductor firms, particularly Japanese businesses at the time. The consortium was so successful that Sematech has a variety of different purposes today, although its general focus remains on improving knowledge in the semiconductor industry.

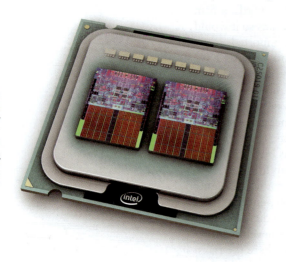

Of critical importance is the amount of knowledge a firm holds. In fact, some argue that firms holding greater stocks of knowledge often have a competitive advantage. For this reason, many alliances are formed to gain access to a partner's valuable knowledge. So a primary reason for developing alliances is to learn from partners, which can contribute to higher performance by the firm.[9] In some cases, firms may attempt to learn from partners in order to explore new areas (such as R&D alliances as in the Nokia example). In other cases, firms may want to learn from partners in order to know how to better use their current capabilities. For example, large multinational corporations often enter emerging markets to exploit their current technological knowledge. To do so, they must learn the local culture and marketplace. They must also learn how to deal with the foreign government and distributors. This knowledge can be obtained from local partners, as illustrated in Focusing on Strategy.

A final reason why firms develop alliances is to outsource an important function or activity of their business. *Outsourcing* (defined in Chapter 4) involves acquiring a capability from an external supplier that contributes to creating value for customers. As we explained in Chapter 4, outsourcing is a popular trend among U.S. firms. Even though much outsourcing occurs in manufacturing, outsourcing of information technology, human resources, and other internal staff functions has become more frequent as well.

Outsourcing is commonly used to reduce costs. However, firms also outsource to gain access to special skills for higher-quality output. For example, many pharmaceutical firms outsource R&D to improve the effectiveness of the research operations.[10] For example, Groupe Bolloré, a French firm, has formed an outsourcing deal with Pininfarina, an Italian car designer and manufacturer, to produce a "zero-emissions electric car." Many other car companies, such as Ford/Volvo and Fiat's Alpha Romeo, have used the design services of Pininfarina to improve the design and manufacturing ability of many of their car models. The outsourcing deal also included financial incentives for the customer by the availability of leasing the car in a further alliance with the French car company through the electric utility firm Electricité De France SA.[11]

Because international outsourcing is believed to be responsible for exporting jobs to other countries, it is controversial. A significant amount of outsourcing has occurred by firms seeking to reduce their expenditures in information technology and services. Three large firms in India have made a big business of receiving this high-technology outsourcing, Infosys Technologies, Tata Consultancy Services (TCS), and Wipro. Approximately 10 percent of the global technology service is now outsourced to foreign service providers, and Indian companies hold about 70 percent of the market share in this large and growing segment. Outsourcing often occurs as companies seek to cut costs. When the U.S. economy is weak, an increase in the outsourcing trend is more likely.[12] However, from a strategic management perspective, outsourcing has the potential to help firms successfully implement their strategies and to earn returns for shareholders as a result. You will read more about outsourcing in this chapter's Mini-Case.

Firms form alliances for use at different levels in their hierarchy of strategies. First, we'll explore business-level alliances.

Business-Level Strategic Alliances

Two types of business-level strategic alliances are vertical alliances and horizontal alliances. Next, we explore how a firm can use either type of business-level alliance to help create or maintain a competitive advantage.

Vertical Strategic Alliances

A **vertical strategic alliance** is an alliance that involves cooperative partnerships across the value chain. (The value chain was discussed in Chapter 4.) A relationship between buyers and suppliers is a common type of vertical alliance. Some firms use vertical alliances to produce their products. Nike uses quite a few vertical alliances to produce many of its athletic shoes. These alliances are a part of the value chain discussed in Chapter 4.

Although contracts are usually written to form them, vertical alliances are most effective when partners trust each other.[13] Trust enables partners to invest less time and effort to ensure that a contract's terms are fulfilled. Trust also helps partners learn from each other in ways that benefit both firms. In fact, when developed and sustained over long periods of time, trust even facilitates the transfer of technological knowledge from buyers to suppliers: The supplier is more likely to help improve the performance of the buyer, and the alliance is more likely to be successful.[14]

Many firms are finding it necessary to manage their supply chain through strategic alliances and relationships rather than use an arm's-length pricing strategy focused on purchasing stuff as cheaply as possible. For example, Nike sought to manage its relationships with contract manufacturers for its shoes by having different types of suppliers. Tier 1 suppliers are firms with a stronger relationship to the main contracting company (Nike), more like a strategic alliance than a pure contractual relationship. However, Tier 2 manufacturers may be associated with pricing and may be managed by Tier 1 suppliers or more closely related manufacturers.[15] This more relationship-oriented approach has required that supply-chain managers develop a whole new set of skills in alliance management.[16]

Horizontal Strategic Alliances

A **horizontal strategic alliance** is an alliance that involves cooperative partnerships in which firms at the same stage of the value chain share resources and capabilities. Horizontal alliances are often intended to enhance the capabilities of the partners to compete in their markets. Firms sometimes develop horizontal alliances to

vertical strategic alliance
an alliance that involves cooperative partnerships across the value chain

horizontal strategic alliance
an alliance that involves cooperative partnerships in which firms at the same stage of the value chain share resources and capabilities

Horizontal Alliances in the Chemistry and Seed Businesses

Dow AgroSciences and Monsanto Inc. are rivals in agricultural seed production. However, to foster both of their competitive advantages as well as compete more fully with other competitors, they are forming a horizontal alliance to produce new corn seeds. Through the research that these companies have already established in this area, Dow and Monsanto will each contribute four genetic traits for each new seed, as part of the design of this alliance. These genes will fight pests as well as ward off weeds. Each firm has specialized in genes that overcome problems with some pests but not others; the same is true with weeds. Accordingly, if they can create genetic strains that combine their strengths, they will be able to compete more fully and offer better value to their consumers.

This deal responds to mounting competition in this particular seed sector. In 2006, Syngenta and Dupont, two additional rivals in the seed business, signed a similar partnership arrangement to compete against Monsanto. Dow and Monsanto, once they have the eight-gene combined corn seed, will also be able to create additional seeds on their own that they can market under their own brand besides the SmartStax brand, which will be the combined brand name.

As such, the agreement will allow Monsanto to expand its market share by increasing the number of products that it can

© Digital Vision/Getty Images

offer. Likewise, for Dow, the agreement will provide access to more customers and give a substantial boost to its agricultural unit, which does not have the same level of market share as some of its rivals.

As these examples show, horizontal alliances are often used when competition is strong and one firm does not have all of the capabilities needed to produce the next advance to keep it competitive. Furthermore, firms observe rivals who have already pursued strategic alliances and believe it important to enter into a cooperative agreement in order to maintain a stronger level of competitiveness with those rivals that have already formed an alliance. When a great deal of uncertainty characterizes the industry and it is necessary to maintain competitive strength, rivals at the same level of the value chain often cooperate to make progress and competitive advances. These cooperative agreements often lead to improved performance and create value for the potential customers of the products.

Sources: L. Aetter, 2007, Dupont's biotech bet; Ethanol boom inspired the drive to catch up, *Wall Street Journal*, January 22, A10; M. Bryner, 2007, Dow and Monsanto team up for eight-gene stacked corn, *Chemical Week*, September 26, 7; A. Campoy, 2007, Seed giants join forces, *Wall Street Journal*, September 15–16, A4; B. Hindo, 2007, One little seed, eight special genes; Monsanto plans a super corn seed to ward off weeds and bugs, *BusinessWeek*, December 17, 40.

respond to competitors' actions or to reduce the competition they face. Understanding Strategy: Learning from Success illustrates several horizontal alliances.

Because of dynamic and highly competitive markets, firms often face substantial uncertainty. To buffer against this uncertainty, they frequently form alliances to share the risks (as noted earlier in the chapter). High uncertainty has become increasingly common in many markets, not just markets that you would expect to be highly uncertain, such as high-technology markets. For example, markets for banks have become highly competitive as they experience significant change. One response has been to acquire other banks to increase market power. However, compared to acquisitions, alliances can accomplish similar objectives, but with a smaller investment of a bank's financial capital. Of course, care must be taken in horizontal alliances to avoid explicit or tacit collusion.

Although explicit collusion is illegal, tacit collusion is more difficult to identify.[17] *Tacit collusion* occurs when firms signal intentions to one another through their actions. The market signaling observed when firms tacitly collude is more likely to occur in concentrated industries with only a few large competitors. For example,

Kellogg, General Mills, Post (Kraft sold this brand to Ralcorp in 2007), and Quaker have almost 80 percent of the ready-to-eat cereal market.[18] An example of tacit collusion in this industry would be if most or all of these four competitors took no action to reduce the price of their products when the demand for them declined.[19]

Vertical alliances often have the highest probability of producing positive returns, while horizontal alliances usually are the most difficult to manage and sustain. In particular, vertical alliances in which partners have complementary capabilities and the relationship between the partners is strong are likely to be successful. Horizontal alliances are difficult because often the partners are also competitors. Firms in these alliances must guard against opportunistic actions (being unfairly taken advantage of) by their partners because of the potentially serious implications those actions might have for the firms' ability to remain competitive. Also, because of the differences between competitors, horizontal alliances are ripe for conflict.

Even though business-level partnerships are important, corporate-level alliances also can have substantial effects on firm performance. We examine these types of alliances next.

Corporate-Level Strategic Alliances

Corporate-level strategic alliances usually focus on the firm's product line and are designed to enhance firm growth. Corporate-level alliances are particularly attractive because they often have the same purpose as acquisitions but are much less costly.[20] Corporate-level strategic alliances include those for diversification, for synergy, and for franchising.

Diversification by Alliance

R&D strategic alliances may be formed with the intent to develop new products that serve markets distinct from those that the partners currently serve. Partners operating in different industries may be able to integrate unique knowledge stocks to create products that serve new markets and customers. In this way, the new products add to each partner's current product line. In fact, developing new products for markets different from those served may be difficult for firms without help from partners who have the additional knowledge needed. The knowledge held by a firm can be valuable but also may create a *path dependence* whereby it is difficult to learn something new that does not fit with the firm's current knowledge base.[21] Diversification alliances can be especially valuable if the new products developed are related to the current products in some way such that synergy can be created.

However, alliances can also be used to refocus the firm and reduce its level of diversification, changing its direction into new businesses. Using joint ventures to create new businesses in combination with other firms can lead to organization restructuring and renewal.[22] For example, in Focusing on Strategy, China's SAIC Motorcorp and Nanjing Automobile Corp. formed a joint venture to develop a "national car company" to challenge foreign automakers in China. Their expansion using the Rover and MG brands may allow them to compete more effectively as a stand-alone car company in the Chinese domestic market and may launch them as global auto producers.

Synergy by Alliance

Strategic alliances at the corporate level between firms can be used to create synergy. Synergy is created when partners share resources or integrate complementary capabilities to build economies of scope. In fact, a synergistic strategic alliance is similar to a complementary business-level alliance in that both types of alliances are intended to synergistically involve partners with new businesses. Coca-Cola and Cargill Inc. created a strategic alliance to produce a new calorie-free, "natural" sweetener they hope will appeal to health-conscious consumers. The product, tentatively named "Rebiana," will likely become an ingredient in Coke's soft drink products and will be a new product for Cargill Inc. to sell. Rebiana is derived from stevia, a plant native to South America. This move by both firms will put pressure on makers of synthetic sweeteners such as NutraSweet and Equal. If approved by food regulators in the United States, it could be a significant innovation and diversification for both Coke and Cargill. Currently, sugar-related products that are high in calories and the synthetic products that are not natural are criticized by various consumer groups. A "natural" sweetener might create a big demand in the market, especially if the new product can be produced without a great deal of cost, and thus lead to a significant transition in these associated industries.[23]

Franchising

Franchising is a well-established and successful type of corporate-level strategic alliance. As defined in Chapter 8, *franchising* is the licensing of a good or service and business model to partners for specified fees (usually a signing fee and a percentage of the franchisee's revenues or profits). Franchising allows a firm to expand a successful venture and earn additional returns without taking large financial risks. Franchising has the added advantage of allowing the franchisor to maintain control of its product and business model. Usually, the franchisor establishes tight controls on the actions a franchisee can take with its product and business name.

Many well-known firms franchise. McDonald's, Hilton International, and 7-Eleven all have franchisees operating some of the businesses carrying their name and products. For example Choice Hotels International franchises hotels under the following brands: Comfort Inn, Comfort Suites, Quality Inn, Sleep Inn, Clarion, Cambria Suites, MainStay Suites, Suburban Extended Stay Hotel, Econo Lodge, and Rodeway Inn. As of December 31, 2007, it had franchises for more than 5,500 hotels representing more than 450,000 rooms in the United States and in 37 countries and territories.[24]

For franchising to be highly effective, the partners must cooperate. The franchisor must develop and transfer successful programs and means of managing the operation to the franchisee. The franchisee must have the knowledge and capabilities necessary to compete in the local market. And franchisees must provide feedback to the franchisor about activities that work and those that do not. Franchisees should also inform the franchisor about the important characteristics of competitors and market conditions in their local markets. Franchising can also enable a franchisor to gain a first-mover advantage without some of the risks involved in being a first mover.[25]

Sony is trying to develop highly related new products using alliances. The most ambitious and probably the most important alliance is the joint venture with Samsung, a competitor. This venture has much potential for Sony, particularly with Samsung's technology and its market-leading position in flat panel displays. Interestingly, Sony's alliances with Ericsson and Samsung are both cross-border alliances, the next topic of discussion.

International Strategic Alliances

Cross-border strategic alliances have become the most prominent means of entering foreign markets. One reason is that some countries require that firms form joint ventures with local firms in order to enter their markets. This is the case for many industries in China, as explained in Focusing on Strategy. Additionally, foreign firms need knowledge and perhaps other resources to understand and compete effectively in the newly entered markets. As noted earlier, even if the Chinese government did not require joint ventures, foreign firms would do well to form them anyway. They could use the alliances to learn about the different culture and characteristics of the market, and to develop relationships with distributors and important government units. Also, outsourcing to businesses in foreign countries with lower labor costs increases the number of cross-border strategic alliances. Therefore, as noted in Chapter 8, entering foreign markets through cooperative strategies is an attractive option for many firms.[26]

All strategic alliances carry risks. However, the use of international strategic alliances, a popular strategy for entering markets or gaining access to special skills and resources, carries some additional risks and potential costs. In the Danone and Wahaha joint venture noted in Focusing on Strategy, the differing strategic intents and cultures of the two companies' executives created an early barrier to an effective alliance. Different cultures and a lack of trust can hinder the transfer of knowledge or sharing of other resources necessary to make an alliance successful. Top executives warn against making assumptions when moving into new international markets. A firm's products often must be adapted to the local market. These adaptations require close cooperation of local partners. Firms may have to adapt their products and use different distribution channels as they cross into new international markets. For example, India does not allow foreign retailers to sell directly to consumers. Accordingly, Wal-Mart has chosen to enter the market through a wholesaling operation in a joint venture with India's Bharti Enterprises Ltd. Wal-Mart plans to open its first cash-and-carry wholesale joint venture store by December 2008, followed by more stores in 2009. Additionally, Wal-Mart can develop "back office operations" in which it intends to have a significant amount of investment to help modernize India's retail industry and supply chains. To quell potential protests by mom-and-pop store owners and the intermediaries that supply them, Wal-Mart announced "our goal is to work with India's existing supply chain infrastructure and improve efficiency to minimize wastage and maximize value for farmers and manufacturers as well as retailers."[27]

Managing Risks in Strategic Alliances

© Kevin Winter/Getty Images

Each type of strategic alliance (business-level, corporate-level, and cross-border) has its own risks and potentially generic risks as well. Many strategic alliances fail, even some that were formerly successful, as in the case of Disney and Pixar. Estimates of alliance failure range from 50 percent to 70 percent. The failure of alliances is an important issue because often value creation and up to a third of revenues for many companies come through alliances, which can account for up to 25 percent of annual growth in revenues.[28]

One major issue is the development of trust. Given the substantial conflict in the Danone and Wahaha alliance, the risks related to lack of trust are evident. When partners don't trust each other, they are less likely to share resources, particularly the most valuable ones. Without trust, partners also must invest more time and energy (resulting in extra costs) to guard against possible opportunistic behavior by the other firm. As a result, alliances without trust between partners are unlikely to meet their goals.

Of course, all alliances suffer from the potential differences in corporate and national cultures. These differences reflect emphases on separate values and may lead to communication problems between partners as well as an inability to understand each other's intentions. Additionally, because it is impossible to know all of a firm's capabilities before alliances are formed, participants in alliances often discover that the partner's competencies are not as strong or complementary as assumed.

Firms also may be unwilling to share important resources as assumed when the alliance was formed.[29] For example, Pixar's market power grew considerably during the time of its alliance with Disney because of the substantial success of their jointly produced animated films, so Pixar likely became unwilling to share its creative talent with Disney, at least under the old arrangement. When the alliance ended, Disney may have needed Pixar more than Pixar needed Disney, as evidenced by Disney's later acquisition of Pixar.[30]

Effectively managing alliances can reduce some of their risks. But it isn't easy to manage the risks of alliances, as evidenced in the demise of successful alliances such as those between Disney and Pixar and Danone and Wahaha. Some firms use detailed contracts to try to guard against opportunistic behavior by a partner. A detailed contract can help, but it isn't possible to identify and then specify in a contract all partner actions that are acceptable as alliance partners.[31] Thus, problems with overseas alliance partners can have a substantial negative effect on a firm's performance and can lead to a loss of control, as the Danone and Wahaha joint venture illustrates.

Indeed, the best action that most firms can take is to attempt to develop a trusting relationship. Trust is the best preventive medicine against opportunistic behavior. In addition, trust promotes the sharing of resources and even the willingness to cooperate with and help alliance partners. We emphasize the importance of trust in our discussion of managing alliances.

Managing Strategic Alliances

Given the importance of strategic alliances and their potential effects on firm performance, businesses have started to emphasize the management of alliances as a way to develop a competitive advantage and create value for their shareholders.[32] As a result, firms are even creating units with the responsibility of managing their multiple strategic alliances.[33] The actions required to successfully manage alliances and their outcomes are shown in Figure 9.1.

Selecting partners is the first step in managing alliances to make them successful. If an incompatible partner is selected, the alliance is likely to fail. Furthermore,

Figure 9.1 Managing Alliances

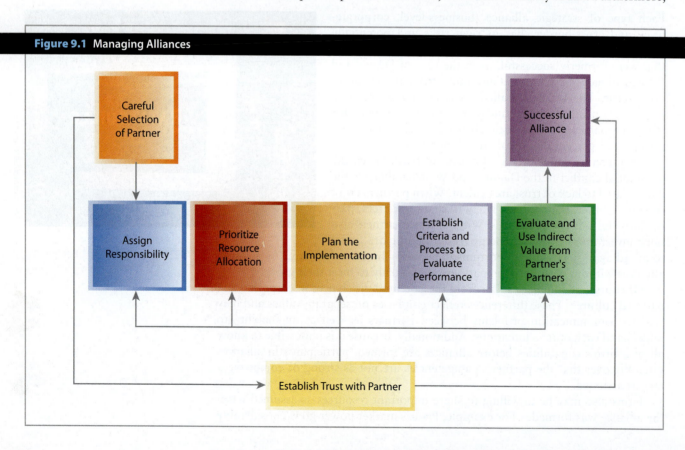

the firm should understand its partner well enough to ensure that it has the resources desired. An important part of the analysis and selection of a partner is to understand the context in which the partner operates, its competitive landscape, and the institutional forces (such as banks and government policies) with which it must deal (especially for international alliances).[34]

After selecting the partner and starting the alliance, each partner must access the resources desired from the other partner and learn the knowledge needed to successfully participate in the alliance. If either or both partners fail to achieve their goals, the alliance will fail. To increase the probability of alliance success, then, both partners must provide access to resources and be willing to help the other partner learn. The willingness to help partners may require extra effort until trust between the firms grows. Firms should attempt to build trust with the intent of establishing social capital in the alliance.[35] Trust is the base for social capital, which in turn leads to cooperation between partners. Social capital implies that firms will help their partners gain value from an alliance. Of course, the partner is expected to reciprocate. Because of the difficulty in building trust and social capital, firms often form alliances with former partners with whom social capital already exists.

One measure of an alliance's success, in addition to its longevity, is the extent to which knowledge is transferred between partners and integrated into the alliance operations. Integrating separate knowledge sets is important because this helps produce synergy and innovation, as illustrated in Understanding Strategy: Learning from Success on the Monsanto and Dow AgroScience joint venture to produce corn seeds that are both weed- and pest-resistant. Thus, alliance managers should invest time and effort to ensure that both partners learn (add knowledge) from the alliance and that their two complementary knowledge stocks are integrated to create value in the alliance.

According to some recent research, firms would do well to pay careful attention to equity investments in the alliances. The failure rate is high in alliances in which the foreign investors have a low equity investment. However, the success rate is higher when the foreign investor makes a large equity investment.[36] Obviously, when the equity is high, the investor has an incentive to ensure that the alliance succeeds. As such, more effort also is invested to make the alliance work. Additionally, foreign investors are likely to have greater technological and management expertise. Therefore, a higher equity stake encourages them to use more of their expertise to make the alliance successful.

Alliance success also is more likely when alliances are managed to identify and take advantage of opportunities rather than to minimize costs. Alliances formed on the basis of detailed formal contracts with extensive monitoring mechanisms are more likely to fail. Rather, firms should build trust in order to take maximum advantage of opportunities generated by forming the alliance. Such outcomes require careful and dedicated management to ensure cooperative efforts in strategic alliances.[37]

In addition to the actions suggested previously, the following steps are recommended as guidelines for effectively managing strategic alliances:

1. Even if the firm has a unit with the overall responsibility of managing its network of alliances, a manager or sponsor should be named for each alliance (and a similar person should be named by the partner). These managers keep each other informed of major alliance activities, resource allocations, and outcomes.
2. The organization should analyze the alliance's priority within its resource allocations and ensure the commitment needed for each alliance to succeed.
3. A clear plan for implementing the alliance should be created and activated after the partners have agreed to the alliance.
4. The means for analyzing the performance of the alliance and distribution of performance outcomes to the partners should be clearly established. Important stakeholders' interests need to be considered when establishing the performance criteria.
5. In the evaluation of an alliance's value, the partners' partners in other alliances should be considered. The indirect network of partners from other alliances may

How to End Failed Strategic Alliances or Those That Reach the End of Their Useful Life

Abbott Laboratories and Takeda Pharmaceuticals have ended their joint venture that created Tap Pharmaceutical Products Inc. and earned revenue of $3.1 billion in 2007. This joint venture lasted for more than 31 years, created a number of useful products for both companies, and made the venture profitable. However, both companies found that ending the venture made sense financially and strategically. Accordingly, they ended the venture amicably with Abbott retaining the rights to Lupron, a prostate cancer drug that had $640 million in sales in 2007. Abbott also will retain 300 employees who work on the product, as well as receive a cash payment of $1.5 million over seven years. Alternatively, Takeda will retain Prevacid, a heartburn drug that reached more than $2 billion in sales in 2007, along with the research team of about 800 people in the United States.

© Susan Van Etten

Although the Tap joint venture ended in a friendly way, many do not, as shown in the Danone and Wahaha venture. Because so many joint ventures and alliances end in failure or prematurely, a wise approach is to make sure that both parties agree beforehand on how the venture will end. Like a prenuptial agreement, if a divorce occurs between two firms, negotiating exit options before the venture is formed seems rational, although it often goes counter to the euphoria leading up to an exciting new agreement. However, partners may ignore the issue at their own risk.

Predictable patterns seem to be rationally observed. One partner might grow dissatisfied and seek to exit but has no reasonable options in the contract. Accordingly, this partner may attempt to covertly appropriate much of the value from the alliance before it moves completely into negative territory. The dissatisfied partner might also seek to establish a trail that would blame the other partner for the failed venture. If partner B discovers such maneuvering, the executives might become angry and, as such, lead the firm to take counter moves. This situation is much like what happened within the Danone-Wahaha joint venture in China.

A successful disengagement plan might observe the following steps. First, make sure that exit triggers are clearly defined by both parties in the event that circumstances dictate motivation toward exiting. Second, clearly try to specify the rights of each party to create a fair separation of the joint venture assets and products, as was done in the Abbott and Takeda joint venture. Finally, develop a plan of communication and flow of information between partners, customers, suppliers, and other parties involved to specify the dissolution process. Not clearly stating the triggers that will end the partnership and some specification about timing when differences occur may lead to lengthy and expensive haggling in court.

Maintaining transparency with partners, customers, and employees (and even rivals) can help manage the impact of the news of the breakup, especially the impact from financial markets. When a company mishandles the communication during a breakup, it can severely damage a company's image and reputation, which will hinder its chances of finding future partners for additional ventures that the company might want to undertake.

Sources: S. Wang, 2008, Abbott, Takeda to end joint venture, *Wall Street Journal*, March 20, D5; C. M. Wittman, 2008, Strategic alliances: What can we learn when they fail? *Journal of Business-to-Business Marketing*, 14(3): 1–19; J. T. Areddy & L. Chao, 2007, Groupe Danone gets a cool reception in peace offering to partner in China, *Wall Street Journal*, December 17, B2; R. Gulati, M. Sytch, & P. Mehrotra, 2007, Business insight (A special report); Preparing for the exit when forming a business alliance, don't ignore one of the most crucial ingredients: How to break up, *Wall Street Journal*, March 3, R1.

be of value for future alliances or got providing indirect value through the benefits derived by the firm's partner.[38]

Of course, even with these guidelines, a number of strategic alliances will fail or reach the end of their useful life. Understanding Strategy: Learning from Failure illustrates how a firm can manage such failure and learn from it in order to improve its capability to better manage cooperative strategy in the future.

SUMMARY

The purpose of this chapter is to explain how a firm can develop and manage strategic alliances to develop or maintain a competitive advantage. In doing so, we examined the following topics:

- A strategic alliance is a relationship between firms in which the partners agree to cooperate in ways that provide benefits to each of them. In an equity alliance, each partner owns a specified percentage of the equity in a separate venture. These ventures are often called joint ventures. In a nonequity alliance, a contractual relationship is established between two or more firms that allows them to share resources or capabilities.
- Firms form alliances for many reasons. Alliances can be helpful for entering new markets, especially those that are restricted (e.g., by governments). Alliances can be useful for sharing the risks of entering markets or in developing new products. In some cases, alliances help firms expand their economies of scale and market power. Oftentimes, strategic alliances are helpful in meeting competitive challenges, especially when the firms involved gain access to complementary resources or learn new capabilities. Finally, strategic alliances have played a major role in the recent outsourcing trend.
- Strategic alliances can be established at the business level. They may be vertical alliances across separate activities in the value chain or horizontal alliances between competitors.

- Corporate-level strategic alliances include alliances for diversification and/or those designed to create synergy. Additionally, franchising is a form of strategic alliance and international strategic alliances have become common for entering new foreign markets.
- While strategic alliances can provide several benefits to the partners, they also present some important risks. A major risk is the potential for opportunism by one of the partners. There is a high alliance failure rate often because of differences in corporate or national culture and due to information asymmetries. Differences in culture may produce conflicts, and information asymmetries can lead to inaccurate assumptions about resources and capabilities held by partners.
- To increase the probability of success, strategic alliances need to be managed. First, firms should take great care in selecting compatible partners that have the needed resources. Examining the amount of equity used in forming an alliance is also important. After the alliance is formed, the partners should invest in establishing trust, which will ensure the transfer of resources and learning. They should also assign responsibilities within the firm, develop priorities for allocating resources, plan for the alliances' implementation, and develop means for evaluating its performance and distributing performance outcomes back to partners.

KEY TERMS

complementary resources 171
cooperative strategy 170
equity alliance 170

horizontal strategic alliance 173
joint venture 170
nonequity alliance 170

strategic alliance 170
vertical strategic alliance 173

DISCUSSION QUESTIONS

1. What is a strategic alliance, and what are the differences between equity and nonequity alliances?
2. Why do firms form alliances? Explain.
3. What are vertical and horizontal business-level alliances?
4. What are corporate-level strategic alliances?
5. Why do firm commonly use strategic alliances to enter international markets?

6. What are the major risks involved in forming strategic alliances?
7. What can firms do to manage strategic alliances in ways that increase their probability of success?
8. What is the best way to end a strategic alliance or joint venture?

STRATEGY TOOLBOX

Introduction

Before entering a strategic alliance, a firm must carefully analyze the supporting logic and rationale. It is a good time to consider external consultants, even though the initial assessment process can be done internally. This chapter's tool—the Alliance Decision Evaluation Grid—can be a helpful way to evaluate whether the alliance makes sense.

Alliance Decision Evaluation Grid

Rationale	A. Relative Importance [1 (low) to 5 (high)]	B. Support for Alliance [1 (low) to 5 (high)]	Calculated Attractiveness [A × B]
Gain access to a restricted market			
Develop new goods or services			
Facilitate new market entry			
Share significant R&D investments			
Share risks and buffer against uncertainty			
Develop market power			
Gain access to complementary resources			
Build economies of scale			
Meet competitive challenges			
Learn new skills and capabilities			
Outsource for lower costs and higher-quality output			

MINI-CASE

Is Outsourcing Good or Bad for Firms?

Outsourcing by U.S. firms has increased significantly in recent years as a way to lower costs and improve their focus on their capabilities. However, firms are now outsourcing professional jobs done by white-collar workers (engineering and software development jobs); most previous outsourcing involved blue-collar manufacturing jobs. Because it is affecting a large number of all types of jobs, outsourcing has become a political issue. However, some argue that outsourcing, such as in the automobile industry, will lead to production and sales in foreign countries with growing demand, such as China. In fact, as we noted in Focusing on Strategy at the beginning of the chapter, China's SAIC Motorcorp and Nanjing Automobile Corp., both of which produce cars for foreign manufacturers, have formed a joint venture to develop a "national car company" to become a domestic competitor and to produce cars for export. More broadly, some argue that trade with foreign countries such as China has fostered moves away from past political repression toward more economic freedom. Thus,

as discussed next, most of the focus of outsourcing is to improve efficiency and effectiveness, but political ramifications must also be considered.

Many of the products listed on Dell's Web site are developed for Dell by contract manufacturers. The list of products it buys from these sources includes TVs, DVD players, portable music devices, and digital cameras. Most of these products have become commodity items, as is the case with the personal computer (PC). Even Japanese firms such as Toshiba are outsourcing the manufacture of PCs. Even though outsourcing to low-cost manufacturers has been common for some time, software development, programming, and even high-technology professional activities such as interpreting medical X-rays are more recent examples of work activities being outsourced.

For example, AstraZeneca, a large U.K. pharmaceutical firm, plans on contracting much of its drug production and even some of its R&D to manufacturers in China and India in the coming decade. One executive indicated that "manufacturing is not a core activity for the company" and "that there are a lot of organizations that are better at manufacturing." However, he also pointed out that "it will never make sense for a major pharmaceutical company to outsource 100 percent of its manufacturing requirements." In fact, the decision will be based on keeping knowledge of important products and processes in house to protect intellectual property, as well as basic supply (sourcing and transportation), financial, regulatory, and restructuring considerations.

Outsourcing professional activities means that higher-paying jobs are going overseas and may become a political liability for organizations doing such outsourcing. Yet businesses argue that outsourcing is necessary to remain competitive in global markets. In fact, managers suggest that outsourcing important activities not only saves money (by reducing costs) but also increases quality in some cases because those doing the outsourced work are specialists. Still, drawbacks are a factor. Outsourcing firms lose the capability to perform the activity when they outsource it, meaning that it will be difficult and costly to redevelop that capability at a later date, if desired. Additionally, even though outsourcing provides flexibility that is important in a dynamic competitive landscape, firms must be careful not to outsource key areas. Managers must also ensure that the firm does not lose a core competence or an activity important for supporting a core competence because of their outsourcing decisions. Additionally, outsourcing may involve risks to reputation and even legal liability problems if work is done poorly.

The outsourcing trend has reached Japan and Europe. However, the cost of outsourcing in Europe is more expensive. For example, in Denmark, although firms have more flexibility to decide to outsource than most European companies, workers can receive up to 90 percent of their wages for six months as severance paid by the company before they receive any unemployment payments from the government insurance program. By law, they also receive up to six weeks of retraining to facilitate movement into new jobs. However, the reverse trend toward outsourcing to higher-level capabilities are evident. For example, many U.S. financial service firms expect to receive significant levels of outsourcing by sovereign wealth funds (national governments that often have funds due to trade surpluses, such as Saudi Arabia) to provide expertise in portfolio management.

Many arguments are made on both sides about the costs and benefits of outsourcing. Firms must decide whether outsourcing is positively linked to performance, what to outsource, and to whom to outsource. They may have to fend off politicians who provide incentives not to outsource. In addition, legislation may be introduced that calls for a tax to be levied on imported goods or services that have been developed through outsourcing. The problems managers face related to outsourcing are complex, and the solutions may not be simple.

Sources: J. Howells, D. Gagliardi, & K. Malik, 2008, The growth and management of R&D outsourcing: Evidence from U.K. pharmaceuticals, *R&D Management*, 38(2): 205–219; L. M. Ellram, W. L. Tate, & C. Billington, 2008, Offshore outsourcing of professional services: A transaction cost economics perspective, *Journal of Operations Management*, 26(2): 148–163; M. H. Weier, 2008, Study finds outsourcing delivers ROI, but not innovation, *InformationWeek*, www.informationweek.com, February 15; S. Fitch, 2007, Copenhagen capitalism, *Forbes*, March, 98; A. Jack, 2007, AstraZeneca set to buy more Chinese drugs, *Financial Times*, September 18, 22; J. Miller, 2007, Mixed message, *Pharmaceutical Technology*, November, 102, 104.

Questions

1. From the perspective of strategic management, what are the costs and benefits of outsourcing?
2. As a manager, what type of information would you gather and what analyses would you conduct to decide whether to outsource an activity?
3. How do you predict that outsourcing from U.S., Japanese, and European firms to China, Taiwan, and India will affect the economies and firms in the three sourcing countries?

EXPERIENTIAL EXERCISES

Exercise One: Alliances in the Airline Industry

In Groups

Each group will be assigned one of the following airline alliances. Use the alliance Web site and other information sources to answer the following questions:

1. What kind of alliance is used? Equity or nonequity? Horizontal or vertical?
2. When was the alliance formed, and which airlines are members of the alliance?
3. How do airlines cooperate within this alliance (e.g., what kinds of resources are shared), and what are the specific benefits to the airlines and customers?
4. Refer to Table 9.1 in the chapter. Which of the reasons for strategic alliances are most applicable to this alliance?

5. What are the main risks associated with being a member of this alliance?

Whole Class

Each group should present its answers to the preceding questions, and the class should discuss the similarities and differences among the three alliances. To what extent do these alliances help airlines overcome the current challenges facing them?

Airline Alliances

oneworld: www.oneworld.com
SkyTeam: http://skyteam.com
Star Alliance: www.staralliance.com

BIZ FLIX

Erin Brockovich: **Rocky Start to a Critical Partnership**

As discussed in this chapter, partnerships are a type of strategic alliance. This scene from *Erin Brockovich* quickly shows you some issues that a firm must consider when entering such an alliance.

Erin Brockovich (Julia Roberts), a single mother of three, needs a job and persuades skeptical attorney Ed Masry (Albert Finney) to hire her. She quickly discovers a potentially large case against Pacific Gas & Electric Company (PG&E) for environmental pollution. Based on a true story, the film has many dramatic and funny moments. Roberts received the 2000 Best Actress Academy Award.

This scene is an edited segment from the "Erin finds out about their new partner" sequence about 90 minutes into the film. Ed Masry has just entered into a partnership with another attorney who has extensive experience in toxic litigation. He had not discussed his idea of the partnership for the PG&E case with Erin. It begins with Erin and Ed Masry discussing the new partner. The film continues after this scene to its dramatic conclusion.

What to Watch for and Ask Yourself

1. Does Ed Masry describe a clear need for entering into this partnership?
2. What strengths does the partnership bring to litigation against PG&E?
3. What type of strategic alliance discussed in this chapter best describes this partnership? Is it a business-level, corporate-level, or international strategic alliance?

ENDNOTES

1. W. H. Hoffmann, 2007, Strategies for managing a portfolio of alliances, *Strategic Management Journal*, 28: 827–853; R. D. Ireland, M. A. Hitt, & D. Vaidyanath, 2002, Alliance management as a source of competitive advantage, *Journal of Management*, 28: 413–446.
2. Y. Wang & S. Nicholas, 2007, The formation and evolution of non-equity strategic alliances in China, *Asia Pacific Journal of Management*, 24:131–150; S. S. Lui & H. -Y. Ngo, 2004, Trust and contractual safeguards on cooperation in non-equity alliances, *Journal of Management*, 30: 471–485.
3. D. Lavie, 2007, Alliance portfolios and firm performance: A study of value creation and appropriation in the U.S. software industry, *Strategic Management Journal*, 28:1187–1212.
4. R. C. Sampson, 2007, R&D alliances and firm performance: The impact of technological diversity and alliance organization on innovation, *Academy of Management Journal*, 50: 364–386.
5. S. Kurokawa, S. Iwata, & E. B. Roberts, 2007, Global R&D activities of Japanese MNCs in the US: A triangulation approach, *Research Policy*, 36: 3–36.
6. K. Dittrich & G. Duysters, 2007, Networking as a means to strategy change: The case of open innovation in mobile telephony, *Journal of Product Innovation Management*, 24: 510–521.
7. Y. -S. Hwang & S. H. Park, 2007, The organizational life cycle as a determinant of strategic alliance tactics: Research propositions, *International Journal of Management*, 24(3): 427–435; M. A. Hitt, M. T. Dacin, E. Levitas, J. -L. Arregle, & A. Borza, 2000, Partner selection in emerging and developed market contexts: Resource-based and organizational learning perspectives, *Academy of Management Journal*, 43: 449–467.
8. G. Wiesmann, 2008, Lufthansa plans JFK hub link with JetBlue, *Financial Times*, March 13, 18.
9. C. Lakshman & R. C. Parente, 2008, Supplier-focused knowledge management in the automobile industry and its implications product performance, *Journal of Management Studies*, 45: 317–342.
10. J. Howells, D. Goiardi, & K. Malik, 2008, The growth and management of R&D outsourcing: Evidence from U.K. Pharmaceuticals, *R&D Management*, 38(2): 205–219.
11. 2007, Pininfarina, Bolloré reach deal to form electric-car joint venture, *Wall Street Journal*, December 24, B3.
12. J. Range, 2007, Are the big three outsourcing firms worth a flier? *Wall Street Journal*, December 17, C3.
13. R. Gulati & M. Sytch, 2008, Does familiarity breed trust? Revisiting the antecedents of trust, *Managerial and Decision Economics*, 29: 165–190.
14. J. Yang, J. Wang, C. W. Y. Wong, & J. -H. Lin, 2008, Relational stability and alliance performance in supply chain, *Omega*, 36(4): 600–608.
15. R. Locke & M. Romis, 2007, Improving work conditions in a global supply-chain, *MIT Sloan Management Review*, 48(2): 54–62.
16. L. C. Giunipero, R. B. Handfield, & D. L. Johansen, 2008, Beyond buying: Supply-chain managers used to have one main job: Purchasing stuff cheaply; They need a whole new skill set now, *Wall Street Journal*, March 10, R8.
17. J. B. Barney, 2007, *Gaining and Sustaining a Competitive Advantage*, 3rd ed., Upper Saddle River, NJ: Prentice Hall.
18. B. Chidmi & R. A. Lopez, 2007, Brand-supermarket demand for breakfast cereals and retail competition, *American Journal of Agricultural Economics*, 89: 324–337; L. C. Strauss, 2006, They're grrrreat! *Barron's*, January 2, 19.
19. Barney, *Gaining and Sustaining a Competitive Advantage*, 276.
20. J. S. Harrison, M. A. Hitt, R. E. Hoskisson, & R. D. Ireland, 2001, Resource complementarity in business combinations: Extending the logic to organizational alliances, *Journal of Management*, 27: 679–699.
21. P. Kale & H. Singh, 2007, Building firm capabilities through learning: The role of the alliance learning process in alliance capability and firm-level alliance success, *Strategic Management Journal*, 28: 981–1000.
22. E. Garnsey, G. Lorenzoni, & S. Ferriani, 2008, Speciation through entrepreneurial spin-off: The Acorn-Arm story, Research Policy, 37: 210–224.
23. L. Etter & B. McKay, 2007, Coke, Cargill set ambitious push for sweetener; Partners tout Rebiana as natural, no calorie; Steep hill remains, *Wall Street Journal*, May 31, A1, A10.
24. 2008, www.choicehotelsfranchise.com.
25. S. C. Michael, 2003, First mover advantage through franchising, *Journal of Business Venturing*, 18: 61–80.
26. A. C. Inkpen, 2008, Knowledge transfer and international joint ventures: The case of NUMMI and General Motors, *Strategic Management Journal*, 29: 447–453.
27. G. Raghuvanshi & E. Bellman, 2008, Wal-Mart sets India plans, Aims to back local players, *Wall Street Journal*, February 21, B4.

28. J. Hughes & J. Weiss, 2007, Simple rules for making alliances work, *Harvard Business Review*, 85(11): 122–131; D. C. Hambrick, J. Li, K. Xin, & A. S. Tsui, 2001, Compositional gaps and downward spirals in international joint venture management groups, *Strategic Management Journal*, 22: 1033–1053.

29. Hitt, Dacin, Levitas, Arregle, & Borza, op. cit.

30. R. Grover, 2007, How Bob Iger unchained Disney, *BusinessWeek*, February 5, 74–79.

31. J. J. Reuer & A. Arino, 2007, Strategic alliance contracts: Dimensions and determinants of contractual complexity, *Strategic Management Journal*, 28: 313–330.

32. Lavie, op. cit.

33. Hughes & Weiss, Simple rules for making alliances work; J. H. Dyer, P. Kale, & H. Singh, 2001, How to make strategic alliances work, *MIT Sloan Management Review*, 42(4): 37–43.

34. J. W. Spencer, 2008, The impact of multinational enterprise strategy on indigenous enterprises: Horizontal spillovers and crowding out in developing countries, *Academy of Management Review*, 33: 352–361; M. A. Hitt, D. Ahlstrom, M. T. Dacin, E. Levitas, & L. Svobodina, 2004, The institutional effects on strategic alliance partner selection in transition economies: China versus Russia, *Organization Science*, 15: 173–185.

35. M. H. Hansen, R. E. Hoskisson, & J. B. Barney, 2008, Competitive advantage in alliance governance: Resolving the opportunism minimization-gain maximization paradox, *Managerial and Decision Economics*, 29(2/3): 191–208.

36. C. Dhanaraj & P. W. Beamish, 2004, Effect of equity ownership on the survival of international joint ventures, *Strategic Management Journal*, 25: 295–305.

37. R. D. Ireland & J. W. Webb, 2007, A multi-theoretic perspective on trust and power in strategic supply chains, *Journal of Operations Management*, 25: 482–497; J. H. Dyer & C. Wujin, 2003, The role of trustworthiness in reducing transaction costs and improving performance: Empirical evidence from the United States, Japan and Korea, *Organization Science*, 9: 285–305.

38. Hughes & Weiss, op. cit.; K. E. Klein, 2004, Fine-tune that alliance, *BusinessWeek Online*, www.businessweek.com, February 10.

CHAPTER 10
Strategy, Innovation and Entrepreneurship

Knowledge Objectives

Reading and studying this chapter should enable you to:

1. Define innovation, entrepreneurship, and entrepreneurs.

2. Describe entrepreneurial opportunities and entrepreneurial capabilities.

3. Understand strategic entrepreneurship and explain how organizations use it.

4. Describe how firms internally develop innovations.

5. Explain how firms use cooperative strategies to develop innovations.

6. Discuss acquisitions as a means of innovation.

7. Summarize the use of strategic entrepreneurship as a means of innovation and market entry.

© BrandX Pictures

Google's Capabilities and Approaches for Successful Innovation

This chapter discusses how firms are able to reinvent themselves by taking advantage of opportunities through entrepreneurial actions. Google is a prime example of a firm that has strong innovative capabilities and uses all three approaches that we mention in this chapter.

First, Google has an internal innovation system that can be characterized as the "Patient Strategy," or incremental gradualism. In other words, Google has developed an operating system that is scalable, meaning that when a new application is present, the flexibility built into the system allows Google to simply download the application. Once in the system, the application can address the large, varied content database. Google has also made huge investments in data movement and database management tools that accelerate the product development life cycle. Its data versions evolve over time and can be improved and customized based on continual customer feedback.

© Eros Hoagland/Redux

Second, Google's basic software and operating capability allow cooperative relationships with third-party creators. Such relationships created services such as Gmail, Google Maps, Google AdWords, and Outsense (an advertising placement system). For instance, *Zillo.com,* by displaying elements on Google Maps for customers, can provide high-quality data on real estate properties for sale, which benefits both the third-party provider as well as Google. Similar combinations have been found through *housingmaps.com,* which combines data from Craig's List and Google Maps for those seeking apartments for rent or houses for sale plotted on a map of a local area. Comparable software applications, available for advertisers as well as content providers, allow Google's system to create working relationships with consumers, innovators, advertisers, and content providers in an "innovation ecosystem" that facilitates cooperation among all parties.

Third, when Google executives realize they do not have critical capabilities or information management tools needed, they seek to obtain them via significant acquisitions such as Picasa for photo management, YouTube for online videos, Double Click for Web ads, Keyhole for satellite photos (now Google Earth), and Urchin for Web analytics (now Google Analytics).

To foster this system of creativity, Google has developed a culture of invention and innovation. For example, it allows its engineers to focus 20 percent of their time on new ventures they would like to see developed further. In other words, innovation is literally built into job descriptions at Google. "Managers spend 70 percent of their time on core business, 20 percent on related but different projects, and 10 percent on anything else. Technical employees spend 80 percent of their time on core business and 20 percent on projects of their own choosing."

In summary, Google has built an internal culture focused on innovation and has developed the infrastructure necessary to facilitate this culture. Additionally, the company has built a structure so that it can cooperate with customers and strategic partners, advertisers, and content providers to facilitate innovation. Finally, as mentioned previously, when Google does not have an application that it needs or foresees as a new development opportunity, it makes an acquisition of another firm that has the capabilities to develop a new product or service. All of these efforts combined have made Google into a "true innovation machine."

Sources: P. J. Hane, 2008, Google 2.0 as "Calculating Predator," *Information Today*, January, 1–3; B. Iyer & T. H. Davenport, 2008, Reverse engineering Google's innovation machine, *Harvard Business Review*, 86(4): 58–68; K. Melymuka & T. H. Davenport, 2008, Deconstructing Google, *Computer World*, April 7, 32–33; G. Ambers, 2007, Business: Why Google inspires diverging case studies, *Wall Street Journal*, August 15, A2; R. Rigby, 2007, Trailblazers with tinkering time on their hands: Giving workers the chance to pursue pet projects can pay off, *Financial Times*, November 6, 16; S. Wunker & G. Pohle, 2007, Built for innovation, *Forbes*, November 12, 137.

The purpose of this chapter is to explain the use of innovation as a means for firms to enter new markets or to create entirely new markets. Essentially, when innovating, companies develop unique and successful solutions to problems facing customers and users. For example, in Focusing on Strategy, innovation is critical to continuing Google's success. Increasingly, innovation is proving to be vital to the success of virtually all companies. In fact, a number of studies found a positive link between innovation and firm performance.[1] These findings corroborate Google's experience as well as many other companies' experiences that will be mentioned throughout this chapter. As is true for Google, many organizations, especially larger ones, use three methods to innovate: internal development, cooperative relationships, and acquisitions. This chapter will address these three means for developing innovation.

Additionally, we discuss several topics in this chapter to describe firms' use of innovation as a means of market entry and market creation. We first define innovation and then describe innovation's relationships with entrepreneurship and entrepreneurs. We also introduce the characteristics and behaviors of entrepreneurs and explain the concept of strategic entrepreneurship (the pursuit of entrepreneurial opportunities using a strategic perspective). The chapter then describes the three ways firms innovate when engaging in strategic entrepreneurship. After discussing internal innovation, we examine innovation through cooperative relationships and then through acquisitions. We close the chapter with a summary analysis of how firms can create value by successfully using strategic entrepreneurship.

Our focus in this chapter is on innovation and entrepreneurship in existing organizations. This phenomenon is called **corporate entrepreneurship,** which is an organization-wide reliance on entrepreneurship and innovation as the link to solid financial performance.[2] Thus, our concern is with entrepreneurship and the innovation it spawns within established firms rather than how entrepreneurship is the bedrock for starting new ventures. Courses in entrepreneurship describe how innovation often is the foundation on which new entrepreneurial ventures are built.

Before beginning our discussions of these topics, you should know that uncertainty surrounds innovation. Uncertainty exists when the probability of a certain outcome being achieved is unknown.[3] Even when firms do everything the way it should be done, they have no guarantees that what they are doing will lead to successful innovations. Firms must accept uncertainty when dealing with innovation. Uncertainty does not diminish the value of innovation at all, although firms can't expect every innovative effort to succeed. Of course, many actions that firms take are uncertain in terms of their outcomes. Uncertainty is reduced, however, when the firm successfully follows the steps in the strategic management process. We will add to the basic model in this chapter by suggesting under what circumstances certain approaches to innovation are better than others. We first define innovation.

corporate entrepreneurship

an organization-wide reliance on entrepreneurship and innovation as the link to solid financial performance

innovation

the development of something new— a new good, a new type of service, or a new way of presenting a good or service

Innovation, Entrepreneurship, and Entrepreneurs

Innovation

What image comes to mind when you think of *innovation?* Are you thinking of some new product or service offered? If so, your thoughts are on target: **Innovation** is the development of something new—a new good, a new type of service, or a new way of presenting a good or service to the market. Newness sometimes finds a firm creating a new market niche (e.g., Subway's creation of the "health-conscious" niche in the fast-food industry) or even redefining an industry as Apple did in the music industry with iTunes. Television shows such as *Cops, America's Most Wanted, In Living Color,* and *American Idol* seem to be redefining parts of the entertainment industry. Who created these shows? Not ABC, CBS, or NBC. Newcomer FOX Television developed and introduced all of these shows. Indeed, some analysts suggest

© AP Photo/Dan Steinberg

that for the first 15-plus years of its life, FOX has been redefining the television industry as a result of its ability to shape trends through its programming choices (*Cops* and *America's Most Wanted* are early examples of reality TV). Moreover, unlike its counterparts, FOX has managed to create a brand that provides customers with programming that is hip, young, and sometimes outrageous.[4]

As customers, we are familiar with innovative goods and services. Process and administrative innovations are also important to firms and their efforts to enter new markets, although we may not be aware of them as customers. **Process innovations** are new means of producing, selling, and supporting goods and services.[5] Dell's famous direct-sales model is an example of a process innovation. Before Dell, personal computers (PCs) were sold through store-front retailers. Seeing an opportunity, Michael Dell developed a new process to sell PCs, which was to sell directly to customers rather than indirectly through retailers.

During his time at the helm of General Motors, Alfred P. Sloan, Jr., "invented the very idea of the modern American corporation."[6] An **administrative innovation** is a new way of organizing or handling the organizational tasks firms use to complete their work.[7] Sloan's administrative innovation was to break General Motors into smaller divisions that could operate autonomously as long as they met their financial goals. Initially, the divisions focused on different products (Chevrolet, Buick, Pontiac, Oldsmobile, and Cadillac) that were intended to meet customers' different needs (family transportation, sporty performance, luxury, and so forth). Sloan believed that his innovative organizational structure would enable employees to work more independently in each division. Division independence from the direct control of the firm's upper-level managers, he thought, would cause employees in those divisions to be more creative and productive.

Therefore, innovation is concerned with bringing something new into use. As we've described, the newness of an innovation can take the form of a new good; a new service; a new process to manufacture, sell, and support a good or service; or a new way of managing and directing how a firm operates. From the perspective of a consumer of an innovation, innovation is all about a new opportunity to choose.[8]

It is important to recognize that the purpose of innovation is to increase the firm's performance. Recently, firms producing innovative flat-screen televisions based on different technologies such as LCD, DLP, and plasma gas, as well as companies making components for flat screens, earned significant and record profits. Some business analysts believe that the amount devoted to R&D by firms in the flat-panel industry suggests that additional innovations will stimulate still more growth and profitability in the industry.[9]

What helps firms in their efforts to consistently innovate? As we discuss next, entrepreneurship and the entrepreneurs who are its foundation play important roles in a firm's ability to innovate.

Entrepreneurship

Joseph Schumpeter, the famous economist, saw **entrepreneurship** as a process of "creative destruction" through which existing products, methods of production, or ways of administering or managing the firm are destroyed and replaced with new ones.[10] Firms encouraging entrepreneurship are willing to take risks as well as to be creative while trying to outperform competitors.[11] Peter Drucker provided a classic description that directly describes the relationship between innovation and entrepreneurship: "Innovation is the specific form of entrepreneurship, whether in an existing business, a public service institution, or a new venture started by a lone individual."[12]

The specific focus of entrepreneurship is on discovering and exploiting profitable entrepreneurial opportunities. **Entrepreneurial opportunities** are circumstances suggesting that new goods or services can be sold at a price exceeding the costs incurred to create, make, sell, and support them.[13]

process innovations
new means of producing, selling, and supporting goods and services

administrative innovation
a new way of organizing or handling the organizational tasks firms use to complete their work

entrepreneurship
a process of "creative destruction" through which existing products, methods of production, or ways of administering or managing the firm are destroyed and replaced with new ones

entrepreneurial opportunities
circumstances suggesting that new goods or services can be sold at a price exceeding the costs incurred to create, make, sell, and support them

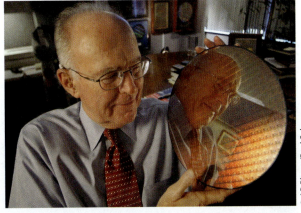
© AP Photo/Paul Sakuma

Sometimes opportunities are borne out of cold-hard realities. Moore's Law suggests that the number of transistors (the microscopic, silicon-based switches that process the digital world's ones and zeros) on a chip roughly doubles every two years. This doubling creates more features, increased performance, and reduced cost per transistor. But in the 1990s, it became obvious that the limitations of existing technologies would rather quickly prevent continuing repetition of Moore's Law. Essentially, the problem facing chip manufacturers such as Intel was that as microcircuits continue to shrink while becoming more powerful, they run hotter and hotter, making it impossible to satisfactorily provide cooling. Intel's decision makers concluded that a different type of transistor had to be developed if the PC industry was to continue growing (and Intel along with it). As we discuss next, entrepreneurs are people in organizations who identify entrepreneurial opportunities and then convert those opportunities into successful innovations.

Entrepreneurs

Entrepreneurs are people who recognize entrepreneurial opportunities and then take risks to develop an innovation to pursue them. Entrepreneurs are found throughout an organization, meaning that those actually making a firm's good or service are just as capable of being entrepreneurs as are managers and staff personnel.

A number of characteristics describe entrepreneurs. For example, entrepreneurs are optimistic,[14] highly motivated, courageous, and willing to take greater financial responsibility for their projects and accept uncertain outcomes.[15] By responding to the issues in Table 10.1, you will have some perspective about the degree to which these characteristics describe you.

The characteristics of an entrepreneur certainly describe Thomas J. Watson, Jr. As the CEO of IBM, Watson was an innovator who bet his firm's future when he decided in 1964 to replace all of the firm's existing computer lines with a radically different type of machine called the System/360. Before the introduction of this innovative product line, firms required different software programs for every computer model. In contrast, the System/360 was a family of computers that allowed programs written for one computer to work on another computer in the family. Questioned at the time about his decision to push IBM in this direction, Watson is now thought of as a courageous and brilliant innovator. Entrepreneurs such as Watson make unique connections among seemingly unconnected events and see possibilities others haven't noticed.[16] Of course, these possibilities are actually entrepreneurial opportunities.

After identifying entrepreneurial opportunities, entrepreneurs turn their attention to developing capabilities that will be the basis of the competitive advantages required

entrepreneurs

people who recognize entrepreneurial opportunities and then take risks to develop an innovation to pursue them

---

Table 10.1 Characteristics of Entrepreneurs—Where Do I Stand?

Entrepreneurs are known to have certain characteristics. For each characteristic, rate yourself on a scale of 1–4 with the following scale values:

1   This characteristic does not describe me.
2   This characteristic slightly describes me.
3   This characteristic accurately describes me.
4   This characteristic strongly describes me.

Characteristic	Rating
Highly motivated	____
Very optimistic	____
Very willing to take responsibility for the outcomes of projects	____
Consistently view uncertainty as an opportunity	____
Highly tolerant of ambiguous situations	____
Highly committed to the importance of innovation	____
Very willing to tackle tasks, even with insufficient resources	____

The higher your score, the greater the probability that you have many of the characteristics of entrepreneurs.

to make a profit from pursuing the opportunities.[17] Although a necessary step, identifying entrepreneurial opportunities is insufficient for innovation and, subsequently, for corporate success. As we learned in Chapter 4, to successfully exploit opportunities, firms must develop capabilities that are valuable, rare, difficult to imitate, and nonsubstitutable. Capabilities satisfying these four criteria are competitive advantages and are the basis on which entrepreneurial opportunities can be successfully pursued.

Therefore, to innovate and to use innovation as a path to enter new markets, firms must identify opportunities *and* determine how to take advantage of them. As you may have already concluded, identifying opportunities is an entrepreneurial process, while developing the capabilities needed to exploit them is a strategic process. When innovations are exploited, they contribute to maintaining or creating competitive advantages. Both processes are concerned with growth and creating value for customers and wealth for shareholders.

Strategic entrepreneurship is the process of taking entrepreneurial actions using a strategic perspective by combining entrepreneurial and strategic management processes to enhance the firm's ability to innovate, enter new markets, and improve its performance. Strategic entrepreneurship allows the firm to first identify and then exploit entrepreneurial opportunities. Strategic entrepreneurship also helps the firm balance its need to find and exploit tomorrow's "new products" while exploiting its current marketplace successes.

As we said earlier, firms can use strategic entrepreneurship to innovate in three ways. Next, we examine these methods, summarized in Table 10.2.

Table 10.2 Three Ways to Innovate

Internal Innovation

- Using a firm's own resources and capabilities to innovate

Cooperating to Innovate

- Two or more firms forming an agreement to join some of their resources and capabilities to innovate

Acquiring Innovation

- Buying ownership of another firm's innovations and innovation capabilities

---

Three Ways to Innovate

Internal Innovation

A firm uses its own resources and capabilities when engaging in *internal innovation*. Of the organizational functions around which resources and capabilities are developed, R&D is most critical for developing innovations internally. Indeed, in most industries, the battle to innovate and use innovation to enter new markets begins in R&D labs. Industries that are highly dependent on innovations for continuing success, such as pharmaceuticals, devote large amounts of their total sales to R&D. For example, in 2007, both software and health care (e.g., pharmaceutical firms) industries averaged 13.3 percent of sales allocated to R&D spending, while the aerospace and auto industries allocated 4.9 and 3.8 percent, respectively.[18]

Often firms in high-technology industries grapple with two conflicting pressures: the need to boost profit margins and the need to invest in new technologies to fuel future growth. In a market that is in a significant downturn, this pressure is even more salient. In 2007, for instance, Hewlett-Packard and IBM, two of the largest information technology firms by revenues, increased their overall research and development budget by 1 percent. At the same time, IBM placed fewer but larger bets on its research projects. Similarly, HP Labs, HP's basic research arm, decided to move from funding 150 smaller projects to focusing on 20 to 30 more significant projects in order to sharpen its research focus.[19]

strategic entrepreneurship

the process of taking entrepreneurial actions using a strategic perspective by combining entrepreneurial and strategic management processes to enhance the firm's ability to innovate, enter new markets, and improve its performance

The internal innovation process can also change low-tech firms such as those found in the food industry. The R&D expenditure relative to sales in the food-processing sector is estimated to be about 0.3 percent compared with a 2.1 percent average in the manufacturing sector as a whole. Although many firms such as Procter and Gamble (P&G) have been successful at creating new products through internal innovation, this process is accelerating through additional biotechnology discoveries in basic agricultural firms. The firms that have experimented with biotechnology have significantly increased the rate of R&D expenditure per dollar of sales. Accordingly, these firms also have been correlated with significant increases in new product developments.[20] For example, the way farmers use sophisticated computer systems and global positioning satellites can help modify the amount of fertilizer, seeds, and water applied in a single field and raise efficiencies from 7 to 15 percent. Additionally, the genomic revolution is influencing the rate of scientific discovery for food producers as well. Seed producers are identifying gene traits for various crops faster and more inexpensively. As such, they can help specify certain crops, such as corn and sugar, to be raised as fuel or food and thereby improve agricultural productivity and the food supply, which is important when basic foods, such as rice, are scarcer than in the past.[21]

When firms pursue an internal innovation process, competitors may try to imitate the R&D processes, but it will be difficult for them to do so. The main reason for the difficulty, of course, is that each firm is using unique capabilities in unique ways to internally develop innovations such as Apple's iPod. Although firms may ultimately copy the product successfully, the time to do so often gives the pioneer time to establish brand recognition and thereby first mover advantages.

Some innovations are incremental, while some are radical. Procter & Gamble's new toothpastes are primarily *incremental innovations,* meaning that each one builds on the firm's existing knowledge about toothpaste to extend the breadth and depth of its offerings. Product line extensions such as those we see in laundry detergents (e.g., liquid Tide as an extension of Tide powder) are another example of incremental innovations. On the other hand, the handheld cellular phone was a radical innovation relative to landline phones. Once a radical innovation is established, incremental innovations are then possible. Radical innovations usually involve technology breakthroughs and the discovery of new knowledge such as the move to integrated circuits from single transistors in the electronics industry.

Both incremental and radical innovations have the potential to create value. However, radical innovations may lead to more substantial improvements in a firm's performance. Nonetheless, it is important to understand that incremental innovations can be particularly profitable. (P&G's introduction of Crest Whitestrips is an example of a successful incremental innovation.) In general, though, the firm can use its current capabilities to successfully exploit incremental innovations and maintain its competitive advantages. In contrast, new capabilities are usually required to gain full value from radical innovations, thereby creating new competitive advantages.

Firms accept risks when innovating through internal means. The most prominent risk is that internal innovations tend to take a great deal of time to develop in order to realize commercial successes. This issue can be serious when rapid innovation is important to a firm's success. As the chairperson and CEO of Charles River Laboratories International says, "Everything in this business is about speed to market."[22]

In the final analysis, firms learn a great deal from their efforts to innovate internally, especially when radical innovations are developed. However, firms also learn from internally created innovations that become product failures. In other words, a fine balance exists between learning from failure and overcoming the trauma of failure, as explained by the experience of P&G and Sun Microsystems in Understanding Strategy: Learning from Failure. While reading about these firms, think about the type of culture required for a firm to risk failure, one that is open and receptive to radically different ideas even while it remains supportive enough to overcome the trauma of failure.

Allowing People to Take Risk and Pursue Innovation While Overcoming the Trauma of Failure

Procter & Gamble was in need of a significant turnaround when A. G. Lafley took over as CEO in 2000. The company was experiencing slow growth and listless older brands. Lafley decided that P&G needed to pursue innovation more vigorously. He created a new development division, Future Works, with a focus on internal innovation through measuring it and rewarding it more consistently. Furthermore, he recruited teams of talented designers to enhance packaging design.

Interestingly, the company's most significant successes, the Olay, Febreze, and Swiffer brands, arose from

Courtesy, SunRay

possible failures. The company aims for a success rate of 60 percent with its innovations. The leaders suggest that "it is as high as P&G wants to go. Any higher would be playing it too safe." Because this goal suggests a 40 percent product failure rate, P&G also stresses a disciplined focus on controlled innovation so that it will not become too difficult and painful to get rid of a bad product before it significantly affects profits.

P&G experienced double-digit growth from its new products and 4 to 6 percent organic growth from established products. Like other firms noted in this chapter, it expects to focus on "fewer, bigger projects" in the future in order to maintain the innovation success that it has had.

Another interesting example is the SunRay computer created by Sun Microsystems in September 1999. Notwithstanding its many competitive advantages relative to the PC, this potential innovation never succeeded even though it had a radical

approach relative to the PC and would have sold for half the cost of a PC. A recent article suggests that this innovation failed because of prior innovation failures that hindered the organization's effort to refine and promote this potentially positive innovation. The JavaStation product was cancelled a month before SunRay's official release in 1999. In 2001, Sun began to experience the trauma of its first downsizing in the company's history. The JavaStation merger killed SunRay's morale and the product's momentum. Furthermore, a constant leadership change triggered turnover in the SunRay team, which contributed to the lack of leadership attention. Grossly overly optimistic sales expectations were never met, and Sun's internal budgeting system was not able to accommodate the new product and its existing product portfolio and control system.

In this classic "innovator's dilemma," a disruptive innovation is unable to fit into the current organizational structure. Instead of creating success, the new innovation adds to the failure. The legacy of the JavaStation merger failure and the subsequent introduction of SunRay led to a downward spiral and loss of momentum for SunRay's team. Instead of a culture of success, Sun realized a "culture of failure."

Organizations need to strike a balance between taking risks and understanding the trauma associated with too much failure. A desirable level of tension in the system can be managed through an appropriate culture within the organization.

Sources: J. Birchall, 2008, Tales of brand revolution from P&G, *Financial Times*, April 10, 16; S. Brown, 2008, Learning from failure, *Director*, February, 31; J. Moldenhauer-Salazar & L. Valikangas, 2008, SunRay's struggle to overcome innovation trauma, *Strategy & Leadership*, March, 15–20; 2008, Innovation and leadership; Executives fail to foster innovation, *Strategic Direction*, 24(5): 36–38.

Innovating by Cooperating

As we previously noted, firms pursuing internal innovations use their own resources and capabilities to innovate. When an organization partners with one or more other firms to combine two sets of resources and capabilities as the source of innovation, it is labeled *innovating by cooperating*. Strategic alliances and joint ventures are common organizational forms used by partner firms to cooperatively develop innovations.

One reason firms decide to cooperate on innovation is that it is becoming increasingly rare for a single company to have all the resources and capabilities needed to successfully innovate in today's dynamic marketplaces. Discussing the complexity of continuous innovation, Andy Ruben, senior director of mobile platforms at Google, suggests that the company is building "an open-source platform for mobile phones called Android. . . . Google can't do everything. And we shouldn't. That's why we formed the Open Handset Alliance with more than 34 partners."[23] As Google develops software for mobile phones, especially the iPhone product, it is using an open approach with many partners on both the supplier side and the service delivery side (customer). As such, it is using strategic partnerships in a cooperative fashion to develop its strategy for mobile phones. Through another collaborative project with MIT students, Google is creating software that meets the needs of young people. For example, one student group created a potential product labeled GeoLife. It uses "to-do" lists that are triggered by geographic locations; for instance, the software provides reminders when a person with the software on his or her mobile phone walks by a grocery market. For example, if the to-do list contained a task "pick up milk," the phone would send a message indicating that this task could be marked off the to-do list by entering the store.[24]

From a strategic entrepreneurship perspective, a partnership formed to innovate can involve one partner bringing to the cooperative relationship its capability to identify entrepreneurial opportunities while the other partner brings its capability to exploit opportunities and create competitive advantages. Strategic entrepreneurship is often practiced in relationships between large pharmaceutical companies and more entrepreneurial biotechnology companies. In these instances, the smaller biotechnology company provides its capability to identify entrepreneurial opportunities and develop innovative products in light of them. The larger organization in the partnership commonly has the skills (often called complementary assets[25]) needed to exploit those innovations (i.e., manufacturing, marketing, and distribution) and to form competitive advantages in the marketplace.

An interesting example of innovating by cooperating is the set of relationships between companies and researchers housed in different universities and research centers located throughout the world. For example, as previously mentioned, Google partnered with MIT by asking a professor to teach a class in which the students help create software applications for Google's forthcoming mobile-operating system labeled Android. To facilitate this interaction, Google established an office across the street from MIT's campus so that the student projects could be conveniently mentored by Google professionals.

Cooperating to innovate is not without risk, however. One firm might "steal" its partner's knowledge with the intention of improving its own competitive ability. A second risk is that before the work of a partnership actually commences, the partners may feel uncertainty about the true level of skills each possesses. Because of these types of risks, a firm needs to be careful in choosing its partner before trying to cooperate to innovate.

On a more positive note, partnering with others shares the risks, which can be substantial, so that one firm does not have to shoulder all of the risk and uncertainty with pathbreaking innovation. Additionally, partners share the cost of developing the innovation, which can be especially useful when the innovation is expensive to develop.

Innovating Through Acquisitions

A firm that acquires a fully developed product from another entity or acquires an innovation capability by buying another company is *innovating through acquisitions*.[26] A firm may go this route for several reasons: to add a complementary product to its existing line, to gain immediate access to different markets or market segments, to substitute an acquired firm's superior technology for its own less effective technology, to add talented scientists and innovative personnel to the firm's labor pool, and to achieve firm growth. Clearly, acquiring innovations allows much faster growth compared to cooperative alliances or internal development. During the 1990s, Cisco Systems acquired a number of firms to gain access to their product innovations and often their innovative capabilities. As emphasized in Understanding

Cisco's Capability in Acquisitions to Create New Business Platforms

Cisco has historically been famous for acquiring emerging firms and digesting them completely through a system that installs its own executives and leaves little trace of the original target's identity. This system has been used by other firms such as Microsoft and Oracle. This approach allowed the networking giant to become the largest network hardware provider of equipment that has been the backbone of the Internet as it has developed.

After the Internet bubble burst in 2000 and 2001, Cisco had to develop a new way to create innovation through acquisitions. Similar to its earlier approach, it continues to buy small, innovative firms rather than develop new technology from scratch to help it stay ahead of the competition and continually develop a new stream of products. Its new approach has been to buy companies in which it finds a platform in new business areas and allows the former managers of the small business to stay in place and retains the core human capital as well, avoiding layoffs that would hurt the innovation capabilities for which the system was purchased.

In 2003, Cisco pursued this approach by acquiring Linksys Group Inc., a home-networking equipment manufacturer. The Linksys networking equipment allows multiple personal computers to simultaneously connect to the Internet and share and print files. The standard Cisco large-firm networking gear could cost $100,000, compared to the Linksys consumer product that starts at less than $100. This acquisition provided a new source for revenue, but Cisco had little experience with this type of consumer product.

© Susan Van Etten

Accordingly, it needed the Linksys brand name and reputation—and especially its experienced sales team—to provide the knowledge needed to expand with this innovative company.

In 2006, Cisco acquired Scientific-Atlanta for $6.9 billion. Again, it used the hands-off approach to manage this set-top-box manufacturer, a mainline producer of cable converters for in-home television sets hooked to cable systems.

In 2007, it purchased WebEx for $3.2 billion and IronPort Systems for $830 million. WebEx provides software and support for conducting meetings through Internet technology. IronPort Systems is part of the network security software business, protecting e-mail from spam viruses and hacking attempts on a subscription basis with updates and new features delivered frequently.

Cisco's hands-off strategy appears to be working. For example, Scientific-Atlanta contributed $2.7 billion, about 8 percent of Cisco's 2007 revenue of $34.9 billion. Although the company does not break down numbers for the WebEx and Linksys divisions, these divisions remain market leaders with strong brand recognition. Cisco expects similar results from the IronPort acquisition.

As you can see, Cisco uses an acquisition approach to build its technological base, speed up the process of innovation, and allow increased growth relative to an internal innovation approach.

Sources: R. Sachitanand & K. Mitra, 2008, Networking India, *Business Today*, www.businesstoday .com, March 4; B. White & B. Vara, 2008, Rerouted: Cisco changes tack in takeover game, *Wall Street Journal*, April 17, A1, A16; J. Brodkin, 2007, Three IT deals that matter, *Network World*, December 20, 26–27; R. Kirkland, 2007, Cisco's display of strength, *Fortune*, November 12, 90, G. A. Moore, 2007, To succeed in the long-term, focus on the middle-term, *Harvard Business Review*, 85(7–8): 84–90.

Strategy: Learning from Success, Cisco has recently changed its approach from the 1990s, but still uses acquisitions to develop and foster new products.

As with the other two means of innovating, acquiring innovations isn't risk-free. A key risk is that acquiring innovation may reduce a firm's ability to innovate internally. Indeed, a failure to support R&D as the base for internal innovations can cause bright and talented people to leave a firm. Research evidence indicates that firms acquiring innovations introduce fewer new products into the market-place, highlighting the dangers of relying heavily on acquisitions as a means of innovating. Additional research suggests that firms pursuing innovation through acquisition need to maintain internal expenditures for R&D in order to continue to create value through such acquisitions.[27]

Across time and events, the most successful firms learn how to innovate inter-nally through cooperative relationships and by acquiring other companies. How-ever, the firm must balance its use of the three innovation methods in ways that create maximum additional value for customers as well as enhance the wealth of its shareholders. In the final section, we discuss how firms can create this balance by identifying and exploiting entrepreneurial opportunities.

Innovation and Strategic Entrepreneurship

As already discussed, strategic entrepreneurship involves identifying an opportu-nity and creating innovation to pursue that opportunity to create value for cus-tomers and wealth for shareholders. *Fast Company* writers also suggested strategic entrepreneurship's importance when presenting its 2008 list of "the world's most innovative companies."[28] To be on this list, firms must be able to use entrepre-neurial capabilities to identify entrepreneurial opportunities and to develop inno-vations in light of them *as well as* to use strategic capabilities to exploit the innovations and opportunities and build competitive advantages.

An important skill is the ability to choose among the alternatives for pursuing an entrepreneurial opportunity: internal innovation, cooperative innovation, and innovation from acquisitions.[29] A central issue in determining whether a firm should pursue an internal venture focuses on its internal skills and abilities. If the firm has a strong set of skills and capabilities to innovate, the targeted innovation should largely remain internal. Firms that have developed strong, intangible capabilities in a specific domain are often in an excellent position to leverage these capabilities through a new internal venture when a related opportunity is perceived.

If a firm's executives perceive a significant entrepreneurial opportunity that is also important strategically to the firm but circumstances suggest that the firm does not currently have the skills and capabilities to take advantage of the opportunity, one of the external options (cooperation or acquisition) should be considered.[30] We suggest that a cooperative venture is the appropriate mode of entry choice to facili-tate rapid development of the skills needed to take advantage of an opportunity, especially in the face of significant uncertainty about whether the technology is available or whether the market will accept the potential prototype good or service. The uncertainty of success suggests that it would be wise to share this risk with partners who have complementary skills; combining those skills with other part-ners provides sufficient incentive to take advantage of the opportunity.

If, on the other hand, the opportunity is less uncertain and more speed is required, an acquisition approach might be more successful. Acquisitions attempt to create value by uniting the complementary innovative resources or capabilities of the acquiring firm and the acquired firm in order to create whole capabilities that did not exist previously. Companies that seek to enhance their technical capa-bilities with speed and efficiency often target innovative firms with expertise in the area of the perceived entrepreneurial opportunity and complementary R&D capa-bilities necessary for the acquiring firm to succeed. Cisco has used this approach to acquire start-up firms to speedily build new niche products in the network gear market, as noted in Understanding Strategy: Learning from Success.

Combining entrepreneurial and strategic skills to successfully innovate and enter new markets is a relatively new concept. But companies that can do so out-perform those that cannot. In increasingly competitive markets, the highest returns accrue to companies that can quickly identify entrepreneurial opportunities, inno-vate, and then use novel capabilities to exploit innovations and develop them into commercial successes.

SUMMARY

The primary purpose of this chapter is to describe how a firm's entrepreneurs can rely on entrepreneurship and strategic entrepreneurship to create innovation as the foundation for entering new markets. In doing so, we examined the following topics:

- **Innovation** is concerned with the creation of newness, especially new products—that is, with bringing something new into use. New goods (e.g., a medicine that significantly improves a patient's chance of recovering from an illness) and services (e.g., the ability to purchase low-cost tickets for travel and entertainment from Internet vendors) are commonly used to satisfy consumers' needs. However, for firms, **process innovations** (e.g., discovering a new way to create value in the primary activities part of the value chain) and **administrative innovations** (e.g., developing value-creating methods to operate the firm) are also important. Effective innovation helps firms create value for customers and wealth for shareholders and can be the basis for entering new markets. Innovation helps firms differentiate their goods and services from competitors' goods and services and facilitates organizational efforts to rapidly move products to the marketplace.

- As a process of creative destruction, **entrepreneurship** is an organizational process through which firms innovate. Entrepreneurial firms are willing to take risks and strive to innovate to quickly introduce goods or services to the marketplace.

- **Entrepreneurs** are people who recognize entrepreneurial opportunities and are willing to take risks to develop an innovation to pursue them. Entrepreneurs have certain characteristics, including being highly motivated, tolerant of uncertainty, and willing to take greater financial responsibility for the outcomes attained through their innovation-focused efforts.

- **Entrepreneurial opportunities** are the product of entrepreneurial behaviors, while pursuing opportunities results from strategic behavior. The most effective firms rely on strategic entrepreneurship as their source of innovation. **Strategic entrepreneurship** is the process of taking entrepreneurial actions with a strategic perspective. Strategic entrepreneurship is becoming increasingly important for firms trying to innovate and to use innovation as a means of entering new markets.

- Firms use one or more of three means to innovate (increasingly, firms use all three means). Internal innovation takes place when the firm uses its own resources and capabilities to innovate. Each firm develops an innovation process that is unique to it. When that process satisfies the criteria of a core competence and can be sustained as discussed in Chapter 4, it can be a source of competitive advantage. Because most firms lack all resources and capabilities required for consistently effective innovation, they also form cooperative relationships such as strategic alliances and joint ventures to innovate. Finally, firms may acquire specific innovations as well as another firm's innovative capabilities. Each means of innovation has benefits and risks. The most effective firm learns how *and* when to use each means of innovation.

- If a firm finds an entrepreneurial opportunity that fits its skills and abilities, it probably should use an internal innovation process to pursue such an opportunity. Alternatively, if a firm's skills do not currently fit the opportunity, it probably should use one of the external approaches (cooperatively develop the skills or acquire the skills) to pursue the opportunity. The cooperative option is more likely to be successful in situations involving significant uncertainty about the technology or market because it allows risk sharing. The acquisition approach might be better when the opportunity is more certain because speed to market becomes more important in developing the necessary skills.

KEY TERMS

administrative innovation, 189
corporate entrepreneurship, 188
entrepreneurial opportunities, 189

entrepreneurs, 190
entrepreneurship, 189
innovation, 188

process innovations, 189
strategic entrepreneurship, 191

DISCUSSION QUESTIONS

1. What is innovation, and what is entrepreneurship? Who are entrepreneurs? What is the relationship between entrepreneurship and entrepreneurs?
2. What are entrepreneurial opportunities and entrepreneurial capabilities? Why must a firm have entrepreneurial capabilities as well as entrepreneurial opportunities to use innovation as a means of entering new markets?
3. What is strategic entrepreneurship? Why do firms use strategic entrepreneurship when innovating?

4. How do firms develop innovations internally?
5. How are cooperative strategies used to develop innovations?
6. How do firms use acquisitions as a way to innovate?
7. How is strategic entrepreneurship important to firms committed to innovation and to the use of innovation as a way to enter markets that are new to them? Under what circumstances would you use each of the three approaches (internal innovation, cooperative relationships, and acquisition) to pursue a new entrepreneurial opportunity?

STRATEGY TOOLBOX

STRATEGY TOOLBOX

Introduction

CEOs need to have some of the key skills associated with entrepreneurship, such as being willing to change and being able to articulate the long-term vision. That being said, pure entrepreneurs are somewhat of a different breed, as they often find the confines of corporate hierarchies constraining. The last tool of this book—the Entrepreneurial Mind-Set Checklist—is a way to quickly assess whether you would be better suited as a corporate CEO or an entrepreneur.

The Entrepreneurial Mind-Set Checklist

1	Do I generally enjoy taking chances?	Yes / No
2	Am I more comfortable with an established infrastructure?	Yes / No
3	Do I generally accept situations rather than try to change them?	Yes / No
4	Do I think I would prefer a guaranteed base pay over commission?	Yes / No
5	Am I comfortable in situations of high ambiguity?	Yes / No
6	Am I creative?	Yes / No
7	Do I generally rely on the opinion of others to guide my actions?	Yes / No
8	Have I ever brainstormed carefully about an unmet business need?	Yes / No
9	Do I generally have problems articulating my ideas to others?	Yes / No
10	Do I occasionally have difficulty fitting in when others seem comfortable?	Yes / No

continued on next page

MINI-CASE

Innovation Through Acquisition: Is It a Good Idea Compared to Other Approaches?

After $4.8 trillion worth of mega-mergers and acquisitions worldwide in industries ranging from automobiles to video games in 2007, which was a 23 percent increase from 2006, *BusinessWeek* analysts asked whether this significant activity has a positive affect on innovation. Roger Martin, Dean of the Rotman School of Management, discussed with the analyst from *BusinessWeek* the potential pitfalls and rewards of seeking to "buy innovation through acquisitions." He suggested that acquisitions represent at least two basic approaches: (1) an attempt to buy innovations that are disruptive and represent game-changing technology developed by an early start-up firm or a firm that might be a potential competitor and (2) alternatively, an attempt to bring in human capital that can help the acquiring firm be more consistently profitable with its creative output.

For instance, analysts widely agreed that Electronic Arts' attempt to acquire Take-Two Interactive Software was an effort to gain control of Take-Two's Grand Theft Auto video game franchise, which is popular among game enthusiasts. Similarly, Microsoft's attempt to acquire Yahoo! seemed to be a hedge against the emerging dominance of Google as it continues to innovate beyond the current abilities of both Microsoft and Yahoo!

Similar acquisitions have been both successful and ruinous in attempts to buy such innovations. For instance, Disney's 2006 acquisition of innovative Pixar seems to have been a boon for Disney. However, TimeWarner's merger with AOL in 2000 was a disaster.

Another example is Ford. In the 34 months that Jack Nasser was CEO of Ford, he tried to reshape Ford through acquisitions. In the process, day-to-day business as well as future innovation was neglected. Ford's market share slid from 25 percent to 15.6 percent between the years 1997 and 2007. Although Bill Ford increased the emphasis on research, new product introduction slowed. However, Alan Mulally, the most recent CEO of Ford, is emphasizing the ingredients that make Ford a great brand and is seeking to create products on a global scale using these same ingredients that have been successful in the past. It remains to be seen whether Ford—which has lacked new product introductions that meet the needs of consumers—can come out of the slump that it is in.

Essentially, many acquirers scan the environment for small innovative firms with potential and then collaborate with them to develop an understanding of the business or buy them outright. For instance, in 2007, IBM bought Cognos and SAP bought Business Objects. Firms seek to buy businesses to integrate a current business that demonstrates an opportunity or to start a new business with which to build a new set of products. Often these firms watch venture capitalists as they help to develop new start-up companies and then seek to buy them from the owners after they have proved to be successful. Cisco, Yahoo!, and Microsoft, as well as Google, have pursued this approach. What created a situation in which these large software makers need to acquire innovative companies? Is it because their R&D budgets were reduced? With the downturn in the economy experienced in 2007 and 2008, will R&D allocations for internal innovation be cut during such lean years? If possible, it would seem that wise companies would use the downturn to gain market share and be even more innovative. Perhaps they can be innovative in a more efficient manner. Alternatively, would it be better to buy innovative and potentially lucrative start-up firms when market prices are down? Instead of doing acquisitions, should they pursue more cooperative agreements with smaller start-up firms in order to cover more opportunities that might be found in the marketplace? These important questions need answers and analysis. It will be interesting to see what these large firms do (i.e., which of the three strategic approaches to strategic entrepreneurship are employed) and what the ultimate outcome will be.

Sources: C. Holahan, 2008, Microsoft swoops in on Yahoo!, *BusinessWeek*, www.businessweek.com, February 1; C. Hymowitz, 2008, In deal-making, keep people in mind, *Wall Street Journal*, May 12, B2; T. Laamanen & T. Keil, 2008, Performance of serial acquirers: Toward an acquisition program perspective, *Strategic Management Journal*, 29: 663–672; J. McGregor, 2008, The world's most innovative companies, *BusinessWeek*, www.businessweek.com, April 17; A. Taylor III, 2008, Can this car save Ford? *Fortune*, May 19, 170; M. Vella, 2008, Electronic Arts tries to snatch Take-Two, *BusinessWeek*, www.businessweek.com, February 25; M. Vella, 2008, Innovation through acquisition, *BusinessWeek*, www.businessweek.com, February 29.

Questions

1. Based on the materials you read in this chapter, do you think it is wise for the larger software producers to be acquiring companies? Why or why not? When do you think it would be appropriate to use other strategic approaches to foster innovation or entrepreneurial activities?
2. Search the Web sites of Google, Yahoo!, and Microsoft to identify what has happened with their previous acquisitions and cooperative agreements. What does your search suggest about the acquisitions and cooperative agreements versus internally developed innovations? Which appear to have been the most successful? Why?

EXPERIENTIAL EXERCISES

Exercise One: Innovating in the World's Most Innovative Companies

Chapter 10 mentioned *Fast Company's* 2008 list of "Fast 50: The World's Most Innovative Companies." *Fast Company* notes that top innovators range from "visionary upstarts" (such as Facebook) to "storied stalwarts" (such as GE). The group includes a wide range of industries and firm sizes.

Complete this exercise in teams of two or three. Each team should choose one of the firms listed and answer the following questions for each firm:

1. What approaches were used to create innovations (i.e., internal development, cooperative relationships, or acquisitions)? If other approaches were used to generate innovations, explain them.
2. Are the firm's innovations incremental, radical, or both?
3. What role do entrepreneurs play in the innovation process in the firm?

Top 15 of the World's 50 Most Innovative Companies

1. Google	9. Amazon
2. Apple	10. Nintendo
3. Facebook	11. Procter & Gamble
4. GE	12. News Corp.
5. Ideo	13. Affymetrix
6. Nike	14. Disney
7. Nokia	15. Samsung
8. Alibaba	

Source: Chuck Salter, "Fast 50: The World's Most Innovative Companies," *Fast Company*, March 2008.

BIZ FLIX

October Sky: **The Ultimate in Innovation**

Watch the *October Sky* scenes after you have studied the discussion of innovation and strategic entrepreneurship in this chapter. The film tells the true story of Homer Hickam's (Jake Gyllenhaal) rise from a West Virginia coal-mining town to become a NASA engineer. Homer and his friends experiment with building small rockets as a way of winning college scholarships and getting out of working in the coal mines. Hickam's *Rocket Boys* memoir was the basis of the screenplay. This film is an enjoyable, uplifting story of building a better future for oneself.

The scenes are an edited composite of parts of the "Rocket Roulette" and "Splitting the Sky" sequences that appear a third of the way into the film. Although Homer and his friends are not developing a new product for sale, the process they use to develop their rocket has many characteristics of innovation described in this chapter.

What to Watch for and Ask Yourself

1. What aspects of innovation discussed in this chapter appear in these scenes? Does the process Homer and his friends use have the characteristics of "creative destruction" discussed earlier? Why or why not?
2. Is Homer Hickam behaving like an entrepreneur as described earlier in this chapter?
3. Do the scenes show internal innovation or innovating by cooperating? Refer to the earlier discussion in this chapter for details.

ENDNOTES

1. B. A. Gilbert, P. P. McDougall, & D. B. Audretsch, 2008, Clusters, knowledge spillovers, and new venture performance: An empirical examination, *Journal of Business Venturing*, 23: 405–422; Y. Zhang, H. Li, M. A. Hitt, & G. Cui, 2007, R&D intensity and international joint venture performance in an emerging market: Moderating affects of market focus and ownership structure, *Journal of International Business Studies*, 38: 944–960.
2. J. G. Covin & M. P. Miles, 2007, Strategic use of corporate venturing, *Entrepreneurship Theory and Practice*, 31(2): 183–207.
3. F. H. Knight, 1921, *Risk, Uncertainty, and Profit*. Houghton Mifflin (reprint ed.). Chicago: University of Chicago Press
4. D. Kimmel, 2004, *The Fourth Network: How FOX broke the rules and reinvented Television*, Chicago: Ivan R. Dee Publisher.
5. C. B. Bingham, K. N. Eisenhardt, & N. R. Furr, 2007, What makes a process a capability? Heuristics, strategy, and effective capture of opportunities, *Strategic Entrepreneurship Journal*, 1: 11–32.
6. D. Welch, 2004, Reinventing the company, *BusinessWeek*, March 22: 24.
7. A. M. Kleinbaum & M. L. Tushman, 2007, Building bridges: The social structure of interdependent innovation, *Strategic Entrepreneurship Journal*, 1: 103–122.
8. S. A. Alvarez & J. B. Barney, 2007, Discovery and creation: Alternative theories of entrepreneurial action, *Strategic Entrepreneurship Journal*, 1: 33–48.
9. J. A. Hart, 2008, Flat panel displays, in J. T. Macher & D. C. Mowery (eds.), *Innovation in Local Industries: U.S. Firms Competing in A New World*, National Academies Press: Science, Technology and Economic Policy, 141–162.
10. J. Schumpeter, 1934, *The Theory of Economic Development*, Cambridge, MA: Harvard University Press; R. Agarwal, D. Audretsch, & M. B. Sarkar, 2007, The process of creative destruction: Knowledge spillovers, entrepreneurship, and economic growth, *Strategic Entrepreneurship Journal*, 3: 263–286.
11. K. D. Miller, 2007, Risk and rationality in entrepreneurial processes, *Strategic Entrepreneurship Journal*, 1: 57–74.
12. P. F. Drucker, 1998, The discipline of innovation, *Harvard Business Review*, 76(6): 149–157.
13. D. A. Shepherd, J. S. McMullen, & P. D. Jennings, 2007, The formation of opportunity beliefs: Overcoming ignorance and reducing doubt, *Strategic Entrepreneurship Journal*, 1: 75–96.
14. 2004, Rules to live by, and break, Knowledge @ Wharton, http://knowledge.wharton.upenn.edu, June 17.
15. D. Duffy, 2004, Corporate entrepreneurship: Entrepreneurial skills for personal and corporate success, *Center for Excellence*, www.centerforexcellence.net, June 14.
16. M. M. Crossan, H. W. Lane, & R. E. White, 1999, An organizational learning framework: From intuition to institution, *Academy of Management Review*, 24: 522–537.
17. H. L. Sirkin, J. P. Andrew, & J. Butnam, 2007, *Payback: Reaping the Rewards of Innovation*, Cambridge, MA: Harvard Business School Press.
18. B. Jaruzelski & K. Dehoff, 2008, Customer connection: The innovation 1000, *Strategic Finance*, February, 17–19.
19. K. Allison & R. Waters, 2008, High-tech companies focus their R&D spending, *Financial Times*, www.ft.com, March 16.
20. J. K. Sankaran & B. S. Mouly, 2008, Managing innovation in an emerging sector: The case of marine-based Nutraceuticals, *R&D Management*, 37: 329–344.
21. S. Hamm & J. Karey, 2008, Solutions from a hunger crisis; The global food shortage could lead to lower trade barriers and innovation that may raise farm productivity, *BusinessWeek*, May 12, 26.
22. A. Barrett, C. Palmeri, & S. A. Forest, 2004, The 100 best small companies, *BusinessWeek*, June 7: 86–90.
23. C. Salter, 2008, The faces and voices of Google, *Fast Company*, www.fastcompany.com, February 14.
24. B. Bergstein, 2008, Cell phone innovations rival Web, *Arizona Republic*, May 17, D3.
25. D. J. Teece, 1986, Profiting from technological innovation, *Research Policy*, 15: 285–305.
26. T. Laamanen & T. Keil, 2008, Performance of serial acquirers: Toward an acquisition program perspective, *Strategic Management Journal*, 29: 663–672; D. Mauricio, 2008, Building world-class M&A competencies, *Mergers and Acquisitions*, 43(4): 82–83.
27. K.-H. Tsai & J.-C. Wang, 2008, External technology acquisition and firm performance: A longitudinal study, *Journal of Business Venturing*, 23: 91–112.
28. C. Salter, 2008, Fast 50: The world's most innovative companies, *Fast Company*, www.fastcompany.com, March.
29. L. A. Plummer, J. M. Haynie, & J. Godesiabois, 2007, An essay on the origins of entrepreneurial opportunity, *Small Business Economics*, 28: 363–379; R. E. Hoskisson & L. W. Busenitz, 2002, Market uncertainty and learning distance in corporate entrepreneurship entry mode choice, in M. A. Hitt, R. D. Ireland, S. M. Camp, & D. L. Sexton (eds.), *Strategic Entrepreneurship: Creating a New Mindset*, Oxford, U.K.: Blackwell, 151–172.
30. S. A. Hill & J. Birkinshaw, 2008, Strategy-Organization configurations in corporate venture units: Impact on performance and survival, *Journal of Business Venturing*, 23: 423–444.

A

acquisition a transaction in which a firm buys a controlling interest in another firm with the intention of either making it a subsidiary business or combining it with its current business or businesses

acquisition strategy an action plan that the firm develops to successfully acquire other companies

administrative innovation a new way of organizing and/or handling the organizational tasks firms use to complete their work

B

balanced scorecard provides a framework for evaluating the simultaneous use of financial controls and strategic controls

benchmarking the process of identifying the best practices of competitors and other high-performing firms, analyzing them, and comparing them with the organization's own practices

business-level strategy an action plan the firm develops to describe how it will compete in its chosen industry or market segment

C

capabilities result when the firm integrates several different resources to complete a task or a series of related tasks

competitive advantage when the firm's core competencies allow it to create value for customers by performing a key activity *better* than competitors or when a distinctive competence allows it to perform an activity that creates value for customers that competitors can't perform

competitive M-form an organizational structure in which there is complete independence between the firm's divisions

competitive rivalry the set of actions and reactions between competitors as they compete for an advantageous market position

complementary resources resources that each partner brings to the partnership that, when combined, allow for new resources or capabilities that neither firm could readily create alone

complementors the network of companies that sell goods or services that are complementary to another firm's good or service

cooperative M-form an organizational structure in which horizontal integration is used so that resources and activities can be shared between product divisions

cooperative strategy an action plan the firm develops to form cooperative relationships with other firms

core competencies capabilities the firm emphasizes and performs especially well while pursuing its vision

corporate entrepreneurship an organization-wide reliance on entrepreneurship and innovation as the link to solid financial performance

Corporate-level core competencies complex sets of resources and capabilities that link different businesses, primarily through managerial and technological knowledge, experience, and expertise

corporate relatedness achieved when corporate-level core competencies are successfully transferred between some of the firm's businesses

cost leadership strategy an action plan the firm develops to produce goods or services at the lowest cost

country specific or location advantages advantages that concern the desirability of producing in the home country versus locating production and distribution assets in the host country

D

demographic trends changes in population size, age structure, geographic distribution, ethnic mix, and income distribution

differentiation strategy an action plan the firm develops to produce goods or services that customers perceive as being unique in ways that are important to them

distinctive competencies core competencies that differ from those held by competitors

divestiture a transaction in which businesses are sold to other firms or spun off as independent enterprises

due diligence the rational process by which acquiring firms evaluate target firms

E

economic trends the direction of the economy in which a firm competes or may choose to compete

economies of scale the improvements in efficiency a firm experiences as it incrementally increases its size

economies of scope cost savings that the firm accrues when it successfully shares some of its resources and activities or some of its core competencies between its businesses

entrepreneurial culture encourages employees to identify and exploit new opportunities

entrepreneurial opportunities circumstances suggesting that new goods or services can be sold at a price exceeding the costs incurred to create, make, sell, and support them

entrepreneurs people who recognize entrepreneurial opportunities and then take risks to develop an innovation to pursue them

entrepreneurship a process of "creative destruction" through which existing products, methods of production, or ways of administering or managing the firm are destroyed and replaced with new ones

equity alliance an alliance in which each partner owns a percentage of the equity in a venture that the firms have jointly formed

exporting the process of sending goods and services from one country to another for distribution, sale, and service

external environment a set of conditions outside the firm that affect the firm's performance

F

financial controls focus on shorter-term financial outcomes

financial economies cost savings or higher returns generated when the firm effectively allocates its financial resources based on investments either inside or outside the firm

focus strategy an action plan the firm develops to produce goods or services to serve the needs of a specific market segment

focused cost leadership strategy an action plan the firm develops to produce goods or services for a narrow market segment at the lowest cost

focused differentiation strategy an action plan the firm develops to produce goods or services that a narrow group of customers perceive as being unique in ways that are important to them

foreign direct investment a process through which a firm directly invests (beyond exporting and licensing) in a market outside its home country

franchising the licensing of a good or service and business model to partners for specified fees (usually a signing fee and a percentage of the franchisee's revenues or profits)

functional structure an organizational structure consisting of a CEO and a small corporate staff

G

general environment the trends in the broader society that influence an industry and the firms in it

geographic-area divisional structure a decentralized organizational structure that enables each division to focus on a geographic area, region, or country

global matrix structure an organizational structure in which both functional and product expertise are integrated into teams so the teams will be able to quickly respond to requirements in the global marketplace

global mind-set cognitive model that motivates a manager to search for opportunities in foreign markets; to develop strategies that exploit those opportunities; and to coordinate units, tasks, and people in multiple geographic locations throughout the world

global strategy an action plan that the firm develops to produce and sell standardized products in different markets

global trends changes in relevant emerging and developed country global markets, important international political events, and critical changes in cultural and institutional characteristics of global markets

greenfield venture a venture in which a firm buys or leases land, constructs a new facility and hires or transfers managers and employees, and then independently launches a new operation (commonly called a wholly owned subsidiary) without involvement of a partner

H

horizontal acquisition the purchase of a competitor competing in the same market or markets as the acquiring firm

horizontal strategic alliance an alliance that involves cooperative partnerships in which firms at the same stage of the value chain share resources and capabilities

human capital includes the knowledge and skills of those working for the firm

I

industry a group of firms producing similar products

innovation the development of a new good, a new type of service, or a new way of presenting a good or service

intangible resources assets that contribute to creating value for customers but are not physically identifiable

integrated cost leadership/differentiation strategy an action plan the firm develops to produce goods or services with a strong emphasis on both differentiation and low cost

internal environment the set of conditions (such as strengths, resources and capabilities, and so forth) inside the firm affecting the choice and use of strategies

internal-coordination or administrative advantages advantages that make it desirable for a firm to produce the good or service rather than contracting with another firm to produce or distribute it

J

joint venture a separate business that is created by an equity alliance

L

leveraged buyout (LBO) a restructuring strategy in which a party buys all or part of a firm's assets in order to take the firm or a part of the firm private

liability of foreignness the costs and risks of doing business outside a firm's domestic market

licensing the process of entering an international market by leasing the right to use the firm's intellectual property—technology, work methods, patents, copyrights, brand names, or trademarks—to a firm doing business in the desired international market

M

market power power that exists when the firm sells its products above competitive prices or when its costs are below those of its primary competitors

merger a transaction in which firms agree to combine their operations on a relatively equal basis

mission defines the firm's core intent and the business or businesses in which it intends to operate

multidivisional (M-form) structure an organizational structure in which the firm is organized to generate either economies of scope or financial economies

multidomestic strategy an action plan that the firm develops to produce and sell unique products in different markets

multiproduct strategy an action plan that the firm develops to compete in different product markets

N

nonequity alliance a contractual relationship between two or more firms in which each partner agrees to share some of its resources or capabilities

O

operational relatedness achieved when the firm's businesses successfully share resources and activities to produce and sell their products

opportunities conditions in the firm's external environment that may help the firm reach its vision

organizational culture the set of values and beliefs that are shared throughout the firm

organizational structure specifies the firm's formal reporting relationships, procedures, controls, and authority and decision-making processes

outsourcing acquiring a capability from an external supplier that contributes to creating value for the customer

P

physical environment trends changes in the physical environment and the business practices that are intended to sustain it

political/legal trends the changes in organizations and interest groups that compete for a voice in developing and overseeing the body of laws and regulations that guide interactions among firms and nations

premium occurs when firms pay more than the current market value to acquire another firm

primary activities inbound logistics (such as sources of parts), operations (such as manufacturing, if dealing with a physical product), sales and distribution of products, and after-sales service

process innovations new means of producing, selling, and supporting goods and services

R

related-party transactions paying a person who has a relationship with the firm extra money for reasons other than his or her normal activities on the firm's behalf

resources the tangible and intangible assets held by the firm

S

simple structure an organizational structure in which the owner/manager makes all of the major decisions and oversees all of the staff's activities

social capital includes all internal and external relationships that help the firm provide value to customers and ultimately to its other stakeholders

sociocultural trends changes in a society's attitudes and cultural values

stakeholders individuals and groups who have an interest in a firm's performance and an ability to influence its actions

strategic alliance a relationship between firms in which the partners agree to cooperate in ways that provide benefits to each firm

strategic business unit (SBU) a semiautonomous unit of a diversified firm with a collection of related businesses

strategic business unit (SBU) M-form an organizational structure in which corporate headquarters personnel try to transfer corporate-level core competencies into the firm's businesses

strategic controls focus on the content of strategic actions rather than on their outcomes

strategic entrepreneurship the process of taking entrepreneurial actions using a strategic perspective by combining entrepreneurial and strategic management processes to enhance the firm's ability to innovate, enter new markets, and improve its performance

strategic intent the firm's motivation to leverage its resources and capabilities to reach its vision

strategic leaders the individuals practicing strategic leadership

strategic leadership developing a vision for the firm, designing strategic actions to achieve this vision, and empowering others to carry out those strategic actions

strategic management the ongoing process companies use to form a *vision, analyze* their external environment and their internal environment, and select one or more *strategies* to use to create value for customers and other stakeholders, especially shareholders

strategy an action plan designed to move an organization toward achievement of its vision

strategy implementation the set of actions firms take to use a strategy after it has been selected

strengths resources and capabilities that allow the firm to complete important tasks

substitute products goods or services that perform similar functions to an existing product

support activities provide support to the primary activities so that they can be completed effectively

switching costs the one-time costs customers incur when they decide to buy a product from a different supplier

T

takeover a specialized type of acquisition in which the target firm does not solicit the acquiring firm's offer

tangible resources valuable assets that can be seen or quantified, such as manufacturing equipment and financial capital

technological trends changes in the activities involved with creating new knowledge and translating that knowledge into new products, processes, and materials

threats conditions in the firm's external environment that may prevent the firm from reaching its vision

top management team the group of managers charged with the responsibility to develop and implement the firm's strategies

transnational strategy an action plan that the firm develops to produce and sell somewhat unique, yet somewhat standardized products in different markets

V

value chain consists of the structure of activities that firms use to implement their business-level strategy

value the satisfaction a firm's product creates for customers; can be measured by the price customers are willing to pay for the firm's product

vertical acquisition the purchase of a supplier or distributor of one or more of a firm's goods or services

vertical strategic alliance an alliance that involves cooperative partnerships across the value chain

vision contains at least two components—a mission that describes the firm's DNA and the "picture" of the firm as it hopes to exist in a future time period

W

weaknesses the firm's resource and capability deficiencies that make it difficult for the firm to complete important tasks

worldwide divisional structure a centralized organizational structure in which each product group is housed in a globally focused worldwide division or worldwide profit center